Managing People
in Public Agencies

MANAGING PEOPLE IN PUBLIC AGENCIES
Personnel and Labor Relations

Jonathan Brock
University of Washington

UNIVERSITY
PRESS OF
AMERICA

Lanham • New York • London

University Press of America,® Inc.
4720 Boston Way
Lanham, MD 20706

3 Henrietta Street
London WC2E 8LU England

British Cataloging in Publication Information Available

This edition was reprinted in 1989 by
University Press of America, Inc.

Library of Congress Cataloging-in-Publication Data

Brock, Jonathan, 1949–
Managing people in public agencies : personnel and labor relations
/ Jonathan Brock.
p.   cm.
Reprint. Originally published: Boston, Little, Brown, © 1984.
Includes bibliographies.
1. Civil service– –United States– –Personnel management. 2. Civil
service– –United States– –Personnel management– –Case studies.
I. Title.
JK765.B68   1988   88–36475 CIP
350.1'0973– –dc19
ISBN 0–8191–7277–4 (alk. paper)

All University Press of America books are produced on acid-free paper.
The paper used in this publication meets the minimum requirements of American
National Standard for Information Sciences—Permanence of Paper for Printed Library
Materials, ANSI Z39.48–1984.   ∞

To Professor Dunlop

Preface

A Managerial Perspective

Unlike much of the material in public personnel management, this book emphasizes the role of the program — or line — manager rather than that of the personnel officer. It emphasizes accomplishment of public programs rather than technical personnel activities, such as classification, or specific areas of law, such as labor law or affirmative action. Yet, technical personnel activities, labor relations, and affirmative action are dealt with in the book — but from the perspective of a program manager. Although the book provides the necessary exposure to the technical and procedural side of government personnel management, those areas are treated in the context of providing better services and of improving employee satisfaction, not as ends in themselves. The book is intended to develop judgment and abilities for managing people within a variety of programmatic, bureaucratic, and political settings, and to develop skills and strategies for dealing with various experts and other "actors" who might otherwise restrain a program manager's range of action.

A Case Approach

To serve these purposes, this volume relies largely on case studies, which allow students to view human resource management as one part of a manager's overall approach to delivering effective public services. Suggested readings provide some basic managerial and behavioral concepts helpful in analyzing each case. (More experienced audiences usually have less need for such readings.) The cases provide typical management problems set within their typically complex political and organizational environments. Discussion and analysis of the cases by students and professors provide the forum through which useful lessons can be gleaned.

Twelve of the fourteen cases are drawn from typical governmental personnel situations. They deal with real and recent problems and were selected and written with the concept of this book in mind. In addition, two cases are drawn from business settings on issues for which good cases from a public agency were not available, or where the differences in tradition or approach suggest additional lessons or techniques for public managers.

In order for students to obtain the necessary technical knowledge, most of the cases contain excerpts from applicable personnel regulations in areas such as classification, reduction in force, labor contracts, and the like — information too boring to be tolerated on its own. By making these technical issues part of the case, students are forced to tackle them as they attempt to resolve the managerial problem. They thereby can become adept at understanding or influencing the impact of these regulatory constraints on a manager's options and obligations.

In resolving the case problems, students must also consider means of developing constructive working relationships with those who can influence their ability to manage effectively — including personnel specialists, budget officers, union leaders, political officials, and others.

In concentrating on the manager as the link between program goals and effective management of people, the book aims to help managers identify the managerial tools, personnel management strategy, and style appropriate to each program, organizational, or political context in which they find themselves. Different cases suggest different styles and judgments depending on the problems and opportunities at hand.

The book also recognizes that personnel decisions can be difficult to make and implement, especially when the issues are complex, time is short, or pressure from other quarters is strong. Thus, studying the approach in the first two chapters and then working through the cases will help students develop better diagnostic abilities, quicken their analysis, and add depth to their decisions in personnel matters. Developing practical solutions is emphasized. Study of this book also offers a means of developing criteria to guide decisions that must be made under severe or competing pressures.

Organization of The Book

A personnel management problem rarely presents or resolves itself simply as a "compensation" problem or a "promotion" problem. Rather, management situations have many interactive elements and a variety of possible consequences. Yet, from a learning standpoint some topic-by-topic focus seems necessary. Therefore, although cases from other parts of the book may touch on some similar points, each part of the book and each case focuses on a different aspect of personnel management, without sacrificing the richness of the real situation depicted. The lessons progress from case to case, solidifying and integrating management tools and concepts, developing analytic and diagnostic abilities, and using the cultural and technical knowledge from analysis of previous cases to work on each new case.

The introductions and questions preceding each case are intended to highlight the major issues. These introductions are brief, leaving to the student the process of analysis and discovery. The cases present real situations in which the manager had no assignment sheet — and so it will be for future managers.

This book will easily fill a quarter or a semester course covering the basic issues of public sector human resource management. This material is assembled as a survey course in which a wide range of personnel management problems is presented. Cases or readings may be added or deleted to fit the time available, coverage desired, or other instructional criteria. Each case can be taught at a level of conceptual or operational detail appropriate to the course, audience, or time constraints.

Civil Service Reform

The Federal Civil Service Reform Act of 1978 and parallel state and local reforms were taking place as this material was first developed and taught, and much of it explicitly reflects post-reform issues. Thus, the advent of civil service reform motivated inclusion of the case on the "Merit System Protection Board" and the material on performance appraisal, an important and often confusing subject. The remaining material focuses on developing universal tools for analysis and problem solving in personnel matters.

Genesis and Limitations

This material is largely a product of the four years I spent on the faculty of the John F. Kennedy School of Government at Harvard University. It has been taught to hundreds of graduate students, ranging in age from 20 to 61, at major universities. Some students had substantial work experience and some did not. Selected portions have been used in special programs for in-service executives from various state and local governments and from a plethora of program areas.

As I was leaving government in 1977, I consulted respected government managers and observers to develop a list of the human resource issues and skills with which a public manager ought to be most familiar. Lamenting the lack of good curricular material, I wrote or supervised cases where resources were available and where a manager and agency were willing to permit a case to be written. Inevitably, resources cannot support all one's ambitions, nor can a semester's course swallow them. However, a substantial portion of the original list is represented here. As one consequence of time and resource constraints, the preponderance of the cases are from federal agencies, a balance that could stand correction but that has not negated the material's value in teaching those students with state and local interests. Rather than wait until a more balanced set of cases was available, I decided to go ahead and publish this grouping. The purists may argue; in the meantime, students of management and those they manage can benefit.

Learning and Teaching

Learning with this collection comes not just from reading the words, but through careful, head-scratching analysis and discussion of the cases; through a search for realistic solutions; and through a systematic attempt by students and instructors to distill the lessons from each case and apply them to the next case and to reality. Depending on experience and perspective, the lessons will vary in each class or for each student, but study and discussion will advance each student's thinking and consequent ability to handle real situations.

Typically, the study of these cases and the underlying concept of management has generated interesting, and often exciting, discussions on issues that, presented in other forms, often seem either too abstract or too pedestrian. When personnel management is related to the mission of a public agency or to the accomplishment or aspirations of a given manager, personnel management becomes a vital and interesting subject.

The course represented by this book has been challenging and fun to teach and — if student evaluations are to be believed — challenging and fun to take. It has demonstrated its practical relevance to managers in public agencies. That was my intent when research on the first case was begun. It is my continued interest, therefore, that this text contribute to the better training and awareness of public managers in managing people. The public deserves it, public employees deserve it, and managers owe it to themselves to gain the satisfaction of doing the best possible job for themselves, for public employees, and for the public.

Acknowledgments

This book owes its genesis to John T. Dunlop, Lamont University Professor at Harvard University, and over the last four decades, frequently a government manager. As an academic and as a practitioner, he recognized well the importance of "personnel questions" in public management and employment. He also saw these personnel management questions as intertwined with public policy formulation and implementation. Thus, my thinking and perspective have benefited greatly from my exposure to Professor Dunlop, as his junior colleague both in government and in the university. True to the principles of management delegation, Dunlop provided resources, encouragement, and wise counsel, yet left me to develop my own means of approaching the issue. To the extent that the work of public managers is helped by this collection and its offshoots, it is as a result of his astute observations of the workings of government and politics and his conception of the role of universities in helping to bring ideas to the practical work of government.

Through his efforts, funding came from the Ford and Sloan Foundations for the early cases and conceptual development; later from the program in Business and Government, sponsored jointly between the Harvard Business School and the John F. Kennedy School of Government. Dean Graham T. Allison of the Kennedy School provided an institutional home and encouragement for my efforts, and Dean John McArthur of the Business School had years earlier taught me the value of feedback by his example as a teacher and manager. Jared E. Hazleton, Dean of the School of Public Affairs at the University of Washington provided me with a peaceful year as a visiting faculty member that allowed the manuscript to be completed. It was my wife, Lois Schwennesen, who convinced me that the material, if worthy of a Harvard graduate program, perhaps deserved to be shown to a publisher.

Twenty years ago, the aborted presidency of John F. Kennedy kindled my awareness of the arts of governance and leadership, and of the importance of public service. Some years later, my understanding of government management was advanced by Dan H. Fenn, Jr., a warm and gifted teacher at the Harvard Business School and Director of the John F. Kennedy Memorial Library.

The hard work of Nancy Griesemer, Sue Forman, Tom Fagan, Rina Spence, Tom Sellers, and Phil Sharpless, who, under my direction, researched and wrote many of the cases, is acknowledged here, with admiration for their perseverance and dedication.

Many government managers, employees, and other colleagues contributed generously of their time and insight as the cases and concepts were developed. Among them were Bert Concklin, Roland Droitsch, Hank Perritt, Dave Kuechle, Bert Lewis, Dave Williams, Bill Usery, Jim Hibarger, John Heiss, Liz Gordon, Quinn Mills, Colin Diver, Wick Skinner, Mike Dukakis, the late Gordon Chase, Larry Lorber, Richard Shakman, Peter Bower, John Schwartz, Hale Champion. A special note of appreciation is given for the encouragement and example of my late colleague, Manny Carballo, the archetype of the practitioner/academician. Also helpful were many friends in the International Personnel Management Association (IPMA), whose publications director, Ken Fischer, circulated drafts of this material among members for technical and substantive review. An IPMA board member, Jack Golden, spent many hours introducing me to his colleagues and helping me understand better the role of personnel professionals in the government personnel process.

I received many detailed and thoughtful comments on the manuscript from faculty members at universities across the country: among them, David Lipsky, Duane Thompson, Walter Broadnax, Bill McGregor, Shirley Teeter, Jim Doig, Dick Loverd, Frank Havelick, Ben Burdetsky, James Perry, Gilbert B. Siegal, Mary Hall, and Fremont Lyden; and from countless former students. Captain Richard Martin provided an especially detailed review. Alexander Greene, my editor at Little, Brown, consistently provided thoughtful and helpful suggestions and support. The manuscript is greatly strengthened as a result of all their efforts. Any weaknesses remain only as a result of my own stubbornness and limitations.

I am especially indebted to my teaching assistants, who helped to integrate the use of the material and develop the teaching approaches to the cases. David Wilhelm's perception on management issues, his instincts for pedagogy, and his extreme dedication laid a firm foundation for structuring and teaching the original course. Kevin Murphy's help in refining the concepts added to the integration of the material. In the first year that I taught the course, Anne L. Spillane worked diligently against my centrifugal tendencies to keep the materials in a form and order upon which future work could be built. Mary Spillane provided an important suggestion concerning presentation of the conceptual framework in the book.

On other aspects of the work, Ele Jaynes added immeasurably to the quality of the cases with her skills in word processing, never complaining about numerous revisions. During the bulk of the project, Robin Berberian Bianchi was a loyal secretary to whom I owe a great debt for skill, calm, and good humor throughout. The text portions and final manuscript were prepared at the Business Service Center of Bellevue, Washington, under the competent direction of Tammy Erickson.

Finally, I will be ever grateful to my students, who motivated me as no manager could.

Jonathan Brock
Seattle, Washington
February 1984

Contents

PART V
Feedback and Information   202

PART VI
Resolving and Avoiding Conflict   264

Managing People
in Public Agencies

PART I

Problems
and Opportunities
in Managing People

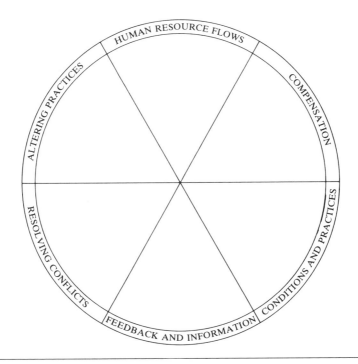

Even well-developed policy ideas require implementation before they can serve a useful social purpose. Most government activity is carried on through the efforts of people. Therefore, the deployment, management, and motivation of human resources are critical to the success or failure of a government program or function — as well as to the success or failure of an individual manager. Because many of the formal and informal elements of personnel administration are not under the direct control of an individual manager, personnel management is an especially complex task in public agencies. Effective management of people is difficult enough in any setting, but management within civil service rules and within political, labor-management, and bureaucratic constraints is especially complex.

The object of the material in this book is to develop managers of public programs and functions. Through case studies, most of them depicting actual public managers, the book takes an integrated view of managing people in the context of program purposes and political and bureaucratic reality. The content, the order of the cases, and the underlying analytic scheme reflect conceptual, technical, and "cultural" knowledge that will be useful in a wide variety of managerial situations. Where appropriate and illustrative, comparisons are made with the private sector.

The cases focus on issues such as motivation, hiring, firing, compensation, performance evaluation, organizational change, and labor relations. While each case highlights a specific topic or managerial technique, the combination of them provides an overview of the formal and informal workings of public personnel systems as viewed by a manager. Taken together, the case collection develops managerial tools for diagnosing and resolving human resource problems in public management. This material also highlights the important power relationships between operating managers and other, often unexpected, actors and institutions who participate in the personnel management process. Overall, attention is focused on methods by which a manager can use these techniques, tools, and power relationships in the interest of program purposes, the organization, and its employees. While a later chapter considers the need for change in the formal systems and in other personnel management practices, the view of the book is that better results can be achieved even within existing constraints.

The first chapter in Part I provides an overview that describes typical problems and opportunities for a public manager in human resource management. The second chapter includes a conceptual framework that can be used to diagnose and make use of each agency's managerial environment as it affects the management of people. By presenting a case study about a controversial promotion, the third chapter in Part I illustrates this environment and the manager's role in it.

CHAPTER 1

Management in the Public Sector: Tools and Constraints

The Role of Human Resource Management

Government is a service operation. People, not machines, deliver government services. Therefore, any action to change or improve the output or service of a government operation must somehow affect the way people do their jobs. Because human resources are so central to obtaining organizational results, public managers with an interest in results must make the management of people a major and conscious aspect of their job.

This book is focused on the management of people from the standpoint of a manager with program or functional responsibilities. It is presented from the viewpoint of a manager, not from the viewpoint of a personnel specialist, a labor lawyer, or a policy analyst — all of whom frequently have active roles in aspects of personnel management — for it is the manager who has to use the various aspects of personnel policy to further the purposes of the organization by integrating those purposes with the personal needs and talents of individuals in the work unit. The manager is ultimately responsible for making the organization work. A manager's point of view, therefore, may be different from these specialists.

The cases in this book depict a variety of middle- and upper-level managers. One runs a policy and economic analysis office; another is the Commissioner of Social Services in a large state; yet another runs a staffing function in a regional civil service office. Some are "general" managers presiding over large, multi-program, multi-function, self-contained agencies. Some are "program" managers responsible for providing a particular public service, often within a large agency. Others are "function" managers, overseeing specific functions such as budgeting, policy analysis, or data processing within an agency or program. While we can identify differences of perspective, complexity of mission, and external relations among these three types of managers, strict categorization is difficult. Managerial functions differ according to the variety of organizational hierarchies and program structures in different governmental jurisdictions and agencies. For simplicity and to emphasize the program responsibility of a manager, most references in the book will be to a program manager, although the other terms will appear from time to time.[1]

To one degree or another, formally or informally, managers in such positions help in planning and goal setting for their organization. Their objectives may range from new program development to improvement of on-time case completion or planning for a conversion to automatic data processing. In pursuing their objectives, managers usually have the help or hindrance of others, such as their supervisors, legislators, interest groups, the media, and other actors in their political and governmental orbit.

A manager is also responsible for maintaining and building organizational capacity. To varying degrees obtaining or allocating financial resources will be part of the managerial job, as will handling media, constituents, politicians, and interest groups. With greater or lesser involvement of supervisors and other parties, a program manager tries to translate surrounding pressures and expectations into some coherent direction and accomplishment for the organization or work unit. And managing human resources is a central duty of virtually any manager who hopes to accomplish the basic mission, or anything else useful, in a public agency.

Managing people requires more than good social and interpersonal instincts. As individuals, people are complex enough, but several dimensions of complexity are added when they interact within their own work organization and with other organizations.[2] Where a manager has responsibility for directing organizational tasks and meeting objectives, a dimension is added to human relations that is simply not part of other interpersonal relationships. For effective management, therefore, skills beyond the interpersonal are necessary. This set of skills must be addressed both to organizational goals and to employee concerns.

During periods of fiscal limitations, the effective management of people may be at the same time more difficult and more important to continued service delivery. Despite a decreased level of resources, the need to perform a demanding task or mission remains. Where people are the primary production resource, maintaining service levels during and after resource cutbacks may involve even more creative planning and management of human resources. Simply asking people to work harder is not sufficient.

Because of the importance of people in providing, changing, and improving public services, the management of people in public settings must be studied at a

[1] There are many discussions of a manager's role. Some examples: Peter Drucker, *Management: Tasks, Responsibilities, Practices* (New York: Harper and Row, 1974), Chester Barnard, *The Functions of the Executive* (Cambridge, Massachusetts: Harvard University Press, 1942), Herbert Kaufman, *The Administrative Behavior of Federal Bureau Chiefs* (Washington, D.C.: Brookings Institution, 1981), and Laurence E. Lynn, *Managing the Public's Business: The Job of the Government Executive* (New York: Basic Books, 1981).

[2] The literature on organizational behavior and complex organizations discusses these issues. For one example, see Jay Lorsch and Alan Sheldon, "The Individual and the Organization: A Systems View," in Jay W. Lorsch and Paul Lawrence, *Managing Group and Intergroup Relations*, pp. 161–182 (Homewood: Richard D. Irwin and the Dorsey Press, 1972).

level of detail not ordinarily handled by policy analysis, economics, or political science — disciplines that provide insight into many other aspects of government activity. Nevertheless, the policy analyst and the politician could usefully consider the effect of human resource management issues on public programs and service delivery. Successful policy and programs require that human resource policy and the deployment of human resources be explicitly considered both at the planning stage *and* in implementation.

In contrast to legislators and policy makers, for example, a manager must be concerned with the effects of procedures and activities involved with recruiting, and with providing pay and working conditions that will attract and motivate people. He or she must establish and operate reward and accountability systems that will provide direction, maintain quality, and give feedback on the tasks to be performed. A manager must handle labor relations policy and strategy and carry on day-to-day employee relations that support program objectives and that respect employee rights. He or she must have the capacity to resolve conflicts and make adjustments in the organizations' practices as experience dictates.

Even if a manager masters the art of recruitment or is an expert on management control systems or labor-management relations, in public organizations there is an added dimension that often makes public management difficult and frustrating for employees and managers alike: Outside actors, institutions, and processes commonly affect decisions and judgments concerning human resources. Because of the influence of outside factors, it is necessary to examine human resource management specifically as it takes place in the public sector. Direct application of even the most proven private sector techniques will not suffice. Because of the separate priorities and points of view of these other actors and institutions, a public manager needs to be especially attentive to his or her own priorities. Otherwise, personnel decisions can be influenced excessively by the priorities of actors other than the manager. To help make personnel decisions in the interest of a program or policy objective, a manager must keep in mind the effect of each personnel decision on the program and total group of employees for which he or she is responsible. Using decision criteria related to program and organizational needs can greatly simplify diagnosis and decision making on personnel issues.

Special Dimensions of the Public Culture

The next four sections of this chapter describe aspects of the public sector that have generally made it difficult to manage people conscientiously and effectively. Some generalizations, to which there are always exceptions, are made about the actors, institutions, and processes that are part of a typical public manager's human resource environment. The next chapter presents a framework to assist in the effective management of people in this environment.

History and Politics. Historical and political developments have had a profound impact on the shape and availability of personnel management tools. Public personnel practices in the United States have many of their roots in the prevention of inappropriate political influence. The original purposes of civil service systems can be summarized as (1) protecting individual employees from politically motivated work orders or firings and (2) minimizing frequent turnover of the government work force as a result of electoral turnover of top officials. Since the advent of American civil service systems in the latter part of the 1800s, there has been a major ideological and operational commitment to the use of civil service personnel systems, or "merit" systems, as they are usually called.[3]

In the development and study of civil service systems, there has long been a preoccupation with potential abuse and procedural considerations. There also has been a corresponding neglect of the management perspective.[4] This preoccupation has influenced the design of many formal personnel systems toward curtailment of managerial action, rather than toward achievement of a manager's goals. A system intended to *prevent* managers from doing things is not likely to be a personnel system that can *assist* managers to motivate human resources usefully.

It is well acknowledged by political scientists and managers — many of whom themselves are tenured civil servants — that the *effort* (whether considered successful or not) to protect employees from managers has gone too far off the track and has, in fact, become so procedurally and ideologically rigid that it prevents effective management. Herbert Kaufman has noted that as civil service systems have evolved, ". . . managers [now] pray for deliverance from their guardians," and, ". . . like the spoilsmen, managers are treated like the enemy."[5] Hardly a useful result.

Efforts in the late 1970s to reform civil service sought to restore some of the flexibility to manage that had been removed over the years in response to the continued concern over spoils and the subsequent over-complication of personnel rules.[6] On balance, however, political and historical factors — and related rhetoric — have continued to exert a major influence on the presence and power of important actors, institutions, traditions, and procedures related to managing people.

Interest Group Politics. A number of interest groups play central roles in shaping personnel policy and in pressuring managers for particular personnel decisions. The operation of interest groups in the legislative arena has had a great impact on federal, state, and local personnel policy. For example, veterans' groups

---

[3] There are countless descriptions of the development of civil service systems. For a clear discussion of the evolution of civil service systems, see Herbert Kaufman, "The Growth of the Federal Personnel System" in Wallace S. Sayre, editor, *The Federal Government Service* (Englewood Cliffs, Prentice Hall, 1965).

[4] See Kaufman, "Growth of the Federal Personnel System," and *Staff Report of the Federal Personnel Management Project,* U.S. Civil Service Commission and Office of Management and Budget, 1978; respectively, for some critiques; see O. Glenn Stahl, *Public Personnel Administration,* 7th Edition (New York: Harper and Row, 1976) for an example.

[5] Kaufman, "Growth of the Federal Personnel System," pp. 58 and 59.

[6] *Staff Report of the Federal Personnel Management Project,* and Civil Service Reform Act of 1978, P.L. 95-454.

at state and federal levels traditionally have been active in lobbying legislative committees and administrative decision makers. They have been effective in securing employment advantages for those who have served in the armed forces. Unions, which often have well-developed lobbying channels, behave very much like a political interest group on personnel policy questions.[7] More recently, groups representing the interests of blacks, women, the handicapped, and others have been seeking to influence governmental personnel policies and decisions that affect their interests.

In contrast to groups that routinely seek to influence personnel policy, managers have a more limited history of behaving effectively as an interest group. Consequently, management's interests in the structure of formal personnel policy have often been poorly represented. Even where a desirable policy objective has been enacted into law and regulation, without management input, many features of these laws or regulations have often impeded program management and occasionally have had results or consequences antithetical to their initial purposes.[8]

Politically Appointed Managers. In some agencies politically appointed managers may be prone to even greater difficulty in managing human resources than are career managers. For one thing, appointees may be automatically suspect and cast as spoilsmen or political hacks. Thus, their direction may be resisted unless their reputation, experience, or performance on the job can convince the workers otherwise.

Usually politically appointed managers are not familiar with the formal civil service personnel system and may run afoul of the rules, perhaps by accident — thereby increasing suspicion about their intentions or competence — or be stymied by the rules — thereby decreasing their effectiveness. And by the time they learn enough about the personnel rules and regulations to make a credible attempt at management in that environment, they're gone: The average tenure of a politically appointed executive in the federal government is widely pegged at 18 months to two years.[9] To the extent that such managers run afoul of the rules or traditions, the argument to protect employees from "political abuse" is strengthened despite the relatively small proportion of political appointees to employees in most governmental jurisdictions.[10]

---

[7] For a brief discussion of the history of this phenomenon, see Jonathan Brock, *Bargaining Beyond Impasse: Joint Resolution of Public Sector Labor Disputes* (Boston: Auburn House Publishing Company, 1982), Chapter 1, pp. 6 and 7.

[8] See, for recent examples, the federal Department of Energy Organization Act of 1977 P.L. 95-91 and performance appraisal provisions of Washington State's Civil Service Reform Law of 1982, RCW 41.06 and Chapter 53, Laws of 1982.

[9] See, for example, E. Pendleton James, "Lifting Barriers to Public Service," *Business Week,* April 19, 1982.

[10] See, for example, *Policy and Supporting Positions in the U.S. Government, 1980* (U.S. Government Printing Office) for the relatively small number of politically appointed positions in the federal work force.

Management Development. Most government jurisdictions have been less active than private industry in developing general managers, particularly in developing their managers' skills in personnel management. Part of the reason may lie in the strong, separate establishment of personnel rules and personnel offices, which has caused personnel management to become the province of specialists. Also, in many high-level government positions there is an informal emphasis on political, policy development, and external activities related to program design and development. Much of the professional feedback and recognition in high-level government jobs goes to policy makers and others on the "front end." You get your name in the papers if you make policy; if you are a good manager and implement difficult programs, nobody may ever hear of you.

Overall, there has been more attention in private companies to developing managerial skills.[11] Very few public sector managers come from the private sector into senior levels of government; about 82 percent of the senior managers in the federal sector have never left the government since they entered, and most entered at an early stage in their careers.[12] Except for some of the very senior positions, most government managerial positions are filled by career civil servants rather than by those from outside the government. Among other factors, cultural and institutional barriers combine with conflict of interest regulations to minimize late-career entry by private managers.[13] As a result, there's a further barrier to informal transfusion of human resource management know-how from the private to the public sector, despite attempts by a number of executive interchange programs.

Another traditional problem is that technicians with little management background frequently become managers. People live in a system, grow up in a system, and become very good at the substance of their work. However, this does not prepare them to be managers. Supervisors in engineering, nursing, and even among doctors often find themselves on uncertain ground when they ascend to managerial positions. Yet senior, skilled technicians are appointed as managers, often without reference to their managerial aptitude. This tradition, while seemingly considerate of the senior technicians, has consequences for their job satisfaction and that of the people they are to manage. It is difficult for managers promoted under such circumstances to serve as examples or to develop management

[11] See, for example, "How G.M. Picks Managers," *The New York Times*, September 11, 1980, p. D1. For a discussion of public management and some contrasts with private management, see Joseph L. Bower, "Effective Public Management," *Harvard Business Review*, March-April, 1977. For a number of essays on some special problems in attracting, compensating, and developing public managers, see Robert W. Hartman and Arnold R. Weber, *The Rewards of Public Service: Compensating Top Federal Officials* (Washington, D.C.: The Brookings Institution, 1980).

[12] Unpublished study by the author based on Executive Inventory data of the U.S. Civil Service Commission (now U.S. Office of Personnel Management), 1978.

[13] In addition to the study just cited, see E. Pendleton James, "Lifting Barriers . . . ," Clark Kerr, "The Balkanization of Labor Markets," reprinted in Lloyd G. Reynolds, *et al.*, *Readings in Labor Economics and Labor Relations*, second edition (Englewood Cliffs: Prentice Hall, 1978), and the federal Ethics in Government Act of 1978, P.L. 95-521, for discussions and an example of various barriers.

skills of others coming through the ranks. Insufficient or inadequate training in supervision and management has also hampered development of prospective managers, although a few public organizations and institutions have done well in this regard.

Diffusion of Management Authority

In government, authority over personnel activities, like most government decisions and activities, is split up as a result of the constitutional separation of powers. The laws are passed and money appropriated by the legislative branch, the executive branch carries on day-to-day management, and the courts interpret application of the laws. In addition, as in private employment, managers frequently must deal with union representatives and quasi-judicial proceedings such as employee grievances and appeals. However, in public employment the separation of personnel authority does not stop with the constitutional separation of powers. Even within executive branches of most government jurisdictions personnel authority is further diffused.[14] Typically a manager shares authority and influence with personnel officers, classifiers, job analysts, budget officers, civil service boards and commissions, selection panels, and a host of others who have technical or other roles to play in personnel selection, compensation, and other matters.

The presence of these institutions and actors may circumscribe the flexibility of a public manager to respond rapidly or effectively to a personnel or program issue. In order to determine whether a particular strategy, tactic, or action would be useful or feasible, a manager must consider the influence, role, and probable response of other actors with influence over the issue in question. In selecting the best response to a human resource problem, a manager must determine also if that response is worth the price in management time and its effects on the relationship between the manager and other actors who might be interested or involved. He or she must also assess the effect of a particular response on the relationship between the manager and his or her employees. For example, independent actions taken by other actors in pursuit of their own priorities and missions can directly affect employees' perceptions of the work environment and employees' perceptions of the manager's influence. The following situation, in which a budget office took an action to cut costs, is illustrative:

> Robert F., Deputy Director of the Data Processing Division, had been acting as director of the unit ever since Bill S., the director, had been hospitalized for heart trouble. In offering Robert the temporary assignment and in watching him performing in it over the last six months, the department head told Robert that he would be a strong candidate for the director's job should Bill retire or move to a less stressful job. Robert was excited by the prospect.
>
> Bill subsequently retired a few months before the annual budgeting process

---

[14]See Dan H. Fenn, Jr. "Finding Where the Power Lies in Government," *Harvard Business Review,* September-October, 1979.

began. In a package of cost cutting measures, the budget office recommended that the director's job be downgraded and the deputy's job be eliminated: It was apparent to them that the job was being adequately filled by a lower-salaried person, functioning without a deputy. The department head hoped to reverse their recommendation. He knew that while Robert was anxious to fill the job on an acting basis when the possibility of advancement existed, Robert would be a lot less enthusiastic under the conditions recommended by the budget office.

As in this example, there are many different actors or institutions who affect human resource management, but with priorities and missions that differ from those of the program manager. Yet they have a unifying characteristic: The central principles or criteria guiding *their* activities are unlikely to be the same as those of a program manager. First, such institutions and actors will have their own program mandate and objectives. Second, they have their own legislative and interest group constituencies to satisfy. To the degree that their mandate, their constituencies, and the pressures to which they respond differ from those of the program agency, their priorities will conflict with those of management. Third, many such institutions have their own procedural and paperwork requirements that by law, regulation, or tradition must be satisfied. These differences in values, priorities, or criteria can make for arguments, delays, or competition, which are usually to the detriment of employees and to future relations with these important external actors. It is not useful to try to judge whose values or priorities are right. If a manager understands the criteria and procedures by which these actors operate, he or she can create significant opportunities for better human resource management.

Described below are the roles of some actors and institutions with whom managers typically share power in the process of managing people.

Civil Service Systems and Personnel Offices. Generally, a manager must deal directly or indirectly with one or more separate, central personnel agencies with policy making, audit, oversight, and appeals authority on a wide range of personnel matters. Civil service systems and the civil service agencies are the primary institutional means by which the formal aspects of personnel systems are applied in the public sector. In most government jurisdictions, civil service systems have grown up as a source of authority in personnel matters separate from the authority of managers. Although specific arrangements vary among towns, cities, counties, states, and the federal government, there is usually a central civil service body in each jurisdiction that determines significant aspects of personnel policy. It may be a board or commission, a central personnel department, or, often, both. A city, town, or county may have its own system or in some jurisdictions may be subject to the state civil service system.

Depending on the size of the agency or governmental jurisdiction, there is usually a personnel office or officer within a manager's program agency. The personnel office is a major actor in the process of managing people. Such offices or officers typically have responsibility for policing management's personnel actions as well as some mandate for advising and assisting management. To be successful in human resource management, each manager must deal effectively with the personnel office.

Even though the personnel function may be housed within an agency and officially reports to the agency head, it will have important professional and legal responsibilities to a central authority such as a civil service commission or board, where basic formal personnel procedures and standards are dictated. Because of the need to adhere to professional and statutory procedures, most personnel offices within a public program agency can be viewed as having at least an indirect or "dotted line" relationship with their local civil service authorities. See Figure 1–1. Even where personnel officers emphasize their responsibilities to the program agency, their flexibility is restricted by the need to comply with the requirements and professional values of the established civil service system.

As government activities have grown more diverse and skill requirements more complex, it has become increasingly difficult for a central commission or a personnel office in a large agency to understand and make timely or good judgments regarding job matches and other personnel issues that relate to a particular program's mission. For example, unless they work closely with a program, personnel specialists outside the program agency are necessarily limited in their familiarity with the skills and personal qualities required in a given position. A manager, on the other hand, if attentive to his or her responsibilities, is familiar with the overall organization, so that the substantive program needs in a particular job can be matched

Figure 1-1. Formal and informal reporting relationships of a personnel office

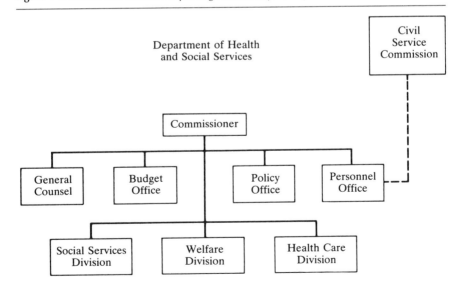

with the needs and abilities of an applicant or employee. The restraints imposed by many civil service rules and their application can make it difficult, however, for a program manager to exercise that program-related judgment and make timely decisions in the interest of the candidate, the organization, and its employees.[15] Many of the cases, including those in Chapters 3 and 4, explore the relationships between managers and other actors in the formal personnel system.

A well-designed personnel system can impose order, assist in equitable treatment of employees, and strengthen organizational performance. It will not do so very effectively, however, if the priorities of the central system are developed separately from the mission-related priorities of the program agency. Therefore, the procedures and judgments of a given central civil service system or personnel office may not match the values and priorities of the program agency. In addition, the emphasis on procedures in many civil service systems can lead to a concentration on standardized administrative and record keeping activities rather than on a responsive approach to mission-related priorities and actual fairness to applicants.

Where this is the case, a manager can avoid frustration and improve results by understanding the source of the priorities and values of the civil service commission and personnel department with which he or she must deal. Then a manager must plan personnel actions accordingly. Certainly, managers must respect the professional needs and be realistic about the institutional and personal needs of these actors. Successful managers develop an understanding of these values and the technical personnel practices that arise from them. Armed with that knowledge, they establish productive professional, and often personal, relationships with their personnel officer and civil service commission counterparts.[16]

Budget Offices. Because of the connections among money, pay issues, and the number and level of positions, the budget bureaucracy is a powerful factor in the personnel business, even though it may have no formal or direct personnel management authority. A manager may encounter the budget office in his or her own agency. The budget office in this situation is likely to be closely aligned with program priorities. On the other hand, there may be a central budget office for the jurisdiction, i.e., the budget office or bureau in a town, city, county or state. Such budget offices are more removed from a manager's program and may have different priorities.

Higher level managers or political executives commonly use the budget as an instrument to set priorities or allocate resources.[17] For this and other reasons, bud-

---

[15] Reports of long delays and referral of inappropriate candidates by the formal procedures abound among public managers. One recently documented and published source may be found in the *Appendix to the Staff Reports of the Federal Personnel Management Project.*

[16] For an illuminating discussion of the importance of personal/professional relationships in running the federal government, see Hugh Heclo, *A Government of Strangers: Executive Politics in Washington* (Washington: The Brookings Institution, 1977).

[17] Joseph L. Bower and Charles J. Christensen make this point in *Public Management: Text and Cases* (Homewood: Richard D. Irwin, 1978), Part Four in both the text and cases therein.

get authorities may be driven more by overall spending priorities, availability of dollars, or political considerations than by the particular effect of budget proposals or procedures on programs or employees of an agency. The difference between priorities of the program office and those of budget office may be especially evident when saving money is a primary driving force. As suggested by the example of Robert F. provided on page 11, under severe fiscal limitations a manager's control over promotions or filling vacancies can be severely affected by budgetary edicts and actions aimed at controlling costs. While a program manager may share a goal of efficiency with the budget office, he or she shares it in the specific context of program purposes and a manager's interest in the welfare and motivation of his or her employees. The case in Chapter 16 contains an example of the influence of budget processes and institutions on personnel decisions.

The Legislative Branch. The legislative branch presents another category of actors and processes that affect personnel management and policy. Legislators become involved as they pursue their role in the lawmaking, budget, and appropriation processes, through legislative oversight and as players in the game of interest-group politics.

Legislatures make specific policies and rules that a civil service commission, personnel board, or other body must implement and follow. Most government programs are created by legislative acts, and often their staffing and organizational structures are defined in law. Legislatures have been known to initiate reorganizations, and recently there have been instances of legislators specifying performance targets for individual managers under a formal performance appraisal system.[18]

Other less structured activities are carried on in response to more immediate constituent pressure. These might include constituent service to an aggrieved employee or angry constituent (who may recently have been mistreated by one of your employees!) or by an unsuccessful job seeker. The legislative branch may also pressure an agency in response to complaints or objections from the interest groups that were discussed earlier. Legislators may be involved in different ways and to varying degrees in job selections. This sort of activity varies with civil service rules and traditions in each jurisdiction and with the characteristics of particular legislators.

These constituent and job selection activities are more or less accepted parts of the legislators' role as elected representatives. These activities have, however different roots, less tangible criteria, and less accountability than the legislator's appropriations, authorization, and oversight responsibilities. Less legitimate but no less real are occasional efforts, frequently by legislative staff, to influence day-to-day management matters of an executive agency. This may be done indirectly

---

[18] For an example, see "Immigration and Naturalization Service Records Management Problems; Twenty-Ninth Report by the Committee on Government Operators," (House Report No. 96-1459, October 17, 1980). See the recommendations, p. 70 and preceding discussion and p. 80.

through activities in the oversight or appropriations processes or more directly by threatening a manager with unwanted legislative involvement or restrictions. Many of the cases in the book reflect various forms of legislative influence in personnel matters, especially Chapters 5, 11, and 14.

Audit Agencies. Inspectors general, state or local auditors, and agencies like the U.S. General Accounting Office perform activities to promote efficiency and prevent fraud and waste. Among their activities, such agencies "audit" government programs and agencies for compliance with the law, administrative rules, or practices. They also may study implementation of a particular program and its resource utilization. They often render judgments about such things as the number of people used or required in a program, skill requirements, skill utilization, or the overall effectiveness of a program or agency. Such reports and activities may at times be constructive and may motivate change. At other times they generate little real pressure to alter practices. Whether an audit activity is constructive or not, appearances count for a lot in the public sector. The activities of audit agencies, therefore, can exert pressure on managers to take up or avoid a practice, or they may excite other actors to pressure management.

Many civil service-type agencies perform audits of personnel procedures that can be quite relevant to the behavior of a personnel office. Judgments and activities by personnel offices in response to an audit — or in fear of one — may directly affect a manager's flexibility in processing personnel actions through the personnel office in his or her agency. The cases in Chapters 3 and 14 contain two such examples.

Procurement and Supply. Agencies and offices that handle supplies, equipment, and facilities have influence over variables affecting working conditions, environment, and work technology. Even where there is a general willingness to provide such facilities or services, the time taken by requisition procedures and related technical justification can affect the timing and appearance of management action. As with civil service bureaucracies, budget offices, and personnel offices, these procurement and supply institutions have priorities and values emerging from different sources than do program priorities. A district attorney may consider it critical that the new task force, formed to solve a string of murders, get offices and telephones immediately. The procurement office, however, may not respond until written justification and budget approval are obtained.

To the extent that values and priorities in regard to facilities are developed away from the program agency in question, management will find it more complicated to provide proper working conditions and equipment. Lest employees become disillusioned about management's power or commitment to them, management actions aimed at altering working conditions or technology must take into account the procedures, values, and pressures on agencies and actors in these logistical functions. Chapters 7 and 8 contain cases that involve these actors and institutions.

Equal Employment Opportunity Enforcement. Most government jurisdictions have a formal office or advocate for issues of equal employment opportunity (EEO). In larger government bodies there may be an office or department of human rights or other entity charged with EEO oversight or enforcement. Equal employment opportunity is a matter of social and personnel policy that affects, among other things, recruitment, selection, and promotions. Since the 1960s, many special procedures and requirements have been added to formal personnel systems, often as separate advocacy or grievance machinery. This machinery and related advocates add another group of processes and actors to the personnel management process. Many procedural requirements in this area have sometimes become divorced from social and ethical purposes of EEO and can affect the flexibility, timing, and appearances of management action on many recruitment, hiring, and promotion matters. Also, less formal but influential pressures can be generated by interest groups or other actors on either side of a case or controversy. Resolving the case problems in Chapters 3 and 14 requires consideration of these factors.

The Judicial System. Through precedential decisions and in considering individual cases, the courts and other adjudicatory forums may set and interpret personnel policy. In this arena, the legal system is concerned largely with due process, equity, and constitutional and civil rights of an aggrieved employee, rather than with management issues, with the organization's program objectives or clients, or with the effects of judicial actions on other employees. The judicial system is an important forum for resolving employment-related conflicts.

Legal challenges take time. During the period that the challenged policy or action is under review, a manager's authority and the status of the affected individuals are left unclear. During that time, uncertainty and antagonism may get in the way of the employment relationship with the aggrieved individual and with others. Legal challenges also add attorneys as actors in the personnel process and, if a challenge goes to an administrative hearing or to court, hearing officers and judges join the fray. While the role of appeals channels is important in protecting employee rights, the degree and type of litigiousness we have been experiencing may not be having as constructive an effect on the employment environment as we might like. Chapter 3 and Chapters 12–16 deal with several aspects of judicial and quasi-judicial activities.

Labor Groups and Neutral Agencies. The development of labor-management contracts make organized employee groups important actors in developing personnel policies. Labor laws in most government jurisdictions give public employee unions the right to bargain over a range of issues that can affect management flexibility.[19] Much as they do in private employment, unions, through collective bar-

---

[19] See *Summary of Public Sector Labor Relations Policies* (U.S. Department of Labor, Labor-Management Services Administration) for a periodic state-by-state compilation of bargainable issues and other aspects of labor management relations.

gaining or representation in the grievance process, can seek to alter or challenge a management policy or action. Where there are poor or unstable labor-management relations, managers may find confusing or restrictive contract provisions and an antagonistic union. In the public sector, about 50 percent of employees are represented by unions, whch is more than double the proportion of membership in the private sector.[20] Most public managers are likely, therefore, to be involved in labor-management issues and in dealing with neutral agencies (such as mediation services, public employee relations boards, or arbitrators) and unions.

Widespread unionism is relatively new to the public sector, so in many jurisdictions both parties have had little experience in labor-management relations. In many occupations and jurisdictions, the same inexperience has left the legal parameters and traditions of bargaining and dispute settlement undeveloped. In most private sector labor relations, longer years of formal experience, development of concepts and traditions, and a more unified string of decisions by federal courts and the National Labor Relations Board point the way. Simple borrowing of private sector practices does not fit the public sector and cannot, therefore, assist very much in catching up. In fact, many public bargaining laws reflect ill-suited adaptations of private sector techniques. Thus, new mechanisms have to evolve in many areas of public labor relations. Where practices and institutional arrangements are still unsettled, a bit of additional confusion will complicate labor-management relations in public employment.[21]

Even as these problems of inexperience and lack of structure are resolved, other characteristics of public sector labor relations will continue to affect the management of human resources in ways distinct from those of the private sector. Most of these distinctive characteristics are a product of our political system. Many, therefore, relate to the history of political involvement by public unions.

In the years before public employees began to gain bargaining rights, some employees — especially those in public safety — formed union-like groups and lobbied the legislative body that voted on their wages, benefits, and other conditions of work. In many state and local jurisdictions these lobbying relationships remain strong; elsewhere, new relationships have developed in the same tradition. Unions may also be active in supporting candidates for legislative or executive positions. Thus, the activities of public unions are not limited to dealing with management across the table or in the work place. They can influence personnel policy decisions through their electoral or lobbying activities. These activities are aimed at federal, state, and local legislators and at elected and appointed members of the executive branch in which their members work.[22] The cases in Chapters 12 and 13 focus on the role of labor groups and neutral agencies.

---

[20] *Statistical Abstract of the United States* (U.S. Department of Commerce, Bureau of the Census, 1980).

[21] See Brock, *Bargaining Beyond Impasse,* Chapter 1, especially pp. 3–6 and 8–16, and Chapter 8, pp. 205–207.

[22] *Ibid,* especially Chapter 1, pp. 5–8 and Chapter 8, pp. 211–212.

Prospects in a Diffused Environment

Traditions and institutions like those discussed above do not die easily; they reflect central aspects of government structure and philosophy in the United States. As an example of the endurance of civil service practices, it has taken nearly 100 years for even a modest degree of civil service reform to gain momentum.[23] This endurance is surprising since many formal practices are vestigial and serve no useful purpose, even in maintaining order and fairness.[24] In jurisdictions where it has begun, reform often has not affected the most important problems in formal personnel systems. Further, by their legislative and regulatory nature, such reforms can't easily address actors, institutions or other factors outside the formal personnel system that are also of critical importance to the management of people.

It is unlikely that managers can make significant changes in the formal personnel system or otherwise narrow the diffusion of formal authority affecting human resource management. The forces, traditions, and structures are, in general, too much a part of the fabric of government. However, public managers can improve human resource management in their organizations by improving their knowledge of management principles; by understanding the workings of the formal personnel system, institutions, and actors in the process; and by honing their skills at working within this system.

The public workplace represents a special case of human resource management. There, standard concepts of managerial, human, and organizational behavior can be useful, but only if seen against the backdrop of political, institutional, and technical complications.[25] Therefore, knowledge of the technical rules and requirements and of the relationships between managers and other actors are as central to managing people in a public agency as are concepts of management and of human and organizational behavior.

Consider the following example of using technical knowledge and an understanding of the priorities of other actors to gain a desired action:

> Helen P. was hired as an entry-level clerk-typist after 15 years out of the work force to raise a family. Paid less than others performing tasks of similar skill and responsibility, she soon demonstrated her skills as an administrator, supervisor, editor, and word processing operator, among many others. Her supervisor, Jack B., believed that people should be paid fairly for their contribution to the

---

[23] See the Federal Civil Service Reform Act of 1978, the many proposed state statutes that followed and the great and sudden interest evident in the literature in the 1977–1982 period. For example, the journals *Public Administration Review* and *Public Personnnel Management* devoted much space to the issue during this period.

[24] For some horror stories see the *Appendix to the Staff Report of the Federal Personnel Management Project.*

[25] For an apocryphal and humorous, yet illuminating, account of how a civil service merit system affects management flexibility on a baseball team, see Alan Jacobs, "The Civil Service Giants: A Story of Baseball and Bureaucracy." *Harper's,* October, 1978.

work unit and submitted by memorandum to the personnel office a positive and detailed recommendation for an increase in pay level. It was returned a few months later with a form letter noting "insufficient justification." In the meantime, Jack had learned that the type of personnel action most appropriate to a person whose responsibilities had increased was called a "promotion based on material modification of duties," a process with specific paperwork requirements and criteria for changes in the work. In the course of other personnel duties, Jack had also gotten to know several of the people in the personnel office, including a job classifier. He also learned a good bit about the way they do their jobs and the way in which their performance is measured and audited by their superiors.

On one occasion he mentioned to the classifier Helen's progress and accomplishments. The classifier suggested that Jack stop by to discuss the circumstances. With the advice of the classifier Jack filled out the proper forms and sent a revised memo of justification and a clear description of the duties that had been modified. The next week a classifier interviewed Helen and observed her at work. The promotion came through in the next paycheck.

Working Outside the Formal System. In addition to operating within the formal personnel system and knowing its customs, a public manager must understand the effect of variables and actors outside the formal personnel system. In any well-managed organization the tools for managing people are drawn, in fact, from a far broader spectrum of the job and job environment than simply from the formal personnel system. Each task and its environment are part of a broader system of variables that influence the productivity and satisfaction of employees. The better these aspects or elements of the work setting can be arranged to enhance productivity and satisfaction, the more effective the organization is likely to be. In addition to traditional personnel tools like promotions or pay raises, employee motivation and performance are affected by such things as opportunities for learning or training, unusual or challenging projects, good working conditions, positive supervision, and positive personal and professional experience on the job. While the constraints on these less traditional tools are usually less rigid than for most formal tools, there may be some external considerations affecting their use.

Expanding the Spectrum of Tools. By combining the other elements of the job environment with the features of a formal personnel system, a broader personnel system is made possible. We define this expanded system as that larger group of variables that affects people in their work and over which a manager can exercise some influence. We might differentiate this extended system from a civil service-type or formal personnel system by calling it a "managerial" personnel system: a system viewed from the vantage point of a program manager. The purpose of a managerial personnel system is to help accomplish organizational goals rather than to police or restrict the actions of managers or promote and protect viewpoints that are unrelated to organizational needs and purposes. A managerial personnel system contains more variables than a formal civil service system and is connected more directly both to the purposes and to the needs of a particular organization or work unit. Viewing the entire range of tools, a manager has an opportunity to fashion a managerial personnel system that matches the purposes and structure of his or her organization.

Since so many factors affect people on the job, this altered and broadened view can provide a more effective framework for predicting and diagnosing personnel problems as they relate to individuals, to the culture and characteristics of each work unit, or to the task. This view also reveals a wider array of options for affecting the behavior and satisfaction of employees. The greater number of options increases the possibilities for selecting the variable or tool that best fits a particular employee or group in each circumstance and organizational context.

Consider the case of an outstanding employee — call him David S. — blocked from promotion for a long period to come because of his low seniority. David's supervisor wanted to avoid his becoming discouraged and seeking a job elsewhere but thought there was no means by which to reinforce the employee's efforts.

> David S. had recently transferred from one portion of the state agricultural department, where his career had languished, to the state veterinary service. A doctor of veterinary medicine, David dug into the job and, among other things, was responsible for diagnosing and arresting a rare animal disease epidemic in the agricultural region of the state. With promotions blocked and budgets dry, his supervisor hoped for a chance to acknowledge the vet's talents and contribution and encourage his level of commitment. Toward the end of David's first year, his supervisor received a request to nominate a veterinarian for a prestigious training program. A few weeks later, David was selected over more senior vets. He was proud that his hard work and skill were being acknowledged and appreciated the opportunity for learning. He saw for himself a real future in the agency. He has since become one of the most energetic and sought-after veterinarians in the state, seniority notwithstanding.

Depending on the person, his or her interests, the task, and the employment setting, there usually is likely to be a variety of tools available to a manager that can affect a person's motivation, encourage growth, and provide recognition. Increases in salary and promotions are not necessarily the only tools, nor are they necessarily most important. There may be available a cash bonus, a desirable training program (as in the example above), a challenging task force, a nicer office, more advanced equipment, an alteration in job structure, expanded resources, or greater authority.[26] By assessing the extended, or managerial personnel system in each circumstance, the likelihood increases of finding an action or policy that can enhance employee satisfaction and performance.

The prospects for effective personnel management, given the diffusion of formal personnel practices and actors, depend on each manager's skill in identifying and operating within the managerial personnel system in his or her environment.

[26] For a discussion of some of these individually applied tools, see the article by Rosabeth Moss Kanter and Barry A. Stein, "Value Change and the Public Workforce: Labor Force Trends, the Salience of Opportunity and Power, and the Implications for Public Sector Management," a paper prepared for the U.S. Office of Personnel Management 1980 Public Management Conference, Washington, D.C., November 17–18, 1980.

That means dealing within the formal and traditional systems, dealing with other actors, and dealing with other aspects — outside the formal system — of the work and work environment that affect employees. The ability of a manager to select and apply parts of this extended personnel system will vary from organization to organization and jurisdiction to jurisdiction. It will depend most on the energy, creativity, and skill of each manager in linking employee talents and needs with program purposes in the context of each organization's culture. Although they may not all construe it quite this way, successful managers behave in ways that reflect a broadened, managerial view of the personnel system.

A broadened, managerial personnel system has many tools to motivate, recognize, or alter employee behavior. When a variable is used for managerial purposes it becomes a tool, rather than an impediment. One purpose of the framework in the next chapter and in the cases that follow in the remainder of the book is to develop the reader's ability to diagnose personnel problems and to find and use the variables or tools available in each work environment. The better the diagnosis and the more tools that are apparent, the more likely it is that effective strategies and tools can be applied to managing people.

CHAPTER 2

A Managerial Personnel System

Every organization contains an implicit managerial personnel system. Unlike a formal or civil service system, the broader, less formal managerial personnel system can not be written down. It takes shape and becomes a working system only as a manager makes use of it. How, then, can a manager recognize this extended system and make use of its tools? This chapter sketches out a general framework and describes some typical features of a managerial personnel system. These examples and principles are intended to help managers identify such a "system" in each organization and use it to diagnose problems and identify opportunities present in each specific circumstance.

The following discussion of this broader personnel system consists of four primary parts: (1) a description of the categories of management tools that exist in most organizations; (2) examples of the tools that typically fall within those categories and which, therefore, comprise a managerial personnel system; (3) a brief discussion of how the use of those tools is affected by the surrounding organizational, political, and bureaucratic culture; and (4) the development and use of program-related criteria for selecting strategies and tools and for making human resource management decisions.

The Categories of Management Tools: Processes and Practices

Observations in dozens of public agencies suggest that there are a number of basic processes that take place, almost of necessity, to handle human resource management in a work organization. Organizational practices — and managers — will differ in handling these. Yet all organizations carry on certain basic human resource functions that affect the way people experience their work and perform their job.[1]

Regardless of how these functions are handled, every work organization

---

[1] See John T. Dunlop, *Industrial Relations Systems* (Carbondale and Edwardsville: Southern Illinois University Press, 1977), Chapters 1 and 2, for a rigorous development of a generalized system applied to industrial relations.

somehow (1) hires people and causes people to leave, (2) pays people well or poorly, (3) has better or worse working conditions, (4) provides feedback more consciously or less, (5) settles or doesn't settle its conflicts or disagreements very well, and (6) has an easy or a difficult way to change personnel practices. These types of activities allow an organization to function — whether or not they are done well or whether or not a manager takes an active role in them.

Some of these processes and practices may be handled largely through a personnel office; others may be defined in a union contract. Still others may simply be handled by informal traditions that have grown up — and which no one in the agency may be consciously aware of. Elsewhere, an autocratic manager may call the shots. However these functions are handled, most work organizations carry them out in some form or fashion. Of course, the better these functions are handled, the more likely it is that the organization will perform well.

Other groupings of the functions are possible. But for purposes of this discussion these processes and practices are grouped into six major categories, described briefly in the list below and then explained in the paragraphs that follow. The remainder of the book is organized in accordance with this division. The six categories are depicted in the circle diagram in Figures 2-1 through 2-3.

1. *Human Resource Flows:* processes and practices that move people into, around, or out of positions in an organization, or into or out of the organization itself.

2. *Compensation:* processes and practices that determine and distribute pay and benefits.

3. *Work Practices and Conditions:* psychological, physical, social, technological, and procedural aspects of the job and workplace.

4. *Feedback and Information:* means by which employees receive information on what they are doing and how well they are doing it.

5. *Conflict Resolution:* ways in which conflicts are avoided, handled, or resolved.

6. *Altering Practices:* means of making changes in human resource management policy and practices.

As the cases in the book suggest, variables in and around these categories often overlap and interact to affect employees. Division into these categories, therefore, is somewhat arbitrary. Such division is intended to help in the analysis of human resource management situations by breaking them into somewhat more manageable pieces.

The Tools and Their Uses

Most organizations use a mixture of formal and informal processes and practices, some of these variables working purposefully and some unplanned, for carrying out activities in each of these six categories. The more of these variables a man-

Figure 2-1. A managerial personnel system: categories of variables

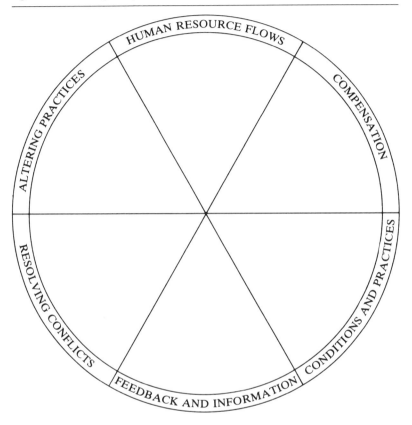

ager can call upon in a purposeful way, the more tools he or she will have to influence the work behavior and experience of employees. The following descriptions of each category provide examples of common variables, or tools, and their importance to managers. Their uses are illustrated in the cases found throughout the book. Most of the tools mentioned in this discussion are also depicted in the circle diagram in Figure 2-2.

Human Resource Flows. Included in this first category are things that affect the movement of people into, through, and out of an organization. They include management processes such as recruiting and hiring, promotion, reorganization, transfer, layoffs, and removal (including retirement and firing) and practices such as tenure, seniority, and preference.

Figure 2-2. Tools of human resource management: examples of processes and practices

This set of processes and practices, among other things, help to determine whether or not there is a good match between people and their jobs. A good job match is a primary ingredient to productivity, low turnover, and job satisfaction. Also, promotion and retirement practices will affect the nature and frequency of job opportunities and employees' expectations of the employment prospects that result. The flexibility and skill with which practices in this area are developed and applied can have an important effect on the character and quality of the work force that is attracted to or remains in an organization. The cases in Part II concentrate on human resource flows.

Compensation. In addition to wages and salaries, compensation can come in the form of health, pension, and other benefits and occasionally as incentive pay or bonuses. Raises, of course, are also in this category.

Public managers frequently feel that they have limited control over the compensation an individual employee receives. Compensation, nevertheless, affects the way people perceive their value and that of others as members of an organization. These perceptions can affect job performance and the degree of cooperation or competition among employees. Compensation is also a critical factor in attracting candidates to an organization and in retaining people who might otherwise leave for better opportunities. Compensation is sometimes used to make up for other deficiencies or difficulties in a job or job environment. Examples include hazard pay, night differentials, or even a raise to mollify someone passed over for promotion. In some instances, usually where pay is collectively bargained, monetary compensation may be offered in exchange for changes in work practices aimed at productivity improvement.

Overall, compensation can be a major focus of attention. Because it is a major budget item, it will receive attention. It will also receive attention where there is disagreement on its proper distribution or use. Despite constraints on its use as a management tool, public managers should be cognizant of its effects and seek ways to influence or mitigate those effects. Part III deals with the effects of compensation practices on employee motivation and management control.

Work Practices and Conditions. Variables in this category include physical and psychological conditions, the technology used, hours worked, supervisory practices, social conditions, and work rules. Office location, atmosphere, the work flow, flexibility in work hours, availability of computers or other equipment might be some examples of tools in this category.

Work practices and conditions may arise directly from work technology or skills in a particular setting; they can affect the availability and efficiency of resources used to do the job. Alternatively, practices and conditions may be related to the degree of personal freedom on the job and other emotional and psychological aspects of work. By affecting a person's attitude as well as the way the job is physically or mentally carried out, conditions and practices affect motivation and productivity. Since many work practices and conditions lie outside of formal personnel systems, they represent important aspects of the broader personnel system that a manager ought to consider in seeking to improve job performance and satisfaction. Part IV suggests the importance of these factors in managing people.

Feedback and Information. There are many ways that an employee gets information about performing his or her job and feedback about job performance. In the formal system, job training and orientation provide information about *what* to do, and a variety of rewards and punishments or formal evaluation systems can provide feedback about *how* well it was done. Part V focuses on a number of these factors. Variables in other categories are frequently used as, or provide, feedback. Thus, most parts of the book contain cases in which feedback is a factor. For example, changes in compensation, promotions, and assignment of a bigger (or smaller!) office may be used or seen as feedback. See Figure 2-2.

A less formal but no less important set of feedback tools exists or can be created according to what has value in an organization or suborganization: thank you's; a prestigious assignment; expanded responsibilities; frequent discussions of a project or developments in the organization; a letter or other acknowledgment of accomplishment from a client, a respected official, or an expert; a meeting with the President or the County Executive.

Individuals may respond differently to the same form of feedback depending upon their personality and perceptions. Also, through misunderstanding, misinterpretation, or thoughtlessness, employees may receive information and feedback that management does not intend. Many management actions — or lapses — have the potential to send a signal to employees about expectations or performance. As a consequence, management should be aware of the signals that employees are receiving, not just what management intends to send. Making conscious use of the channels and actions that provide information and feedback help a manager send more consistent, clearer signals about what activities are called for and how well those activities have been performed.

Conflict Resolution. People's personalities and priorities sometimes clash, and some people will inevitably disagree with one another on some aspect of work or management judgment. Conflicts can arise over many issues, including promotions, pay, space, and other features within the extended personnel system. Where no effective means exist to resolve conflicts, they may escalate. The more complicated a problem gets — or the stronger feelings of the parties are — the more difficult it may be to resolve and the greater the chances for an unfortunate or uncontrollable outcome. If conflicts persist or fester, a contentious atmosphere (or more obvious symptoms such as high turnover) can prevail.

Despite the difficulties that conflicts can cause, they often highlight more basic problems in need of repair. Although disputes can be helpful in illuminating problems, there still must be a means to resolve those underlying issues.

Some types of disputes occur in a labor-management context. Others arise out of application or interpretation of the formal personnel rules. There are many ways to avoid or settle such clashes. Labor-management negotiations and mediation are processes used to resolve certain classes of disputes, as are appeals, grievances, and arbitration mechanisms. In many organizations such problems are handled through less defined mechanisms, perhaps by informal intervention or mediation by someone who is generally looked to for advice. Elsewhere, conflicts may be handled through *ad hoc* means in response to a problem. Conflicts may be handled early or not until they provoke an obvious crisis.

Unnecessary or unnecessarily virulent conflicts divert time and energy away from more productive and inherently more satisfying tasks. For this reason, and because conflicts frequently identify problems requiring remedial attention, it is important to have a means of resolving quickly whatever disputes an organization experiences. Part VI of the book concentrates on many of these issues.

Altering Personnel Practices. The capacity of an organization to alter personnel processes and practices determines the speed or quality with which some of the elements in the previous five categories can be adjusted or improved. As there are changes in an agency's mission, the surrounding society, or the work force, it may be necessary or desirable to seek changes in formal practices, prevailing customs, or management approaches. Few policies or practices are immune to improvement as experience is gained. If a fundamental problem is exposed by conflict or by the unresponsiveness of a policy or practice to a changing labor force or labor market, the organization must be able to adjust. The more sensibly organizations or managers are able to alter formal and informal personnel practices, the better they can function in the existing environment.

Leaving in place inappropriate traditions or practices can be frustrating for managers and employees alike and possibly damaging to the agency. However, changing practices too rapidly with insufficient thought or consultation also has its risks. For example, if important actors or parties feel that their concerns were not properly factored into the change, they could adversely affect implementation of the change, adding to instability and confusion.

Another risk is that changes in one category can affect perceptions or flexibility in another. A unilateral loosening of discharge rules might cause a conflict over an ensuing firing, or a precipitous discharge could negate the goodwill engendered by a recent increase in pay scale. Linkages among categories, actors, and actions must be considered in contemplating each change. One way of altering practices is addressed in the case in Part VII, but less formal instances pervade other cases in the book.

Cultural Considerations: Constraints on the Use of Management Tools

Practices and traditions differ among agencies and jurisdictions because of differing histories, organizational needs, leadership, and peer relationships and because of the effects of the surrounding institutional and political culture. Therefore, the specific means available for carrying out human resource management functions can vary greatly even among units within a single government jurisdiction or agency. Further, individuals' histories and preferences also will be of importance to a manager in selecting tools or in making decisions that affect people. For example, a highly competent economist may be gratified by a promotion into a managerial position; another economist in a similar professional position may simply prefer a more challenging technical assignment.

In addition to considerations of internal organizational culture and individual differences, a public manager must deal with the institutions, actors, and processes that are part of the organization's external culture. These actors and the processes that govern them (or which they govern) can affect management actions in human resources and can otherwise affect employees directly. The better a manager understands these processes and institutions and the needs of these actors the more creative and successful he or she can be in developing and applying managerial tools.

As discussed in Chapter 1, there are certain types of institutions, actors, and processes that affect managers in using the tools in the categories just described. The following paragraphs provide examples of these external factors as they affect each of the categories in the managerial personnel system. Examples of these actors, institutions, and other constraints can be found as we traverse each section of the diagram in Figure 2-3. The specific array of actors, institutions, and processes will vary among organizations or over time, but we can cite some general examples. Many of them appear in the cases found in the rest of the book.

Following is a review of the categories in the managerial personnel system and the external factors that affect them.

Human resource flows, discussed in Part II and in Chapters 12, 14, and 15, are typically affected by some of the following actors, institutions, and processes: (1) civil service statutes and regulations; (2) interpretations and judgments by the civil service commission and (3) civil service commission staff; (4) interpretations and judgments by internal personnel offices (probably the most frequently encountered); (5) legislative action and oversight; (6) provisions of collective bargaining agreements, such as hiring and seniority; and (7) activity by unions representing employees in the agency through contract negotiations and grievances.

Compensation is one of the most constrained variables in a public manager's personnel system. Many actors, institutions, and related procedures affect it: (1) legislation determining pay scales; (2) legislative actors and committees in the pay setting process; (3) classification policy and practices of the civil service commission and (4) of the agency personnel office; (5) decisions by qualifications examiners or (6) classifiers; (7) the content of job descriptions; (8) provisions in labor contracts; (9) a union in a collective bargaining process and relationship; (10) arbitrators who may decide wage increases if the parties reach impasse; (11) budgets; (12) budget offices; and (13) traditional concern over possible misuse of public funds and fear of spoils or cronyism. Chapters 3, 4, 6, 7, 9, 11, and 12 introduce many of these factors.

Work practices and conditions are affected by the actors, institutions, and processes that affect the availability and use of funds, equipment, or space. Although frequently outside of the formal personnel system, these are nonetheless important. They include (1) budget offices; (2) legislative bodies and committees that affect an agency's budget; (3) procurement and supply policies and those who set and interpret the policies; i.e. (4) central supply agencies, (5) contracting offices, (6) procurement offices; (7) work rules and other provisions of collective bargaining agreements; (8) unions, through their bargaining and grievance behavior; (9) traditional ways of doing the work; and (10) other group norms. Part IV addresses many of these.

Figure 2-3. Constraints in a managerial personnel system: actors, institutions, and processes

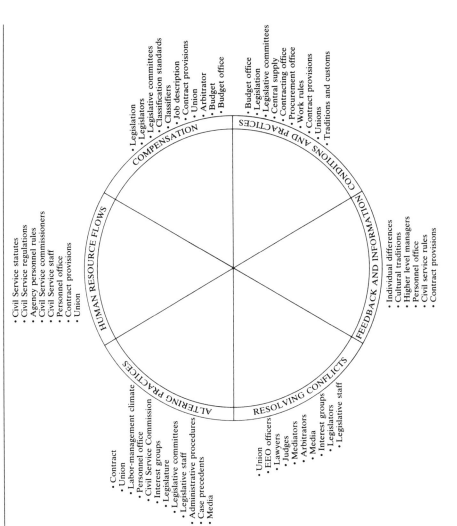

Feedback and information may come in many forms and may involve less severe constraints than will tools in most of the other categories. Thus, this may be a fruitful area in which to seek flexible management tools. The cases in Chapter 3 and in Chapters 7 through 11 will help to explore the important considerations in choosing feedback and information channels. Such considerations might include (1) individual differences and (2) organizational customs and history. However, when appraisal and reward systems are used to provide feedback or information, they typically will involve (3) requirements and practices of an appraisal system; (4) higher levels of managerial review; and (5) design, policy, or review input of a personnel office. Similarly, when feedback or information is provided by means of human resource flows (such as promotion), or by changes in compensation or in working conditions, it probably will involve the actors, institutions, and processes that affect those categories, such as (6) classification and other regulations, (7) classifiers, (8) civil service commissions and/or staff, (9) unions, (10) procurement offices and their practices, (11) budget offices, and (12) legislative committees and staff.

Resolving conflicts, the subject of Part VI, always includes the parties actually involved, but often they are not alone. Other common adversaries, participants, or interested parties might include (1) a union in negotiations or grievances; (2) an EEO officer or agency; (3) someone's lawyer; (4) a higher level manager and/or a designee; (5) a hearing officer or judge; (6) a mediator; (7) an arbitrator; and, if the conflict gets big or interesting enough, (8) an interest group representative, (9) perhaps members of the legislature or their staff, or (10) the media.

Alterations in practices can sometimes be effected by changing local traditions and by different interpretations of existing rules. Alterations can occur within subunits or in situations in which there is room for such interpretation, where there is consensus regarding the change, or where there are relatively few actors with a strong interest in the issue at hand. In order to avoid mistakes or fatal opposition, significant changes or departures, even in many informal practices, will usually require direct negotiation by a manager or at least consultation with key actors, institutions, or employees.

More obvious constraints are likely to be in evidence when changes in formal practices or firmly held traditions are sought. Explored primarily in the case in Part VII, some of the actors, processes, and institutions that may be encountered are (1) the union (both in contract negotiations and in lobbying to influence laws and administrative rules); (2) contract provisions and contract administration machinery; (3) the structure and climate of labor-management relations; (4) the personnel office; (5) the civil service commission; (6) interest groups such as those representing veterans and minorities; (7) "good government" groups such as Common Cause, the League of Women Voters, the Civil Service League; (8) the legislature; (9) legislative committees and (10) legislative staff; (11) procedural requirements for administrative changes (such as administrative procedures or open meeting rules); (12) grievance, judicial, or other proceedings that result in changed practices; and, if the change is large or controversial enough, (13) the media.

The Extended System. By surrounding the circle in Figure 2-3 with these actors, institutions and processes, the extended personnel system in a typical public organization can be illustrated. It is not just a formal system with forms and procedures. It is a more comprehensive, and accurate, view of the personnel management system that really exists, with pressures and judgments and behavioral effects. It has many more variables than those suggested by descriptions of formal personnel systems. In the latter, a much more limited menu of tools is typically presented, without the dynamic, task-related, or idiosyncratic elements present in each organization or subunit, and without taking into account the many other forces that affect the management of people.[2] Thus, the formulation in this discussion and accompanying Figures 2-1 through 2-3 is more representative of the actual system of variables and constraints that affect job performance and employee satisfaction in a public organization. Although other actors, institutions, rules, and constraints could be added to these examples, it's clear that a manager is rarely alone in developing or applying human resource policies or tools.

Strategic Considerations

The constellation of actors will differ with the place, time, and quality of the relationship between the key actors and the manager. An issue that seems important one year may be less important the next or may differ when different personalities and stakes are involved. These relationships constantly shift, and part of a manager's job is to assess the culture, constraints, and stakes represented in each decision. Each time, he or she must gauge the impact of these external factors on timing, direction, or choice of management tools or strategy. Therefore, each of the cases provides an opportunity to think both strategically and practically about human resource decisions or policies.

In assessing these factors prior to a decision, a manager may perceive that an important actor or institution will hold a different view. The probable or expected visceral response of an actor shouldn't suggest abandonment of an action important to the organization. Nor should a manager move precipitously. Rather, by knowing the modus operandi and concerns of relevant actors, a manager often can devise a strategy that will mitigate opposition.

For example, the fact that a manager might expect union opposition to a dismissal might suggest, for substantive or political reasons, reconsideration of the dismissal in light of the union's underlying concerns. Perhaps other disciplinary steps should be taken first. If upon review of the situation, dismissal still seemed the most appropriate action, the position and response of the union should be anticipated, at least, and steps taken to limit damage to the labor-management relationship. Perhaps explanations should be made to key union leaders or a tradeoff made on the means or timing of the dismissal to meet some of the union's insti-

---

[2] See the personnel manual of almost any public agency or its table of contents for an example.

tutional needs or priorities. Their concerns are certainly important, but not necessarily determinative.

A manager cannot always expect to eliminate opposition or resistance, but it is possible and important to limit the secondary effects of an action on future relationships with key actors. Consideration of other actors may dictate an entirely different decision on a given matter. However, in an extended managerial system, such consideration would often simply suggest different tools or possibly altered or more painstaking tactics for gaining the same result. It is the objective or purpose of a personnel action as it relates to organizational purposes, not the specific tool or action, that should be of paramount concern.

Up to this point we have discussed two sets of ingredients for successful human resource management: (1) an understanding and creative use of management tools provided by an extended, managerially focused personnel system; and (2) application of specific tools within the cultural constraints that may be deliberately or inadvertently imposed by other institutions, actors, and processes in the extended personnel system. Next, we look at a manager's use of criteria to select the tools or make decisions that will be most effective in each management situation. The following section is intended to further set the stage. Analysis of the cases later in the book will provide vicarious practice at such selection and decision making.

Criteria for Selection of Management Tools: Program Objectives and Institutional Capacity

Centrifugal Force vs. Management Direction. The elements of an extended personnel system will affect people even if the manager does not actively use parts of the system as tools. Because of the diffusion of personnel power among other actors and institutions, many elements in an employment setting will be influenced directly or indirectly by actors whose judgments are divorced from a manager's program priorities and who are unfamiliar with the internal culture or with characteristics of individuals in the manager's organization. In addition, the values and priorities of disparate actors may not agree and, therefore, can exert conflicting pressures on personnel policy matters or on individuals. Unless this potentially independent or passive character of personnel variables is unified by the program manager, policies and actions that affect people in the unit may be inconsistent with organizational purposes or with each other — even within the same organization, agency, or subunit. The confusing effects on employees can divert energy, resources, and behavior from organizational purposes and job satisfaction.

For example, people will be promoted or hired whether or not a manager becomes involved in the process. But the quality of the match between position and person can be affected greatly by a manager's active participation in defining the job and its requirements and in carefully screening candidates. Otherwise the job requirements are likely to be identified and screening done primarily by those in the civil service commission or personnel office, often with insufficient knowledge about the specific position, with less connection to program goals, and less exposure to the consequences of a poor match. While these actors have a role to play, so does a manager. A poor job match means lower productivity for the organization and less satisfaction for the employee and for others who may be affected. And whether or not the manager is active in the process, employees and others will hold him or her responsible for the quality and perceived fairness of the selection process and its result.

Many of the cases in this book demonstrate that, despite the imposition of merit systems, few decisions on promotions or on disciplinary or other actions are without some element of judgment. The question is, whose judgment will be dominant? Although a manager may have nominal decision making power, there may be considerable pressure from outsiders to make a decision in a certain way. Some quick examples:

1) In promotion or disciplinary actions, a manager may be influenced by the union's viewpoint or probable reaction, or he or she may be concerned about appearances of fairness or the inferences that may be made about his or her EEO record, or by what other employees might later expect of the manager. These pressures often conflict and decisions can be pushed one way or the other by the intensity of the pressure or the apparent power of persuasion of one of the actors or of the considerations put forth. But a decision primarily based on such pressures may not be in the best interest of employees or of program goals, nor will it demonstrate consistency or evidence fairness in the eyes of employees.

2) Even when there is no immediate event forcing a decision, there are many reasons for a manager to participate or try to influence variables in the extended personnel system. For example, as personnel policies are established, or a new performance evaluation system is being designed, managers have a choice: They can let such policies or systems be imposed, or they can involve themselves in the design and selection of the system they later will have to use.

3) A manager can choose to make use of feedback and reinforcement to direct and encourage the efforts of an employee or work group. Alternatively, a manager can simply assign work and presume that the formal evaluation or compensation system provides sufficient feedback. The following example reflects different degrees of involvement in supervision and use of feedback on a task:

> Joe F., an economist, had recently been assigned to work on an analytic staff for John R. Joe's previous supervisors had said that Joe was just a lazy old bureaucrat, came in at 9:00, left at 5:00, wasn't very creative or responsive between those hours, and it took weeks to get anything out of him. They'd never had much use for him. John R. received a draft of Joe's first project. As it turned out, John

read it that evening. When he came in the next morning about 8:00 A.M. he found Joe walking down the corridor looking at him expectantly.

"Good morning, Joe. I read your draft last night."

Joe stopped, his eyebrows went up, his head turned.

"Your approach is real creative. I wrote some comments in the margins kind of as a non-expert reader; let me dig it out of my briefcase and send it down to you. After you look at it why don't we have a cup of coffee and talk about it?"

Joe waited. Seeing Joe out of the corner of his eye, John immediately dug the draft out of his briefcase. They had coffee later in the day, and in three days a new draft was on John's desk. And so it went. John could hardly keep up with Joe, and the analysis progressed extremely well. When the study was passed on to John R.'s supervisors, John kept Joe informed on how it was being used. The next project went about the same way: very well.

A few years later after they had each moved on to other positions, they met for a drink.

"Joe, you did a great job when you were on my staff. Why didn't things work out for you with Bill and Sam? You're a talented guy. Why didn't they think so?"

"Those sons-of-bitches were always asking me to write things in time for yesterday. After I'd bust my ass to get it done, I'd never hear a thing. After a while it was hard to get interested in putting much energy into something when it looked as if they didn't even read it. At that point, I simply did the minimum necessary to get by. I like to discuss my ideas and find out if they're on target. That turns me on."

An active role by a manager in using the extended personnel system provided motivation and a spur to productivity, and it helped accomplish the primary mission of the office. A passive role by previous supervisors left the same employee feeling incompetent and unappreciated and thereby deprived their office of his best analytic work. In this instance, aspects of the extended, or managerial, personnel system — active supervision, and feedback on an assignment — were used with good results. Active use of tools *outside* the formal system were directed at an employee's personal needs and work style and resulted in better analytic work for the agency.

Criteria for Personnel Decisions. With or without active management effort, employees constantly are affected by elements in the extended personnel system. And these effects generally have implications for organizational performance. Intervention and use of the elements in the extended, or managerial, personnel system can be made simpler and more effective by employing decision criteria. Managers in the public sector lack unified and agreed-upon criteria such as profits, market share, or solvency, as is the case with those involved in other types of organizations. However, some unifying criterion or set of criteria is necessary for consistent handling of personnel issues and to promote the interests of fairness and organizational accomplishment. What can a public program manager use as a guidepost in developing and carrying out constructive human resource management decisions?

Mission-based criteria seem to hold the most promise. When considering a human resource issue of almost any type, a program manager's first consideration should be the potential effect of his or her decisions on the achievement of organizational purposes.

Management can achieve greater consistency in policies and actions affecting employees by reviewing each personnel issue in the context of the organization's central purposes, tendencies, and needs. For example, a recruitment policy or decision should be formulated and carried out to attract and hire people who have the skills and characteristics that can best help the organization at that time, not simply those who happen to meet minimum standards and happen to walk in on the day of the vacancy or who happened to be at a recent cocktail party. Nor will simply meeting the formal procedural requirements for screening candidates be sufficient to strengthen the organization. In considering the design and operation of a bonus system, fairness and equity will be important criteria. Still, the ability of the system to motivate employees toward useful, productive behavior will be most critical.

In addition to gaining immediate program results, an important organizational purpose usually will be to maintain or enhance the long-term capacity of an agency or work unit to fulfill its function. In a public organization the major ingredient of that capacity is the work force. Therefore, a manager must consider the long-term effect of a personnel policy or a decision on the development and quality of the work force.

Similarly, personnel policies or decisions can have repercussions on the viability of the organizational infrastructure and on prospects for political survival. For example, if a manager seeks to move a problem employee by reorganizing that person's job out of existence, the resulting structure may or may not be conducive to smooth-running operations. If an action is taken or policy established that irreconcilably offends employees, a militant union may be formed or an existing union galvanized against management. Along the same lines, a manager should be careful not to make an implacable enemy of a personnel office, a key legislator, a union leader or others who may be crucial to the manager's or the organization's influence or flexibility in the future.

To achieve consistency in the eyes of employees and to make progress toward program objectives, each decision should transcend the exigencies of the moment, even the temptation to be kind — or ruthless — to a particularly deserving employee or outside actor. While interest in individual job satisfaction and principles of equal treatment are central, there is frequently pressure simply to appease an employee or an actor in the personnel system without consideration of the impact of the action on immediate program goals or future organizational capacity.

It is frequently difficult to make a personnel decision when there are conflicting perspectives and pressures on what should be done. Such factors can more logically be sorted out and key considerations prioritized when filtered through a screen consisting of program purposes and ingredients of organizational success. The framework presented in this chapter can be used as a general checklist to see if a decision in one area might affect other variables or actors in the system. Also, asking questions like the following can serve as a rudder to a manager beset by conflicting considerations:

What are the overriding needs and objectives of the organization?

What are its primary purposes?

What must it do well to survive?

How will this decision affect those needs and purposes?

How will this policy or decision affect the speed and quality of service that clients receive?

Will it help or hurt this employee's motivation to provide that service?

Will it help or hurt the motivation of others?

Will it affect turnover or cause conflict?

How will it affect employee attitudes toward clients? Toward management?

What will that do to management control over the service?

Are there financial implications that may not be immediately apparent?

Will there be other costs?

Will any outside actors be incited to block this action or otherwise restrict future management flexibility or mission-related activities?

Right, Wrong, and Compromise. Other actors in the management process will have their own priorities, some of which may be of value to the organization. For example, there may be safeguards to ensure equal employment opportunity or certain procedures designed to ensure that only qualified candidates have access to jobs. Surely, these are helpful priorities to have in mind. But there may simply be arguments between managers and other actors over what is an equitable decision, over what's fair or who has a right to a job, bonus, or assignment. The dominant concern of each manager should be the effect of each such argument on the organization's mission and its organizational capacity. To maintain that capacity or fulfill other aspects of a mission, the values or requirements of especially powerful outside actors will have to be factored explicitly into a personnel policy or decision, whether or not those concerns assist in the agency's immediate program accomplishment. When dealing with especially powerful outside actors, a manager must on occasion negotiate or compromise in order to ensure the inclusion of management considerations in a policy or decision. A seemingly courageous, but unilateral, decision can result in wholesale dilution of program purposes if a powerful actor prevails and causes an opposite result. A decision for its own sake is an empty gesture without at least modest accomplishment of its intended effect. Also, because a powerful actor can be vengeful, the manager's or the organization's bureaucratic or political power can suffer, as can the organization's overall ability to accomplish its objectives. The art of compromise must therefore be part of a manager's repertoire in seeking to use the extended personnel system.[3] But knowing the extended system, good planning, and building the necessary knowledge and relationships can minimize the occasions for sacrificing organizational needs.

A Manager's Role in Applying Criteria. Unless mission-based criteria are applied with consistency, the formal and informal operations of the personnel environment are left to happen either (1) according to the priorities and activities of others in the system, (2) at random, or (3) according to transient pressures on the decision maker. Priorities of other actors may not only be different from those of a manager trying to accomplish a program goal, but the various actors will differ from one another in values and desires — even on the same case or policy and over time. Left on their own, the elements of the extended personnel system may affect employees with little apparent logic or consistency or with little relationship to the purposes of an agency or work unit. It is up to the manager to inject organizational priorities as much as possible into decisions and actions that affect people in his or her organization. While other types of consistency may be possible, no other actor in the process is in as good a position or has as much responsibility as the manager to exercise a stabilizing and unifying influence on the organization's success. By knowing his or her priorities and by viewing individual decisions in terms of those priorities, a manager can counterbalance strong pressures to the contrary and minimize counterproductive decisions.

The missions, organizational structures, and values of the other actors and institutions make it unlikely that their independent actions will coincide regularly with the central interests of a given government program and its manager. Their influence and pressures can, however, affect employees. Thus, a manager must take an active role if the employment environment is to have any consistent relationship to the organization's purpose. A program manager is the institutional linkage between the organization, with its purposes and resources, and the abilities and needs of the people who must do the work. A manager has to work with, influence, and often compromise with the other actors to ensure the best match between their actions and the needs of the program organization. If a manager has program and institutional objectives consistently and clearly in mind, he or she can more easily resist transient pressures, provide direction, and greatly simplify and stabilize the employment environment. Without those as criteria, a manager's personnel decisions may be vitiated by simplistic diagnosis and interpretations, neglect, or by recommendations and pressures from those with other agendas.

---

[3] For a discussion of the sorts of trade-offs and relationships that characterize actors in a bureaucracy, see Heclo, *A Government of Strangers*, especially Chapter 4.

Summary

The impact of politics, history, and the diffusion of power in governmental institutions has created an environment in which a manager's human resource responsibilities require not only skilled internal management but also require facility at "managing" the surrounding bureaucratic and political environment. The management of human resources can be effective when a manager looks broadly at and seeks to influence the larger array of variables that affect employee productivity and satisfaction.

Knowing the "Extended" Personnel System. By increasing the degree of awareness and influence over the many things that affect people on the job, a manager can develop greater influence in managing people. While each organization presents a different constellation of actors and variables, the entire task and employment environment falls more or less within a manager's purview. The task-related variables lie largely outside the formal personnel system and present many tools that a manager can use to affect the employment setting with limited interference by outside actors. Taken together, the ability to work within the formal system and an awareness of other tools in the extended or managerial personnel system presents a set of important management opportunities for gaining results. Combined with more active use of the tools provided by the formal system, this larger set of possibilities for affecting human resource management can be created or shaped by a manager in response to program purposes and the needs and talents of people in each organization. More tools thereby become available to be applied toward achieving a stable employment environment directed at organizational effectiveness. This case collection exposes and provides practice at identifying such tools.

Dealing with Other Actors. Many management tools can be applied effectively only if a manager can, and chooses to, deal with other actors holding the power to influence personnel matters. Without conscious management activity, the direction and influence of variables in the extended system will be affected significantly by the inertia of other actors and values within and surrounding the employment environment. Awareness, anticipation, and creative handling of the values, technical requirements, and priorities of other actors and institutions enable a manager to operate in a way that benefits organizational purposes and the well-being of employees, but which does not cause damaging confrontations with others in the system.

The other actors and institutions are not malevolent. Rather, their values and agendas will correspond to the needs and objectives of their own organizations, their professional values, and the technical and statutory requirements of their missions. No one actor or manager need be considered right or wrong, but the differences in values and needs and their sources must be understood and explicitly dealt with by a manager who intends to be successful. A successful manager must form and maintain relationships with, or have a strategy that deals with, others who have power in the managerial personnel system. This book offers an opportunity to identify these actors and the proper ways to deal with them.

Criteria for Decisions. A manager needs criteria to guide specific applications of personnel policy and interventions. A set of criteria should contribute to consistency for employees and to actions consistently in support of organizational purposes. Criteria based on organizational purposes can provide a manager courage in the face of the conflicting pressures that inevitably arise. With criteria for selecting tools and making decisions, a manager has greater reason and, therefore, greater power to resist transitory pressures and thereby maintain a consistent and productive employment setting. Such a setting can better support both organizational purposes and individual interests and keep them in harmony. The first case in the book finds a manager trying to balance these interests against pressures of the moment, and each subsequent case requires that appropriate criteria be identified in order to find a stable solution.

Diagnostic Abilities. For a manager to see the tools that are available, to identify the views of the actors present, and to apply criteria constructively in each work setting, he or she will need well-honed diagnostic abilities. These include the ability to recognize problems in human resource management; to anticipate or predict problems; to find the cause of the problem; to think through the consequences of a policy or decision; and to come up with creative solutions that fit each situation and which resolve the underlying issues, not just fix the symptoms. Analyzing the fourteen cases in this book will help to develop these diagnostic abilities.

Commitment to Managing People. Finally, a manager has to recognize his or her central and unique responsibility to make and implement the decisions that concern the people in his or her organization. The more a manager acts on this responsibility and utilizes his or her freedom of action, the greater will be that manager's influence over the success of a public program.

That is what this book is about — to develop a manager's abilities and awareness in these five areas:

1. an awareness of the extended or managerial personnel system in his or her organization

2. an understanding of and relationships with other actors in that system

3. an ability to develop and apply mission-based decision criteria

4. the development of diagnostic skills

5. an operational commitment to making and carrying out active, consistent, and constructive human resource management decisions.

To develop these skills, the cases in the seven sections of this book explore each category of tools in the managerial personnel system with explicit consideration of the institutional actors that are typically encountered. The cases are actual instances of managerial decisions involving typical human resource considerations. Practice in diagnosis and in identifying and applying the proper tools can be gained through analysis and discussion of the cases. As you progress through the book, more tools should become apparent and your abilities should be enhanced to diagnose problems, develop and apply criteria, and create specific and practical solutions under most organizational circumstances.

The case collection in this book is intended to help managers gain and utilize the appropriate degree of influence over human resource matters—in a form that can contribute to the better and more sensitive management of people in public agencies.

CHAPTER 3

The Managerial Climate

The case in this chapter draws on the description of the extended personnel system in the previous chapters and begins our exploration of the program manager's role in managing people. With this case, we can examine the use of decision criteria, start to develop a diagnostic approach to human resource problems, and begin to understand and deal with the presence, priorities, and values of other actors and institutions in the system. Further, we are able to use the case to examine how the formal personnel system and its interpretation can affect human resource policy and decisions.

We begin the discussion by talking about the manager's influence and dependence on the employment environment, a setting shaped in part by the variables in the managerial, or extended, personnel system.

To help an organization perform and at the same time provide satisfaction and security to people in the organization, a manager must play the central role in establishing a climate that can move the organization toward accomplishment of its objectives. As Chapter 2 suggested, a manager has to establish an environment that supports the organization's needs and purposes. To do so requires that the manager have influence over elements in the environment — in the extended personnel system — that affect the way people perceive the organization and the way they do their jobs.

Douglas McGregor, in the *Human Side of Enterprise,* articulates this point well: "If a boss cannot carry substantial influence with respect to decisions on salary increases, promotions or working conditions, his subordinates will have little confidence in him no matter what his attitude." [1] If McGregor is right, public managers have an especially difficult task in gaining that confidence.

In the public sector, many factors impede the fair and productive management of human resources. Chapter 1 described the diffusion of personnel authority among various actors and institutions. This diffusion contributes to the proliferation of impediments. Nevertheless, there are actions and tools that can positively affect

---

[1] Douglas McGregor, *The Human Side of Enterprise* (McGraw-Hill, 1960), Chapter 10, "The Managerial Climate," p. 136.

43

employees as well as the degree of influence a manager can have. The case study in this chapter — a true situation in a disguised location — allows us to diagnose the dilemma of a top manager who sought to gain influence in an organization characterized previously as "chaotic," "highly personalized," "erratic," and "without concern for employees." He tried to stabilize this employment environment through a combination of formal and informal management tools that he perceived to be at his disposal. By examining the context of his decision on a promotion, we see many of the structural, procedural, and institutional impediments to effective management of people. In seeking a solution to his dilemma, we find ourselves fashioning criteria to meet his organizational objectives while at the same time seeking ways in which he can take into account the actors and institutions that have a stake in the situation.

The manager in this case was committed to good human resource management and had a strategy in mind for stabilizing the organizational climate. He intended to make explicit and active use of the extended personnel system. By analyzing the case, we can evaluate his use of the tools and instrumentalities available for achieving his objectives. By analysis we have an opportunity to think about how his human resource strategy — or any other — might best be implemented in a public organization and how the decision he faces in this case will affect that implementation.

STUDY QUESTIONS

The following questions may be helpful in reaching a decision and recommending a plan of action to Jeff Scinton, the manager in the case.

1. What are Scinton's goals and objectives for this organization? What does his strategy depend upon?

2. Given his goals and strategy for the organization, what criteria should Scinton use in deciding the issue of Samson's promotion?

3. Should Scinton promote Sue Samson? Why or why not?

4. Which actors or institutions are likely to react positively or negatively to such a decision? Is their reaction of interest to Scinton? Why? Why not? How should he take any such reactions into account?

5. What will be the consequences of the decision you recommend to his organizational strategy and goals? What aspects of the decision or its implementation will lead to those consequences?

6. Would you modify your initial recommendation or suggest any specific implementation steps to lessen any negative consequences?

RECOMMENDED READING

Douglas McGregor, *The Human Side of Enterprise* (McGraw-Hill Book Co., 1960), Chapter 10, "The Managerial Climate."

SELECTED REFERENCES

Wickham Skinner, ''Big Hat, No Cattle,'' *Harvard Business Review,* September-October, 1981.

Nathan Glazer, *Affirmative Discrimination, Ethnic Inequality and Public Policy* (New York: Basic Books, 1975), Chapter 2.

Theodore Purcell, ''How G.E. Measures Managers in Fair Employment,'' *Harvard Business Review,* November-December, 1974.

Equal Employment Opportunity in the U.S. Department of Health, Labor and Commerce (A)

On February 25, 1977, Jeff Scinton was preparing to convene a meeting of his key staff aide, the personnel director and the administrative director of his organization to discuss a pending promotion action. In the United States Civil Service, most promotions must be approved by the employee's immediate supervisor and by the next level supervisor in the chain of command. In this instance, Mr. Scinton was not only the second-line supervisor, he was the presidentially appointed Assistant Secretary of the Environmental Regulation Agency (ERA) of the Department of Health, Labor and Commerce, a large federal cabinet agency.

He knew that some of the people walking into his office were about to argue strenuously that Susan Samson, a black female, should be promoted to the next pay level in the grade scale as a secretary, while another in the group was prepared to recommend that her promotion be denied. Ordinarily Scinton thought his subordinate managers should determine their own promotion policies, even though he technically held final approval authority. This case was a bit out of the ordinary since the matter might reflect importantly on the agency's treatment of employees, especially where discrimination issues were concerned. ERA had an abysmal record of employing and promoting minorities and was also known for a chaotic management and organizational atmosphere. One of his advisers felt strongly that he should exercise his authority to intervene rather than follow his more usual policy of perfunctorily signing the document.

Scinton was a graduate of the United States Military Academy and had served in the army with distinction for 10 years. He later worked in a number of private engineering and consulting firms and then entered the civilian Executive Branch of the Federal government where he took on a variety of complex managerial assignments as a GS-18, the highest pay grade and responsibility level for civil servants who are not appointed by the President or one of his appointees. He had earned a reputation for his ability to manage complex organizations, set priorities and accomplish the impossible, largely through a management style characterized as tough and fair. He was known for a highly developed sense of ethics and for demonstrating loyalty downward as well as upward in organizations of which he had been a part.

This organization was characterized by weak middle managers, most of whom had technical or other specialized background, although there were some exceptions. Despite their weakness, Scinton still believed in delegating most day-to-day management authority, and reserving only major policy issues for top management. He sought to alter and strengthen management behavior by delegating, by conducting ongoing and constructive performance appraisals of each manager and by using systems management techniques to promote accountability. He instituted frequent management staff meetings so that

This case was prepared by Jon Brock, lecturer at the John F. Kennedy School of Government, Harvard University. Funds for its development were supplied by the Ford Foundation and the Alfred P. Sloan Foundation. The case is intended to serve as a basis for class discussion rather than to illustrate either effective or ineffective handling of an administrative situation. While based upon a factual situation, the names of the organization and individuals are disguised and other information has been altered in the interest of confidentiality.

senior staff would be fully informed of policy issues and management priorities.

Finally, he sought to create a consistent and fair organizational environment through his example of being an orderly, tough and fair manager: He believed strongly that people in an organization needed to know what was expected of them and what they could expect in return.

As part of his campaign to promote a stable organizational environment, he encouraged managers to administer rewards and punishments fairly and consistently. For example, managers in the agency consistently had been asked by Scinton to give accurate and tough performance appraisals despite the prevailing tradition in government to give everyone "satisfactory" ratings. Ninety-eight percent of all performance ratings in the Federal government are "satisfactory." Indeed, when Scinton appraised his subordinate managers, word would often filter up from the receiving manager that Scinton was taking it all too seriously; the traditional practice, they said, would never change.

In a previous organizational affiliation, he forswore several employment opportunities for himself after his operational responsibilities had ended in order to spend several full-time months helping to find jobs for employees previously under his supervision who were being terminated as a result of a lack of funding for the agency.

Job Classification and Hints of Discrimination

The decision that Scinton faced concerned a 26-year-old black woman, Susan Samson, whose supervisor had recently sent through papers recommending her for a promotion. Ms. Samson was one of some 23 secretarial and clerical employees of the ERA who, a year earlier, had their jobs audited by the Civil Service Commission. Under the laws and procedures governing federal personnel practices, most government agencies possessed authority, delegated by the Civil Service Commission, to classify jobs at grade levels that they deemed appropriate to the task. This was usually determined by examining a job description prepared by the line organization. A classifier in the personnel office was responsible for completing the classification action. That individual either approves or disapproves the requested grade level after examining the job description. Occasionally, a manager simply submits job requirements and allows the classifier to determine the appropriate grade level. It is not an exact science, even though the award of grade level is determined in accordance with an elaborate manual of classification standards which specifies point scores for each job element. (See excerpts in Exhibit 3-1.) The total number of points indicates the GS level of the job.

Typically, there is a lot of judgment and considerable negotiation on the specific level awarded to a job. A classifier's decision is subject to an audit review by the Civil Service Commission, which periodically sweeps through federal agencies in order to curb what they consider improper classification and abuse of the system of classification and pay scales. Oftentimes overclassification contains a stigma of "political abuse" of the personnel system — a stigma to which civil servants are particularly averse. Classifiers, although they have some latitude, are typically conservative when classifying jobs since the audit by the Civil Service Commission can reflect significantly on their professional standing and abilities. Many managers feel that classifiers are unduly unresponsive to line management because of the sanction implicit in a "bad" audit. Top management in this case felt that the ERA classifiers were even less responsive to those managers whose tenure is determined more closely by electoral politics rather than by civil service status.

In this case the Civil Service Commission performed an audit, found that the jobs held by 23 secretaries to be overgraded, and ordered in late 1975 that the jobs be properly reclassified. The agency elected not to appeal the decision and proceeded to carry out the reclassification.*

The result of the audit was to rate 23 of the jobs one grade level lower. This is generally perceived as loss in status, although Civil Service rules specified that the incumbents to those jobs maintain their pay level for at least two years. "Downgrading" is also perceived as impeding or "ratcheting back" the individual's ability to progress to the next grade. These "down-grade" actions caused considerable consternation among those affected, since it appeared to reflect on their abilities and accomplishments in their jobs, in addition to the prospective loss of pay and perceived impediments to promotion potential. (In fact, an employee can actually compete for a job one level above the highest grade he or she has ever actually held for one year.) The local union, which was an affiliate of the AFL-CIO and an outspoken critic of management generally, took up the cause of these employees and exerted pressure on management seeking to gain some redress. Formal appeals of the reclassification were filed by a number of the women. Scinton recognized that the issue could severely undermine morale in the agency and perpetuate a widely held perception of lack of management commitment to employees of the agency. Since all of the downgraded employees were black, the racial overtones added an additional dimension of concern. The agency already had a history of racial difficulties and a poor record of minority employment. This situation could have a great, if unknown, impact on Scinton's efforts to redirect the agency and alter the organizational environment from one of chaos and uncertainty to one of fairness and consistency.

*Had the agency been unsuccessful in appealing the decision, their flexibility in the future to alter the questioned jobs would have been restricted by the requirement to obtain Civil Service Commission approval for any subsequent changes in those positions.

Scinton and Samuel Allen had become, respectively, Assistant and Deputy Assistant Secretary for Environmental Regulation just after the downgrade was ordered by the Commission. Scinton took the lead in seeking to defuse the situation. It was his view that the most important objective was to protect the interest of the employees and demonstrate management's resolve to do so. He immediately called together the agency's top managers as well as personnel experts and specialists in equal employment opportunity. Jointly they searched for possible solutions. He also met with union representatives and the affected employees and informed them of his progress. Finally, Scinton met with the top personnel and administrative people in the Department of Health, Labor and Commerce as well as with the personal assistant of the Secretary of Health, Labor and Commerce. As a result of his efforts at persuasion, Scinton was assured cooperation from the Assistant Secretary for Management, who recognized that the implications of the outcome were as important to the department's overall reputation as it was to ERA's. He was, therefore, more than willing to cooperate. The department had publicly made several strong statements about its commitment to equal employment opportunity and had directed all managers, by a Secretarial order, to be conscious of EEO goals as a major departmental policy. (See Exhibit 3-2.) All managers in the Department had included in their job descriptions and performance appraisal forms a category regarding commitment to equal employment opportunity and affirmative action.

After a few months of negotiations Scinton managed to work out an agreement with the union and with the individuals affected that specified a very clear and measurable commitment. Each of the affected individuals would receive, during the course of the next 12 months, an offer of secretarial jobs in ERA at least at the level of her old grade. If at the end of the year the agency was not able to make an offer to each of the individuals, secretarial jobs available elsewhere in the department would open up to them on a priority basis until each individual had received at least one fair and reasonable offer. Anyone who received but did not accept an offer waived her rights thereafter under the agreement, although individuals could and did receive more than one offer.

Samson's History in the Agency

Sue Samson was among those downgraded by the Civil Service Commission audit. She had been a GS-7, a relatively high grade for a secretary in the federal government. Her job had been rated by the auditors as a GS-6. In the ensuing confusion, she had been attached to a task force writing a report on environmental problems related to offshore drilling, which had become a "hot topic" about which the agency knew little. Thus, several crack analysts and managers were assigned to the task. Although a variety of officials for whom Samson had previously worked expressed mixed opinions regarding her performance and job attitude, Jim Safire, the project leader on the offshore oil project, spoke well of her skills and performance. Safire was respected throughout the agency for his good judgment and insistence on performance.

At about the time the project was completed there was a GS-7 secretarial opening in the office of Assistant Secretary Scinton. The secretarial job, while open, had no one to report to. This was due to the fact that the job of Special Assistant for Scientific Liaison, a special assistant to Deputy Assistant Secretary Allen, had not yet been filled. Nevertheless, the office manager, Gary Lomond, judged it desirable to fill the job now; since it would be filled ultimately by one of the persons on the "downgraded" list, he reasoned that the best performers would be selected first, and he wanted to fill the job with someone from the top of the list. Lomond later noted that Susan was regarded as a person with good skills, although her attitude and dedication had frequently fluctuated, but recalled that her recent association with the task force had been positive for all concerned. She officially occupied the position beginning in January, 1976.

Supervision

In the meantime, Samson worked informally for Lomond, who was not assigned a secretary, in the 5th floor suite of offices directly upstairs from the 4th floor suite in which Scinton, Allen, their secretaries and Scinton's assistant were housed. Samson would occasionally be asked to fill in at lunch time on the fourth floor. After about three months of this arrangement, a Scientific Liaison was hired and Samson had an official supervisor. Willard Cranston had never supervised anyone before and had never worked for the government. He had sought his job as he desired to leave his position as a researcher at a small midwestern college following a traumatic divorce.

About a month after Cranston arrived, during which time Samson was frequently absent and tardy, Ms. Samson, without explanation, did not appear at work. After informal attempts to reach her for several days, a telegram was drafted and sent with the assistance of Lomond and the director of personnel, informing her that she was absent without official leave (AWOL) and could face termination if she did not immediately make known her whereabouts and return to work shortly thereafter. Technically, a federal employee must request leave in writing ahead of time from his or her supervisor, who may or may not approve it depending upon workload and staffing considerations.

Ms. Samson returned to work a few days later just after Henry Dowitt had begun his employment as Scinton's executive assistant. Dowitt was a graduate of a well-known western business school and had several years experience in management and policy analysis elsewhere in the government. Dowitt was to provide advice on policy matters and was to improve the follow-through on the implementation of policy decisions. He was also to structure a more orderly environment and process for these top management decisions. Part of the latter task was to ensure smooth operation of the "front office" staff — those who served directly the Assistant and Deputy Assistant Secretary and their principal assistants. (See Exhibit 3-3.)

Dowitt was acutely aware of the downgrade problem and the ERA's reputation for callously treating employees and had heard much about the highly personalized and erratic management style of Scinton's predecessors. Lomond briefed Dowitt on the structure, personnel and operations of the front office and told Dowitt of the recent Samson absence. After she returned Dowitt observed her for a few weeks, noticing her frequent absences from her desk and numerous sick days.

Dowitt told the case writer: "It was clear to me that she didn't like being there. Otherwise, why would she be absent that much? The front office sets an example for the rest of the organization. It was management's responsibility to provide a decent work environment and to challenge people. Cranston was pretty flaky and didn't come in regularly or on time. How the hell could he expect her to? When my secretary went on vacation, I asked Samson to type a couple of things for me and she did a careful and thorough job. It's one thing when someone doesn't have the ability to do good work and feels frustrated; there's not much you can do. But with a skilled person who is unhappy, I really felt an obligation and saw possibilities.

"Pretty shortly thereafter, Cranston came to me and said he was having problems with her. She was uncooperative, surly, frequently absent and did poor work at least fifty percent of the time. If possible, he would like a different secretary. I decided I would try and talk with her

to find out if perhaps she was unhappy with Cranston as a supervisor, which wouldn't have shocked me, or to see if there wasn't something else going on that perhaps could be fixed. Besides Cranston's problems, the other secretaries in the office were grumbling about her frequent absences, the fact that she didn't carry her share of the common workload, didn't come in on time, etc. I felt it would be useful to have an informal chat with her."

The First Attempt at Change

"Well, it was one of the hardest conversations I ever had. I put it in the context of a series of 'get-to-know-you' conversations I had with everyone in the office during my first month; asking what each person's job was, how they liked it, what the problems were, etc. She said it was fine, couldn't be better. Boy, was I surprised. I wondered if there wasn't something we were doing that made it unpleasant for her to be there, wondering if working for a boss who didn't originally hire her was perhaps difficult. That was the wrong thing to say: 'No one has ever questioned my work performance. Why don't you ask Mr. Cranston? He's my boss, not you. You don't have any right to complain, or do anything. You aren't my official supervisor.'

"The conversation was inconclusive, and I suggested to Cranston that he try having a conversation with her, since she was more or less throwing the rulebook at me: She knew I could execute no official authority in connection with her. I told Cranston I would cooperate in trying to find her a different job, if either or both of them were willing to express their dissatisfaction and press for a change. He was her official supervisor; I wasn't and my attempt at informal intervention had failed.

"Increasingly he came to me seeking secretarial help. I knew the assignments he was getting from Sam Allen and he came for help every time he'd miss the deadline and Sam would put the heat on him.

"She went AWOL again and a more serious telegram went out. Cranston, the personnel people and I then agreed that something had to be done. Recognizing that she was competent, we thought that a 'change of venue' would be a good idea and began to work with the personnel office to identify offices that had vacancies. Most managers in the agency complained of inadequate numbers and quality of secretaries, so we thought that several people would be interested in hiring Susan. The personnel people, however, were rather certain that she would resist a change from what was perceived as the higher status job in the front office. When Safire approached her about a possible change, she apparently went to see the Equal Opportunity counselor for advice and we thought she might have been preparing to file a grievance.

"After she had returned, Cranston wouldn't press the point, said he'd handle it. I told him that I was happy to have him handle it, but that I would be completely unresponsive to his requests for secretarial help. He told me he'd had a couple of productive conversations with Samson about the need for her to perform better and be at work. For a while, at least, she kept pretty regular hours and I didn't hear much from Willard. Subsequently I asked him what he had done: I was actually quite amazed to see things going so smoothly. He told me that he had decided to hold out a carrot and told her he'd see about a promotion for her if her performance improved."

The Election

In November of 1976 the presidential election was won by Jimmy Carter of Georgia and in January of 1977 new cabinet and subcabinet appointments were made. A new Secretary of Health, Labor and Commerce was appointed and he proceeded to appoint his own group of As-sistant Secretaries to head the various parts of his department. Scinton and Allen served at the pleasure of the President and the Secretary and were, as members of the old administration, therefore slated to leave. Allen quickly resigned to begin a private law practice. Scinton, as Assistant Secretary, and Dowitt, as Scinton's executive assistant, were asked to stay on for a transition period until a suitable replacement for Scinton could be found, nominated by the President, and confirmed by the Senate, typically a two- to four-month process.

Samson Is Measured

On January 20, 1977, a set of performance appraisal documents (see Exhibit 3-4) was hand-carried to Dowitt by his administrative assistant, Jane Bando. Ms. Bando gave Dowitt his daily dose of a one-inch-thick pile of paper to review prior to submission to Scinton for decision or signature. She separately handed him the set of performance appraisal papers for Susan Samson.

"Look at that! She never does a damn thing — excuse my language. Why, she's never here and he gives her 'excellents' in all categories. But I'll tell you something, she wrote it and handed it to him all typed up like that. I heard her yelling and screaming about it. Next day, she walked out of his office, papers in hand, smiling like a Cheshire cat. Pardon me for saying so, 'cause it's none of my business, but if you-all sign that it just won't be right. Willard ought to be more grown up, but you shouldn't let him get away with that."

Dowitt had in his hand a set of documents signed by Cranston evaluating Samson's job performance as uniformly excellent. Bando was a high performer who as a GS-11 was actually two grades below the grade level (GS-13) she had previously achieved in a temporary agency where she had been employed in the early '70's.

Her dedication and high performance had resulted there in rapid promotions. When that agency was forced to reduce its staff when its legal mandate expired, she was returned to ERA, where she had "reemployment" rights — rights that are used to encourage employees to join temporary agencies.

Often, in order to attract staff, these temporary agencies are permitted to waive certain Civil Service requirements and to offer higher grade levels and promote rapidly. Since the agency guaranteeing the reemployment is only required to ensure a job for the individual, many people return to lower grades than they have achieved in the new agency. Oftentimes the personnel office of the original agency is less than sympathetic and views it as a burden to accept the returning "expatriate." Bando thus was "busted" when she returned. She was placed in a temporary position on which Dowitt had expended considerable time and effort to establish as permanent in an attempt to reward with job security her loyalty and good performance. She, however, had expressed interest in a promotion — both for the status and for the additional dollars it would mean to her and her family. The personnel office told Dowitt that it would be impossible to justify her position at any higher level.

A Promotion

The next day a set of blue papers was carried in by Bando. (See Exhibit 3-5a, 3-5b.) "Now look at these! First he gives her a flattering performance evaluation and now he promotes her. What about the rest of us who work for a living?" Dowitt looked at the papers just handed to him. They were the government's standard form 52, filled out to request a promotion for Samson and a job description describing her "new" duties.

A few days later Cranston came into Dowitt's office to discuss some difficulties he was having with the print shop. Dowitt made some phone calls and got the print shop to alter a few priorities so Cranston's project would get done. Dowitt asked him about the performance appraisal and promotion. "Will, I know that you don't think she's this good. What the hell is going on?"

"Well, she came in with the performance appraisal one day, said she knew I was leaving since administrations were changing and that I owed it to her. There was no talking her out of it. She said she'd just sit in my office until I signed it. I tried to reason with her, but she just sat there and called me all sorts of names, saying I promised her a promotion. She couldn't get a promotion without a good rating and if I refused, she'd know I was a racist. It was five o'clock and I wanted to go home, so I told her I'd think about it. She told me that there was no thinking about it, but said she'd come back in the morning and expect it to be signed. The next morning I came in and there she was. She got real nasty and just wouldn't leave. She had brought the promotion papers. We must have been in there another hour or two. I finally agreed to sign them both. I didn't know what else to do." He shook his head and smiled weakly.

"Will, this is a fraud. We all know she's been a problem. These evaluations have to be taken seriously, if we're going to improve this organization. It's not in the organization's interest or in hers to have this happen. I'd like to hand this back to you and have you deal with it in a more straightforward way."

Cranston shrugged his shoulders, a bit of sweat on his upper lip. "No, I, uh, don't really see what that would do. You guys handle it however you think best."

"Will, you're leaving. What difference does it make to you? No one can do anything to you, but leaving us with this kind of document leaves us very little flexibility. Jeff and I have to keep managing the place during the transition and this won't make it any easier to command loyalty and respect and get the other managers to continue to run a tight ship.''

''No, I just don't think I can do anything,'' Cranston said and hurriedly walked out. Since Cranston seemed unwilling to take responsibility and Dowitt could think of no way to leverage Cranston into action, he began to think of ways to work it out with Scinton and with Jim Safire, head of administration with responsibility for personnel. He called Safire to alert him.

Political Appointee

Two days later, on January 30, Cranston came into Dowitt's office holding a letter in his hand signed by the Administrative Assistant to the Secretary of Health, Labor and Commerce.

Since he was a political appointee, Cranston's tenure was being terminated as of February 15, 1977. Cranston wanted to know if Dowitt could do anything to delay that date. Although exceptions were being made so that the transition of administrations would be eased by maintaining for a few months a number of key people, he told Cranston, ''Those dates are final. I hardly think we can justify requesting an exception.'' Cranston pressed the matter for a few minutes but Dowitt was unshakable. They parted cordially.

Dowitt went into Scinton's office. ''Will Cranston — the son of a bitch — does no work for a year, gets paid $35,000, doesn't manage the one damn employee who works for him and leaves us holding the bag with a fraudulent promotion — and then has the nerve to come in looking to be kept on. The man has no pride.''

Early Strategy

Scinton asked how Dowitt was going to handle the promotion situation. ''Let me talk to Safire and the personnel people and see what the options are. As I see it, we don't have a GS-8 secretarial slot in our staffing pattern. The personnel people will almost never create a slot for you. For ten more reasons they'll rarely go for

a 'material modification'* of the duties of an existing job. [Exhibits 3-5b and 3-6 show ''new'' and old jobs.]

''They typically like to have open competition for an upgraded job so that, even if a material modification were appropriate, they aren't accused of favoring one employee over another. You know the union jumps on every promotion looking for evidence of preselection. I've been trying to have the personnel people materially modify two of our GS-2 mail clerks to GS-3, but they won't do it. I've been trying to get the personnel shop to modify Bando's job up one grade. She's been saving us from chaos all year. But they won't budge. They don't like her because she runs our assignment tracking system — and they're always behind. Anyway, Samson has literally no work to do, so a desk audit — which is a necessary part of a material modification — will probably be negative. It seems to me that we have grounds to deny the promotion that are completely non-personal and thus not subject to a grievance. The SF-52 is technically a *request* for a promotion which can be refused by you as the approving official on your own or on the technical advice of the personnel people. The thing that ought to concern us is the perception of inequality that will rebound among the rest of the front office and other secretarial and administrative people. Also, other managers won't be encouraged to resist similar kinds of pressure if we let this one by.''

In the meantime, Ms. Samson had persis-

---

* A ''material modification'' is a promotion resulting from a rewritten job description (see Exhibit 3-5b) based on new duties which, in the view of the supervisor, ''materially modify'' the job such that a higher rate of pay is in order. Usually, a ''desk audit'' takes place whereby the classifier seeks to confirm that the new duties in the rewritten description are indeed part of the job *and* worthy of a higher classificaton. Rather than gaining a promotion by seeking a new job, the material modification route results in promotion on the basis of growth in the existing job as measured by additional duties taken on and provides financial reward for growth in a job.

tently asked Cranston where her promotion papers were, recognizing that he would soon be gone. She also went to see the head personnel officer to explore her options and courses of action if the request were turned down. She knew the procedure for receiving a promotion based on "material modification of duties" and insisted that a desk audit be performed immediately to establish the level of her duties at the next GS salary level. She also went to see the equal employment opportunity counselor for the Environmental Regulation Agency, who was responsible, as in most agencies, for counseling and acting as an agent for employees in protecting their rights against discrimination in employment. The rumor mill had it that, if she did not receive the promotion she intended to file a grievance charging discrimination on the part of management.

Her visits to the personnel office prompted Jim Safire, the head of management services, under whom the personnel officer worked, to call Dowitt, who was a close colleague.

Safire: "You've had the Samson promotion papers for a couple of weeks."

Dowitt: "I've tried to get Cranston to rescind them but he won't do it and I called George [George Jonston, the personnel officer] to see what options we had, and he hasn't gotten back to me. I'm hoping we can deny it on the basis of no GS-8 slot and insufficient duties to support the desk audit."

Safire: "Well, she wants a 'material' and has been lobbying for a desk audit, but we don't even have the papers from you. Officially, we don't know about it, but it's getting pretty hot down here."

Dowitt: "O.K., I'll send the papers down, but no one gives her any work to do and she's never there, so I don't see how she'll get promoted on the basis of a desk audit."

Safire: "Henry, she *can* get promoted on the basis of a desk audit."

Dowitt: "What kind of an operation are you guys running?? I tried to get those GS-2 clerks in the records receipt division promoted to GS-3 so they could make a piddling $8,000 a year. They work hard and are loyal as hell. Your classifier said the job wasn't worth a GS-3. People ought to get a GS-3 if they can write their name."

Safire: "Well, Henry, this is different."

Dowitt: "Why, because she's making a fuss and going to file a grievance? Why should we reward incompetence and poor attitudes when there are lots of people who are breaking their asses and getting no reward? It just isn't a good example to set for managers or employees."

Safire: "Henry, look, I respect your judgment, but Jeff is the guy that has to sign it, not you, so quit trying to finesse the damn thing. Put the papers in front of him and ask him to take the action one way or another. If he wants to take it on, O.K., but it's up to him, not you. Now cut it out, will you? Apart from how I feel, it's up to him to make the decision. He's legally responsible, so let's move it out."

Meeting with Scinton

Safire, Jonston, and Dowitt entered Scinton's office on the following Monday. Jonston began by explaining his point of view: "We're not on very strong ground here. She was one of the twenty-three which immediately presupposes that she at least once had been badly treated by management. Cranston promised her a promotion if she behaved well. He signed a paper saying she behaved well — the performance appraisal — and delivered on the promotion. You have to have some direct evidence and reason to refuse to approve the performance appraisal or she'll have us dead to rights on that. The promotion, well, she knows that a material modification will do the trick. She's checked that out pretty carefully and has been all over the building to our local EEO counselor and to the head of departmental EEO. We really don't have any grounds on which to deny it that I find to be particularly strong. Any denial that you make of either action will almost undoubtedly be seen as discrimination imposed by you individually. She'll likely win the case and even if she doesn't, we'll be tied up in it for months, maybe years. . . ."

"If the grievance goes on," Safire added, "the disruption she'll cause to other people in the office will make it not worth the hassle. It could be a managerial nightmare and you guys are leaving: It'll be our headache."

"Henry, I know you have strong views. What do you think?"

"I think it's a travesty. She's a notorious bad actor. If we give her a promotion, what will the other secretaries think? They all do their jobs, to one degree or another and frequently complain or at least notice that Susan doesn't carry her load. Every one of them out there has done Samson's work at one time or another. And the rest of the managers in the organization will see us bowing to pressure; oiling the squeaky wheel, not being firm and fair as we urge them to do."

Jonston: "But, outside of this immediate office, I think most of the secretaries in the agency will see Susan as a martyr, shafted again by white management. I don't think your argument carries much weight as a matter of local public opinion."

Dowitt: "Maybe not, and we don't have time for a public opinion poll. Nevertheless, we shouldn't be cowed by the threat of a grievance. So what? I'd rather see us do what's right and what we've been telling other managers to do — 'hang tough' — and lose the grievance. I agree that it might be difficult for Jeff not to sign the performance appraisal, since he had no knowledge of her performance except for hearsay. The promotion is another thing. Why can't he make an evaluation of the workload, grade levels, etc. in his immediate office and deny the promotion? Besides, she's been AWOL twice. Doesn't that give us any credibility in denying a promotion? We've promoted two other black women in this office in the last two years. Doesn't that

help to establish that we aren't bigots? Regarding your point on all the trouble she can cause, she's already sitting in a room separate from the rest of the secretaries now that my secretary and I have moved downstairs. She hasn't done any productive work for anyone in months, so we won't miss her work. She can go ahead and create a tempest in a teapot up on the 5th floor if she wants to. With respect to our options you know and I know that a desk audit would show her job level to be about a GS-4. Even when Cranston was here, she barely typed 30 pages a week. A legitimate audit would make it a moot issue and your auditor is known as the tightest in the business."

"Henry," Johnson interrupted, "you can't go trying to get out of this on a technically. If Jeff decides to go with it, we go with it."

Safire: "She will have a strong grievance, given the history of this place, the good performance appraisal from her supervisor and a promise to grant a promotion."

Dowitt: "Do the rules say that managers making unreasonable promises contrary to other regulations and practices can be held up as evidence in the employees' favor?"

Jonston: "He didn't have the authority to tender a promotion. But that's not her problem when it comes to an EEO grievance. We have to go with it."

Dowitt: "If you're certain that we have to do this, shouldn't we get something for it? George, couldn't we deliver on the promotion by putting her into a GS-8 job in another office? Whether we give her the promotion or not, her usefulness in this office has long since finished. Don't we have some leverage now to get her into a different situation where the waters aren't poisoned? Even with the promotion she's going to feel that she was treated badly here; she thinks that she's had the promotion coming. It's not perceived as a reward. At least if she were somewhere else, the rest of our staff won't have a constant reminder of bad management and inequity in their midst. Also, she'd have a fresh start. In fact, the rules say that management has the right to transfer an employee laterally at management's initiative.''

Safire: ''She won't go peacefully. Remember we tried that back the last time she went AWOL and it didn't work. We should just do it and get it over with. If we try to move her and she's already filed the grievance, we'll be charged with a reprisal. It'll take years to unravel.''

Dowitt: ''Jeff, you're really going against yourself if you do this.''

Scinton: ''Let me think about this overnight and I'll give you my decision in the morning.''

Exhibit 3-1. Excerpts from U.S. Civil Service Commission
technical standards for position classification

GS-318   SECRETARY SERIES

This series covers all classes of positions the duties of which are to serve as personal assistant, generally to one individual, by performing a variety of clerical and administrative duties which are auxiliary to the work of the supervisor and which do not require a technical or professional knowledge of a specialized subject-matter area.

→ This standard has been edited for the purpose of referring to employees in this occupation and to their supervisors in a manner which eliminates implications of sex-stereotyping and to integrate the substance of Classification Standard Explanatory Memorandum No. 1 (TS 52) into this standard. This standard is a complete reprint of the standard for this series which was issued in April 1959, amended in December 1959, August 1961, October 1963, reprinted in June 1964, and December 1969. ←

*Basic Problems in Classifying
Secretarial Positions*

A secretary performs a variety of duties which are usually unrelated in kind and also as to the qualifications required for each. These dissimilar tasks are all auxiliary to the work of one individual — the supervisor. This constitutes a common thread which binds the individual tasks of the secretary into a unified position.

Not only are the individual tasks performed by a secretary different in kind, but they may also be different in grade-level value within any one position. In short, the secretarial position is a "mixed" position with tasks typical of different occupations or series and usually of different grade levels.

Most secretarial positions are equal to more than the sum of their individual parts. The relative degree to which this is so in any specific position depends on many things. The nature of the supervisor's position, the level of supervisory responsibility, the willingness of the supervisor to delegate authority, the individual level of ability of the secretary, and the variety of tasks to be performed usually loom largest in fixing the dimensions of the secretary's position. It should be added also that most secretarial positions are characterized by lesser supervision received, fewer and less specific guidelines, greater opportunity to use initiative, and more commitment responsibility than are other types of clerical positions.

Because all of the individual tasks of secretaries are related to the work of their supervisors there are unique opportunities available for secretaries to increase the scope of their position. For example, there is a possibility of what the automation engineer terms "feedback" among the individual tasks. That is, by utilizing information and insights obtained in performing one task secretaries can enlarge the scope and effectiveness of their performance of others. There is also a special opportunity for secretaries and supervisors to build a mutual work relationship which results in a secretary's acting and speaking for the supervisor with an authority not common in other clerical positions.

To the extent the work of the supervisor affords these kinds of opportunities, to the extent the supervisor is willing and able to permit and encourage the secretary to exploit these possibilities, and to the extent the secretary possesses the capacity and initiative to recognize and act on the opportunities available, the position of the

(Exhibit continues on following page.)

Exhibit 3-1. Continued

secretary may be substantially enlarged beyond the more routine performance of the assigned individual tasks.

However, secretarial positions vary widely in the nature and degree of the opportunities which are present and in extent to which they are exploited. This variation presents a special problem in the classification of some secretarial positions.

Characteristic of positions in this series is the close working relationship between the supervisor and the secretary. The secretary described herein either performs or supervises the performance of a variety of duties, including performing telephone and receptionist duties; keeping the supervisor's calendar and scheduling appointments and conferences; performing liaison duties as necessary between the supervisor and the other subordinates, and other offices; receiving and distributing incoming mail and preparing replies; arranging for recording of proceedings of conferences; channeling and reviewing outgoing mail; maintaining records and files; performing stenographic and typing services for the supervisor; making travel arrangements for the supervisor and the staff; and performing miscellaneous clerical duties. . . .

ELEMENT 1. SCOPE OF SUPERVISOR'S
ADMINISTRATIVE RESPONSIBILITY

The scope of the supervisor's administrative and/or program responsibility, although not an exclusive determinant, has a direct relationship to the potential scope and nature of the secretary's duties, the degree of complexity of the overall function in which the secretary participates, the amount of knowledge of procedures, rules, regulations, policies, and programs which is required, and the amount of guidance which is exerted. This element has been defined in five levels in ascending order of

scope and complexity in terms of typical organizational patterns as found in Government agencies. Each level or situation described here covers a range of executive positions. The cut-off between levels is made at a point where the increased scope of the supervisor's position normally has a sufficient effect upon the secretary's position to warrant recognition at the next more responsible level. Every possible situation has not been specifically described. Therefore, that level applies which is most nearly like the one present in the position being evaluated, except of course positions clearly at program and organizational levels higher than those defined.

To avoid any possible misinterpretation of these situations as classification by "grade attraction" it is emphasized that neither echelon nor grade of the supervisor is the automatic determinant of the secretary's grade. Rather, the scope of the supervisor's administrative responsibility is used to define the potential range of the secretary's duties and responsibilities. It is also emphasized that this element is not intended to evaluate the supervisor's position but rather, it is used to measure these aspects of the supervisor's responsibilities which might affect the secretary's position. For example, the fact that the supervisor reports to a very high level official in an executive department (or equivalent) does not, by itself, mean that a high "level" must be assigned to the job for the purposes of this standard. The nature and complexity of the position, the number and level of contacts, the size and complexity of the organization and other qualitative elements of the job which could have an impact on the secretary's assignment are the elements to be considered in determining the "level" to be assigned.

(Exhibit continues on following page.)

Exhibit 3-1. Continued

Nature of the Relationship Between the Secretarial and Supervisory Positions

A relationship does in fact exist between the grade of a secretary's position and the grade of organizational level of the supervisor's position. This relationship, while roughly parallel, is complicated by a number of elements so that it is misleading to make direct comparisons. The relationship is not constant, not simple, and certainly not mechanically assessable. The reasons that the grade or organizational level of the supervisor's position frequently offers no more than a clue to the possible potential of the secretarial position can be described in terms of the following elements:

1. *The nature of the work for which the supervisor is responsible.* — Some kinds of work afford more opportunities for the secretary than do others. Those which afford the greater opportunities do not necessarily result in the higher grades for the supervisor's position. A secretary to a public information officer GS-12 may have more responsibility for personal contacts, for gathering information, for composing correspondence, for establishing files, etc., than does the secretary for a research scientist at a higher grade.

2. *The capacity and willingness of the supervisor to delegate.* — This capacity and willingness is independent of the grade of the supervisor. Even when the supervisor can and does delegate widely there may be staff assistants who lighten much of the burden which in theory at least might otherwise fall to the secretary.

3. *The size of the organization for which the supervisor is responsible.* — Broadly speaking, in the larger organization the

supervisor may rely more on the secretary than is the case in smaller organizations. However, the size of the organization is not in direct proportion to the grade of supervisor's position. The position of the supervisor of a very large mail and file unit may be several grades below the position of the supervisor of a small management analysis unit.

4. *The confidence of the supervisor in the secretary.* — This again is independent of the grade of the supervisor's position. Instead, the supervisor's confidence may be conditioned by the apparent ability of the secretary, the length of time the secretary has worked in the organization, the length of time the secretary has worked for the supervisor, the length of time the supervisor has worked in the organization, the inherent attitude of the supervisor toward the secretary and other subordinates, etc.

5. *The intellectual ability of the secretary to master various possible tasks.* — Inherent capacities will condition the secretary's ability to master the full potential of the job. The grade level of the supervisor is certainly not a valid prediction of the secretary's ability.

6. *The willingness of the secretary to assume responsibility.* — Not every one has the desire to function at the peak of his ability. Whether the reason is health, family, lack of confidence, lack of ambition, or other cause, the gap between what is possible and what exists is sometimes wide.

7. *The overall personality of the secretary.* — A secretary with ample intellectual ability and a high level of am-
(Exhibit continues on following page.)

Exhibit 3-1. Continued

bition may still be deprived by the supervisor of possible higher level opportunities because of personality shortcomings, e.g., inability to work smoothly with other subordinates of the supervisor. Once again, the grade of the supervisor's position is hardly a measure of this.

Not only do these forces tend to operate independently of the grade of the supervisor's position, but also they change in their effect from time to time. The most noticeable change occurs when either the supervisor or secretary is replaced or the organization in which the supervisor functions is altered.

The operation of these forces on the secretary's position cannot be measured by examining only the supervisor's position.

The effect of these forces can be accurately evaluated by an examination of the duties which are performed and the responsibilities which are assumed.

It is the duties performed and the responsibilities assumed that reveal the true worth of the secretarial position. Any mechanically established relationship to the grade, rank, or organizational level of the supervisor's position must necessarily ignore realities in most situations and must therefore run counter to the goals of good personnel management.

It is a fact, however, that the nature of the supervisor's position establishes limits within which the secretary necessarily functions. The nature of the supervisor's position, therefore, is considered as one major factor in the standard. . . .

Originally issued April 1959   TS 18   May 1974

Exhibit 3-2. Equal Employment Opportunity Policy in the
Department of Health, Labor and Commerce

DEPARTMENT OF HEALTH, LABOR AND COMMERCE

Office of the Secretary

Washington

March 17, 197

SECRETARY'S ORDER 4-78

SUBJECT: Equal Employment Opportunity Policy, Delegations of Authority,
          and Assignment of Responsibility

1. Purpose. To set forth Department of Health, Labor and Commerce policy
and to delegate authority and assign responsibility for the establishment
and maintenance of the Equal Employment Opportunity (EEO) Program for
Federal employees within the Department of Health, Labor and Commerce.

2. Authority and Directives Affected

   a. Authority. This Order is issed pursuant to, and in implementation
of, P.L. 92-261, the Equal Employment Opportunity Act of 1972; P.L. 93-259,
the Fair Labor Standards Amendments of 1974 amending the Equal Pay Act;
P.L. 90-202, the Age Discrimination in Employment Act of 1967; Executive
Order 11478; and Subpart B of Part 713 of the Civil Service Commission (CSC)
regulations.

   b. Directives Affected. Secretary's Order 19-74 is canceled.

3. Policy. It is the policy of the HLC to provide equal opportunity
for all employees in every aspect of their employment and working conditions,
and for all applicants for employment, regardless of their race, color,
religion, national origin, sex, or age. The Department's management
programs shall reflect this policy. In addition to making equality of
opportunity a part of the day-to-day management of the Department, there
will be special programs developed and implemented to assure proper emphasis
on equal employment opportunity, including the Federal Women's Program
and the Hispanic Program. The EEO Program will include the use of goals
and timetables and will assure prompt action to redress and correct an
act of discrimination against any job applicant or HLC Federal employee,
by any HLC Federal employee or official, or consultant or expert under
contract to the Department.

DISTRIBUTION: SO-1

(Exhibit continues on following page.)

Exhibit 3-2. Continued

---

4. Delegation of Authority and Assignment of Responsibility

    a. The Assistant Secretary for Management is hereby delegated authority to take necessary action for ensuring the coordination and cooperation of all components of the HLC in carrying out the department's EEO policy. The Assistant Secretary will make the final decision on all formal discrimination complaints, except for those complaints against the Office of the Assistant Secretary for the Management or one of its organizational components, in which case the final decision will be made by the Solicitor of Health, Labor and Commerce.

    b. The Deputy Assistant Secretary for the Management is hereby delegated authority to make the proposed disposition of all formal discrimination complaints, except for those complaints against the Office of the Assistant Secretary for the Management or one of its organizational compenents, in which case the proposed disposition will be made by the Deputy Solicitor of Health, Labor and Commerce.

    c. The Director of Equal Employment is delegated authority and assigned responsibility for:

      (1) Implementing the Department's EEO policy in a manner consistent with P.L. 92-261, as set forth in Sub-part B of Part 713 of the CSC rules and regulations, and Executive Order 11478.

      (2) Evaluating systematically the effectiveness of the Department's EEO Program and recommending to the Secretary of HLC any improvements or corrections which are needed.

      (3) Administering the discrimination complaint process in the Department.

    d. HLC Agency Heads are hereby delegated authority and assigned responsibility for:

      (1) Developing and implementing a National Office Agency EEO Plan, which includes EEO goals and timetables and is consistent with Departmental guidelines and CSC regulations.

      (2) Providing each Regional HLC Agency Head with the number of regional positions that are expected to be allocated and filled during the time period covered by the upcoming Regional EEO Plan. These figures will be used in establishing regional recruitment goals and timetables.

      (3) Establishing in the National Office specific funding allocations sufficient for EEO Program development and implementation, and allocating to the Regional HLC Agency Administrators sufficient funds to assure EEO Program development and implementation in the regions.

      (4) Providing a quarterly review and analysis to the Director of Equal Employment Opportunity on the National Office EEO progress.

(Exhibit continues on following page.)

Exhibit 3-2. Continued

(5) Assuring that the EEO policies of the Department, as expressed in EEO Plans, are carried out at both the National and Regional levels.

e. The Regional Administrators for Management are hereby delegated authority and assigned responsibility for:

(1) Ensuring the coordination and cooperation of all Regional Agencies in complying with Departmental EEO policy.

(2) Providing for the development and administration of a region-wide EEO Plan which includes EEO goals and timetables, is consistent with Departmental guidelines and CSC regulations, and is based on HLC Agency input.

(3) Assisting and advising Regional HLC Agency Heads in the implementation of the regionwide EEO Plan.

(4) Providing a quarterly review and analysis to the Director of Equal Employment Opportunity on regionwide EEO progress.

f. Regional HLC Agency Heads are hereby delegated authority and assigned responsibility for:

(1) Providing input to, support for, and implementation of the regionwide EEO Plan.

(2) Allocating sufficient funds to assure EEO Program development and implementation.

(3) Providing a quarterly review and analysis of Agency progress to the Regional Administrator for Management and the National Office Agency Head for inclusion in the reports required by the Assistant Secretary for Management.

Secretary of Health, Labor and Commerce

Exhibit 3-3. Organization of Environmental Regulation Agency

ENVIRONMENTAL REGULATION AGENCY

Assistant Secretary
(J.Scinton)

Deputy Assistant Secretary
(S. Allen)

Executive Assistant
Admin. Assistants
(J. Bando, G.Lomond
H. Dowitt)

Special Assistant
for Scientific Liason
(W. Cranston)

Office of Policy and Program Evaluation

Office of Enforcement

Office of Environmental Rulemaking

Office of Management Service
(J. Safire)

Personnel
(Jonston)

Finance

Office of Research and Technology

Office of Congressional and Public Affairs

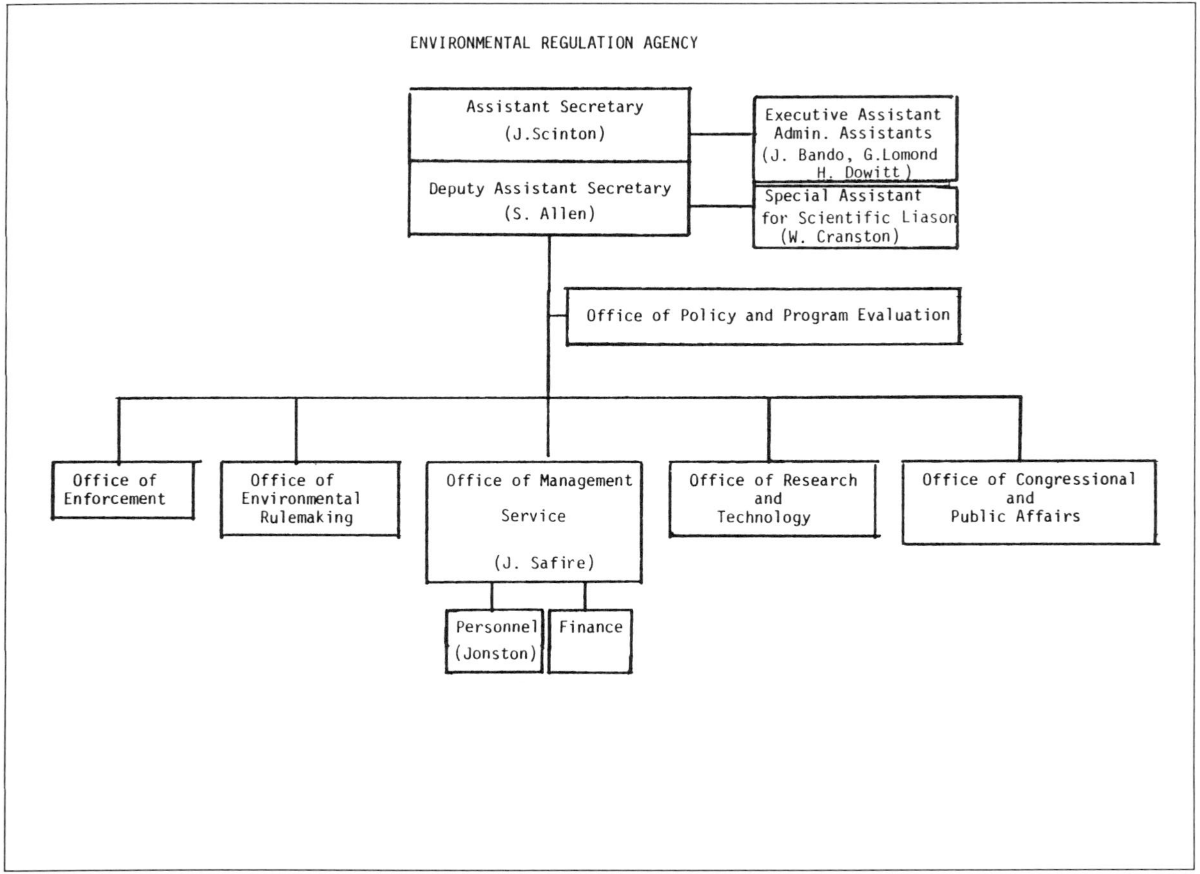

Exhibit 3-4. Performance requirements and evaluation

U.S DEPT. OF HEALTH, LABOR AND COMMERCE	PERFORMANCE REQUIREMENTS AND EVALUATION FOR POSITIONS IN THE UNION BARGAINING UNIT
1. Name of Employee Susan Samson	3. Organizational Location Office of the Assistant Secretary, Environmental Regulation Agency
2. Title and Grade Secretary (steno) GS-7	

4. Instructions to Supervisors in Establishing Performance Requirements

Performance requirements, in terms of principal work assignments and results expected, are to be recorded on this form in the spaces provided. The results achieved by the employee are to be added in the appropriate space. The performance evaluation is prepared annually or in accordance with instructions from your Administration or Office.

A. Establishing Performance Requirements. Develop with your employee a brief description of the principal work assignments of his job and a clear, brief and realistic description of what results and levels of achievement you expect. As work changes or new goals are set, update the requirements and indicate date when effective. It is your responsibility to make sure that the employee understands what is expected of him. This should be done at the beginning of the evaluation period or when you begin supervising the employee.

In addition to the performance requirements that are unique for the employee's job or occupation, there are several requirements that are found in most jobs. If the employee's job has these requirements, be sure to include them in the principal work assignments and results expected. They are divided into requirements commonly found in non-supervisory jobs and those commonly found in supervisory jobs having some elements of supervision, such as a straw-boss or crew leader.

(1) Non-supervisory Positions.

  (a) Person-to-person relationships that must be established to accomplish goals and objectives, as for example, teamwork, leadership in group tasks, training and advising others.

  (b) Organizing and planning required, including resourcefulness, perceptiveness in identifying and analyzing problems, and finding solutions and new approaches.

  (c) Oral communication required in individual work contacts, speaking before groups and so on.

  (d) Written communication required in accomplishing goals and objectives.

  (e) Assignments accomplished, which should be reflected in performance requirements under each individual task and also may be reported on separately. Be specific in terms of quality, quantity, timeliness, accuracy, completeness of work product, and consequences of poor performance.

(Exhibit continues on following page.)

Exhibit 3-4. Continued

(2) Positions Having Some Elements of Supervision.

   (a) Person-to-person relationships required. Consider communication and cooperation with subordinates, his superiors and with persons outside his organization; handling of human relations matters so that morale and productivity are maintained; skill in resolving day-to-day problems; obtaining high performance from his subordinates. Consider also ability required in furthering equal employment opportunity, such as encouragement and recognition of employee achievements, fair treatment of minority group employees, sensitivity to the developmental needs of all employees, including minority groups and women.

   (b) Supervisory skills required. Consider motivation, development, utilization of his subordinates; day-to-day direction of work; response to emergencies, pressure, changes; work decisions, including timeliness and soundness; review of work of subordinates, including timeliness and completeness.

D/L 1-390
December 1970

(Exhibit continues on following page.)

Exhibit 3-4. Continued

6. PERFORMANCE REQUIREMENTS AND EVALUATION ON PRINCIPAL WORK ASSIGNMENTS

Principal work assignments	Program objectives Results expected	Facts about performance Results achieved	Needs some improvement to meet expectations	Meets expectations	Exceeds expectations	Greatly exceeds expectations
1. Keeps in touch with all regular & special assignments & action officers on those assignments under Special Assistant's Supervision. 2. Screens phone calls & visitors. 3. Receives & reads incoming mail.	1. Helps keep projects on schedule by reminding responsible official. Keeps Special Assistant apprised of progress and problems. 2. Expected to use tact and judgment, maintaining good relations with all visitors.	1. Aware of all projects & action officers under Special Assistant's supervision. Tracks projects in an orderly manner & uses good judgment in reporting on progress on problems. 2. Very tactful & uses good judgment in referring calls & handling visitors.				X X
4. Reviews outgoing correspondence, checking for conformance with administrative instructions. 5. Maintains calendar, arranges meetings. 6. Takes dictation, types and performs other secretarial duties as required.	3. Refers minimum amount of correspondence to Special Assistant. 4. Error free correspondence should leave the office. 5. Exercises judgment regarding time, place, attendance and documents necessary for meetings. 6. Error-free, rapid performance of duties.	3. & 4. Overall, handles all correspondence duties without error. Has full responsibility for this area. 5. Consistently shows good taste & judgment, anticipating needs for and at meetings. 6. Excellent secretarial skills, responsive and quick turnaround on all projects.				X X X
7. Is consistently available and on time for work at duty station. 8. Office conduct is appropriate to duties.	7. Because of high-pressure environment, consistent attendance is a requirement. 8. Visitors and other staff are willing to deal with routine matters.	7. Punctuality and attendance are among best in the agency. Always available. 8. Creates pleasant and productive work environment for all who deal with the office.				X X

(Exhibit continues on following page.)

Exhibit 3-4. Continued

7. Instructions to Supervisors in Evaluating Performance

Your employee's performance should be evaluated continually in informal discussions. You should make a point of commenting on his performance in the course of the daily work. In addition, you are required to make an annual written evaluation of his performance on this form. This should represent your cumulative evaluation of the employee and be consistent with what you have told him in informal discussions during the year. The process should be carried out with the emphasis on developing factual data which will assist in improving the employee's performance, identifying needed skills and training, determining meritorious performance, and clarifying work assignments.

Using the "Work Assignments" and "Results Expected," which you have discussed with the employee and recorded on this form, complete the third column under "Facts about Performance-Results Achieved." Compare the employee's performance on each assignment against the results expected, in terms of what he actually accomplished. Describe the actual outcome of his major assignments and include factual data to support your judgments. Indicate any factors beyond the control of the employee which affected his performance on the assignment. Consider changes in requirements that occurred since you last up-dated them.

If the employee displayed unusual initiative or originality in accomplishing over-all objectives, be sure to give examples. If the employee spent only part of the year on a given principal work assignment indicate the length of time spent. Use additional pages, if necessary, to describe the employee's performance.

The proposed evaluation report should be discussed with the employee on an informal basis to avoid misunderstandings and possible inaccuracies.

After you have completed your evaluation, forward it to your supervisor for review, comment and signature. Be sure that both you and your supervisor have signed and dated the form. Discuss the final report with the employee personally and give him a copy of it.

8. Signature of Supervisor _Willard Cranston_   Date _1/20/77_

Indicate the length of time you have supervised this employee _4/76_ to _1/77_
                                                          Date   Date

9. Signature of Reviewer _____ Date _____

10. Instructions to Employees

Your supervisor will have a personal discussion with you about your performance and give you a copy of this completed Performance Requirements and Evaluation form. KEEP A COPY OF THIS COMPLETED FORM AS YOU MAY WISH TO FURNISH IT WITH YOUR APPLICATION WHEN APPLYING FOR FUTURE PROMOTION OPPORTUNITIES.

(Exhibit continues on following page.)

Exhibit 3-4. Continued

You will have 10 work days from the date you receive this Form to check either Box A or B below, sign and date the Form, and return it to your supervisor. If you do not sign or otherwise respond in writing by the end of the 10-day period, this form will be forwarded to your personnel office as your official performance evaluation.

If you do not agree with the evaluation and intend to file a grievance, your check in Box B below will constitute your notice of intent to submit a grievance.

Box C is to be checked only under special circumstances. If the Form is needed for a merit staffing action before the final version of the evaluation has been decided upon, either by agreement or adjudication, you are entitled to attach a statement. This statement will then accompany the official Form when it is sent for merit staffing evaluation.

CHECK THE APPROPRIATE BOXES BELOW, THEN SIGN AND DATE THIS FORM AND FORWARD IT TO YOUR SUPERVISOR.

My signature below signifies that:

A. ☑ My supervisor has discussed his evaluation of my performance with me and has given me a copy of the evaluation.

B. ☐ I do not agree with this evaluation and intend to file a grievance.

C. (For use when the evaluation is needed prior to agreement or adjudication.)

  ☐ I have no comments

  ☐ My comments are attached.

11. Signature of Employee: _____*Susan Samson*_____ Date: __1/20/77__

Exhibit 3-5a. Request for personnel action

Standard Form S2—Rev. July 1968
U.S. Civil Service Commission
PPM Ch. 295

PART I. REQUESTING OFFICE: Unless otherwise instructed, fill in all items in this part *except those inside the heavy lines.*
If applicable, obtain resignation and separation data on reverse side.

1. NAME (CAPS) LAST–FIRST–MIDDLE MR.–MISS–MRS.	2. *(For agency use)*	3. BIRTH DATE *(Mo., Day, Year)*	4. SOCIAL SECURITY NO.
Samson, Susan		1 15 50	127-38-7228

A. KIND OF ACTION REQUESTED	B. REQUEST NUMBER	C. DATE OF REQUEST
(1) PERSONNEL *(Specify appointment, resignment, resignation, etc.)* Promotion - material modification		Jan. 19, 1977

(2) POSITION *(Specify, establish, reverse, abolish, etc.)*	D. PROPOSED EFFECTIVE DATE ASAP	E. POSITION SENSITIVITY

5. VETERAN PREFERENCE 1—NO 3—10 PT. DISAB. 5—10 PT. OTHER 2—5 PT. 4—10 PT. COMP.	6. TENURE GROUP	7. SERVICE COMP. DATE	8. HANDICAP CODE

9. FEGLI 1—COVERED (REGULAR ONLY—DECLINED OPTICAL) 2—INELIGIBLE 3—WAIVED 4—COVERED (REG. & OPT.)	10. RETIREMENT 1—CS 3—FS 5—OTHER 2—FICA 4—NONE	11. *(For CSC use)*

12. NATURE OF ACTION CODE	13. EFFECTIVE DATE *(Mo., Day, Year)*	14. CIVIL SERVICE OR OTHER LEGAL AUTHORITY

15. FROM: POSITION TITLE AND NUMBER Secretary (steno)	16. PAY PLAN AND OCCUPATION CODE GS-318	17.(a) GRADE (b) STEP OR OR LEVEL RATE 7 3	18. SALARY

19. NAME AND LOCATION OF EMPLOYING OFFICE

Office of the Assistant Secretary, Environmental Regulation Agency

20. TO: POSITION TITLE AND NUMBER Secretary (steno)	21. PAY PLAN AND OCCUPATION CODE GS-318	22.(a) GRADE (b) STEP OR OR LEVEL RATE 8 1	23. SALARY

24. NAME AND LOCATION OF EMPLOYING OFFICE

Office of the Assistant Secretary, Environmental Regulation Agency

25. DUTY STATION *(City—Community.—State)* Metro Washington, D.C.	26. LOCATION CODE

27. APPROPRIATION	28. POSITION OCCUPIED 1—COMPETITIVE SERVICE 2—EXCEPTED SERVICE	29. APPORTIONED POSITION FROM: TO: STATE 1—PROVED–1 2—WAIVED–2

F. REMARKS BY REQUESTING OFFICE *(Continue in item F on reverse side, if necessary)*
Please review position for material modification of duties.

G. REQUESTED BY *(Signature and title)* *(Leave blank on resignations)* *Willard Cranston*	I. REQUEST APPROVED BY: SIGNATURE
H. FOR ADDITIONAL INFORMATION—CALL *(Name and telephone number)* *Susan Samson*	TITLE:

PART II. TO BE COMPLETED BY PERSONNEL OFFICE *(Items inside heavy lines in Part I above also to be completed)*

J. POSITION CLASSIFICATION ACTION ☐ IDENTICAL ADDITIONAL	☐ NEW	☐ VICE	☐ REGRADED

K. CLEARANCES	Initials or Signature	Date	(7) REMARKS *(Note: Use item 30 on reverse for Standard Form 50 remarks)*
(1)			
(2) COIL OR POS CONTROL			QUALIFICATION STANDARD
(3) CLASSIFICATION			
(4) PLACEMENT OR EMPL.			
(5)			
(6) APPROVED BY:			

(Exhibit continues on following page.)

Exhibit 3-5b. Samson's proposed "new" job description

Optional Form 8 July 1959 U.S. CIVIL SERVICE COMMISSION PPM Ch. 295 1008-104-01 POSITION DESCRIPTION CLASSIFICATION ACTION	1. Check one: Dept'l ☒ Field ☐ 3. Reason for submission: (a) If this position replaces another (i.e., a change of duties in an existing position), identify such position by title, allocation (service, series, grade), and position number. GS-301K-7 OS 73-32 (b) Other (specify)	2. Official headquarters: Washington, D.C.	4. Agency position No. 08 76-194 5. C.S.C. certification No. 6. Date of certification 7. Date received from C.S.C.

ALLOCATION BY	CLASS TITLE OF POSITION	CLASS Service	Series	Grade	INITIALS	DATE
Civil Service Comm.						
Department, agency, or establishment	Secretary (Steno)	GS	318	8		
Bureau						
Field office						
Recommended by initiating office	Secretary (Steno)	GS	318	8		

Organizational title of position (if any)	10. Name of employee (If vacancy, specify V-1, 2, 3, or 4)

11. Department, agency, or establishment Department of Health, Labor and Commerce	c. Third subdivision
First subdivision Environmental Regulation Agency	d. Fourth subdivision
Second subdivision Office of the Assistant Secretary	e. Fifth subdivision

12. This is a complete and accurate description of the duties and responsibilities of my position *Susan Samson* (Signature of employee) (Date)	13. This is a complete and accurate description of the duties and responsibilities of this position New Item 13 certification statement below required by CSC (Signature of immediate supervisor) (Date) Title:
14. Certification by head of bureau, division, field office, or designated representative (Signature) (Date) Title:	15. Certification by department, agency, or establishment (Signature) (Date) Title: Office of the Assistant Secretary

16. Description of duties and responsibilities

I certify that this is an accurate statement of the major duties and responsibilities of this position and its organizational relationships, and that the position is necessary to carry out government functions for which I am responsible. This certification is made with the knowledge that this information is to be used for statutory purposes relating to appointment and payment of public funds, and that false or misleading statements may constitute violations of such statutes or their implementing regulations.

————————————————————   ———————
(Signature of Immediate Supervisor)   Date

NOTICE TO EMPLOYEE

You have the right to appeal the classification of your position at any time, either within the Department or to the U.S. Civil Service Commission. Your bureau administrative office can tell you how to appeal.

(Exhibit continues on following page.)

Exhibit 3-5b. Continued

I. INTRODUCTION

Incumbent serves as secretary to the Special Assistant for Scientific Liaison, who is responsible for providing overall direction to the planning, initiating, implementing, and maintaining a program of interaction with the scientific community. As secretary, incumbent utilizes a comprehensive knowledge of overall changing ERA policies and procedures and uses initiative in interpreting them for the operation of the Special Assistant. Incumbent is responsible for relieving him of numerous administrative details and keeps him advised of important decisions made or actions taken on matters of importance or special interest to him.

II. DUTIES AND RESPONSIBILITIES

Serves as liaison between the Special Assistant for Scientific Liaison and the Office Director of the Agency and the scientific community, reporting to him in connection with instructions or assignments on specific programs, requests, etc., taking independent action as necessary or advisable on many of the assignments. Keeps in touch with the progress of all regular and special projects undertaken by the Special Assistant or assigned by him or her, discussing any problems or difficulties which they may have, or questions which may arise.

Receives and screens telephone calls for the Special Assistant and receives visitors including heads of the scientific and environmental organizations, officials of Federal agencies, representatives of industrial associations, employers, State officials, local officers and officials of both the Administration and the Department. Ascertains purpose of calls or visits and personally answers many of the various projects. Personally decides when to refer caller or visitor to her supervisor. Upon request, listens in on local and long distance calls to the supervisor, making notes on important phases of the conversation and keeping necessary records for follow-up on commitments made by the supervisor.

Receives and reads incoming mail and refers to the appropriate Office Director or Division Chief that which can be answered without referral to the supervisor. It is the incumbent's responsibility to see that a minimum amount of correspondence is referred to the Special Assistant, while at the same time assuring that all correspondence is rapidly and correctly handled. Incumbent has the ability and knowledge to prepare replies in superior's name, manner and style, utilizing a high degree of discretion and judgment so as to require a minimum of attention and correction by superior to his correspondence.

Reviews for appropriateness, style, form, responsiveness and policy implications, correspondence originated by Office Directors or Division Chiefs and prepared for supervisor's signature, as well as correspondence prepared for the signature of the Assistant Secretary of ERA and the Secretary of HLC. Returns letters to staff members which do not conform to established policies or procedures of ERA and advises what changes are required.

Maintains Supervisor's calendar of appointments and in his absence, or if he is unavailable, makes arrangements for future fulfillment. Reminds him of appointments and administrative matters requiring his personal attention and provides him at the proper time with a brief summary about the persons to be seen and their business with him, or with other necessary materials.

(Exhibit continues on following page.)

Exhibit 3-5b. Continued

Exercises primary responsibility for administrative details incident to conferences and meetings he attends, assembles pertinent material and as required or requested attends meetings and takes notes of proceedings in order to prepare resumes of the decisions reached.

Takes dictation from supervisor and participates in a variety of miscellaneous secretarial and clerical duties.

III. SUPERVISORY CONTROLS

Incumbent performs the duties set forth above and exercises responsibilities under the general supervision of the Special Assistant for Scientific Liaison. Except for unusual situations incumbent's actions and decisions are not reviewed. The duties require that incumbent demonstrate a thorough knowledge and understanding of the work done daily within the immediate office and the work of other components of the agency with whom incumbent deals. Incumbent is required to exercise tact, diplomacy, courtesy and patience in order to deal effectively with ERA employees and the general public.

Exhibit 3-6. Samson's current job description

Optional Form 8 July 1959 U.S. CIVIL SERVICE COMMISSION PPM Ch. 295 1008-104-01 POSITION DESCRIPTION CLASSIFICATION ACTION	1. Check one: Dept'l ☒ Field ☐	2. Official headquarters: Washington, D.C.	4. Agency position No. OS 76-194
	3. Reason for submission: (a) If this position replaces another (i.e., a change of duties in an existing position), identify such position by title, allocation (service, series, grade), and position number. GS-301K-7 OS 73-32	5. C.S.C. certification No.
		6. Date of certification
	(b) Other (specify)	7. Date received from C.S.C.

ALLOCATION BY	CLASS TITLE OF POSITION	CLASS			INITIALS	DATE
		Service	Series	Grade		
Civil Service Comm.						
Department, agency, or establishment	Secretary (Steno)	GS	318	7		
Bureau						
Field office						
Recommended by initiating office	Secretary (Steno)	GS	318	7		

Organizational title of position (if any)	10. Name of employee (If vacancy, specify V-1, 2, 3, or 4)
11. Department, agency, or establishment Department of Health, Labor and Commerce	c. Third subdivision
First subdivision Environmental Regulation Agency	d. Fourth subdivision
Second subdivision Office of the Assistant Secretary	e. Fifth subdivision
12. This is a complete and accurate description of the duties and responsibilities of my position	13. This is a complete and accurate description of the duties and responsibilities of this position New Item 13 certification statement below required by CSC

Susan Samson   1/76

(Signature of employee) (Date)	(Signature of immediate supervisor) (Date) Title:
14. Certification by head of bureau, division, field office, or designated representative _____ _____ (Signature) (Date) Title:	15. Certification by department, agency, or establishment *James Safire* 1/11/76 (Signature) (Date) Title: Office of the Assistant Secretary

16. Description of duties and responsibilities

I certify that this is an accurate statement of the major duties and responsibilities of this position and its organizational relationships, and that the position is necessary to carry out the government functions for which I am responsible. This certification is made with the knowledge that this information is to be used for statutory purposes relating to appointment and payment of public funds, and that false or misleading statements may constitute violations of such statutes or their implementing regulations.

Willard Cranston

_____   _____
(Signature of Immediate Supervisor)   Date

NOTICE TO EMPLOYEE

You have the right to appeal the classification of your position at any time, either within the Department or to the U.S. Civil Service Commission. Your bureau administrative office can tell you how to appeal.

(Exhibit continues on following page.)

INTRODUCTION

This position is located in the Office of the Assistant Secretary which is responsible for serving as the principal source of agency expertise with respect to scientific and engineering issues involving ERA and to provide technical assistance and support to the National Office and liaison with the scientific community.

The incumbent of this position serves as the principal secretary to the Special Asst. and acts as a personal assistant in performing a variety of administrative and clerical duties to assist him/her in effectively accomplishing various internal administrative and management objectives.

DUTIES AND RESPONSIBILITIES

As secretary to the Special Assistant for Scientific Liaison, the incumbent's duties include personal and telephone contacts; liaison with subordinate officials and with officials in the Department and other Agencies concerned with environmental regulation; obtains and presents information; correspondence preparation and review; and a variety of duties of a clerical and administrative nature that are a necessary adjunct to the duties and responsibilities of the supervisor.

1. Serves as liaison between the supervisor and Office directors and members of the scientific community in connection with transmitting information or assignments on specific programs, requests, etc. Independently takes action as necessary or advisable on many of the assignments and requests. Keeps in close touch with progress on all regular and special projects assigned to the Special Assistant and by him, frequently discussing and resolving any problems or difficulties which occur or answering questions which arise.

2. Receives personal callers and telephone calls for the Special Asst. and serves as the key point for all contacts with him/her. Ascertains the purpose of the contact or call and whether he/she is busy or not, to screen as many as possible either by personally completing them or referring them to other staff members. Insures, when making referrals to other staff members that telephone calls are completed and that the staff member to whom visitors are referred are available. Relieves the Special Assistant of many details on contacts and calls that are subsequently put through by furnishing him/her with information, usually on own initiative and without instructions. If the situation warrants, postpones contacts or calls solely for the purpose of creating the opportunity to obtain and present information that will be required.

3. Maintains the supervisor's calendar of appointments and engagements and, in his/her absence, or if the supervisor is unavailable, makes arrangements for future fulfillment. Reminds supervisor of appointments, engagements and administrative matters requiring his/her personal attention and provides, at the proper time, a brief summary about the individuals to be seen and their business and any other material deemed necessary for the meeting. Arranges all matters requiring the personal attention of the supervisor in order of urgency and calls to his/her attention those which should be given priority consideration.

(Exhibit continues on following page.)

Exhibit 3-6. Continued

4. Receives and processes requests for information, statistical data, or other material from officials inside and outside the Agency. Transmits requests (informing the supervisor) to whichever of the Office Directors can best provide what is required. Follows up on these requests to assure they are satisfactorily processed within reasonable time limits.

5. Receives and reads all incoming mail and refers to the supervisor only that which because of its nature, sensitivity, or prominence of the writer, requires his/her personal attention. Keeps the supervisor informed of all such referrals that are not of a routine nature and follows up to see that they are processed within the time frames established. From brief oral instructions prepares letters and memoranda for his/her signature or that of the Assistant Secretary of ERA to prominent government officials, State government officials, scientific and environmental organizations and others on confidential matters or program or policy questions.

6. Reviews outgoing correspondence prepared in the program offices for accuracy and to determine its conformance with established policy and standards of the ERA and the Department. That which does not meet established standards is returned to the appropriate officials with suggestions for correction or change. This pertains particularly to correspondence prepared for the signature of the Assistant Secretary.

7. Types a variety of materials including notes of conferences and meetings attended by the supervisor, correspondence, reports of travel, discussions and data to Regional and Office Directors. Performs a variety of other clerical and administrative functions necessitated by official requirements.

SUPERVISORY CONTROLS

Incumbent works under the general supervision of the Special Assistant and receives all supervision and guidance from that individual. Overall work is reviewed solely on the basis of his/her appraisal of incumbent's performance plus general office conduct, efficiency and effectiveness.

PART II

Human Resource Flows: Matching Positions and Persons

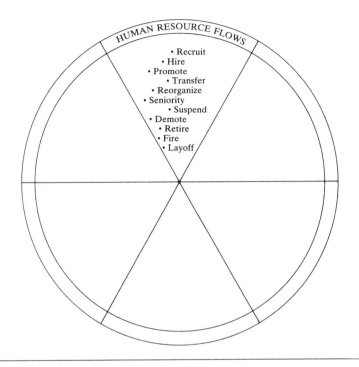

HUMAN RESOURCE FLOWS
- Recruit
- Hire
- Promote
- Transfer
- Reorganize
- Seniority
- Suspend
- Demote
- Retire
- Fire
- Layoff

We discussed in Chapter 2 that purposeful movement of people into, through, and out of an organization affects the quality of job matches. The quality of the match between a person and a task affects the workers' motivation and satisfaction, their productivity, and quality of their work. Matching a person and a job is a basic managerial decision. Effective use of other categories of management tools, such as compensation or feedback, will depend partially upon the efficacy of a given job match. A poor job match, in the extreme, can render other actions and tools ineffective. Trying to motivate a person who is basically mismatched to a task or work unit may be like pushing on a string. Therefore, tools that enhance job matches can contribute powerfully to a productive organization.

This section contains case examples of two managerial tools, hiring and reorganization, that are frequently used to affect the match between people and tasks. These cases also introduce some additional actors and their needs and values and provide a look at some of the technical constraints attached to the use of several management tools.

The case in Chapter 4, "Hiring Quality People in the Executive Office of the President," looks at the policy and actions of a government agency in the recruitment and hiring aspects of a public executive's job. A manager's options within a reorganization are examined in Chapter 5. In that chapter, a very large social service agency is required by law to reorganize. Although the law may cause large numbers of people to be moved, the desired change in service quality is far from assured.

Other cases later in the book involve aspects of job matching, such as the case on job enrichment in Chapter 7, in which specific techniques for altering the job are examined. Later, the misconduct case in Chapter 15 provides a reminder of the importance of fitting a person properly to a job situation.

CHAPTER 4

Recruitment and Selection

"I believe the only game in town is the personnel game. My theory is that if you have the right person in the right place, you don't have to do anything else. If you have the wrong person in the job, there's not a management system known to man that can save you!"[1]

Employees can be selected from within or from outside an organization. In either case it is important that a manager make choices (or establish selection policies) that result in the best possible job match. The match of a person's interests, skills, and personality with an organization's needs in a particular job and work setting will affect significantly the degree of the person's satisfaction and the quality of job performance. A proper match of skills and personal qualities to a given job situation will have an important effect on productivity as well as job satisfaction. It is, therefore, in the mutual interest of a job seeker and a manager to make the best possible match. This is especially important in public organizations wherein firing someone is very difficult. Firing or involuntary transfers are, in any event, extremely unpleasant, and they take up a lot of time and energy. Even in organizations where firing is a simpler matter, it is frequently avoided as too unpleasant to contemplate or carry out. One way to minimize the need for firing is to take extreme care every time a job is filled in the first place, as many performance and attitude difficulties can arise from nothing more than a poor job match. A poor job match also can cause a lot of wasted time in day-to-day management and supervision.

For these reasons, managers need to develop their skills in recruitment and selection, and become familiar with other tools that affect job matching, such as job design, career progression, training, and employee development. A good job match is a sufficiently central ingredient to the smooth running and success of an organization over the long term to merit a manager's devoting considerable time to matters of hiring and recruitment. Some jobs will be especially important to an organization and, therefore, merit a large degree of management attention. There-

[1] This quotation is attributed to Walter Wriston, Chairman of Citicorp. Quoted in Fred K. Foulkes and E. Robert Livernash, *Human Resource Management: Text and Cases* (Englewood Cliffs, Prentice-Hall, 1982), page 43.

fore, a manager should allocate his or her time appropriately, keeping in mind the fact that a person hired into the organization is very likely going to be there a long time.

First Steps

Define the Job. In beginning to think about the hiring or job-filling process a number of general steps can be outlined. First, it's important to define the job. What is the job and what does a person have to do or know to perform it? While a job title may remain the same over many years and the accompanying job description may contain the basic functional elements, the definition of the job and the skill mix or personality traits required to do it well may change from time to time as the organization's priorities shift or as people with similar or overlapping responsibilities come and go and redefine their turf. Therefore, it is desirable to review at least briefly, whenever a particular job becomes vacant, the specific formal and informal responsibilities attached to it. Often, changes in approach or style are desirable if the organization or its environment have been altered or require alteration. While it is sometimes difficult to put such information into a job description or qualifications standard, it is nevertheless of value in selecting the most appropriate candidate.

Job Description. Generally, the functions that must be performed and the characteristics and skills that a strong candidate should possess are put into some sort of job description or qualifications statement. Although a personnel system may or may not require this be done, writing it all down forces a manager to look carefully at what he or she is seeking. Writing the job description gives the manager control over the formal written processes that otherwise might be left to a clerk in the personnel office who knows a good bit less about the job in question than the manager. A good job description or qualifications statement also provides data to others who may participate in the screening process and gives potential candidates information about the job and its requirements. Finally, a well-thought-out job description can be used later to help clarify job requirements and serve as a basis for evaluations and feedback during the course of employment.

Define the Candidate. Once the job itself is defined, it is important to identify the kinds of characteristics and skills that a person would have to possess in order to do well in it. Frequently a formal personnel system will allow or require information on job-related candidate characteristics and background in a qualifications statement or standard. These items will help to screen out inappropriate candidates and more likely lead to selection of an individual who possesses the requisite characteristics. Inadequate discussion of the necessary qualifications can lead to selection on the basis of factors that are not central to job performance or that may even be extraneous, while use of well-considered, job-related criteria helps ensure that personal prejudices and biases are kept out of the process. Active use of these criteria can preclude hiring on the basis of surface impressions that may not have anything to do with a candidate's potential on the job and for which the organization may pay later. The use of clear job-related criteria is important also to meet tests of validity that may later be applied if the process is challenged.

Developing a Pool. There are hundreds of ways to develop a candidate pool, and every organization has its own formal or informal ways of doing so. Some organizations use word-of-mouth through informal networks to attract candidates. Others advertise in the newspapers, or post job announcements. Others hire head-hunters or go to job fairs. Whatever way of generating a pool is chosen, it ought to have a strong likelihood of yielding people with the proper characteristics and skills to perform the particular job being filled. For entry level positions, for example, organizations frequently recruit at educational institutions that grant degrees in areas of expertise necessary for the job. Recruitment at engineering schools or business schools are well-known examples. Frequently there may be other sources of people with similar skills, but the fact that a school through its admissions procedures and degree requirements has already done some screening means that part of the next task is already done.

Similarly, when seeking experienced people it is common to look in organizations or professional associations built around or using the requisite skill areas. This kind of focus can help in the job match and in saving time, both of which are important. If too much time is taken up in unnecessary screening, management time is wasted, and strong candidates that were previously available may have been snapped up in the interim. This defeats the purpose of a careful hiring and screening effort. At the same time, managers should be careful to avoid inappropriate screens that may be antiquated or unresponsive to the current needs of the organization or that inappropriately exclude minorities, women, or others.

Frequently, the formal personnel system will have certain restrictions or requirements for developing a candidate pool or for screening applicants out of that pool. Some such requirements can assist in improving the odds of hiring women or minorities. Usually, however, there is room in the formal practices to vary the method of developing a candidate pool to match organizational needs, while still meeting ethical and statutory obligations. Ordinarily, the more senior or specialized the job, the more likely it will be possible to tailor recruitment procedures. It behooves a manager to be certain that appropriate procedures are in effect for each type of hire.

Screening

Making the actual hiring decision is a matter of judgment. By careful development of criteria and careful screening, better judgment can be applied during the hiring process. Elements of subjective judgment, however, will exist in any process where evaluating people is involved.

Résumés. Résumés or job application forms allow a rough screening for whether or not a candidate possesses the basic skills and background necessary to do the job. Résumés allow a manager or other screener to narrow the field and decide who should be interviewed. If the initial screening is done by someone other than the hiring manager (as it frequently is), a good job description/qualifications statement and discussions between the manager and the screener will give the screener a much better idea of the important things to look for. The time that is spent in such discussions will be repaid with a better job match.

Interviews. An interview permits the manager or screener to get details of a person's experience, and sometimes to probe the veracity of statements in the résumé. It also allows the manager and the candidate to see if they mean the same things when they use terms such as *managed, supervised, analyzed,* or *implemented.* There are degrees of complexity and difficulty in all those terms that can differ from organization to organization and among jobs. The interview also permits an opportunity to experience the personal qualities of the candidate to see if the person meets those dimensions of the job requirements. If a job requires a significant amount of bureaucratic horsetrading, it will be more necessary to gauge the person's ability to get along with others than it would be if the job entailed mainly analysis and working alone. An appropriate interview process may give an indication of the candidates' skills and potential in this area. It is difficult to assess interpersonal characteristics by reading a résumé.

Other interview techniques, such as assessment centers, are also sometimes used, as are a variety of oral interview boards, committee interviews, or having the candidate make a presentation on a subject of interest to the organization. But most commonly a less structured, more informal interview process is used.

References. Finally, references come into play. It is a technique about which there is much controversy. When it is used, it is usually a late step in the process, waiting until no more than several very promising candidates remain in the pool. Choosing the people from whom to get references will be important to getting a full picture. For example, if you are interviewing candidates for a job that will have a lot of contact with the agency finance officer, you might want to talk with a finance officer the candidate has worked with to see how effectively the candidate dealt with that person. Questions for the finance officer ought to probe specific skills and aspects of their dealings and not focus on impressions alone: frequently someone handles their responsibilities effectively but doesn't form a lasting friendship. So plan on some questions that ask about specific types of skills and interactions, and make your own judgments.

References can shed light on how a person actually performed in an employment situation; how he or she worked in groups, how well he or she handled pressure or deadlines and other on-the-job circumstances. Résumés and interviews can only suggest such data. Also, a sense of the complexity and scope of the candidate's prior responsibilities can be sought and the representations from résumés and interviews verified and clarified.

Looking for significant patterns or consistent problems prevents one-time problems or interpersonal animosities from dominating the reference checking process. A consistent, even if subtle, pattern of poor performance on a critical aspect of a job, however, is a strong warning signal and should be heeded, or at least checked out or considered.

Curiously, many people are more capable and accomplished than they represent in a résumé or interview, and references can uncover that as well. For this reason also, references, although delicate, can be an important source of preemployment data.

Selection. A selection should be made as quickly as possible once a sufficient amount of screening has taken place. Good candidates will frequently have other options and may not be willing to wait. Therefore, the more streamlined and efficient the screening process — as long as it is effective — the more likely it is to get the best candidates.

Once the screening process is completed (i.e., the last interviewer satisfied, the references checked), the successful candidate should be called and offered the position right away lest he or she get away. Sometimes a candidate is wined and dined, usually with great encouragement to join. In some rare cases a spouse of the prospective employee is flown to the distant city of the prospective employer to ease the couple's uncertainty and bring harmony back into the domestic relationship.

A Public Sector Example

In a public agency a series of outside actors, institutions, processes, and values make necessary additional requirements. Very rigid procedures, designed originally to ensure fair treatment of applicants, frequently govern hiring. Such procedures are promulgated within the personnel office or the central civil service agency, and the manager may play only a minor role in these official proceedings. However, to get a good job match, the manager must be an active participant in the hiring process. The manager is in a crucial position to define the skills and characteristics that will help the organization most. Personnel specialists can often provide advice, be helpful in recruitment, or help a manager translate the organization's needs into the language and requirements of the formal personnel system. At other times, actors and technical constraints of the formal system can hamper recruitment. These outside actors and institutions may substitute their own values for those of the manager. In examining these issues, the next case describes the activities and values of a manager, an agency personnel office, and a central civil service commission.

While this case — especially the Appendix — transmits some technical information on how and how not to try to hire someone, it has strategic implications as well. On what issues and how should a manager concentrate his or her personnel management time and activities? What are the power relationships among actors and institutions in the personnel business? What is the effect of professional judgment and interpersonal relationships with other actors in accomplishing personnel actions?

While other civil service systems may have different specific rules, requirements, and customs, the essential features of the system in this case are generally parallel to those of most civil service or "merit" systems. In addition to having formal rules, all such systems have some authoritative outside actors and institutions with their own missions and values. Examination of the formal system's role in this hiring action should produce some useful principles for making more effective use of hiring and other human resource management tools.

In analyzing the case, think about the relationships, roles, and powers of the different actors and the pressures placed upon them. Think also about the formal and informal steps in the hiring process and the relative importance of each step to the outcome. In this and other circumstances, an understanding of the constellation of actors and the steps in the process may be used to formulate a strategic approach to hiring that meets the manager's and agency objectives as well as satisfying the values of the other actors and institutions.

STUDY QUESTIONS

1. Why were Smith's and Cronin's intentions frustrated?
2. What were the important steps and who were the important actors in the process?
3. What are the options for the Office of Management and Budget (OMB) as the case ends?
4. What would you advise Smith and Cronin to do?
5. How will your advice affect OMB: its task, employees, and managers? How will it affect the OMB personnel office? The Civil Service Commission?

SELECTED REFERENCES

Fred K. Foulkes and E. Robert Livernash, *Human Resources Management: Text and Cases* (Englewood Cliffs; Prentice-Hall, 1982), Chapter 3, "Employment and Promotion Policy and Administration."

Hiring Quality People in the Executive Office of the President

Introduction

In the summer of 1977, Jim Smith, an assistant director of the Office of Management and Budget (OMB), Executive Office of the President, began interviewing candidates for the position of staff analyst in his office. Smith's area was devoted to the coordination, as the Administration's agent, of agencies throughout the federal government whose missions were related to natural resources, particularly environmental programs and concerns. (See Exhibit 4-1 for an organizational chart of OMB). Most prominent, of course, was the Environmental Protection Agency, although major parts of the Commerce, Interior and Energy Departments were also involved. This area had been the subject of growing public interest in the late 60s and early 70s, and the activities of government agencies, business interest groups and special study groups had grown at least in proportion to this interest. The emerging energy problems of the 1970s clearly intersected this area as did other, related concerns for human health and safety.

Although government policy analysis in the environmental field had been largely dominated by economists, Smith felt that many of the issues required technical expertise in order to consider intelligently the economic and the public policy aspects of environmental protection. He wanted to hire someone with the skills to perform the requisite policy and economic anal-

ysis, and the technical background to understand the policy objectives and problems. After interviewing a number of applicants, he settled on Bob Simmons as his candidate for the position. An engineering student during his undergraduate years, Simmons had just received an M.A. degree from one of the nation's most prestigious universities, where he had taken courses in history, business and management, international business, public policy and government. His Personal Qualifications Statement, the federal government's version of a résumé, is reproduced in Exhibit 4-2.

Simmons was anxious to come to work, and in August of 1977 Smith requested that the personnel office put through the paperwork to hire him. Nearly one year later, the position was still not filled. Despite time-consuming efforts (Smith estimated that 20 percent of his time over the last 12 months had been absorbed by the hiring procedures), neither Smith nor George Cronin, OMB's Director of Personnel, had succeeded in getting Simmons onto the Civil Service Commission's (CSC) list of candidates eligible for the job. Since Simmons could not be hired without CSC certification, Smith and Cronin had to decide what direction to take next: Should they continue their efforts to get Simmons (who in the meantime had taken a job on the West Coast), or should they fill the position in a different manner?

This case was prepared by Jon Brock, lecturer at the John F. Kennedy School of Government, Harvard University. While based upon a factual situation, certain names of the organization and the individuals are disguised and other information has been altered in the interest of confidentiality. Copyright © 1978 by the President and Fellows of Harvard College. Reproduced by permission of the John F. Kennedy School of Government.

Hiring Through Civil Service Procedures

Bob Simmons initially came to Jim Smith's attention through OMB's personnel operation. Personnel director George Cronin described his office with pride:

> We have a very small personnel shop that

concentrates on the basics. We have that luxury because we deal primarily with high level staff and analysts who have an exciting and visible job to do. Most of them are in the agency for the personal and professional challenge and so we don't have to fool with the recreation association and Mickey Mouse complaints that are so typical of line operations in the government. We spend at least 50% of our time recruiting and hiring.

There is generally a turnover of 10% to 20% per year among the professional staff in the Executive Office. We try to keep a pretty good stable of job seekers on tap and try to be sure that most of our managers have seen a good candidate every now and again. As a result, when a vacancy occurs, the process is already in motion and we may even have a first rate candidate or two for that very job. That cuts a lot of time off the front end of the process and ensures that we have quality people interested in applying for those jobs that come open.

Recruitment and hiring really are the key functions of our operation. Finding good people and getting them hired into the right jobs is what maintains the general quality of the organization. Quality people and quality work contribute to making it a good place to work. It keeps the managers and the entire professional staff happy. If we didn't help them get good people, we'd be spending half of our time listening to employee or manager complaints. To help keep the organization's reputation for excellence, we help each supervisor with the recruitment and selection part of his job. We handle the paper work as well as the more interesting recruitment, intake and job matching functions. We try to help managers solve problems, not create problems. We try creatively to use the personnel system on the government's behalf. Some other agencies get used by the personnel system.

When Simmons's resume arrived in the mail at the Personnel Office of the Executive Office

of the President in March 1977, Cronin followed his usual practice by circulating it to a number of high-level managers, in anticipation of vacancies. A few months later, a job opened up in the Natural Resources branch of OMB and, recalling Simmons's qualifications, Smith invited him to Washington for a series of interviews. Once Smith had selected Simmons as his candidate for the position, Cronin began sending into CSC the appropriate forms to set the formal hiring process in motion.

The opening in Smith's area conformed to the general CSC classification of "budget examiner." Cronin described the genesis of this job category:

> We have a preponderance of jobs called "budget examiner." We hire examiners at all levels, from GS-7 to GS-15. As you know, in order to hire anyone in the Civil Service, there must be a properly classified position available for recruitment and filling. The Commission uses it, as we must, as a vehicle to rate candidates who apply for the job. Well, we discovered a number of years ago that there really wasn't a position description in the Civil Service Commission's catalogue of standard positions that was called a budget examiner. There were many budget-related positions in their catalogue, but nothing that looked like the sort of budget examiner we need. We felt that in order to have considered people with the proper skills for our jobs, that an accurate position description would be useful. So with Civil Service Commission concurrence and assistance, we wrote a qualification standard against which we and they could recruit budget examiners. [See Exhibit 4-3, "Single-Agency Qualification Standard."] As the standard reads, there are four basic parts to the job, denoting qualities that all examiners ought to possess at any level. Examiners operate at different levels, and in different substantive areas and they work with varying agencies having different types of programs and problems. These pro-

grams and problems — unlike the written rules and standards — change, so we tried to incorporate flexibility. We are always going back and forth with the Commission on the need for flexibility.

Cronin's first step in the hiring process was to submit to CSC in late August a position description for the job of budget examiner in Smith's office (see Exhibit 4-4), accompanied by a request for a "certificate of eligibles." By law, a certificate, or short list, of eligible candidates must be developed by the Commission for every government job not filled internally; the hiring agency is obliged to make its selection from the top three available names on the certificate. However, Commission practice does allow the hiring party to have its own candidate included in the early stages of the CSC candidate search by submitting a "name request." Cronin explained the procedure:

> Since the Commission runs a search from among the thousands of names in its computer files when they receive a request for a candidate, we often employ the procedure known as "name request," which allows the agency to specify that the Commission consider a particular individual. This ensures that their initial scan of their files doesn't fail to consider the individual. While a name request doesn't guarantee selection, at least it avoids errors of omission. You don't always "get your man," so to speak, although sometimes the register and certificate yield someone better than your original candidate, in which case you're happy to have someone better; but it's hard for a computer and a clerk to select better than we do. That doesn't happen very often. What sometimes happens, however, is that your name request person just doesn't get high enough on the list; people with veterans preference or those who simply get rated better in the eyes of the Commission come out on top in the ranking process. We can't do anything about the vet-

erans preference rules, which are statutory. We can't do much about those who on paper look better than our candidate, but we can usually specify our requirements so that we avoid those who really aren't qualified to do the job. That's why we get so involved up front in the qualifications standard and the selective factors. In this case we name-requested Simmons to ensure his consideration.

> While it's an acceptable procedure, there has been considerable pressure to limit the name request practice, particularly by congressional and union groups who think it gets used to further political favoritism in selection. We recognize the sensitivity, so we proceed accordingly. Between that sensitivity and other factors contributing to the difficulty in getting good candidates from the Civil Service register, which is where all candidates from outside the government must come in, we often find ourselves, when we have to fill a position quickly, restricting our search to internal candidates, or others who already have Civil Service standing, simply to streamline the process. This narrows the candidates to those we feel are qualified. For candidates from within the government, the certificate process is not required. In those instances a simple announcement of the vacancy leads to a process by which qualifications of applicants are reviewed by peers to yield a list of candidates that management must select from. In either case, veterans have preference and you must select one of the top available three names.

The hiring agency is also allowed to designate "selective factors" — skills or experience considered essential for satisfactory job performance. However, there is not always agreement between an agency and the Commission on what constitutes a valid requirement for selection. In keeping with its policy of providing each applicant who meets the minimum qualifications with an opportunity to compete for a job, the CSC disallows any selective factors it considers too restrictive. Cronin expressed dissatisfaction with this system:

It seems that they [CSC staff] don't really comprehend how the qualifications necessary to perform a job change from time to time and how they differ for different budget examiner positions. To them, a job is a job, an examiner an examiner. Their view is that they indeed have been flexible in the way they have helped us to establish the minimum qualifications for the job, which is certainly true. However, they also maintain that candidates meeting these minimums ought to be perfectly adequate. They apply the basic qualifications standard, and rank them in accordance with all applicable rules and regulations. They send us a list — a certificate — that, according to them, meets the minimum qualifications. They don't understand why agencies don't always find it satisfactory to simply choose one from the list so derived. We view our role as one that requires getting the most qualified person selected for the job. We don't want someone who just meets the minimum requirements. In addition, we make decisions based on extensive knowledge of the candidates and the job requirements. That's more than even the best-trained CSC examiners can possibly do. We live here; we know the functions here, we know the mix of skills necessary and can better gauge the needs of the organization at any given time, for any position. The candidates we seek are personally interviewed by those of us in the personnel office, by the line managers and often by others in the organization. We check their references and spend a hell of a lot of time with each candidate.

As part of this tension with the Commission, we continue to maintain that there are elements in addition to those in the classification standard that deserve emphasis in qualifying someone for a particular job. We have frequently tried to include these among the "selective" factors, but have been barred from doing so by the Commission. Instead they have forced us to list these important qualifications as "quality ranking" factors [used to rate applicants who have already passed the early screening] which aren't used to screen their register or applicant list. If the factors are listed as "selective," no one can be considered for the job without those factors in their background. Such factors are used in their initial computer scan. People without those requirements just aren't considered. So it is often useful to provide them with selective factors to make the initial screen more efficient. It's damned hard to include selective factors because of their general philosophy and practice which only screens for minimum qualifications. Since we get the people we want about 75 percent of the time, we haven't yet fought the big battle on the need for flexibility in specifying qualification as program emphasis changes.

The Appendix contains a fuller description of Civil Service hiring procedures and policies.

When the certification of eligibles arrived from CSC in mid-September, Simmons was not among the five names listed. It did include one person whom the agency had already hired into another unrelated job, and another individual with superior qualifications, although according to Smith and Cronin, not as well qualified as the position required. Of the others on the certificate, two were veterans and therefore automatically at the top of the list, and the others lacked any scientific or engineering background. In Cronin's and Smith's view, none of these candidates was acceptable. Cronin explained:

The people on the certificate had scores ranging from 85 to 90, including the veterans, who have had 5 or 10 points automatically added to their raw score depending on the extent of their service-related disability. Simmons, as we later found out, had an 83. The Civil Service ranking system just isn't precise as all that. How can people be ranked based on examining written qualifications only and then use point estimates rather than a range to rank them?

From the looks of the résumés attached to the certificate, it didn't seem that they had considered at all the engineering requirements that we had included as quality ranking factors in the request for a certificate. The engineering requirements were damned important and none of the people they sent us had those qualifications.

On October 3, we wrote back to the Commission noting that none of the candidates on the certificate was qualified and that the technical background we had specified was a crucial part of the job. Thus, we sent a second request for a certificate and name request, asking that the technical engineering requirements among others be included as selective factors. At least if they weren't going to give us our preferred candidate, we wanted to choose from a list someone who was equal to or better than he.

See Exhibits 4-5 through 4-7 for Cronin's letter to CSC and the accompanying name request and selective factors.

On November 14, the second certificate came back, again without Simmons's name on it. Cronin called Smith to suggest that they both look over the backgrounds of the individuals on the new certificate, in the hope of finding someone who matched their standards and requirements. When they finished their review, however, both felt that none of the candidates was as appropriate for the job as Simmons. Smith was insistent on having the best possible candidate. He asked Cronin to consult the Civil Service regulations and search his experience to see what, if anything, could be done to improve the range of choices. Smith was anxious to proceed with the hiring: The major budget and policy review season would soon begin and the job had already been vacant for four months.

Cronin recalled:

We contacted by phone or in writing all of the candidates on the new "cert" to see if they were still on the job market. Three were not. Two of those remaining were veterans, and therefore had to get offers ahead of anyone else on the certificate. On January 10, 1978, we sent a "Statement of Objections" — form SF 62 — to the Commission specifically detailing individually our dissatisfaction with the qualifications of each of these three people. This is the first step along the only avenue of formal appeal. The Commission staff, the same group who had sent over the original cert, did not sustain our objection. Furthermore, they flatly and formally refused to consider engineering as a selective factor.

See Exhibit 4-8 for a Statement of Objections; the Appendix contains a summary of the appeals process.

Cronin continued:

Smith and I met in early February with the Commission people who were responsible for the certificate and we explained to them our view of the standard and the need to allow flexibility in the qualifications as a particular job required. Finally, they agreed to consider informally our viewpoint and asked if they could come over to see what sorts of skills were involved with that activity. A few of them came over and spent an afternoon talking to members of Smith's staff. On March 2 we received a memo from them. They maintained their earlier position. [See Exhibit 4-9.]

We had some further telephone discussions with them, but they held their ground, although they reminded us of our appeal rights to the Director of the Bureau of Recruiting and Examining in the Civil Service Commission. Needless to say, we took our appeal rights and on March 27 sent a detailed letter that Smith and I spent considerable time writing, explaining to the Bureau Director our view of the situation. [See Exhibit 4-10.] We wanted to have the qualifications standard applied as we requested it. We even constructed our own rating scale. In early April the Director called Smith and let him know that the case was being reviewed.

Another personnel officer commented on the appeals procedure:

Generally, when we bring things to a higher level, the perspective is different, less conservative and perhaps more reasonable. If there is a way to resolve the dispute without undermining procedures, staff morale and precedent, the higher-level people usually find a way. The lower-level folks are just blindly following rules, covering their asses. They are more likely to lean on technicalities than deal with the larger question of the quality of personnel. But they are judged by how well they follow their rules, not on how good the selections are.

On April 24, 1978, the Director of the Bureau of Recruiting and Examining sent a letter to George Cronin turning down the appeal on the objection to qualifications. (See Exhibit 4-11.) Smith reacted with anger when Cronin informed him of CSC's decision. Arguing that his area of OMB was under pressure from the president to hold down costs and avoid unnecessary regulation in environmental programs, he insisted that he needed an analyst with technical expertise:

I don't feel like being used by these rules. O.K., they won't certify Simmons for who knows what reasons, but for gosh sake we have to get somebody good into that job. . . . I need people who can help me by understanding the technical stuff as well as the economics and the politics.

Cronin pondered the alternatives. They had already appealed even more broadly than formal CSC procedures allowed. However, Smith was incensed and threatened to talk to the President. At the same time, Simmons was working with a lawyer to take the case to court.

Exhibit 4-1. Organization of OMB

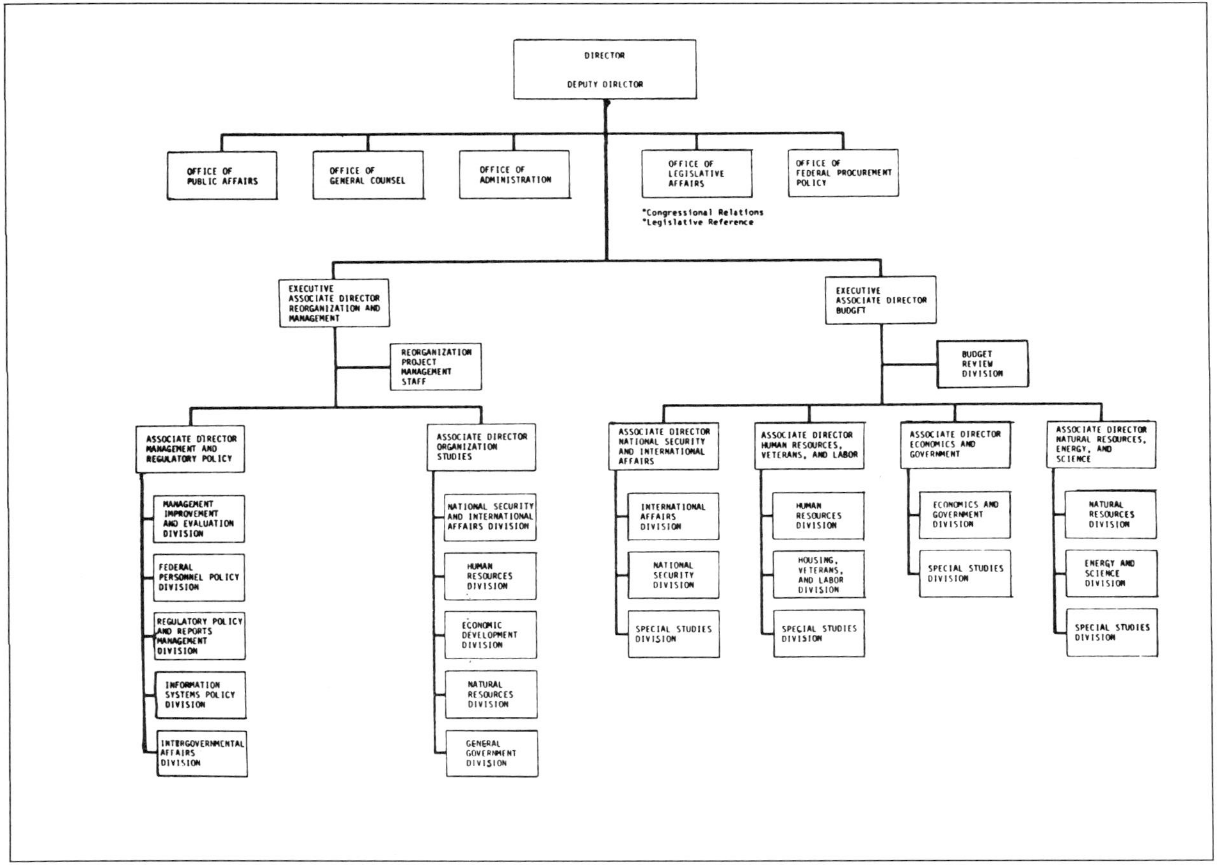

Exhibit 4-2. Personal qualifications statement

Personal Qualifications Statement
Read instructions before completing form

Form Approved:
OMB No. 50-R0387

1. Kind of position *(job)* you are filing for *(or title and number of announcement)*

   N.A.

2. Options for which you wish to be considered *(if listed in the announcement)*

   N.A.

3. Home phone
   Area Code 212 | Number 868-5311

4. Work phone
   Area Code | Number N.A. | Extension

5. Sex *(for statistics only)* [X] Male [ ] Female

6. Other last names ever used

Name *(Last, First, Middle)*

   Simmons Robert

Street address or RFD no. *(include apartment no., if any)*

   2071 West 43rd Street

City	State	ZIP Code
Brooklyn	NY	11210

8. Birthplace *(City & State, or foreign country)*

   Israel

9. Birth date *(Month, day, year)*

   January 7, 1952

10. Social Security Number

    060-44-8418

11. If you have ever been employed by the Federal Government as a civilian, give your highest grade, classification series, and job title.

    Dates of service in highest grade *(Month, day, and year)*
    From N.A. To

12. If you currently have an application on file with the Office of Personnel Management for appointment to a Federal position, list: (a) the name of the area office maintaining your application, (b) the position for which you filed, and *(if appropriate)* (c) the date of your notice of rating, (d) your identification number, and (e) your rating.

    N.A.

13. Lowest pay or grade you will accept:

PAY		GRADE
$	per	OR	11

14. When will you be available for work? *(Month, and year)*

    June 1977

DO NOT WRITE IN THIS BLOCK
FOR USE OF EXAMINING OFFICE ONLY

Material   Entered register:
[ ] Submitted
[ ] Returned

Notations:

Form reviewed:
Form approved:

Option	Grade	Earned Rating	Preference	Aug. Rating

[ ] 5 Points (Tent.)
[ ] 10 Pts. 30% or More Comp. Dis
[ ] 10 Pts. Less Than 30% Comp. Dis
[ ] Other 10 Points
[ ] Disallowed

Initials and date

[ ] Being Investigated

THIS SPACE FOR USE OF APPOINTING OFFICER ONLY
Preference has been verified through proof that the separation was under honorable conditions, and other proof as required.

[ ] 5-Point   [ ] 10 Points 30% or More Compensable Disability   [ ] 10 Points Less Than 30% Compensable Disability   [ ] 10-Point Other

Signature and title

Agency	Date

15. Are you available for temporary employment lasting:

(Acceptance or refusal of temporary employment will not affect your consideration for other appointments.)

	YES	NO
A. Less than 1 month?		★
B. 1 to 4 months?		★
C. 5 to 12 months?		★

16. Are you interested in being considered for employment by:

	YES	NO
A. State and local government agencies?		
B. Congressional and other public offices?		
C. Public international organizations?		

17. Where will you accept a job?

	YES	NO
A. In the Washington, D.C. Metropolitan area?	★	
B. Outside the 50 United States?	★	
C. Anyplace in the United States?	★	
D. Only in *(specify locality)*		

18. Indicate your availability for overnight travel:

A. Not available for overnight travel	
B. 1 to 5 nights per month	
C. 6 to 10 nights per month	
D. 11 or more nights per month	

19. Are you available for part-time positions *(fewer than 40 hours per week)* offering:

	YES	NO
A. 20 or fewer hours per week?		
B. 21 to 31 hours per week?		
C. 32 to 39 hours per week?		

20. Veteran Preference. Answer all parts. If a part does not apply to you, answer "NO".

	YES	NO
A. Have you ever served on active duty in the United States military service? *(Exclude tours of active duty for training in Reserves or National Guard)*		★
B. Have you ever been discharged from the armed services under other than honorable conditions? *You may omit any such discharge changed to honorable or general by a Discharge Review Board or similar authority)* If "YES", give details in item 34.		★
C. Do you claim 5-point preference based on active duty in the armed forces? If "YES", you will be required to furnish records to support your claim at the time you are appointed.		★
D. Do you claim 10-point preference? If "YES," check the type of preference claimed and complete and attach Standard Form 15, "Claim for 10-Point Veteran Preference," together with the proof requested in that form.		★

Type of Preference: [ ] Compensable Disability 30% or More [ ] Compensable Disability Below 30% [ ] Non-compensable Disability [ ] Purple Heart Recipient [ ] Spouse [ ] Widow(er) [ ] Mother

E. List dates, branch, and serial number of all active service *(enter "N/A", if not applicable)*

From N.A. To Branch of Service Serial or Service Number

(Exhibit continues on following page.)

Exhibit 4-2. Continued

21. Experience: Begin with current or most recent job or volunteer experience and work back. Account for periods of unemployment exceeding three months and your residence address at that time on the last line of the experience blocks in order of occurrence

May inquiry be made of your present employer regarding your character, qualifications, and record of employment? (A "NO" will not affect your consideration for employment opportunities except for Administrative Law Judge positions.)   ☒ YES   ☐ NO

A

Name and address of employer's organization (include ZIP code, if known)	Dates employed (give month and year)	Average number of hours per week
student	From 6/1975 To 6/1977	
	Salary or earnings	Place of employment
	Beginning $ per	City
	Ending $ per	State

Exact title of your position	Name of immediate supervisor	Area Code Telephone number	Number and kind of employees you supervise
Kind of business or organization (manufacturing, accounting, social services, etc.)	If Federal service, civilian or military, series, grade or rank, and date of last promotion		Your reason for wanting to leave

Description of work (Describe your specific duties, responsibilities and accomplishments in this job)

N.A.

For agency use (skill codes, etc.)

B

Name and address of employer's organization (include ZIP code, if known)	Dates employed (give month and year)	Average number of hours per week
National Investment Corporation 110 Wentworth Street Westchester, New York	From 9/1974 To 5/1975	40
	Salary or earnings commissions	Place of employment
	Beginning $ per	City Westchester
	Ending $ per	State New York

Exact title of your position	Name of immediate supervisor	Area Code Telephone number	Number and kind of employees you supervised
Salesman	Mr. Cwynar		none
Kind of business or organization (manufacturing, accounting, social services, etc.)	If Federal service, civilian or military, series, grade or rank, and date of last promotion		Your reason for leaving to undertake graduate studies at Harvard University

Description of work (Describe your specific duties, responsibilities and accomplishments in this job)

Sold stocks, bonds and insurance for National Investment Corporation. Increased the number of clients in the company and serviced their accounts.

For agency use (skill codes, etc.)

C

Name and address of employer's organization (include ZIP code, if known)	Dates employed (give month and year)	Average number of hours per week
	From 8/1973 To 8/1974	N.A.
	Salary or earnings N.A.	Place of employment
	Beginning $ per	City
	Ending $ per	State Israel

Exact title of your position	Name of immediate supervisor	Area Code Telephone number	Number and kind of employees you supervised
manager of army platoon			100 soldiers
Kind of business or organization (manufacturing, accounting, social services, etc.)	If Federal service, civilian or military, series, grade or rank, and date of last promotion		Your reason for leaving end of compulsory service
Israeli Army			

Description of work (Describe your specific duties, responsibilities and accomplishments in this job)

My duties as manager were to be in charge of all administrative matters of my platoon and to insure that all vital functions (excluding military) were coordinated and run efficiently. I was responsible directly to my commander and every evening after he was briefed by me, in regard to the day's activities, I participated in the subsequent officers' meetings. My participation in these meetings helped coordinate the activities of the next day and promote unity of action.

For agency use (skill codes, etc.)

Page 2   If you need additional experience blocks, use Standard Form 171-A or blank sheets of paper
SEE INSTRUCTION SHEET

(Exhibit continues on following page.)

Exhibit 4-2. Continued

Attach Supplemental Sheets or Forms Here

22. A. Special qualifications and skills *(skills with machines, patents or inventions; your most important publications [do not submit copies unless requested]; your public speaking and publications experience; membership in professional or scientific societies, etc.)*

N.A.

B. Kind of license or certificate *(pilot, registered nurse, lawyer, radio operator, CPA, etc.)*	C. Latest license or certificate		D. Approximate number of words per minute	
Insurance, Rela Estate	Year	State or other licensing authority	Typing	Shorthand
N.A.S.D.	1975	New York	N.A.	N.A.

23. A. Did you graduate from high school or will you graduate within the next nine months; or do you have a GED high school equivalency certificate?				B. Name and location *(city and State)* of latest high school attended
Yes	Month and Year	No	Highest grade completed	F.D.R. High School
★	01 1969			Brooklyn, New York

C. Name and location *(city, State, and ZIP Code, if known)* of college or university *(if you expect to graduate within nine months, give MONTH and YEAR you expect to receive your degree.*	Dates Attended		Years Completed		No. of Credits Completed		Type of Degree	Year of Degree
	From	To	Day	Night	Semester Hours	Quarter Hours	*(e.g. B.A.)*	
Harvard University, Cambridge, MA	9/75	6/77	2		72 credits		M.A.	1977
City College of New York	2/69	6/73	4		128 credits		B.S.	1973

D. Chief undergraduate college subjects	No. of Credits Completed		E. Chief graduate college subjects	No. of Credits Completed	
	Semester Hours	Quarter Hours		Semester Hours	Quarter Hours
Electrical Engineering	N.A.		Middle East Governments	N.A.	
Math	N.A.		International Business	N.A.	
Physics	N.A.		Management in the U.S. Government		

F. Major field of study at highest level of college work

International Affiars and International Business

G. Other schools or training *(for example, trade, vocational, Armed Forces or business)*. Give for each the name and location *(city, State and ZIP Code, if known)* of school, dates attended, subjects studied, number of classroom hours of instruction per week, certificate, and any other pertinent data.

Eastern School for Real Estate   Attended from 2/1975 - 6/1975.
721 Broadway   Studied real estate for broker.
New York, NY 10003   Classroom hours - 6 hours per week.
                             Received a certificate.

24. Honors, awards, and fellowships received

N.A.

25. Languages other than English. List the languages *(other than English)* in which you are proficient and indicate your level of proficiency by putting a check mark *(✓)* in the appropriate columns. **Candidates for positions requiring conversational ability in a language other than English may be given an interview conducted solely in that language.** Describe in item 34 how you gained your language skills and the amount of experience you have had *(e.g., completed 72 hours of classroom training; spoke language at home for 18 years; self-taught; etc.)*

Name of Language(s)	PROFICIENCY							
	Can Prepare and Deliver Lectures		Can Converse		Have Facility to Translate Articles, Technical Materials, etc.		Can Read Articles, Technical Materials, etc., for Own Use	
	Fluently	With Difficulty	Fluently	Passably	Into English	From English	Easily	With Difficulty
Hebrew								
Arabic								
French								

26. References. List three persons who are NOT related to you and who have definite knowledge of your qualifications and fitness for the position for which you are applying. Do not repeat names of supervisors listed under item 21. Experience.

Full Name	Present Business or Home Address *(Number, Street, City, State and ZIP Code)*	Telephone Number *(include Area Code)*	Business or Occupation
Norman Murray	603 81st Streeet New York, New York 10024		Bank Officer
Prof. Nelson Frew	Middle East Center, Harvard Univ. 1737 Cambridge St., Cambridge, MA 02138		Professor
Prof. E.J. Yargeau	Harvard Business School Cambridge, MA		Professor

Page 3

(Exhibit continues on following page.)

Exhibit 4-2. Continued

Answer items 27 through 33 by placing an X in the proper column	YES	NO
27 Are you a citizen of the United States? If NO give country of which you are a citizen	*	
NOTE: A conviction or a firing does not necessarily mean you cannot be appointed. The circumstances of the occurrence(s) and how long ago it (they) occurred are important. Give all the facts so that a decision can be made		
28 Within the last five years have you been fired from any job for any reason?		*
29 Within the last five years have you quit a job after being notified that you would be fired? If your answer to 28 or 29 above is YES give details in item 34 Show the name and address (including ZIP Code) of employer approximate date and reasons in each case This information should agree with your answers in item 21 Experience		*
30 A Have you ever been convicted forfeited collateral or are you now under charges for any felony or any firearms or explosives offense against the law? (A felony is defined as any offense punishable by imprisonment for a term exceeding one year but does not include any offense classified under the laws of a State as a misdemeanor which is punishable by a term of imprisonment of two years or less		*
B During the past seven years have you been convicted imprisoned on probation or parole or forfeited collateral or are you now under charges for any offense against the law not included in A above?		*
NOTE: When answering A and B above you may omit (1) traffic fines for which you paid a fine of $50.00 or less (2) any offense committed before your 18th birthday which was finally adjudicated in a juvenile court or under a youth offender law (3) any conviction the record of which has been expunged under Federal or State law and (4) any conviction set aside under the Federal Youth Corrections Act or similar State authority		*
31 While in the military service were you ever convicted by a general court-martial? If your answer to 30A 30B or 31 is YES give details in item 34 Show for each offense (1) date (2) charge (3) place (4) court and (5) action taken		*
32 Does the United States Government employ in a civilian capacity or as a member of the Armed Forces any relative of yours (by blood or marriage)? (See item 32 in the attached instruction sheet) If your answer to 32 is YES give in item 34 for such relatives (1) name (2) present address (including ZIP Code) (3) relationship (4) department agency or branch of the armed forces.		*
33 Do you receive or do you have pending application for retirement or retainer pay pension or other compensation based upon military Federal civilian or District of Columbia Government service? If your answer to 33 is YES give details in item 34 If military retired pay include the rank at which you retired		*

Your Statement cannot be processed until you have answered all questions including items 27 through 33 above. Be sure you have placed an X to the left of EVERY marker (◄) above either in the YES or NO column

34 Item No	Space for detailed answers Indicate item numbers to which the answers apply
	N.A.

If more space is required, use full sheets of paper approximately the same size as this page. Write on each sheet your name birth date and announcement or position title. Attach all sheets to this Statement at the top of page 3.

ATTENTION—THIS STATEMENT MUST BE SIGNED
Read the following paragraphs carefully before signing this Statement

A false answer to any question in this Statement may be grounds for not employing you, or for dismissing you after you begin work, and may be punishable by fine or imprisonment (U.S. Code. Title 18. Section 1001). All the information you give will be considered in reviewing your Statement

AUTHORITY FOR RELEASE OF INFORMATION
I have completed this Statement with the knowledge and understanding that any or all items contained herein may be subject to investigation prescribed by law or Presidential directive and I consent to the release of information concerning my capacity and fitness by employers, educational institutions, law enforcement agencies, and other individuals and agencies, to duly accredited Investigators. Personnel Staffing Specialists, and other authorized employees of the Federal Government for that purpose.

CERTIFICATION	SIGNATURE (sign in ink)	DATE
I certify that all of the statements made by me are true, complete and correct to the best of my knowledge and belief, and are made in good faith	*Robert Simmons* Robert Simmons	12/24/76

* U. S. GOVERNMENT PRINTING OFFICE : 1979 O - 281-187 (5005)

Exhibit 4-3. Single agency qualification standard

BUDGET ADMINISTRATION SERIES
(Cancels and Supersedes
PES No 1887 issued
December 10, 1953)

SINGLE-AGENCY QUALIFICATION STANDARD

Budget Examiner and Supervisory Budget Examiner[1]
GS-7/15
Office of Management and Budget

Description of Work

Budget examiners formulate or assist in the formulation of the budget for a
given agency or program. They develop justification data for budget hearings
and other conferences with agency heads and their staffs. They review fiscal
programs to ensure that appropriations are being expended in accordance with
the intent of Congress and the approved program of the agency. They analyze
requests for apportionment of appropriated funds; interpret budget policy in
the evaluation of operating program proposals or in meeting particular
operating situations; and coordinate budget services for various operating
programs which may be unrelated in content or in organizational level. Budget
examiners conduct or assist in conducting studies on improving the organization and management of the agencies for which they are responsible. They
analyze programs to determine program effectiveness and make recommendations
to improve that effectiveness. Examiners analyze legislative proposals and
reports, and draft OMB position papers on such legislation. They visit
field installations" and attend conferences to keep abreast of developments
in their program areas, and provide information to Congress and the White
House Staff concerning various programs.

Applicants must show that they have general and specialized experience as
follows:

Grade	Specialized (years)	General (years)	Total (years)
GS-7----------------------	1	3	4
GS-9----------------------	2	3	5
GS-11 and above----------	3	3	6

[1]This standard is the same as the Handbook X-118 standard for positions in the
Budget Administration Series, GS-560, issued October 1970, except for the
sections on specialized experience and the substitution of education for experience. Except for these two sections, all requirements and provisions set forth
in that standard in the Handbook X-118 apply. The material from Handbook X-118
is reprinted here for the convenience of CSC examining offices and agency
staffing specialists.

(Exhibit continues on following page.)

Exhibit 4-3. Continued

General Experience.

Must have been experience from which the applicant gained a general knowledge of management principles and practices. Experience in specialized fields which are closely related to budget examining, or excess specialized experience, will be accepted as general experience.

Specialized Experience.

Any of the following types of experience may be considered specialized experience:

1. Experience which included the development, evaluation, or revision of budgetary control systems, budget preparation and presentation, or similar duties. It may have been gained as a specialist in budget work, or as a professional worker whose duties provided a knowledge of programs, organization, or operation in a specialized program area.

2. Experience which included the application of the principles and techniques used to improve organizations, programs, procedures, and methods, or the identification and isolation of operating problems similar to those found in a particular activity of the Federal Government.

3. Experience which involved the application of scientific or professional knowledge to the solving of operational problems in a particular program or activity similar to those found in the Federal Government, to the extent that it has given the applicant the knowledges and skills needed to perform the duties of the position.

4. Any combination of the above which clearly shows that the applicant has attained the knowledges and skills needed to perform the duties of the position.

For all grades, the experience shown must have been sufficiently difficult and responsible to demonstrate the ability to carry out the duties and responsibilities of the grade. For positions at GS-12 and above at least one year of the specialized experience must have been of a level of difficulty comparable to that of the next lower grade in the Federal service. For all other positions, applicants must show either 6 months of specialized experience equivalent to that of the next lower grade, or one year equivalent to that of the second lower grade in the Federal service.

Substitution of Education.

1. Successfully completed study in a resident institution above high school level may be substituted for general experience at the rate of 1 year of education for 9 months of experience up to a maximum of 4 years of education for 3 years of general experience.

(Exhibit continues on following page.)

Exhibit 4-3. Continued

2. Full-time* graduate education may be substituted for experience
   on the following basis. The education must have equipped the
   candidate with the knowledge and ability to perform fully the
   work of the position for which he is being considered.

   a. For 1 year of specialized experience. - One full
      academic year of graduate education in (1) public
      administration, business administration, government
      political science, economics, industrial engineering,
      or industrial management; or in (2) the administra-
      tion and organization of public programs, in various
      fields such as public welfare, international organ-
      ization, public health, economic regulation, or
      any other scientific or professional field related
      to the work of the position. (This amount and
      kind of education meets all the requirements for
      grade GS-7.)

   b. For 2 years of specialized experience. - Completion
      of all requirements for a master's or an equivalent
      degree, or 2 full academic years of graduate educa-
      tion, which is in one of the fields described in
      paragraph "a" above. (This amount and kind of
      education meets all the requirements for grade GS-9).

3. The Superior Academic Achievement Standard in section III of
   part II, Instructions to Users of Handbook X-118 is applicable
   at grade GS-7.

4. Some positions may require either specialized knowledge of
   budget techniques or of specific types of operating programs.
   For these positions, selection will be limited to those
   eligibles who have appropriate training or experience.

Quality of Experience.

All applicants for positions at grades GS-13 and above must have had
extensive and significant administrative experience which has provided
a thorough knowledge of methods of supervision, administration and
management, and which has demonstrated ability to deal satisfactorily
with others. This experience must have been of a progressively responsible character and the degree of administrative responsibility involved
must have been proportionately greater for each successively higher
grade. At least 3 years of this experience must have involved responsibility for budget preparation including the study of work plans and
work practices, reporting on their relations to the budget, and making

---

*Part-time graduate education is also accepted at the rate of 30 semester
hours (or the equivalent) for 1 year of specialized experience.

(Exhibit continues on following page.)

Exhibit 4-3. Continued

thorough analyses and review of recommended estimates, and responsibility
for the operation of systems for reporting work performed and funds
expended.

In determining the grade level for which an applicant is qualified on
the basis of experience in the direction, planning, and coordinational
activities, the following elements are involved: (a) Responsibility
for deciding policy or for the interpretation and application of overall policy; (b) responsibility for organizing and carrying through
original programs; (c) responsibility for determining organizational
structure and methods of operation; and (d) extent and complexity of
the work of the organization or that part of it directed by the
applicant.

Supervisory Positions.

For supervisory positions, see the qualification standard for "Supervisory Positions in General Schedule Occupations," in part III of this
handbook.

Written Test.

A written test of learning abilities is required for competitive
appointment at GS-7. The test may not be waived for appointments
outside the register. For inservice placement actions at grade
GS-7, a passing score is not required, but the test may be used,
in combination with other evaluation methods, as one element in
ranking employees for reassignment, promotion, transfer, reinstatement, or other internal placement into this occupation.
(See FPM Supplement 335-1: Evaluation of Employees for Promotion
and Internal Placement, especially Appendix A: Guidelines for
Use of Written Tests.)

**No written test is required for positions at GS-9 and above. Candidates
for these positions will be rated on the basis of the quality and extent
of their total experience, education, and training. Ratings will be
based on statements in their applications and any additional evidence
received.**

Physical Requirements.

**See part II, Physical Requirements, paragraph 3. In addition, applicants
must possess emotional and mental stability.**

Exhibit 4-4. Position description

```
                           POSITION DESCRIPTION

   1.  Duties

   Under the supervision of a senior budget examiner or analyst the examiner
   at this level assists the supervisor in performing general program reviews
   and policy analyses and usually serves as the Office of Management and Budget's
   representative for carrying out the Office's functions for a specific segment
   of the department or the program area for which the supervisor is responsible.
   Programs involved include:  air and water pollution abatement programs,
   radiation programs and other programs associated with the rehabilitation of
   our physical environment.  In this connection, the examiner participates in
   the identification of policy issues, the analysis and development of program
   proposals, the evaluation of on-going programs, the review of pending and
   proposed legislation, the improvement of organization and management practices,
   and the formulation and administration of the budget for the programs and
   activities assigned, including the review and approval of materials submitted
   for inclusion in the President's Budget documents.

   The specific duties of the program examiner at this level include the
   performance of the following activities:

   a.  Assists in policy analysis and development through the performance of
       assigned tasks which involve:  (1) identifying issues or problems
       requiring the attention of policy-level officials, (2) gathering infor-
       mation on these issues, (3) discovering alternatives for resolving them,
       (4) assessing the likely consequences of each alternative, (5) evaluating
       the relative merits of various alternatives, and (6) monitoring agency
       performance in implementing policy decisions.

   b.  Assists in the review and development of program and budget submissions
       and in the administration of the budget for programs concerned with
       environment in general, land use and/or water resources.  Participates
       in an apprenctice relationship with the senior examiner in carrying out
       all or portions of the following specific tasks associated with the
       formulation and administration of the budget:

       1.  Budget Formulation.  Prepares data and assists in making annual and
           multiple year projections of expenditures and appropriation require-
           ments; suggests, and drafts material relative to possible future
           developments, needs, and problems of the programs; assists in
           drafting recommendations of annual budget appropriation and expenditure
           ceilings, and collects and prepares data supporting such recommenda-
           tions; and advises the agency on specific problems of budget prepar-
           ation and presentation.

       2.  Budget Review.  Determines that the submissions are correct and
           complete.  Drafts material and prepares data for use in the conduct
           of agency hearings and other conferences with agency heads and
           their staff; acts as a reference assistant to the senior examiner
           who conducts such hearings; and is sometimes called upon to take
```

(Exhibit continues on following page.)

Exhibit 4-4. Continued

the lead in conducting specific portions of such hearings and conferences. Drafts recommendations and supporting data for presentation to the Director, the Deputy Director, and other officals of the Office, and sometimes gives additional oral testimony before the Director's Review Committee. Keeps notes on decisions, instructions, and information developed in such reviews, hearings, and conferences, and prepares memoranda as a record. Checks and prepares revised budget schedules and appropriation language for printing in the Budget document, and determines that the final document is correct in every detail.

3. Budget Administration. Continually reviews specific fiscal programs to insure that appropriations are being expanded in accordance with the intent of Congress and the approved program of the agency. Reports any unusual developments to his supervisor. Keeps appropriate records and charts showing the status of the appropriations assigned. Analyzes requests for apportionments of appropriated funds, and makes pertinent notes for the supervisor's consideration relative to approving, modifying, or denying such requests. Reviews where necessary agency estimates of receipts, transfers, and expenditures; and reconciles these estimates with Treasury reports and estimates for other agencies.

c. Analyzes and assists in commenting upon proposed and pending legislation and reports thereon; and drafts letters or documents setting forth the position of the Office of Management and Budget, as determined from the program of the President. Monitors the process of pertinent appropriations bills and other legislation and reviews committee reports and publishedrecords of hearings.

d. Participates in the evaluation of on-going federal environmental, land use, and/or water resources programs to identify program strengths and weaknesses. Focuses on activities of high Presidential priority and/or major economic, social or scientific importance and identifies primary objectives and assumptions. Program evaluation, as used here, entails relatively structured systematic analyses of specified operating programs to assess their impact or effectiveness in attaining their stated objectives, or to assess their efficiencey.

e. Assists onstudies and projects for improving the organization and management of programs dealing with environment in general, land use and/or water resources. Works usually as a junior member of a team which may be composed of staff of the division, of the agency, and of the pertinent management division of OMB. In this capacity, collects data, prepares tables and charts and summaries, makes preliminary analyses, and aids in drafting reports and recommendations. Is occasionally assigned, however, as the division representative on such studies and the task then involves recommendations defining the area and scope of the project; identifying policy issues, formulating the manner in which the study is to be carried out, and developing the factual material requried.

(Exhibit continues on following page.)

Exhibit 4-4. Continued

2. SCOPE OF RESPONSIBILITIES:

Although an examiner at this level is completing a professional apprentice-ship, the examiner is expected to perform his/her assigned duties without oversight of another examiner. In all instances, the examiner will report directly to the Branch Chief.

The assigned area usually rivals in importance and difficulty with that of the GS-11 examiner—the primary difference being the degree of work experience in related activities.

It is imperative that the examiner, although junior in actual work experience, demonstrates the likely potential to assume increasingly greater program responsibilities in a short period of time. The incumbent should be aggressive and have the ability to sell his/her ideas to others.

The nature of the issues confronted in the environmental area requires the incumbent to address a wide range of technical issues. To this end, the incumbent must be able to cope with engineering and physical science problems.

The examiner will represent the Office in dealings and contacts with outside agencies, and particularly with the staff of agency budget offices. The incumbent has occasional work contacts with the Deputy and the Associate Director, and with staff of Budget Review and the various program and management divisions of the Office of Management and Budget.

3. QUALIFICATIONS:

    a. Educational background in engineering or related fields.

    b. Ability to understand budget and/or financial concepts and a good facility for thinking and working with numbers.

    c. Familiarity with the workings of the U.S. Government.

    d. The ability to persuade others of the merits of a particular position based upon an analysis of the relevant subject area.

    e. Ability to write and make oral presentations.

Exhibit 4-5. Amended certification request

October 3, 1977

Washington Area Office
Examining Office for Career Entry
  and Mid-Level Positions
U.S. Civil Service Commission
1900 E Street, N.W.
Washington, D.C. 20415

ATTENTION: Ms. Pauline Antil

Dear Ms. Antil:

Following our phone conversation last week, I talked with the selecting
official at some length concerning the primary qualification requirements
for this position. As a result, we have decided to submit a new (amended)
certification request for this position to reflect the importance attached
to the requirement for technical/engineering science knowledge. We have
included this as a selective factor in the amended certificate request
rather than as a quality ranking factor.

As I indicated on the phone, all but one of the individuals on the
attached certificate appear very well qualified for budget examiner
assignments in non-technical program areas. However, none seem to have
the technical/scientific credentials which the selecting official regards
as essential to the proper functioning of this position. I believe we
have demonstrated the need for this qualification in ths SF-39A and
position description.

I would appreciate very much any special handling you might accord our
amendment request. Agency hearings for the FY 79 budget have begun and
it would be very beneficial if the individual selected for this position
could be on board before the end of the month.

Please let me know if there is anything further we might do to assist
in acting on this request. Thanks for your help.

Sincerely,

George Cronin
Personnel Officer

Attachment
cc: Personnel Chron
     Personnel File

Exhibit 4-6. Certification form

STANDARD FORM 39 (Revised) U.S. CIVIL SERVICE COMMISSION JULY 1971—FPM 332	**CERTIFICATION FORM**	CERTIFICATE NO.
		DATE ISSUED

1. REQUEST

DEPARTMENT OR AGENCY	BUREAU OR FIELD ESTABLISHMENT	REQUEST NO.
Executive Office of the President	Office of Management and Budget	DATE September 29, 1977

U. S. Civil Service Commission
Career Entry and Mid-Level
Positions
1900 E Street, N. W.
Washington, D. C. 20415
ATTENTION: Mr. Quantmeyer
Room 2433

This request should be submitted to the office of the Commission having jurisdiction over the work location named unless special prior agreement has been reached with the Commission.

VACANCIES, POSITION TITLE, SERIES CODE, GRADE (SALARY, IF UNGRADED) AND DUTY LOCATION

1   Budget Examiner   GS-560-9

TYPE OF APPOINTMENT
[XX] Career or Career-Conditional
[ ] Temporary not to Exceed_____

TO WHAT EXTENT WILL PERSONS APPOINTED BE REQUIRED TO TRAVEL?
[ ] NOT AT ALL   [XX] OCCASIONALLY   [ ] FREQUENTLY

[XX] D—FOR FILLING DEPARTMENTAL POSITIONS ONLY
[ ] F—FOR FILLING FIELD POSITIONS ONLY

REQUEST RELATES SOLELY TO REQUIREMENTS OF THE MERIT PROMOTION PROGRAM
[ ]

AVAILABLE FOR WORK:
[XX] IMMEDIATELY   [ ] BY_____

REMARKS: *(Give a description of duties where no standard specifications are published, and indicate any special qualifications required)*

Request that the attached SF-171 from Mr. Robert Simmons be evaluated for filling the position described in the accompanying documents and that he be certified for this position if he is within reach on the Mid-Level register. Mr. Simmons requested certain changes in his Mid-Level registration in a letter sent to the Commission dated July 8, 1977 (copy attached). His ID number is 885423, SSN 060-44-8418, DOB - January 7, 1952. The position we are attempting to fill is in the Environment Branch of the Natural Resources Division. The incumbent will have primary responsibility

ADDRESS WHERE CERTIFICATE IS TO BE SENT:

Office of Management and Budget
Personnel Office, Room 2020
NEOB, 726 Jackson Place, N. W.
Washington, D. C. 20503

FOR FURTHER INFORMATION CONTACT:
George Cronin *(Tel.)* 395-3765
George Cronin Personnel Officer *(Title)*

II. CERTIFICATION   *Please Review Instructions on Back of Form*

TO REQUESTING OFFICE:

[ ] The attached list of eligibles is provided in response to the above request.
PLEASE RETURN WITHIN 21 DAYS OF DATE ISSUED OR BY_____.

[ ] Authority is granted to recruit through the open competitive examination for appointment to the position(s) indicated above.
Applications of persons recruited should be FORWARDED WITHIN 30 DAYS OF DATE ISSUED OR BY_____

[ ] Authority is granted to fill the position(s) identified above under CS Reg. 316.402(A).

III. REPORT   *Please Review Instructions on Back of Form*

TO THE ISSUING OFFICE: Report on certificate is submitted and original applications (and attachments) of eligibles not selected for appointment returned.

[ ] WE DESIRE FURTHER CERTIFICATION FOR _____ VACANCIES.

SIGNATURE OF APPOINTING OFFICER	TITLE	DATE
	Personnel Officer	May 4, 1978.

(Exhibit continues on following page.)

Exhibit 4-6. Continued

for budget, legislative, programmatic, and organizational issues
and analysis dealing with programs administered by the
Environmental Protection Agency. The principal task of the
examiner is to maintain a close and continuing review of key program and budget issues as a basis for OMB recommendations concerning budgetary and legislative proposals and to stimulate
management, organizational, and program improvement.

See attached SF-39A for Selective and Quality Ranking Factors.

Attachment

Exhibit 4-7. Request and justification for selective factors and quality ranking factors

REQUEST AND JUSTIFICATION FOR SELECTIVE FACTORS AND QUALITY RANKING FACTORS (ATTACH TO SF 39)	Certificate no.: Date issued:
Requesting agency:	Request no.: Date: September 29, 1977
Title, series, and grade of vacancy: Budget Examiner, GS–560–9	

Definitions. You may request that special qualifications of two types be considered by the csc in its evaluation of eligibles for certification: (1) *Selective Factors* must be skills, knowledges, abilities or other worker characteristics basic to and essential for satisfactory performance of the job; i.e., a prerequisite to appointment. These represent minimum requirements in addition to or more specific than X-118 standards. (2) *Quality Ranking Factors* must be skills, knowledges, abilities, or other worker characteristics which could be expected to result in superior performance on the job. Selective factors may be used for screening (in or out) purposes; quality ranking factors will not be used for screening, but may be used as ranking criteria.

Instructions. This form must be accompanied by a description of the position to be filled. The request and justification for selective and/or quality ranking factors should follow this format: (1) Each selective or quality ranking factor must be stated in terms of a knowledge, a skill, an ability, or other worker characteristic. (2) List the duties or tasks the incumbent will perform that require the possession of the requested knowledge, skill, or ability, or that could better be performed if he or she possessed the knowledge, skill, or ability. (3) Optional: Indicate what experience, education, or other qualifications provide evidence of possession of the knowledge, skill, or ability.

SELECTIVE FACTORS

These special or additional knowledges, skills, or abilities are needed for this position.	Because the incumbent is expected to perform this work (provide a clear description or specific reference to an item in the position description)	These may be appropriate evidences of necessary qualifications (optional).
Familiarity with principles and methods of analysis as a basis for the improvement of public programs.	See Sec. 1, 1–a,d, and e and Single Agency Qualifications Standard.	Graduate level training in public policy formulation, management of public programs, or other evidence of familiarity with modern methods of policy analysis.

(Exhibit continues on following page.)

Exhibit 4-7. Continued

Familiarity with the workings of the U.S. Government.	Reflected throughout the Position Description.	Recent training included courses in Government, public management, and/or public policy.
Ability to present ideas based on analysis and evaluation in a convincing manner as will be useful to decision makers at senior management and policy levels.	See Sec. 1, 1-a,d,e; 2; 3-d of Position Description.	Experience in situations where persuasion skills were utilized.
Analytical ability, to identify the important features of complex problems and to reason logically from the facts available.	See Sec. 1,1-a,c,d; 3-d and Single Agency Qualifications Standard.	Courses requiring the evaluation of federal policy in various areas (e.g., economic policy, domestic social policy, etc.)
Ability to understand budget and/or financial concepts and to work with numbers.	See Sec. 1-b (1,2,3); 3-b of Position Description and Single Agency Qualifications Standard.	Courses in math, statistics, public management, budgeting, and/or finance.
Educational background or other evidence of modern knowledge in engineering, engineering science, or closely related discipline.	See 1, Duties and 1b of Job Description. Background in an engineering or scientific discipline will enable the incumbent to understand the operation of the programs associated with rehabilitation of the environment.	Academic preparation or experience in the physical sciences or engineering.

George Cronin
Personnel Officer
Signature and Title of Appointing Officer

For CSC use:

Signature of CSC Examiner

Exhibit 4-8. Statement of objections

STANDARD FORM 62
MARCH 1967
CIVIL SERVICE COMMISSION
FPM CHAPTER 332

STATEMENT OF REASONS FOR OBJECTING TO AN ELIGIBLE OR PASSING OVER A PREFERENCE ELIGIBLE

63–105

Office of Career Entry and Mid-Level Positions
U.S. Civil Service Commission
1900 E Street, N.W.
Washington, D.C. 20415

Submit in Triplicate to the Interagency Board of U.S. Civil Service Examiners which issued the Certificate; or in the absence of a Certificate, to the office which has examining jurisdiction.

INSTRUCTIONS TO APPOINTING OFFICER FOR USE OF THIS FORM

An *objection* by an appointing officer to an eligible on a certificate, when sustained by the Commission, eliminates that eligible from the group of three from which the appointing officer is entitled to select, and brings the next available eligible within reach. A *veteran passover* is the act on the part of the appointing officer of selecting a nonpreference eligible within a group of three when there is a higher ranking preference eligible within the group. The nonpreference eligible selected may not legally be entered on duty unless the Commission finds that the reasons for passing over the preference eligible are sufficient, or unless a vacancy is reserved for the preference eligible pending receipt of the Commission's decision. Similar provisions apply to temporary appointments made outside of registers. (See Section 8 of the Veterans' Preference Act. Procedures and guides are in Chapter 332 of the Federal Personnel Manual.)

This form should be used to object to an eligible or to request authority to pass over a preference eligible and appoint a nonpreference eligible. One copy will be returned to you with the Commission's decision shown on the reverse. You should submit with the form all available information and documents considered pertinent to the case, such as application, position description, medical certificate, service record, etc.

NAME AND ADDRESS (INCLUDE ZIP CODE) OF ELIGIBLE /	RATING	CERTIFICATE NO.	DATE OF CERTIFICATE
Mark Lynfield 620 Morrisey Blvd. Sacramento, CAL.	88 TP	WA-SM-7-3471-S1	11/14/77
	POSITION BUDGET EXAMINER		
	TITLE OF EXAMINATION AND GRADE MID-LEVEL GS-09		

For the reasons stated below (check appropriate block):
☐ We object to the eligible named hereon.

☒ We propose to pass over the preference eligible named hereon and select a nonpreference eligible.
(*Note:* The Veterans' Preference Act gives the preference eligible the right to request and review the reasons. The reasons, therefore, cannot be considered confidential.)

REASONS (State reasons specifically and clearly so that the significance is readily apparent): Mr. Lynnfield has no budget or related analytic training or experience that would provide familiarity with principles and methods of analysis used in program evaluation as a basis for improvement of public programs. Further there is no indication or evidence of ability to understand budget, financial, or
(Attach additional sheet if necessary)

SIGNATURE AND TITLE OF AGENCY APPOINTING OFFICER		DATE
[signature]	Personnel Officer	1-10-78

Executive Office of the President
Office of Management & Budget
Personnel Office - Room 2020 NEOB
726 Jackson Place, N.W.
Washington, D.C. 20503

NAME OF AGENCY, CITY, STATE, AND ZIP CODE
◄——
(Type return address for use in window envelope)

(Exhibit continues on following page.)

Exhibit 4-8. Continued

Continuation of Page 1 (Reasons)

related concepts. These deficiencies are cruicial to the
performance of this job and were confirmed during a telephone interview by the selecting official on December 15.

Exhibit 4-9. Submission of objections to eligibles

UNITED STATES GOVERNMENT   **U.S. CIVIL SERVICE COMMISSION**

Memorandum

MAR 2 - 1978
Date:

In Reply Refer To:

Subject: Submission of Objections to Eligibles

From: Arthur Lyman, Chief   EWS:EXR
Office of Career Entry and Mid-Level   Your Reference:

Through: Walter Grant, Manager
Washington Area Office

To: George Cronin, Personnel Officer
Office of Management and Budget

Our office received objections to three eligibles (2 veterans) for a
GS-9 Budget Examiner position on Certificate WA-SM-7-3471, S-1. The
reasons supporting the objections were that eligibles did not possess
a knowledge of budget analysis and engineering or another closely
related scientific discipline needed to address the issues and problems
encountered in the environmental program areas of the position. Because
of the continuing problem in the application of selective factors for
these positions we conducted a job analysis of the position.

The results of the job analysis revealed that while a knowledge of both
budget and engineering (or related scientific fields) was desirable for
the position at all grade levels, both knowledges are not essential for
satisfactory performance at the GS-9 level. In our evaluation of the
job analysis, we concluded that this requirement may be reasonable to
expect at the GS-11 and 12 grade levels, but is too restrictive at
grade GS-9 as a minimum qualification requirement.

The GS-9 level is considered to be an advanced trainee level with
independent performance and general supervision. Your single agency
qualification standard for the GS-560 series does not allow for this
requirement. According to the standard, either education and/or experience in budget "or" the specialized subject matter program area is
considered qualifying for these positions. Furthermore, to require both
knowledges would mean that candidates must possess two master's degrees,
one, in the area related to budget and the other in a scientific field,
or a master's degree in the budget area and a year of post-graduate
experience in the subject matter field. This requirement by far exceeds
the minimum qualifications for any GS-9 position.

We noted that the Subject Matter Experts (SME's), Budget Examiners,
GS-13/14, who participated in the job analysis session, did not possess
the technical scientific background at the time they entered into the
positions. The SME's also indicated that because they lacked the

Keep Freedom in Your Future With U.S. Savings Bonds

(Exhibit continues on following page.)

Exhibit 4-9. Continued

technical knowledge, they were not as effective in performing the
duties of the position. However, after a period of on-the-job training,
they were able to perform satisfactorily at the full performance level.
This describes an advanced trainee position as outlined above and further
reinforces our belief that such a knowledge can be learned or developed
within a reasonable period of time on the job.

Because we felt the technical knowledge of engineering was important
but not a minimum qualification to the GS-9 position in question, it
was considered as a critical quality ranking factor and was given
extra weight in the rating process.

Therefore, since the candidates referred meet your single agency qualification standard, we cannot sustain your objections.

Based on our findings of the job analysis, we plan to establish a
standard rating schedule for these types of Budget Examiner positions
at the GS-11 and 12 grade levels. However, since our competitor
inventory does not include candidates who possess an engineering or
other related scientific and budget analysis background, there appears
to be a need to identify potential recruitment sources for the staffing
of these positions. If you wish, we would be glad to assist you in
this endeavor.

Exhibit 4-10. OMB appeal on objections to qualifications

EXECUTIVE OFFICE OF THE PRESIDENT

OFFICE OF MANAGEMENT AND BUDGET

WASHINGTON, D.C. 20503

March 27, 1978

Mr. Warren Morris, Director
Bureau of Recruiting and
  Examining
U.S. Civil Service Commission
1900 E Street, N.W.
Washington, D.C. 20415

Dear Mr. Morris:

We have recently been advised by the Office of Career
Entry and Mid-Level that our objections to three eligibles for a GS-9 Budget Examiner position cannot be
sustained because in the Commission's judgment the
candidates meet our single agency qualification standard.
A copy of this letter is enclosed together with the
certificate of eligibles, request for certification,
position description, and related materials.

We believe the Commission's findings in this instance are
inconsistent with the qualification requirements for this
position including the acknowledged significance of a
quality ranking factor. While the main thrust of our
appeal centers about the rating process and construction
of the rating plan, we also wish to comment on our qualifications standard and the use of selective factors since
this issue has arisen in the past and continues to be a
source of misunderstanding. Several points are worth noting
in this connection.

First, there is nothing in our single agency standard or
to the best of our knowledge in X-118, that limits the use
of selective factors to certain grades, e.g., only at
GS-11 and above. Since the GS-9 Budget Examiner is not
an entry level position, we feel that judicious use of
selective factors is not only legitimate and permissible,
but essential to the identification and selection of
candidates who will meet the standards and expectations of
the Office.

(Exhibit continues on following page.)

Exhibit 4-10. Continued

Second, the Commission's finding that both budget and
engineering knowledge is not essential at the GS-9 level
(but may be at GS-11 or 12) and would be unduly restrictive,
should not preclude selection of the best qualified candidate. Further, we see no valid reason to fill a position
at GS-11 or 12 when the needed skills are available at a
lower grade. Whether or not the "dual knowledge" we seek is
"reasonable" to expect at GS-9, the fact remains that people
with these qualifications do exist, the fact that no one
with "both knowledges" was identified on the Mid-Level
register notwithstanding.

Third, the Commission memo notes in paragraph three that
according to the OMB standard, either education and/or
experience in budget "or" the specialized subject matter-
program area is considered qualifying for these positions.
As we have acknowledged in past discussions with your staff,
the standard was purposely written broadly in order to reflect
the fact that qualification requirements as well as the relative importance of specific knowledges are not identical for
every budget position, even at the same grade level. Thus,
we must make some use of selective and/or quality ranking factors in order to more accurately describe the qualifications
needed for a specific position.

Fourth, the Commission notes that to require both budget and
program/subject matter knowledge "would mean that candidates
must possess two master's degrees, one in the area related
to budget and the other in a scientific field; or a master's
degree in the budget area and a year of post-graduate experience
in the subject matter field." It would seem that another, and
perhaps more realistic combination is a master's in a budget
related field together with an undergraduate major in a subject
matter field, e.g., engineering. Contrary to the impression
given us by the Commission, this combination is not uncommon
and often represents an ideal mix for certain (but not all)
budget examiner positions dealing with scientific and technical programs.

Finally, we have difficulty understanding the rationale which
resulted in the Commission's rating of the eligibles certified
for filling this position. I should mention that at a meeting
with Mid-Level representatives several weeks ago, we expressed
an interest in reviewing the rating plan used in this case.
We were advised that because of privacy considerations,
they could not accommodate our request. The Office of Career
Entry and Mid-Level did acknowledge that because engineering
knowledge was important, it was considered as a critical
quality ranking factor and given extra weight in the rating
process. In addition, we were apprised some time ago that our
name request, although not among those certified, was one

(Exhibit continues on following page.)

Exhibit 4-10. Continued

of several individuals with a score of 83. On that basis, we ask that you consider the following:

- Our name request received the highest number of points, relative to other candidates, for engineering knowledge/training. Yet his total score is identical to Mr. Lynch (prior to veterans points) who has comparable budget qualifications but no engineering credentials.

- Mr. Sheey also received an identical score (prior to veterans points) to our name request and has neither budget nor engineering background.

- Our name request received a lower score than Ms. Jackson who has budget knowledge but no engineering background or knowledge.

There may be a plausible explanation for these apparent inconsistencies but it is difficult to understand the rationale employed without access to the criteria, point system, and weights used in rating the eligibles. To illustrate, we have developed a rating schedule containing four basic criteria, their relative importance and weights, and the basis upon which points might be assigned to the eligibles (as well as our name request) in each category. While there will undoubtedly occur some variance in point assignment according to the rater's understanding of the job and the relative importance ascribed to each rating element, we believe that both the weights and the ratings we have assigned fairly and accurately represent the importance of the various criteria as well as the relative strength of the eligibles in each category. Recognizing that engineering knowledge was treated as a quality ranking factor and may not have weighed as heavily on the Commission's rating schedule, we examined the point scores excluding the engineering criteria and still find our name request with a higher total than two of the eligibles.

We understand and fully appreciate the difficult task assigned to the Commission in identifying the best candidates. At the same time, we believe that an examining system which depends so critically on judgment and understanding of both the position and the environment in which it operates must permit consideration of an agency's needs and unique requirements. We do not feel that the Commission fully grasps the extraordinary demands placed upon an OMB "examiner" or the nature of Presidential staff work. It is a

(Exhibit continues on following page.)

Exhibit 4-10. Continued

gross inequity and a disservice to the Federal merit
system to hire anyone but the most highly qualified
candidate available. And in this instance, we feel
that the legitimate interests of the eligibles and
the Office of Management and Budget have not been
well served.

We would very much appreciate your review of this matter
and look forward to your reply.

Sincerely,

George Cronin
Personnel Officer

Exhibit 4-11. Rejection of OMB appeal

UNITED STATES CIVIL SERVICE COMMISSION
BUREAU OF RECRUITING AND EXAMINING
WASHINGTON, D.C. 20415

IN REPLY PLEASE REFER TO

EPA:EXR

YOUR REFERENCE

April 24, 1978

Mr. George Cronin
Personnel Officer
Office of Management and Budget
Washington, D.C. 20503

Dear Mr. Cronin

This is in response to your recent letter requesting our review of
your objections to three eligibles referred by the Washington Area
Office (WAO) for a Budget Analyst position at the GS-9 level.

We recognize the unique nature of the work of an Office of Management
and Budget (OMB) Budget Analyst and the need for candidates to
understand the program area in which they are working as well as the
budgetary process itself. We gave every consideration to these
factors in reviewing the material you submitted and all additional
background files from WAO on this particular case. In our view, the
single-agency standard, your position description, and the detailed
job analysis conducted by WAO all substantiate the job relatedness of
the rating schedule used to prepare the certificate in question. The
knowledges, skills, and abilities (KSA's) used by WAO in their rating
schedule parallel those included in the rating plan you submitted,
with the addition of factors by WAO relating to budget analysis and
administration.

In response to your documented need for technical program knowledge,
double credit was awarded for this factor; it was not limited, however, to an engineering background but was broadened to include
education and/or experience in the physical, biological, or environmental sciences, all of which are directly related to an understanding
of Environmental Protection Agency (EPA) programs. We were unable to
support the use of this technical background as a selective factor for
this position. Based on information provided by subject-matter
experts (GS-13/14 Budget Analysts from OMB), possession of this
technical background would have improved initial job performance, but
candidates would have been able to perform the duties of the position
without it. The subject-matter experts indicated that the technical
knowledge could be learned after a reasonable period of time on the
job. For these reasons a technical background in the physical,

(Exhibit continues on following page.)

Exhibit 4-11. Continued

biological, or environmental sciences was used as a quality-ranking factor, which could be expected to significantly enhance performance in a position but could not reasonably be considered as essential for job performance.

We also considered the crediting plan submitted by your office and while we are basically in agreement with the factors used, we question the point values for various evidences of possession of the KSA's, e.g., 8 points for an engineering background and a lesser number of points for training in the environmental sciences. Also, we were not in agreement with what appeared to be excessive credit given to an applicant's educational background as opposed to the experience gained by other candidates. This seemed especially significant in the number of points awarded to Mr. Simmons based apparently on two courses he took at the John F. Kennedy School of Government.

In reference to your question on the use of selective factors with a single agency standard, we certainly do not rule out this possibility. Such a factor must have been determined to be essential for job performance and must be supported by a job analysis. As discussed previously, however, program knowledge was not supported as a selective factor in this instance.

We regret that we are unable to sustain your objections but hope you can appreciate our position that based on the material available to us on the duties of the position, the qualifications required, and the applications of the candidates in question, the rankings of the candidates are appropriate as they currently stand. Your certificate and the candidates' applications are enclosed.

Sincerely yours,

Warren Morris
Director

Enclosures

APPENDIX
Procedures for Hiring Mid-Level Employees in the Federal Government

This appendix describes the mandatory procedures (in effect as of July 1979) governing the hiring into the federal government of mid-level employees from among candidates who have not been federal employees. The hiring of current or previous federal employees is covered by a different and less elaborate set of procedures. Even when hiring from outside of the government, there may be variations among agencies in administrative practices, traditions and labor management agreements which will alter the overall hiring process although the actual hire will have to conform to these procedures. All of the practices and procedures discussed here pertain to the Washington, D.C. area office of the Civil Service Commission;* the workload and details of these practices may differ somewhat in their offices in other parts of the country.

"Registers" of Applicants

For the purpose of filling mid-level jobs, the U.S. Civil Service Commission (csc) maintains "registers" of applicants in some 250 occupational categories, most of which are non-technical (i.e., are largely management or social science related). Mid-level jobs are those of the GS 9, 11, and 12 levels, where the starting salary ranges (in 1978) from $15,920 to $23,087 per year. Generally, people at these levels possess a master's degree and/or have five or more

*In January 1978, the Civil Service Commission was reorganized into two agencies, the Office of Personnel Management and the Merit System Protection Board. The procedures described herein are carried on under the Office of Personnel Management. For some job categories these functions can be delegated to individual agencies' personnel offices.

years of job experience. (There is also a senior level register for grades 13, 14, and 15, which will not be considered here.) Some 40,000 applications are contained on all mid-level occupational registers.

To be listed on one of these registers, an applicant must complete Standard Form 171 and a variety of computer coding sheets. (An example can be found in Exhibit 4-2 of this case.) When the csc receives the completed application, the coded characteristics, as coded by the applicant are entered into a master computer file and the application itself is sent to storage, where it remains for a period of one year (applicants must notify the Commission annually to extend their eligibility) or until an applicant is being considered for a job, at which point the application receives its first review; the application is neither screened nor rated. Thus, a coding error cannot be discovered before this review. According to the Civil Service Commission, a great cost saving is effected by this system of "deferred rating" owing to the large number of applicants and the large proportion of those that will never be considered for a job by the time their one year of eligibility runs out.

These registers are the pools from which all candidates from outside the federal government must be selected for mid-level jobs. In order to be considered for a job opening at a federal agency, however, an individual must successfully be screened from a register of hundreds or thousands of applicants to a "certificate of eligibles" through a complex csc review and ranking process described below. A "certificate" is the list of the top-ranked candidates, developed by csc staff from the register appropriate to a job being filled. A hiring agency must by law select one of the top three individuals on the certificate. Therefore, the process by which a certificate is developed is of considerable importance to the outcome of a hiring action.

Submitting a Request, Minimum Qualifications and Selective Factors

An agency wishing to fill a vacancy submits to the Civil Service Commission a request for a "certificate of eligibles" (a ranked list of candidates) along with a description of the position and (usually) a list of "selective factors" — i.e., qualities the agency deems necessary for performing the job (see Exhibits 4-6 and 4-7 in this case). The lists are optional, but the CSC encourages agencies to submit them, since without them Commission staff will have to develop their own factors for screening candidates.

If the agency does submit a list of selective factors, the Commission reserves the right to reject or modify the factors if they appear to be too restrictive or not directly job related. Commission policy is to provide each person possessed of minimum qualifications an opportunity to compete for the job; and since veterans must by law receive priority consideration, the initial screening must be wide enough to give a sufficient number of them an opportunity for consideration. Under law, veterans have 5 points added to their score after the regular scoring takes place. Disabled veterans go to the top of the certificate and must be selected if available. While these mechanisms assure veterans of preferential treatment at the end of the process, there is no parallel mechanism to ensure that they will pass the initial screening. Similar efforts to provide opportunities for other disadvantaged groups have also contributed to the policy decision to cast a wide net. Thus, if the Commission finds that an agency is too narrowly restricting the opportunity to compete for a job, they are likely to modify the selective factors.

Name Requests

An agency submitting a request for a certificate will frequently include a "name request" — i.e., the application of an individual it wishes specifically to have considered for the position (see Exhibit 4-6 in this case). The "name request" guarantees that the individual will receive consideration in the first screening, even if computer scan doesn't turn up his/her application. (In subsequent screenings for the job that applicant is treated like all others.) Unless a register is "closed," * the CSC will consider name request applications, even if they are not on the register, to save the applicant and the agency from waiting for the completion of initial processing onto the register.

Often, before and after a certificate is being requested, informal discussion takes place between the hiring agency and a Civil Service Commission staffing specialist, his or her supervisor, or others. These discussions about job requirements and screening procedures take place among individuals who work together on a daily basis. According to the Commission, large differences on qualifications are rare and are usually worked out. There are frequent negotiations between a CSC examiner or specialist and the agency regarding the factors that will be used to screen the applicants. The Commission staff gets to know the agency people and their needs and as long as these needs are legitimate, the Commission seeks to be flexible. Sometimes there is a legitimate misunderstanding on what is required. It is common for the agency personnel officer or line officials to meet and discuss their requirements with the Commission staff.

Occasionally, basic Commission policy toward minimum qualifications will be modified

---

* At present, registers are "closed" when they become so large as to be administratively unwieldy. The Washington Area Office of the Commission publishes a list of occupational codes quarterly to show which registers are open; as soon as new computerized procedures are installed, the Commission may open all registers on a consistent basis.

as a result of new information thus brought to the Commission's attention. In one case, for example, Commission standards required completion of certain science courses before applicants could be considered for a large number of job openings that a regulatory agency had advertised. The agency did not believe the course requirements were relevant to the job, and in fact had designed its own two-year training course to provide entry-level personnel with a solid background in the necessary sciences. The Commission's requirements were blocking consideration of hundreds of candidates throughout the country, since the classification standard, which was over 20 years old, specified a course that was now offered in fewer than 5 percent of the colleges in the United States. A long series of letters and discussions, culminating in a meeting between Commission staff and an expert in the field, convinced the Commission to revise its standards, freeing up a large pool of applicants. One Commission official said: "We take the position that it's their program, so we want them to lay out the requirements."

Rating and Examining

After the agency request comes in and any changes or clarifications have been made, the master computer file is searched for applications with coded factors matching the selective factors for the job. The codes permit only a very gross screening. These applications are pulled from the files and put into "certificate status," thereby becoming unavailable for consideration for any other jobs. Double application under different occupational codes is not permitted, and spot checks of the computer file cause the last-received of the duplicates to be "kicked out."

The applications drawn from this initial computer pull, which may number as many as five hundred, are sent to a staffing assistant who weeds out those which are improperly coded or which fail to meet the minimum requirements for the job. (The CSC estimates that about 30 percent of applicants mis-code themselves and otherwise do not appear qualified for the positions they seek.) Staffing assistants, who are generally college graduates but not specialists in an occupational field, will often contact applicants and the agencies with questions about qualifications or requirements. Each such contact is carefully documented. Screening by a staff assistant will typically yield 50 to 100 applicants who are considered minimally qualified for the job opening.

The applications are then routed to one of several staffing specialists, a senior examiner into whose occupational specialty the job opening falls. The specialist reviews the position description and qualification standard (the minimum qualifications for the job's civil service category) to set up a rating schedule for ranking applicants: i.e., a list of selective factors, quality ranking factors, and other factors from the position description. No attempt is made to rate people on their ability to meet with, deal with, and otherwise engage in discussions and negotiations with peers and supervisors. The specialist then assigns a weight to each factor, according to its relevance to the particular job, and also lists examples (known as "benchmarks") of appropriate skills and experiences that might indicate a candidate's qualifications relative to that factor. Once the scale is constructed it takes about a half day for an experienced staffing specialist to process 30 to 40 applications. At this point, the staffing specialist sifts through every application, assigning points (from 0 to 10) for each factor according to how well the applicant's qualifications seem to match the factors in the rating scale. This raw score is multiplied by each factor's weight and a composite score is calculated. Applicants with less than 70 points are disqualified from further consideration and the remaining applicants are then ranked according to their scores. Veterans are granted an additional five points and any veteran with a compensable disability who scores at least 70 is granted an extra 10 points and automatically placed at the top of the list. All cases are reviewed by a supervisor to ensure compliance with law and regulation and that all necessary documentation is in the files.

Applicants with scores of 70 and above are grouped as follows, and ranked according to their scores:

70–79 total points: *Minimally qualified.* Meets requirements of qualification standard plus minimal requirements for the job (selective factors).

80–89 total points: *Qualified.* Meets requirements of qualification standard, selective factors plus some of the quality ranking factors.

90–100 total points: *Highly qualified.* Meets requirements of classification standard plus selective factors, quality ranking factors and other aspects of position description.

Generally, about six names are placed on the certificate for each vacancy, although the staffing specialist may use discretion according to his view of the probable availability of individuals on the list. Since many of the people on the register are also seeking other employment, often candidates on a certificate decline job offers. The unavailability rate is estimated to be 30 percent on the average.

Objections and Appeals

The staffing specialist completes the certificate and sends it to the agency, which has 30 days to select a candidate or return the certificate unused. The agency must choose from among the top three available names and must select a veteran ahead of any others, unless the agency can establish — to the Commission's satisfaction — that the top-ranked individuals lack the qualifications necessary for the job. According to the Commission, such "objections" usually only occur when an agency has failed to provide CSC examiners with a complete list of selective factors in its original request. Generally, a specification of selective factors yields a more satisfactory certificate, since better screening is facilitated. (On average, fewer than 250 objections are processed each year out of a total of 200,000 hires.) If an objection is sustained the agency may choose from among the top three remaining qualified.

While providing too little information to the CSC may produce unqualified candidates, specifying job requirements too narrowly produces a more serious problem in the view of the CSC. The Commission guards against this practice, believing it to be inconsistent with its mandate to broaden access to job opportunities. If the Commission agrees that there is a discrepancy between the qualifications used in screening and the qualifications possessed by certified candidates, it will reconsider the qualifications used to construct the certificate or otherwise redo the process. There are five consecutive levels at which objections formally may be ruled on: (1) the staffing specialist; (2) the supervisor; (3) the office chief; (4) the area office manager; and (5) the Director of the Bureau of Recruiting and Examining. In order to resolve differences — often before formal objections are filed — a panel of subject matter experts from the requesting agency or from elsewhere in the government may be employed — at the initiative of the agency or Commission — to rate and examine a job or help resolve an objection.

Avenues of appeal also are open to applicants. If they feel that requirements used to screen them out were not related to the job in question, they may take their objections to a review board especially convened for each case. If not satisfied by the appeal at the Civil Service Commission, applicants may then go to Federal Court to seek redress.

Unused Certificates and Alternatives

About 50 percent of all certificates are returned, and not always for reasons of changing agency needs. Some agencies, because of internal procedural obligations which require them to notify the CSC of job vacancies (perhaps as a result of labor-management agreements), may request a certificate without intending to use it, preferring to fill a vacancy in some other approved way. Other agencies may be looking to choose a specific candidate, and will return the certificate when their preferred candidate does not show up on it. Often in such instances, both the agency's job description and the preferred candidate's application will be resubmitted on a different register, in an attempt to more clearly fit the individual or to place the individual on a different occupational register with fewer candidates, where the odds of selection are greater.

Another way to hook a preferred candidate is through a pattern of collusion, called "fishing expeditions." An agency with a job opening and a preferred candidate calls on other agencies or offices to request certificates for similar job openings; with each new certificate, more names are placed on certificate status (making them ineligible for consideration for a second job). In this way, as each new batch of top applicants is skimmed off, a particular candidate further down the list becomes more "reachable." This is a violation of law, and the Commission has attempted to tighten its procedures to prevent its being used. If the agency is not satisfied with the certificate or wishes to avoid the time and restrictions involved in the certification process, it may use other means to fill the job from within the government. For example, it can promote someone already in the government, transfer someone from elsewhere, or reinstate an individual who has previously been in the Civil Service. The relative flexibility that these alternatives afford will depend upon the parameters of each agency's own "merit promotion plan."

Although a systematic study was not available, there appears to be discernible patterns among agencies.

Audit for Consistency

Once a month, the Washington area office reviews a full day's work to check for accuracy and consistency; and, in addition, the Commission periodically conducts its own audits. Part of the review may consist of re-ranking the candidates for a particular job and comparing the results to those achieved by the original examiner. According to one official in the Civil Service Commission, "There are so many subjective decisions involved, it's amazing how much consistency there is. It's so close, it amazes me. Maybe it's the culture. But it is, nevertheless, amazing." In order to speed the process of certificate production and to make the rating process more objective, the Civil Service Commission (Office of Personal Management) will be implementing a more automated system. The goal is to increase computerization and utilize optical scanning equipment. This is expected also to aid the agency as it becomes subject to scrutiny of the Equal Employment Opportunity Commission.

CHAPTER 5

Agency Reorganization: Isolating the Problem

Reorganization is a common tool of management. In effect it is one type of human resource flow — another tool for moving people within an organization and matching people to jobs. Well used, it can create a more appropriate match of people to tasks. It can establish simpler, more effective channels of professional communication up and down and across an organization and between an organization and its environment. Poorly used, it can cause uncertainty and confusion. While transfers and hiring are also forms of movement within an organization, they move only one person at a time within an existing organizational structure and hierarchy. Reorganization alters that structure and usually moves groups of people within the organization to match the new arrangements.

It almost seems that reorganizations have grown in popularity at the same time as the academic and popular literature on them has expanded. The logic of reorganizing is conceptually appealing and intellectually attractive. On the surface, it seems quite simple to accomplish. Therefore, many analysts, policy makers, and managers see changes in organizational form or structure as a primary way to cause a change in organizational performance. In actual practice, successful use of reorganization is far more complicated. First, reorganization can only help if it actually solves the problems that are hindering organizational results. Second, it can help only if the trauma surrounding the change to a new organizational form does not cause more harm than good. It can be a useful tool, but only if applied to appropriate circumstances and only if well implemented. These conditions are not always simple to meet. Often the planning and organizational design process may cause significant uncertainty and confusion within an organization and may itself lose sight of the problems that originally prompted interest in reorganization. This can leave an elaborate reorganization plan in the position of not addressing the major problems it was intended to fix. Also, implementation of even a well-designed reorganization plan can be very difficult. People's security is affected, and vested interests of one sort or another are offended or aroused. Further, effecting major change while still carrying on the work of the organization is difficult at best; reorganization diverts the time and attention of managers and employees.

Reorganization has also become popular as a way around civil service rules or traditions that make it difficult to move a person out of a job. Reorganizations are sometimes used where a manager finds a mismatch between person and position. In such instances reorganization is used to alter or eliminate that position in order to move the individual or alter his or her influence. In most civil service systems this technique is a prohibited practice, but it is nevertheless employed. While reorganization is often useful to alter a structure or reporting relationships that no longer fit the organization's task or environment, a lot of machinations intended largely to move one individual may not always be worth the price in time and attendant disruption.

Despite its popularity over the last few decades, there are many managers who are not enamored of reorganization, preferring to avoid the trauma and uncertainty associated with it. Rather, they seek other, less radical or more direct methods for increasing the effectiveness of an organization. However, even though a manager may eschew reorganization, reorganization is not always undertaken at a manager's own discretion. The impetus for reorganization arises sometimes from higher-ups and sometimes from other actors in the public policy and management process. The impetus can be from such diverse sources as a campaign pledge or a well-lobbied single-interest idea.

The following case on the Maryland Department of Social Services (a disguised location) provides an opportunity to examine a reorganization from the standpoint of a manager in the middle of one that was someone else's idea. In this case, publicity over a child-abuse death led to legislative lobbying and action mandating organizational change in the state's welfare and social service organization. Thus we find the secretary of a department presiding over an impending reorganization that he did not initiate. When we come to the case, the major organizational boxes have already been redrawn and the manager here is concerned largely with implementation issues. In coming up with an approach, the manager finds himself faced not only with questions of concept and strategy but with some cultural issues — features of the state, its politics, and the personnel-related technical rules that affect the degree of flexibility in carrying out the reorganization. The key question is, "How can this manager make the best of it?"

Organizational change is rarely simple, and often the process of change itself will have an effect on the quality of services offered by the organization. This case provides an opportunity to examine a reorganization that took place in a state social service agency and to assess the sorts of actions that a manager might undertake when faced with an imposed organizational change.

STUDY QUESTIONS

1. In the interest of most improving the effectiveness of the organization, on what aspects of its operations would you concentrate your efforts during this period of adjustment? Overall, what would you be trying to accomplish?

2. As Secretary Patton, what do you have at stake?

3. As one set of criteria for taking action, examine what organizational characteristics might have contributed to the death of Jane Smith. What do these suggest in the way of management action at this point? What other criteria might be important to the Commissioner and the organization? What do they suggest in terms of the utility of organizational realignments or other actions to effect change in the quality of DOSS services?

4. If you were Secretary Patton, what would be your decision on the several issues before you? What are the most important issues?

5. As Secretary Patton, what would be your very next move with respect to this reorganization? Why? How will this help?

6. Be prepared to explain and defend your decisions and answers to the governor. How do these decisions help the agency "make the best of it"?

The Creation of the
Maryland Department of Social Services (A)

The gubernatorial election of November 1978 brought a new governor to the State of Maryland. Shortly after his election, the Governor appointed Bradley Patton to the position of Secretary of Human Resources. A logical choice, Patton came to this position from a well-respected consulting firm where he had long been an advocate for human services. In addition, his previous experience in government during another administration meant he was already familiar with the intricacies of state governing mechanisms. The Secretary of Human Resources position was a demanding one, having under its jurisdiction at least six agencies, among them the Department of Welfare (DOW), with an annual budget of $1.6 billion and 6,000 employees. Of this, $126 million and 2,000 employees were in the area of social services. (See Exhibit 5-1.)

A law had recently been passed to establish a new, separate Department of Social Services (DOSS) to assume this social services component of the Department of Welfare.

Questions surrounding the establishment of the new Department were high on Secretary Patton's agenda and would present him with some of his greatest and most immediate challenges.

Two weeks after he had assumed his position, the Secretary was faced with a decision regarding the appointment of a Commissioner for DOSS, which would represent the official establishment of the new agency. The law called

This case was researched and drafted by Rina Spence, while a candidate for a Masters in Public Administration. It was revised and edited by Carol Ritter Thorn, both under the supervision of Jon Brock, Lecturer at the John F. Kennedy School of Government, Harvard University. While based upon a factual situation, the names of the location, organization, individuals, and other information are disguised to protect confidentiality.

for the appointment of a Commissioner by January 1, 1979. A great deal of politicking for this new agency head position was going on around Secretary Patton; at the same time, however, the appointment became complicated by a growing movement to amend drastically the legislation that created the Department of Social Services, destroying the original legislative intent of the Act. Various interest groups were vigorously lobbying the new administration to so amend the law. If their efforts proved successful, it would mean "business as usual"; however, if their efforts proved futile, Secretary Patton knew he would ultimately be held responsible for the smoothness of the transition and the giant task of getting a major agency up and running.

Confused by these events, Patton decided to put off the appointment of a Commissioner — regardless of the mandated appointment deadline — to look into what had occurred during the planning process for DOSS.

History of Welfare Reorganzation Efforts

In the early 1970s, the U.S. Department of Health, Education and Welfare began to reexamine the structure and delivery of public welfare services in an effort to ensure that national goals were being met. Until then, the national norm was a single welfare agency whose staff served both functions of providing money and social support services to welfare recipients. This meant that often the same worker was responsible for both "handing out" the check and making judgments about the quality of home life being provided to children. There were inherent inconsistencies in this dual nature of the job: On the one hand, it was the worker's responsibility to "police" public funds and reduce the recipient's amount of payment if reason were found to do so; yet the worker was also expected to perform counseling services and be trusted by welfare families with personal information. HEW concluded that an ethical question was at stake here and therefore required that the two functions be separated within welfare agencies. States were informed to take appropriate action to accomplish these results.

At the same time, a major study had been released by Maryland's leading private social service agency, the Baltimore Children's Service Association. This study went a step further than HEW by recommending the establishment of an entirely new social service agency separate from DOW. Its conclusions were based primarily on the grounds that professional social workers were desperately needed to attend to cases of child abuse and foster care placements. The Children's Service Association defined "professionals" as those workers having a Master in Social Work degree or its equivalent.

In compliance with HEW requirements, Maryland in 1974 began to separate its Department of Welfare into two divisions: Assistance Payments and Social Services. Assistance Payments would be made up of workers who handled the delivery of direct payments to eligible recipients (Aid to Families with Dependent Children, Medicaid). Social services divisions would include employees (called social workers or social service workers) responsible for problems of child abuse and neglect, foster care and placements, and for offering personal counseling assistance to welfare recipients. There was little distinction between the qualifications of these two types of employees, who were assigned positions based either on personal preference or available slots.

Collective Bargaining and the Department of Welfare

The first efforts at union organization in Welfare began in 1966 when Chuck Johansen, then

a social service worker, began to think he and others were expected to handle too many cases. The workers agreed that their case-load requirements had become excessive and unreasonable. Case load has traditionally been difficult to quantify and therefore to agree on; a worker could possibly specify how long it takes to process a payment request, but it is difficult to do the same for counseling or home visits. Social workers became increasingly frustrated that administrative officials were unaware of several important aspects of their jobs — for instance, an entire morning spent in court over one case meant that the remainder of a heavy case load was backed up even more. The workers — assisted by Mr. Johansen — began to feel they should have a voice in the issues affecting them.

Johansen organized the workers and was subsequently approached by the Service Employees International Union. The State Labor Relations Commission was reluctant to allow this union to organize DOW workers but, after considerable pressure, certification was granted. Several years later, the union joined the Coalition, the single coordinating body of the several state unions which was recognized to negotiate exclusively with the state. The DOW workers became part of Local 101, a unit of the Coalition.

Dividing the Department of Welfare — 1974

The process of negotiating an agreement between DOW workers represented by Local 101 and the State of Maryland delayed the division of Assistance Payments and Social Services by almost a year. For the worker, this division meant a new job description and possibly new job qualifications. Now that the two functions were separated, employees also wondered what effect this would have on their union contract provisions concerning workload. An agreement had to be reached that would satisfy both the worker, that he or she would not be out of work, and the

State, that qualified persons would be delivering social services.

Workers' concerns included who would be transferred or identified as a social service worker, how the selection would be made, and what the criteria would be. Some employees wanted to be assigned to Assistance Payments because they preferred its more clerical function to actual involvement with families. Others very much wanted to continue their casework because they found the work more interesting and gratifying.

As part of a collective bargaining agreement, an accord was reached which permitted employees to take an exam that would "establish their relative knowledge of social services skills." The test was in-house, producing an in-house list, rather than a uniform civil service exam. It was also optional and intended only for those workers wishing to provide social services, which the administration assumed to be about 60 percent of the staff. Those workers who chose not to test their skills simply remained in Assistance Payments and were relieved of any casework functions. The exam format and questions were developed in cooperation with the union, the Labor Relations Department at DOW, and the DOW administration.

After the exam was administered, a list was created based on numerical scores, those scoring highest at the top. The DOW started its Social Services staff selection from the top of this list, and by the time the process was completed, almost all the workers who opted to take the exam and who were on the list had been transferred to Social Services, although many of their test scores were low.

Child Abuse

No further changes in the DOW took place until April 1978, when two-year-old Jane Smith died tragically as a result of severe abuse. The much publicized incident immediately aroused the interest of the general community, and questions regarding child abuse began to receive serious attention. Among them were how such incidents could be prevented in the future and if the qualifications of social service workers and supervisors were adequate. What had occurred during the four years since the Department was divided was the normal upgrading of social service workers to supervisors on the basis of civil service procedures.

Gail Harrison was the supervisor in charge of the Smith case. The Department determined that Harrison was partly responsible for Jane's death due to a neglect of her duties and a failure to "meet her obligations." The letter terminating Ms. Harrison presented as just cause and reason some of the following incidents:

1. Your October 1977 report to the court recommended that custody of Jane Smith be granted to her natural parents, with the DOW "continuing to provide supportive services." You noted in the case record subsequently that the judge accepted this recommendation, but indicated he believed close contact should be maintained with the family. However, you made only two further visits to the family, both in the month after the court hearing, and there is no evidence of other contact with the family until your response on March 20, 1978 to the report of a crying child at the Smith address.

2. You failed to mention in your October 27, 1978 report to the District Court your observation of a "healing bruise" on Jane Smith's face. You testified that you believed the bruising to be an isolated incident and an accident and yet the record shows you warned Mrs. Smith that such bruising would not be tolerated.

The union filed a grievance challenging the discharge of Harrison, and a hearing was held on September 25, 1978. The arbitrator concluded in his decision of November 3, 1978:

The fact does remain that a child is dead, and the frustration resulting from the failure to prevent it plagues the Department and all who were touched by it in any way. But the charges brought by the Department to justify its discharge of Gail are hardly persuasive. These do not demonstrate any evidence of clear violations of Departmental regulations, procedures, or requirements on the part of Gail Harrison in terms of her involvement in the Smith case. Therefore, the discharge cannot be upheld.

Gail Harrison was directed to be reinstated to her position as Head Social Work Supervisor, with full back pay and benefits from the date of discharge to the date of her reinstatement.

The Department of Social Services Legislation and Mandate

The intense public reaction to Jane Smith's death spurred an emergency law establishing a new freestanding agency, the Department of Social Services. Passed on July 24, 1978, the legislation separated the social services component from the Department of Welfare. (See Exhibit 5-4.) No longer would it be sufficient to have both Social Services and Assistance Payments operating within the same agency, as they had since 1974. Advocated by the Baltimore Children's Service Association and other private agencies, the legislation intended to create a model professional social work agency that would be staffed by professionals credentialed in the field of social work. A Commissioner was to be appointed by January 1, 1979, with a one-year planning period before the agency was scheduled to start up on January 1, 1980.

However, the legislation did not define the qualifications for social workers, nor did it include provisions for staffing the new Department. It was assumed that new positions could be created by vacated positions in the old Social Services component of Welfare — basically a one-for-one exchange. Otherwise, it was never clear how the new agency would be staffed or what would happen to social service workers then at DOW. Two viewpoints began to be held by the workers: Some were confident they would be transferred over to the new Department; others were fearful the State viewed DOSS as an opportunity to hire other workers to staff DOSS.

Just prior to passage of the appropriations statute for the Department of Social Services legislation, the union convinced one of its supporters in the legislature to insert the following as Section 46-A:

> No position or job authorized in this legislation shall be filled unless a position is eliminated in the Department of Welfare.

Carole Boyd, president of Local 101, explained the significance of this section:

> It means that the state can't simply create new positions and leave our workers out. Either they're going to have to transfer them over to the new agency or they have to wait until one leaves the DOW in order to transfer a vacant position to DOSS.

According to an attorney working in the DOW Division of Social Services:

> We don't need any special procedure. We're just going to tap the best social service workers and bring them over to the Department of Social Services.

The Implementation Committee

The legislation called for the Secretary of Human Resources to appoint a committee to plan and implement the new agency. Established in September 1978 by Acting Human Resources Secretary Dorothy Morse, the committee consisted of Jim Morrow, Deputy Commissioner of DOW; Kathleen Cole, Assistant Director for Social Services at DOW; Peter Van Horn, Executive Director of Human Services, Inc.; Janet Ames of the Association for Social Workers, and Margo Williams of the Agency for Children.* The committee recruited and hired as Project Director Mark Swartz, a specialist on government reorganization from New York. Mark arranged to commute for the duration of the four- to six-month implementation process.

Swartz's credentials included a Ph.D. in Organizational Psychology from Columbia University and extensive research and writing on the subject. He had also organized a Conference on Children and had been a consultant to the New York Department of Human Resources on health and drug issues.

Swartz immediately set to work by defining goals and issues for the Implementation Committee:

> For operational purposes, the project's work has been organized into three distinct but overlapping areas. These are: structural issues, services and work environment. In general, structural activities are those which involve the mechanics of setting up a new agency by July 1. The services and work environment areas are likely to be the major determinants of the degree of long term success of the agency. (See Exhibit 5-2.)

After a month on the job, Swartz had put together his staff. He began working closely with the Implementation Committee but there were constraints on the members' time, given that they all had line responsibilities in their respective agencies. As a result, much of the actual planning — including identification of the main issues and key personnel — was based on his own judgment and discussions with Acting Secretary Morse.

Morale at DOW

In the meantime, both Social Service supervisors and direct line workers were affected by

*Human Services, Inc. is an organization which represents the interest of service providers; the Association for Social Workers is a professional organization of social workers who lobby for the maintenance of the profession. The Agency for Children is the State agency responsible for the licensing of public and private child-related programs.

the planning process that rendered their job status ambiguous. Concern for their job security was taking its toll on their performance. Field workers were particularly afraid of layoffs. Employees were also confused as to whether the new agency would offer civil service protection and if they would continue to be part of the Local 101 bargaining unit. One senior supervisor commented:

> The whole process has been very insensitive. The reorganization is happening because of supposed incompetence by our personnel. DOSS is to be a new agency of professionals, they keep telling us — we all wonder if *we* are the incompetents that everyone keeps referring to!

According to another employee:

> The Department has come to a standstill — morale is at an all time low. People don't know how long they'll be carrying their cases. This is affecting their performance. Nobody here feels like working. There's no support from Central Office.

Transfer of Social Service Workers

Reorganization and the creation of the new agency posed several questions dealing with the personnel process: what sort of evaluation mechanisms would be used as a basis for selection, how workers would be selected for the new agency, what procedures would be established, and what criteria would be set.

Selection of workers for transfer to the new agency had been on the implementation staff's agenda since October 1. By November, Swartz's staff began to realize they should be making greater progress on the issue. During long sessions with Swartz, they attempted to analyze the entire process. Great importance was attached to "work environment" and other essentials they agreed were necessary to providing good social services.

The Director of Labor Relations at DOW, Hal Bonati, had also been giving serious thought to the transfer issue and had expected to work closely with Mark Swartz. But although Bonati had been with DOW for eight years and the director of labor relations since 1974, Swartz was not aware of Bonati's existence within the agency. Therefore, he failed to contact Bonati for his input on reorganization and transfer procedures.

"I remember the 1974 agreement process. We're coming up against the same issues in this reorganization," Bonati said. According to him:

DOW better get out to supervisors and managers some of the guidelines saying what we should be looking for so we can evaluate employees and make decisions. I know they're going to have to have some sort of evaluation standards or procedures. There are presently no standards or formal evaluations for DOW social workers. We keep running into the problem of not having a basis to fire someone or even transfer them.

He later reflected:

A lot of people say the DOW doesn't have qualified people in Social Services — but as yet no social services employee has been successfully suspended or terminated as a result of a performance issue. There's no precedent that they are not qualified — therefore it would be a hard argument now to say they're not qualified.

Jim Morrow expressed the view that problems would arise over the lack of written standards for "competence in social services." Without these, he felt, the new agency may simply be an extension of the old, or "business as usual." In order to have a competent staff and professional reputation, he felt an evaluation process would ideally include at least two levels and judgments by professionals who understand social service work. Another, less satisfactory, process would be passing civil service tests as they existed. He offered this suggestion only because he predicted that competency tests would not be established by June 30, 1979, the date they targeted for completion. "Even the social work profession can't agree on one," he claimed.

Not only don't the professionals agree on what should be an evaluation tool but the union doesn't even know what their workers want, so even if we could agree on a format the union wouldn't know what to say. By February 24 [the due date for the Committee's Report] the Implementation Committee will have come up with some evaluation criteria and then we will give it to the union for reaction — but they will battle in March and April over it and then take it to the legislators — it's so predictable.

Social Service workers now think of themselves as professionals, but are not sure they want to be evaluated by those standards.

Given the resistance to defining professional criteria, Morrow anticipated evaluation based on bureaucratic measures.

Jim Donovan, director of social services for DOW and a leading candidate for the new Commissioner of DOSS, offered some novel ideals for evaluation:

Workers do not have rights to jobs in DOSS. Some mechanisms for transfer will occur. We are presently talking to a private college which is proposing "Group Dynamics" meetings as a way of selecting the best workers. The meetings would bring out the workers' views and abilities and therefore provide some criteria for selection.

Meeting with the Union

Acting Human Resources Secretary Morse viewed the State's relationship with the union as a naturally antagonistic one and expressed these feelings to Mark Swartz on several occasions. Swartz himself put off meeting with the union to discuss the reorganization process and the issues of transfer and evaluation. And according to Jim Morrow, Deputy Commissioner of DOW:

We don't need to involve the union in our planning. They never agree with us anyway and their approach is too different. They lose perspective on the planning process.

Because so many workers were frightened about losing their jobs, the union felt keenly its responsibility to protect its members. "They [the State] think the current state employees are worthless and think they're going to get social workers from outside state service — clearly this is not going to happen," according to Carole Boyd, President of Local 101. Ms. Boyd took the position that social service jobs should be offered to existing personnel and training should be expanded. The union was opposed to evaluations because they were viewed as being conducted poorly in the past and as a means "to deny people positions."

On November 1, 1978, Ms. Boyd indicated the union would be willing to negotiate on an evaluation tool. On December 20, the meeting took place between Mark Swartz and Carole Boyd. They sat across from each other for several hours. Afterward, Swartz expressed puzzlement at her antagonistic attitude: "Ms. Boyd did not seem in the least interested in discussing evaluation or transfer procedures. I had been warned about this union, but I never thought a meeting could go so poorly."

On January 5, 1979, a little over five months after the emergency legislation was passed, the union filed legislation under the sponsorship of State Representative George Whalen that would "grandfather" all social service employees from the Department of Welfare to DOSS. In other words, all employees already in place would be transferred to the new agency, although new standards might be applied to new employees. Along with this legislation, the union waged an intense lobbying campaign, favoring no application process, no Master in Social Work requirement, and no interviews.

The proposed legislation was sent to Secretary Patton for review. As Secretary of Human Resources, he must take a position on legislation affecting his agencies. In addition, the law still required him to appoint a Commissioner of Social Services.

Exhibit 5-1. The Department of Human Resources

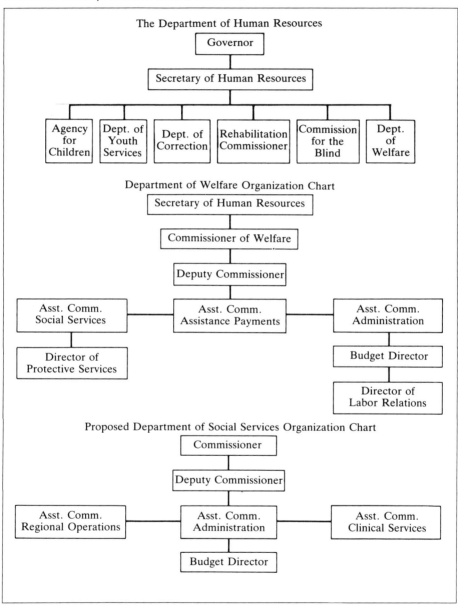

Exhibit 5-2. Plan for Department of Social Services implementation

October 30, 1978

TO: Dorothy Morse, Secretary of Human Services
FROM: Mark Swartz
SUBJECT: Plan for Department of Social Services Implementation

INTRODUCTION

This memorandum represents an outline of the organization of the implementation project. While the project's organization and procedures are
likely to remain relatively unchanged between now and February 24, 1979,
we can expect shifts in the priorities as our information base grows. The
project plan has been developed within a context of a set of specific
goals and assumptions. These follow:

Project Goals

1. Preparation of a clear, comprehensive, and readily usable structural
   and operational plan for the Department of Social Services.

2. Provide for the Implementation Committee and Commissioner the widest
   possible range of choices of service models and methods for enhancing
   the quality of social services programs.

3. Development of a set of departmental processes which will provide for
   ongoing agency flexibility and support systems which are intended to
   assure maximum staff effectiveness at all levels.

4. Provide for an orderly transition with the least possible disruption
   of the operations of the Department of Public Welfare and other service providers, and no disruption of client services.

5. Production of a plan based upon the active participation and support
   of a wide range of constituencies, including the Legislature; Administration; service users; service providers, public and nonpublic advocates; and interested agencies.

6. Provide an overall service framework in which prevention is accen-
   tuated.

Planning Assumptions

1. The most basic assumption made is to sharply limit our assumptions.
   The purpose here is to prevent misdirection, acceptance of ''inevita-
   bilities,'' and the problem of ''things falling between the cracks.''

2. It is assumed that the single overriding responsibility of the implementation staff is to assure the orderly transition to the new agency
   which will begin to function on July 1, 1979.

3. Beyond the mechanical transfer of functions to the new agency, it is
   assumed that the establishment of the Department of Social Services
   represents a one-time opportunity. The next eight months will be critical in at least three specific respects:
   a) Processes can be developed which will address problems of worker
      effectiveness and the work environment at the point of delivery of
      service. In this respect, it is assumed that the ''informal organi-

(Exhibit continues on following page.)

Exhibit 5-2. Continued

zation'' is as important as the formal structure in determining the
quality of services.
  b) A systematic review of all services, mandated and non-mandated, can
     be undertaken for the purpose of designing the most efficacious
     overall program. This opportunity is unlikely to recur once the
     agency is in operation.
  c) Vital linkages with other parts of the system can be formalized and
     strengthened.
4. It is assumed that suspicion and resistance are inherent in the change
   process and that the project must address these conditions, primarily
   through policies of openness in the sharing of information and parti-
   cipatory planning. Within this context, there should <u>not</u> be an attempt
   to minimize the fact that change brings dislocations <u>and</u> requires adjustments.

PROJECT ORGANIZATION

<u>Planning Areas</u>

For operational purposes, the project's work has been organized into
three distinct but overlapping areas. These are: structural issues, services, and the work environment. In general, structural activities are
those which involve the mechanics of setting up a new agency by July 1.
The services and work environment areas are likely to be the major determinants of the degree of long-term success of the agency. A non-ranked
and non-exhaustive breakdown of the major areas follows:

1. Structural Issues
   a) The social services budget: recasting; type; location of budgetary
      authority.
   b) Required legislative revision and other legal actions including
      contractual arrangements, statutes, federal regulations.
   c) Decentralization
   d) Agency Interfaces: with DOW; overhead units; other service provi-
      ders; other agencies.
   e) Definition of services to be provided.
   f) Transition to July 1, 1979: office organization, space, equipment,
      and supplies; payroll, personnel, and purchase functions; vehicles;
      mail; etc.
   g) Area Councils: selection process; roles and linkages; training;
      budget(s).
   h) Overhead systems: personnel; payroll; budget; purchase; grants man-
      agement; fiscal; revenue/payment.
   i) Purchase of Service: contracting; monitoring, evaluation, and au-
      dit; technical assistance.
   j) Management information system(s).
   k) Management and staff support systems: research; training; program
      audit and evaluation.
   l) Procedures for safeguarding client rights.
   m) Entitlements; fee scales; rate setting.
   n) Procedures: procedure manuals; internal and external communication.

(Exhibit continues on following page.)

Exhibit 5-2. Continued

o) Formal structure: job descriptions; lines of authority; civil service, contractual, and other requirements; criteria and procedures
for transfer, hiring, termination, and promotion.

2. Services
   a) Mandated services defined: federal statute; state statute; court
      mandates.
   b) Optional services currently provided: gaps and overlaps.
   c) Definition of goals for services currently provided.
   d) Client criteria and priorities for mandated and non-mandated ser-
      vices defined: need; ability to pay.
   e) Alternative intake and service delivery models.
   f) Continuity of service or care: preventive and early intervention
      approaches; interorganization and intersystem continuity.
   g) The direct service/purchase mix: criteria for choice and policy de-
      velopment.
   h) Monitoring and evaluating services and programs.
   i) Case management: definition; training; plans for installing and
      monitoring.
   j) Crisis-oriented services: design; implications for overall agency
      goals and mission.

3. The Work Environment
   a) Sources of effectiveness and ineffectiveness, satisfaction and dis-
      satisfaction: direct service workers; supervisors; middle manage-
      ment; top management.
   b) Intra-agency communication: horizontal and vertical.
   c) Job design and the organization of work.
   d) Reward systems: career ladder(s); compensation; other possible re-
      wards within framework of civil service.
   e) Time: attendance; vacations; sabbaticals; sick leave; part-time al-
      ternatives.
   f) Internal support systems: assistance in dealing with the stresses
      of work in social services; on-the-job assistance for troubled
      workers.
   g) Expectations; evaluations; equitable systems of accountability;
      grievance and appeal procedures; standards of responsibility and
      performance.
   h) Support systems for supervisors and management.

The Planning Process

The successful completion of the plan will depend heavily upon effective
decision making on the part of the Implementation Committee. The planning
process has been designed with that end in mind. It is built around the
preparation and presentation of well researched and broadly discussed option papers in the areas listed above. In those areas requiring policy
decisions, clear-cut alternatives will be presented to the Implementation
Committee. When longer-range considerations are involved, position papers
will be developed for use by the Commissioner of Social Services. Finally, planning documents and procedures will be developed for use by the
transition staff.

The planning process will consist of the following steps:

(Exhibit continues on following page.)

Exhibit 5-2. Continued

1. Identification of basic issues requiring planning attention.

2. Division of issues into specific tasks leading to policy or option statements for the Implementation Committee or Commissioner, or plans for specific action by implementation staff.

3. Broad discussion and consultation in planning areas.

4. Presentation of papers for decision by the Implementation Committee.

5. Development of plans based upon decisions made.

6. Development of feedback loops based upon planning decisions, branching logic, and broad participation and designed to eliminate oversights and planning inconsistency.

7. Compilation of comprehensive plan.

Staffing

The work will be completed by a mix of directly employed staff and contractors. A core team is being assembled which will provide direction and overall stability to the project. This staff will be complemented by a cadre of specialized contractors who will perform a variety of tasks.

   As of October 30, the implementation team consists of nine full- and part-time members whose immediate activities are directed toward preparation of the budget, the nature of decentralization, staff transfers, transition issues, legal and legislative requirements, and the development of an effective data gathering capability.

November Goals

Project goals for November will be directed toward the development of an effective work team and a research capability; refinement of decision making processes; the letting of key contracts; and the preparation of option papers for decision in the following areas: definition of new agency functions; organizational constraints; staff transfer and recruitment procedures; decentralization; budget; entitlements; and legal requirements.

MS: ej
cc: Implementation Committee Members
    Implementation Staff

Exhibit 5-3. Personnel categories within the state service

EXCERPTS FROM
PERSONNEL CATEGORIES WITHIN THE
STATE SERVICE

Employees within the state service may be described in two different ways: by the appropriations category to which their position belongs (permanent, temporary, or consultant), and by the section of the law governing their hiring and firing (either Civil Service or non-Civil Service). Civil Service employees may be either temporary or permanent; non-Civil Service employees may fall into any of the three appropriations categories. The legislature appropriates personnel funds for each agency under the three different appropriations categories, each of which has its own separate personnel procedures.

Civil Service. About 60% of the employees of the Commonwealth — including both 01 and 02 employees—are selected by Civil Service examination procedures. These employees include most non-professional and most lower-level professional positions. There are two parts to the Civil Service — the official service and the labor service.

Non-Civil Service. A complete list of non-civil service positions would be difficult to compile since the Legislature has included positions under (or excluded them from) Civil Service on a purely ad hoc basis. The Civil Service laws (Chapter 31 of the General Laws) lists some exempt positions, and then includes "such others as are by law exempt from the operation of this chapter." The majority of exempt employees consist of professional employees at the various institutions, for example, nurses and doctors in institutions and hospitals; teachers in correctional institutions; professional librarians. Also exempt are employees in the upper tier of policy mak-

ing and administration in the Executive Branch, including all cabinet secretaries and many of the administrators who report directly to them (such as insurance commissioner, banking commissioner, personnel administrator, department heads).

Employees not selected through Civil Service examinations are neither technically nor customarily considered as being in the Civil Service. However, many of them gain the protection of the tenure provisions of Civil Service after they have served a specified length of time (from six months to three years). For example, all teachers in state institutions gain tenure after three years. Also, the legislature will frequently make a specific position subject to the tenure provisions in order to protect a particular incumbent. Finally, all veterans gain tenure after three years of service, regardless of the type of position they hold or the method by which they were appointed. As a result of these different ways of protecting employees, about three out of four non-Civil Service employees holding non-Civil Service positions actually are protected by the tenure and dismissal provisions of Chapter 31. Only about ten percent of state employees are therefore completely exempt from Civil Service regulations.

Training

The Division of Personnel Administration is responsible for a certain amount of in-service training, but the extent of this responsibility is difficult to determine exactly. The "Blue Book" given to all new employees lists the following courses as having been recently given: Executive Development, Basic Supervisory Management, Human Relations and Communications, Effective Management, Personnel Interviewing and Counseling, and Office Management for Clerical Supervisors,

(Exhibit continues on following page.)

Exhibit 5-3. Continued

among others. More specialized training is occasionally provided by individual departments and agencies.

Evaluation

Maryland does not have any comprehensive system of employee evaluation. Although some attempts have been made to develop evaluation systems for individual state agencies, no state system exists comparable to the regular evaluation system for Federal Civil Service employees. In theory, Civil Service employees serve a six month probationary period (longer for some positions), during which time they should be evaluated and dismissed if not competent; and in the first seven years of an employee's service, an agency can withhold a step increase in pay because of unsatisfactory performance. In practice, however, most employees are not scrutinized at these times. The laws are written so that inaction by appointing authorities results in automatic tenure or step increases for the employees. Although the opportunity to evaluate the employee exists, there is no pressure on the appointing authority to do so.

Except for denial of step increases, an appointing authority has no incentives to give force to whatever evaluations are made. Unlike the Federal Service, there are no quality pay increases or bonuses for outstanding work. After an employee has spent seven years in a pay grade, he or she has reached the maximum step, and so the only negative incentive that can be used is the threat of dismissal.

Promotion

In 1961, a League of Women Voters survey of state agencies showed that "for positions covered by Civil Service, seniority is the ruling factor in promotions and that opportunities for advancement are confined within the unit of government in which the employee works." That summary is still reasonably accurate in 1975. The practice of using seniority as the dominant factor in promotions appears to be the legacy of the many years of a system during which the Division of Civil Service dictated promotional policy to appointing authorities. In fact, the law allows appointing authorities to choose one of several different methods of promotions, subject to the approval of the Personnel Administrator. In the most conservative method, an employee who is one of the three most senior employees in his present grade in the department can be promoted by the appointing authority. Alternatively, an authority can request an examination and can specify that it be oral or written and that it be for departmental employees only, for all employees within the executive office containing the department, for all employees of state government, or for anyone (a normal open competitive examination). While the examination is being prepared, the appointing authority can make a provisional promotion. In the past, agencies have tended to select the most conservative practical method of promotion, as a result of which employees tend to spend their entire career within one office. This practice makes agencies inbred and stifles opportunities for lower-ranking employees of merit. Administrators find it difficult to open up promotional examinations since employee unions can pressure them into seniority-based promotions; administrators may also simply be unwilling to jeopardize office morale by lessening promotional opportunities for a large number of low-ranking employees.

(Exhibit continues on following page.)

Exhibit 5-3. Continued

Dismissal

Dismissal of state employees, although difficult, is not impossible. Provisional employees can be dismissed at any time; temporary employees (02) can be dismissed by the abolition of their positions; and permanent non-Civil Service employees can be dismissed at will, unless their positions have been protected by the tenure provisions of the Civil Service law, or by special legislative provision (often called a "freeze in"). Permanent Civil Service employees can be dismissed during their probationary period; after that they can be dismissed for cause, but the lengthy hearing and appeal processes involved discourage this action.

Exhibit 5-4. Excerpts from the legislation establishing the Department of Social Services

---

1978   Acts and Resolves

Chap. 552   AN ACT ESTABLISHING A DEPARTMENT OF SOCIAL SERVICES AND DEFINING ITS POWERS AND DUTIES.

Whereas, The deferred operation of this act would tend to defeat its purpose which is, in part, to immediately provide for an orderly transfer of certain duties relative to social services to a department of social services, therefore it is declared to be an emergency law, necessary for the immediate preservation of the public convenience. . . .

SECTION 10. The General Laws are hereby amended by inserting after chapter 18A the following chapter:

CHAPTER 18B
DEPARTMENT OF SOCIAL SERVICES

Section 1. There shall be a department of social services, in this chapter called the department.

Section 2. (A) The department shall provide and administer a comprehensive social service program, including the following services:

(1) casework or counseling including social services to families, foster families or individuals;

(2) protective services for children, unmarried mothers, the aging and other adults;

(3) legal services for families, children or individuals as they relate to social problems;

(4) foster family care and specialized foster family care for children, the aging, the disabled and the handicapped;

(5) adoption services;

(6) homemaker services;

(7) day care facilities and services for children, the aging, the disabled and the handicapped;

(8) residential care for children with special needs or aging persons not suited to foster family care, or specialized foster family care;

(9) informal education and group activities as needed for families, children, the aging, the disabled and the handicapped;

(10) training in parenthood and home management for parents, foster parents and prospective parents;

(11) social services for newcomers to an area or community to assist in adjustment to a new environment and new resources;

(Exhibit continues on following page.)

Exhibit 5-4. Continued

(12) camping services;

(13) family services intended to prevent the need for foster care and services to children in foster care;

(14) temporary residential programs providing counseling and supportive assistance for women in transition and their children who because of domestic violence, homelessness, or other situations require temporary shelter and assistance; and

(15) information and referral services.

Section 3. The department shall establish a comprehensive program of social services at the area level and to promote such program shall divide the state into regions and areas consistent with those established by the secretary of human services as provided in section sixteen of chapter six A.

(A) In order that the area-based social services be adapted, organized and coordinated to meet the needs of certain population groups, the department shall provide programs of service for:
  (1) families, children and unmarried parents, which program shall, among other objectives, serve to assist, strengthen and encourage family life for the protection and care of children, assist and encourage the use by any family of all available resources to this end, and provide substitute care of children only when preventive services have failed and the family itself or the resources needed and provided to the family are unable to insure the integrity of the family and the necessary care and protection to guarantee the rights of any child to sound health and normal physical, mental, spiritual and moral development.
  (2) the aging and other adults in need of social, legal, health, rehabilitation, employment or other services.
  (3) other population groups which require special adaptation of the services provided because of special needs.

(B) The department shall:
  (1) formulate the policies, procedures and rules necessary for the full and efficient implementation of programs authorized by the laws of the state and federal laws in the area of social services;
  (2) administer the services, funds, and personnel necessary for such social service programs throughout;
  (3) establish and enforce high standards of social service and strive to elevate such standards;
  (4) provide the range of social services on a fair, just and equitable basis to all people in need of such services;

(Exhibit continues on following page.)

Exhibit 5-4. Continued

(5) collaborate with other departments of the state which are in fields related to social welfare and with voluntary or private agencies or organizations to assure efficient and high-quality social and educational services for persons who are unable for social or economic reasons to provide such services for themselves;

(6) study the social and economic problems in the state and make recommendations to the appropriate branches and agencies of government for broadening and improving the scope and quality of social services.

Section 4. Services of the department shall not be denied to any person because of such person's financial assets or income; provided, however, that the department shall establish a schedule of fees for services which may vary with the ability of the recipient of such services to pay therefor.

Section 5. The department shall make provision for such social services as are required under Title XX and Title IV B of the Social Security Act and the regulations established thereunder and shall provide such additional services as the legislature may determine.

Section 6. The department shall be under the direction, supervision and control of a commissioner of social services, in this chapter called the commissioner who shall be appointed by the governor for a term coterminous with that of the governor. Said commissioner shall be qualified by training and experience to perform the duties of the office and shall at the time of appointment have received a doctorate or other degree beyond the level of the baccalaureate in the field of business, economics, education, government, law, medicine, psychology, public administration, public health, public policy, social work, urban planning, or a field substantially related to one or more of the foregoing and shall have had not less than seven years of responsible administrative experience, at least three of which shall have been in a field related to human services, or said commissioner shall have had experience in one or more of said fields for a period of years equivalent to the number of years required to obtain such other degree beyond that of baccalaureate required herein, and shall have had, in addition thereto, not less than seven years of responsible administrative experience, at least three of which shall have been in a field related to human services. The commissioner shall receive a salary of thirty-six thousand seven hundred and seventy dollars and shall devote full time to the duties of the office. The commissioner shall be the executive and administrative head of the department.

(Exhibit continues on following page.)

Exhibit 5-4. Continued

Section 7.

(a) The commissioner shall establish reasonable caseload rates and shall report the same to the general court in the budget estimates of the department.

(b) The commissioner shall develop and implement a management information system which shall contain fiscal and personnel data, client data, and program data necessary for the ongoing administration or effective service delivery. Said information system shall include but not be limited to a service plan for each client, with provisions for periodic review thereof. The commissioner shall promulgate such rules and regulations as are deemed necessary to ensure the confidentiality of client data collected by the department.

(c) The commissioner shall develop and implement a comprehensive monitoring and evaluation system for all social services under the control of the department and shall collect the necessary program and fiscal data annually.

(d) The commissioner shall conduct an annual needs assessment for all social services under the control of the department.

(e) The commissioner shall report annually to the legislature on all services which report shall reflect program and client data and unit costs.

(f) The commissioner shall develop and implement a plan for the orientation and training of area-based and other staff.

(g) The commissioner shall coordinate the overall service planning of the department with planning under Title XX.

(h) The commissioner shall be authorized to apply for and accept on behalf of the state, federal, local or private grants, bequests, gifts or contributions.

(i) The commissioner subject to the provisions of chapter thirty A shall promulgate such rules and regulations as are deemed necessary to carry out the provisions of this chapter and may amend or repeal the same.

(j) The commissioner shall include in the budget estimates of the department funds for the development and implementation of the aforementioned management information system, monitoring and evaluation system, annual needs assessment, and staff training plan.

Not more than three per cent of the department's annual budget shall be appropriated in a separate account and expended for the purposes set out in subsections (b), (c), and (d), of this section. On or before January first, nineteen hundred and eighty-three the commissioner shall submit to the governor and to the legislature a report evaluating the level of funding and the desirability of continuing separate funding for such activities.

(Exhibit continues on following page.)

Exhibit 5-4. Continued

Section 8. The commissioner shall appoint and may remove a deputy commissioner who shall receive a salary of thirty-two thousand four hundred and seventy-five dollars. The deputy commissioner shall have the same qualifications in training and experience as required by the commissioner. The deputy commissioner shall perform such duties as the commissioner may determine and shall, in the case of a vacancy in the office of the commissioner, or during the commissioner's absence or disability, exercise the powers and perform the duties of the office of commissioner. Said deputy commissioner shall devote full time to the duties of the office.

Section 9. The commissioner may appoint and remove such assistant commissioners as the commissioner shall from time to time determine, not to exceed four in number, who shall be assigned to areas of responsibility to be specified by the commissioner.

Each assistant commissioner shall be qualified by training and experience to perform the duties of the office and shall at the time of appointment have received a masters or higher degree and shall have had professional experience or not less than five years as an administrator in a field related to human services or said assistant commissioner shall have had professional experience in a field related to human services for a period of years equivalent to the number of years required to obtain a master's degree, and shall have had, in addition thereto, professional experience of not less than five years as an administrator in a field related to human services. Each assistant commissioner shall receive a salary of thirty thousand dollars and shall devote full time to the duties of the office. . . .

Section 45. The secretary of human services shall transfer all personal property, including files, records and equipment, which is used by or under the control of the office of social services in the department of public welfare on the effective date of this act, to the department of social services created by section four of this act. Such transfer shall be made at such time as said secretary shall determine but not later than the time provided in the plan submitted by the committee appointed under section ten of this act.

Section 46. Within thirty days after the passage of this act, the secretary of human services shall appoint a committee to prepare a plan for the orderly implementation of the provisions of this act. Said committee shall consist of the secretary of human services who shall act as chairman and five other persons appointed by him. An appropriation shall be authorized to provide staff support for the committee. Said committee may recommend to the legislature changes in the General Laws necessary or desirable to properly carry out the provisions of this act.

Said plan shall include budget estimates for the operation of the de-

(Exhibit continues on following page.)

Exhibit 5-4. Continued

partment of social services for the fiscal year beginning July first, nineteen hundred and seventy-nine.

Said committee shall submit said plan to the governor and the legislature within seven months after the passage of this act for implementation on July first, nineteen hundred and seventy-nine, beginning with a transition period extending until January first, nineteen hundred and eighty.

The commissioner of the department shall be appointed not later than six months before the implementation date of this act.

Section 46A. No position or job authorized in this legislation shall be filled unless a position is eliminated in the department of public welfare.

Section 47. This act shall take effect upon its passage; provided, however, that notwithstanding the provisions of this act, powers and duties vested in the department of public welfare or any board, commission or public office prior to the passage of this act shall continue to be exercised by said department until the time provided for the orderly transfer of such powers in the plan submitted by the committee appointed under section forty-five of this act. Powers and duties exercised by the commissioner of said department, including membership on boards and commissions, shall, notwithstanding the provisions of this act, continue to be exercised by him until the time so provided.

PART III

Compensation: Money as a Motivator

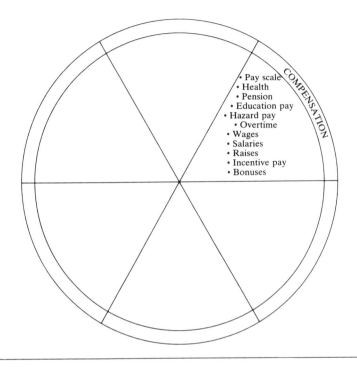

- Pay scale
- Health
- Pension
- Education pay
- Hazard pay
- Overtime
- Wages
- Salaries
- Raises
- Incentive pay
- Bonuses

COMPENSATION

Because compensation is of central importance in the employment relationship and as a cost of operating an agency, this part of the book examines compensation as a management tool. Several cases in other parts of the book deal with aspects of compensation and compensation practices. In Chapter 3 the case, "Equal Employment Opportunity in the Department of Health Commerce and Labor," dealt with the importance of job descriptions and the classification process in determining salaries. Chapter 4, "Hiring Quality People for the Executive Office of the President" dealt further with the classification process and indicated how an individual's rating — and therefore salary — could depend on an evaluation by a qualifications examiner. Chapter 13, on labor-management relations, describes how collective bargaining and related processes may contribute to determining pay. Chapters 9 and 11 on performance appraisal explore methods of determining incentive pay and some of the effects of incentive pay systems on motivation. So, compensation is related to and affected by many other aspects of an extended personnel system.

In this part we look at how compensation governs the way people perform and how they perceive their jobs. As compensation affects satisfaction and performance of individuals, an organization's ability to provide services or otherwise accomplish tasks will be influenced. Despite constraints on affecting compensation, managers interested in performance and satisfaction of employees, therefore, will wish to pay attention to compensation as a variable in the extended personnel system.

As noted in Chapter 2, compensation comes in several forms. Most common are wages and salaries, benefits (health, retirement, educational), incentive compensation, and bonuses. The mix of these will vary among jurisdictions, occupations and organizations, but most public agencies have at least one thing in common concerning employee compensation: It is usually the largest single operating cost. Even where motivational issues related to compensation receive little attention, the cost aspect receives a great deal, especially in periods of retrenchment in government budgets. Policies and practices related to cost control can often conflict with employees' perceptions of fairness in the change and distribution of compensation. Very frequently, actors outside the organization will see compensation only in terms of cost and not in terms of its effect on employees. Budget officers, legislators with fiscal responsibility, the press, and others with concerns about public spending can exert a lot of influence on the amount of money available for public employee pay raises and the manner in which it is distributed. A manager not only has responsibilities for cost control, however; he or she must also evaluate the effects of system-wide financial policy on employees. The manager is often in the middle.

Compensation can also be a management tool for attracting or retaining people. Therefore, to attract well-qualified and well-matched people to a particular public organization, compensation must be competitive with that offered in connection with other options that an individual might have. While precise compensation comparisons are difficult to make, an inadequate or inadequately managed compensation policy can lower the qualifications of a pool of job applicants or can lead to unnecessary and damaging turnover. Like poor job matches, turnover has costs in efficiency: among other things, management and personnel office time spent on repeated recruiting, implicit and explicit training costs, and work loads imposed on other employees. Because of these effects on quality and stability of employment, a manager should have a natural interest in the effects of compensation practices on employees in his or her organization.

Until recently, most public sector pay systems appear to have concentrated on providing uniformity of pay among individuals performing similar functions. The practical result has been an attempt at achieving uniformity of practices used to determine pay. Of necessity this has led to an approach that concentrates on "input" measures, i.e., measurable qualifications of the person such as education or years of experience, and on easily identifiable and ongoing functions in a given job, such as number of people supervised, level of those supervised, or skills or knowledge that must be displayed.

Concentration on these more easily measurable input assumptions may be unrelated either to the quality of the person's work or the potential for handling new challenges, the person's performance on the job, or the results achieved. As a result, the drive toward equity in compensation, focused on input variables, can actually create inequities among people whose performance or conception of ostensibly similar jobs is, in fact, rather different. Against a rigid, input-based compensation system, such differences in individual performance can affect people's perceptions of how fair the compensation system — or the manager administering that system — may be. Recalling Douglas McGregor's injunction quoted in Chapter 3, a perceived lack of fairness in an employee's view of such things as compensation will seriously affect an employee's responsiveness to his or her manager.

Separately, pressures on cost control and the attempt at input uniformity can have a bad effect on workers' responses to their compensation. These factors, while important managerial considerations, ignore the real impact on the workers. These pressures also ignore the way in which compensation affects the achievement of organizational goals and tasks. The pressure of external actors pursuing cost control and input uniformity makes it important that a manager try to mitigate the effects on motivation of such pressures.

Some public pay systems and their application recently have sought to avoid input rigidity or have gone further toward concentrating on output and performance. Such systems have their own difficulties in measurement of output and lack of trust in the measurements. Therefore, progress in reforming civil service compensation systems has been slow, and there have been few experiments or case studies in public environments to help point the way. Experiments and changes going on in the late 1970s and early 1980s may provide some data, as may the cases on performance appraisal and incentive compensation in Chapters 9 and 11.

In my work and research in the public sector, and in advising public managers and policy makers on compensation, I have encountered two opposite, but very strong, impressions about compensation: Most managers both underestimate and overestimate the effect of compensation on performance and satisfaction of employees.

Managers underestimate the adverse impact of insufficient management attention to employee compensation and leave compensation largely to the workings of the formal personnel system. This ignores the possibility that the many actors and processes affecting compensation can divert the motivation and attention of employees toward tangential or secondary tasks or goals. For example, if promotions or bonuses are greatly influenced by someone outside the work unit, a manager can end up competing with other actors or other tasks for an employee's attention. More commonly, compensation policy that does not seem fair or consistent can simply cause dissatisfaction that affects the quality of work and overall responsiveness to management. But managers cannot beg the issue by pointing a finger at the other actors and processes in the compensation business.

On the other hand, managers tend to overestimate the degree of positive effect that changes in compensation or compensation practices can have. Because of the complexity of using compensation as a tool, managers may overestimate their ability to gain quick and direct results with it. First, changes in large, formal compensation systems — even when well conceived — often have perverse and unintended effects on individuals or on group behavior, and in introducing such systems these effects often are unanticipated. Individuals differ and money, therefore, is not a simple factor in a person's work calculus. It is mixed up with and substituted for many tangible and intangible aspects of a work environment and with each individual's psychological, social, and material needs. As this part and Parts IV and V suggest, money may be used as *or* be perceived as a proxy for other things related to status or position in the organization or peer group, or as a signal by a manager regarding an individual's achievement or contribution. What makes things even more difficult is that the manager and the worker may perceive these signals differently or may have differing views of their importance.

The possibility of disruption, displeasure, and uncertainty when altering any organizational system or practice makes it even more difficult to gain positive results from major changes in formal compensation practices. Changes must be thought out carefully, with specific attention to their effect on individuals' reactions to their job and job environment. Not only will the effect on interactions within and among work groups be important, but so will the timing and method of implementing the change. The process of change itself can have as significant an impact as the design of the new system.

Because of its ubiquitous presence in the work setting and in employee perceptions, compensation is a variable in the extended personnel system that deserves careful attention by each manager, even when it seems that the major determinants are out of a manager's direct control. Compensation is not just a cost item — although that is a critical issue — or a matter of strictly applying classification rules. The research and theory on the subject is interesting but offers little guidance unless viewed critically and carefully in the context of particular individuals, particular organizations, and particular circumstances. Still, the effects of compensation on employee behavior and satisfaction can be so strong that a manager must be aware of and try to influence them — if only as a defensive measure.

The following case study examines some of the benefits and risks in planning and carrying on compensation systems. In "Baines Electronics Corporation" management decided that it wished to increase the perceived relationship between compensation and employee performance. It sought to use compensation to enhance the degree of communication and level of motivation in the unit. Until recently, this degree of flexibility in compensation practices has not existed in most public agencies. However, recent interest in such concepts and legislative change have begun to encourage experimentation linking pay more closely with performance. Thus, this case may have a particular currency for public managers.

Because the case is drawn from private business, some of the effects of compensation on individuals and on a work group can be examined momentarily free of the cultural and institutional effects that accompany the subject in most public sector organizations.

CHAPTER 6

The Effects of Compensation

Despite the restrictions on managerial discretion, compensation in public employment is worthy of examination because of the common belief that compensation is an important tool of personnel management. Indeed, many managers and employees talk about compensation as if it were the single most important factor in the employment relationship. This perception alone can make money a significant aspect of the job experience and for this, if for no other reason, it demands attention.

It is important for managers to have some conception of how compensation may be used or perceived. This is true not only for managerial purposes, but also because much of the discussion about reform of public personnel systems centers around compensation reform and seeks to emphasize the relationship between pay and performance. As a result, it is an issue that is likely to come up both in day-to-day management practice and in matters of overall personnel policy.

Pay setting for most public employees will be affected by laws, regulations, and their interpretation by others in the formal personnel system. Still, public employees are likely to be no different from private employees in their basic interest in compensation as a signal of their abilities and worth to the organization — and as a major reason for seeking employment. They will also be interested in whether the process by which compensation is determined seems fair and whether it validates their perceptions about who is carrying the burden in the workplace. Where those perceptions are not aligned, dissatisfaction is possible. Most of the research on pay suggests that dissatisfaction is a common and damaging result of poorly designed or administered compensation practices.

Public managers are constrained by many aspects of the formal compensation system and by other informal pressures imposed in the public arena. Yet we still find that employees are affected by the compensation they receive and by perceptions of what they are receiving. Therefore, a manager, in order to have influence on this important variable, must seek ways to minimize the dissatisfaction that can arise.

In the Equal Employment Opportunity case in Chapter 3 we observed some of the actors and systems that influence compensation in the public sector. To simplify the present examination the following case focuses on a private firm in which statutes and politics impose fewer limitations. Rather, the practices are more endemic to the work unit itself. While other cases in the book illustrate different aspects of public compensation practices, this case focuses largely on the behavioral affects on employees of changes in compensation practices themselves.

STUDY QUESTIONS

1. How is Baines Electronics' new system for pay increases different from their old system? What are the important changes and features?
2. What is it like to work at Baines? How do people there respond to it as a place to work? What are the conditions like?
3. What must they do well in order to succeed at their organizational mission? What has worked well for them so far?
4. What effects will the new system for giving out raises have on the performance of the engineers? Will there be a large or a small difference?
5. What features of the new system account for the results you predict?
6. What characteristics of the engineers account for the results you predict?
7. Would you make any recommendations for adjusting or altering the new system or its implementation?
8. After analyzing this case, what do you think about the proper ways to use money as a motivator? What principles emerge from Baines's approach to using money as a motivator?

RECOMMENDED READING

Maison Haire, Edwin E. Ghiselli, and Lyman W. Porter, "Psychological Research on Pay: An Overview," Industrial Relations, 1963, Vol. 3, 3–8.

Allan N. Nash and Stephen J. Carroll, Jr., *The Management of Compensation* (Monterey: Brooks/Cole Publishing Co., 1975), Chapter 3, "Compensation, Employee Satisfaction, and Motivation."

SELECTED REFERENCES

E. E. Lawler, III, *Pay and Organizational Effectiveness: A Psychological View* (McGraw-Hill, 1971). Chapter 4, "Implications for Practice," pp. 61–75; Chapter 5, "Theories of Motivation," pp. 79–89.

A. Bandura, *Principles of Behavior Modification* (New York: Holt, Rinehart and Winston, 1969). Chapter 4, "Positive Control," especially pp. 217–240, and 261–284; and Chapter 5, "Aversive Control," pp. 293–315 and 338–348. While more theoretical and directed at the psychological community, this is a comprehensive discussion of the principles underlying the effects of positive and negative feedback.

Allan N. Nash and Stephen J. Carroll, Jr., *The Management of Compensation*, Chapter 7, "Direct Compensation," pp. 191–223.

Baines Electronics Corporation (A)

Paul Jefferson, project manager on Baines' air defense missile contract with the U.S. Air Force, returned from a corporate-level meeting late one afternoon in November 1961. The meeting had concerned the corporation's newly announced policy governing salary increases for all employees for the forthcoming year. After reviewing some notes and collecting his thoughts on what had transpired in the meeting, which had been chaired by the president of Baines, Jefferson called his secretary over the intercom and asked her to assemble the project's key leaders for a 4:00 p.m. meeting. The purpose of the meeting was to pass on details of the president's message.

General Company Background

Baines Electronics Corporation, a medium-sized company with annual sales of about $280 million, had its principal plants in a small town located 40 miles outside of Boston. A majority of Baines's 13,000 employees worked at that location. Founded in the late 1930s by Carlton Baines and several other talented engineers from National Electronics, Baines Electronics grew rapidly in the early days of World War II due to heavy involvement in the production of aircraft instruments. The company successfully weathered the postwar transition period, and by the late 1950s Baines had rapidly rising sales and prospects for continued good growth.

An important element of the Baines corporate policy was the fair treatment of employees.

Copyright © 1969 by the President and Fellows of Harvard College. Reprinted by permission of the Harvard Business School. This case was prepared by Jeanne Deschamps from a student report under the supervision of Jay W. Lorsch as a basis for class discussion rather than to illustrate either effective or ineffective handling of an administrative situation.

The company had pioneered in granting real and fringe benefits and had a record of stable employment second to none in the industry. Carlton Baines, up until his death in 1957, had always maintained an "open-door" policy for all his employees. Anyone could enter the president's office and "talk to the boss." Baines had also encouraged the formation of numerous company-sponsored activities, such as bowling and softball, and the founders' overall regard for the workers was an important factor in keeping the company nonunionized. When asked why they worked at Baines, many employees would remark that it was an enjoyable place to work, where friendliness and unanimity of purpose were main motivating factors.

All of Carlton Baines's policies were continued when a new president was selected from within the company to carry on after his death in 1957.

The New Plan

About ten people sat around Jefferson's conference table later that day. None of the men wore suit jackets, and it was apparent from the informal conversation that the missile project was a tightly knit organization, with relatively high morale. Most of the engineers on Jefferson's project and in other engineering groups at Baines had a B.S. or M.S. degree; about 5 percent of the engineers had a Ph.D. Jefferson had always prided himself on the fact that the men in his groups felt free to talk to him about both technical and personal problems. When all were present, he began.

He explained that there had been a growing tendency, according to the president, for salary increases to be handed out annually without appropriate emphasis on the meaning behind the raise. Lately, or so it seemed to upper management, there was not much awareness on the part of either superior or subordinate that such raises were granted because of the specific contribution of the employee and because of a generally favorable overall corporate outlook. It was felt that the merit-raise plan had acquired certain superficial aspects of a cost-of-living increase. Many employees, therefore, expected yearly increases, whether or not their work for the past period truly warranted special recognition and whether or not the company profit picture was favorable.

At this point Jefferson stopped and asked for comments, and in the ensuing discussion it was agreed by all those present that the situation had been accurately described by the president. Some changes certainly seemed in order. Jefferson returned to his notes.

In order to correct the problem and restore proper balance to the merit-raise program, the president had requested that several measures be adopted immediately for the next year:

1. Over and above any plans now in progress, an immediate review was to be made of the salary status of all employees.

2. Those men who "really put out" were to be given raises in January or as soon thereafter as practicable.

3. Whenever a raise was granted, the supervisor was to make a special point — almost an ostentatious gesture of commendation — to highlight the relationship between salary increases and outstanding performance.

4. All raises intended for the next year were to be awarded before August (rather than spread throughout the entire year) with the general expectation that the better the man the earlier he was to receive his raise.

To further enhance the plan, the president announced that the dollar package set aside for raises for 1962 was to be nearly double the amount allotted in previous years. The president had ended his talk by reemphasizing that it was important to let people know where they stood so that they might be encouraged to improve both themselves and their value to the company.

As he summarized the president's remarks, Jefferson added his personal emphasis to the points listed above. He then requested that all his leaders forward their individual raise recommendations to him within one week.

The Old Merit Increase System

Although certain areas within the plants used special practices, all engineering groups used the basic system which is shown in Exhibit 6-1. This curve plots salary against years of experience and was intended to show that for any given number of years of experience a man's salary range was between points A and B. These points were the outer limits of a band of possible salaries shown as "100 percent and 0 percent" lines. Everyone fell somewhere between these extremes, the idea being that everyone had a hypothetical evaluation factor between 100 percent and 0 percent. If one were a 90 percent man it meant that in the company's estimation only 10 percent of the people with similar experience were rated ahead of him. Similarly, if one were a 25 percent man, 75 percent of the men with identical experience were rated superior. The rating factor was accomplished in somewhat subjective terms at the project level and reviewed three times before final corporate approval.

A key point was that the individual ratings and the salary curves (the 100 percent and 0 percent limits) were known only to the evaluator (the immediate superior) and the salary administration group. These facts were not available to the individual employee and no one had any knowledge of his own or his fellow employees' standing, particularly since good and average raises were awarded at random times throughout the year. An engineer who was to be awarded a raise was asked to come to his superior's office for a discussion, and at this meeting he was informed of his increase in salary.

This system had been used for nearly 20 years and had produced little or no griping at any level. Jefferson could recall few instances when he had received complaints about salaries.

Working Out the New Plan

Jefferson spent many hours working over the recommendations of his subordinates and trying to fit these into a workable time-phased series of raises to be granted in 1962. When he finally submitted his project plan in December, both he and his project leaders were enthusiastic about the prospects for the coming year. More money was to be given out, and he felt that that facet of the plan certainly ought to be appreciated, since even the low-rated people would receive a bigger raise than usual.

Exhibit 6-1. Pay Scale

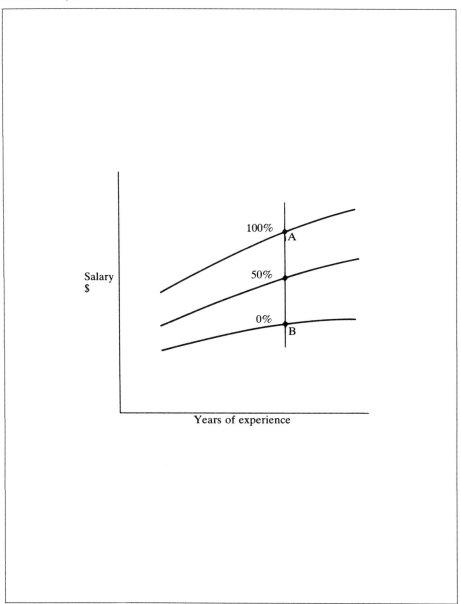

PART IV

Working Conditions and Practices: Sources of Motivation

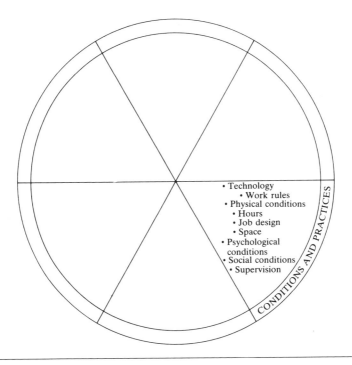

- Technology
- Work rules
- Physical conditions
- Hours
- Job design
- Space
- Psychological conditions
- Social conditions
- Supervision

CONDITIONS AND PRACTICES

Many people believe that changes in compensation and other formal gestures like promotion are the most important motivators; yet public managers generally have relatively little control over monetary rewards and, for many reasons, are restricted in their ability to provide promotions. Therefore, they often lament their lack of tools to affect the behavior of the work force. However, most theory and research suggests that other aspects of work may be even more important as motivators. Because of the strength of this research and the constraints on giving formal rewards, other aspects of the work environment must receive attention as tools to motivate employees. For example, improvements or changes in working conditions and practices may be fruitful sources of such managerial tools. As the next several cases suggest, there are variables in each work setting that can affect employee productivity and satisfaction. Sometimes managers can exert influence on those variables without encountering the constraints that plague many features of formal personnel systems. In the two cases that follow, sources of motivational tools that can be put to use by a public manager will be identified, in effect extending our awareness of a managerial personnel system.

One of the difficulties in applying motivational concepts to specific organizational settings is that human behavior in organizations resists hard, scientific explanations and answers. Part of the purpose of the next two cases is to help sort out our personal assumptions about motivation and to see how those assumptions might affect our management of employees in different work settings.

Assumptions about what motivates people may be influenced by a manager's experience elsewhere and may or may not fit very well in a manager's current situation. It is, therefore, important to develop diagnostic skills that will help identify the key variables in each work setting. It is also important to recognize the effect of one's management style on employees. This can refer to methods of operation, tools of management one commonly uses, or other traits of leadership or personality. While good management is aided by a comfortable style, the tasks and the people in each organization will be different, so alterations in style, as well as in assumptions, may be necessary. To respond effectively a manager should attempt to understand and respond to the opportunities and constraints in each managerial situation. Selection of a style, strategy, and tools to fit each situation is likely to pay dividends in motivation and productivity.

The cases in this part begin to explore the effects on people of several aspects of working conditions and practices. They examine the effects of job structure and the employment environment on job satisfaction, productivity, and on the manager's role. Also, in conjunction with the suggested readings, they provide a chance to examine and develop our personal assumptions about what motivates people on the job, and how a manager can influence that. Since the cases examine several rather different tasks and organizational settings, a number of tools, approaches, and styles can be gleaned from them. For example, in one case the responsible level of management has little day-to-day contact with most of the employees. In the other, the manager is in almost daily contact with all of them. Therefore, different tools must be employed, and personal style may matter more in one than in the other.

Reaching beyond and outside of the formal personnel system into the extended system, some managerial choices were made in each of these cases that produced results that are worthy of analysis. In analyzing these cases, consider what specific aspects of a job, its substance, conditions, and surrounding features can affect people's satisfaction and productivity.

CHAPTER 7

Motivating Employees in a Clerical Task: The Use of Job Enrichment

By focusing on a project to alter working conditions in a large, mass-production-like clerical function, we can begin with this case to consider what aspects of the work and work environment can have an impact on how people are motivated on their jobs. Specifically, the technique used in this case is "job enrichment," a common technique used to make work more interesting and efficient and improve the motivation of employees performing that work. The study of this case gives us not only an opportunity to pick up the vocabulary and explore some assumptions about what motivates people but also gives us an opportunity to study the ingredients of organizational changes that can improve the working conditions and performance of an organization.

In the 1980s, a good deal of attention has been focused on fiscal limitations and related forces that require improvement in the cost-effectiveness and quality of public services. Similarly, a good bit of attention in the business and popular press of this period has been on productivity and quality improvement. Many attempts have been made recently to study methods of management and motivation employed in other cultures, especially those of West Germany and Japan. Many of the features of those management systems — and of the most successful work innovations in this country — have similarities with the situation in the Bureau of Workmen's Compensation, a disguised government agency. The techniques in the case are similar to those used in efforts to improve the "quality-of-work-life" and in the use of "quality circles," now popular concepts in management and in labor-management discussions. This case study gives us an opportunity to see for ourselves what possibilities and impediments there are to adopting some of these motivation and feedback ideas within public organizations. Some organizational and task situations will be amenable to the techniques used in the case; others will not.

Here, management sought to alter the work environment in a way that was based on job enrichment principles and techniques attributed to Frederick Herzberg, a noted industrial psychologist. We can examine the experiment in the case from the standpoint of its effects on motivation by seeking to understand why the experiment had the impact that it had and how the relevant principles from it might be applied in assessing or altering other work settings.

In the next case, many of these same principles can be used to examine how two managers sought to motivate employees in a much smaller work setting that was populated by highly trained professionals. There, we will examine how the differences in the task, the people, and culture affect the specific motivational techniques at a manager's disposal.

STUDY QUESTIONS

1. What are management's intentions and objectives in undertaking this experiment?
2. What accounts for the results of the job enrichment experiment?
3. How well has it met management's objectives?
4. What are the problems at this stage of the experiment? Can they be resolved?
5. What should BWC do about the rest of the experiment?
6. If you think management should proceed, how should they move to implement the remaining teams?
   If they should not, how can they best handle stoppage of the project?
7. What steps and follow-through would you recommend?

RECOMMENDED READING

Frederick Herzberg, "One More Time: How Do You Motivate Employees?" *Harvard Business Review,* January-February 1968.

Douglas McGregor, "Theory X: The Traditional View of Direction and Control," in *The Human Side of Enterprise* (New York: McGraw-Hill Book Company, 1960).

Douglas McGregor, "Theory Y: The Integration of Individual and Organizational Goals," *The Human Side of Enterprise* (New York: McGraw-Hill Book Company, 1960).

SELECTED REFERENCES

Abraham Maslow, "A Theory of Human Motivation," *Psychological Review,* 50 (1943), pp. 370–396.

John M. Greiner, Harry P. Hatry, Margo P. Koss, Annie P. Millar and Jane P. Woodward, *Productivity and Motivation: A Review of State and Local Government Initiatives* (Washington, D.C.: The Urban Institute Press, 1981), Chapter 21 and Chapters 23–25.

William Ouchi, *Theory Z: How American Business Can Meet the Japanese Challenge* (Reading, Mass.: Addison-Wesley Publishing Company, 1981), Chapters 3 and 4.

Job Enrichment in the Bureau of Workmen's Compensation (A)

In mid-1974, the Bureau of Workmen's Compensation of the United States Department of Labor began considering ways in which to restructure its claims processing operation. It was the view of top management that the 7,000 employees involved in the Workmen's Compensation claims procedure were becoming increasingly dissatisfied with their jobs, and, as a result, the quality of their work was suffering.

Management decided to alter the traditional functional organization of the Bureau of Workmen's Compensation (BWC). Under this functional arrangement, there were large, impersonal divisions of several hundred employees in which each employee performed a similar clerical task. Experimenting with the concept of "Semi-Autonomous Task Teams," popularized by Volvo, a Swedish company, they began, in stages, to break the work force into smaller divisions that could work as teams. These "miniature BWCs," as they came to be known, were organized to handle all the tasks and duties of the entire claims processing operation.

By mid-1978, a small portion of BWC was operating successfully in teams, and detailed plans had been devised to convert the rest of the Bureau. However, in the process of "going live," as they put it, management was running into some unexpected delays and difficulties. For example, the acquisition of office space for con-

version into teams had been delayed beyond the usual because of a financial scandal in the agency in charge of obtaining new space. Furthermore, difficulties in matching the team members' duties to traditional government position classifications were creating employee unrest as job security seemed to be at issue. These same sorts of technicalities were thwarting efforts to train and recognize active and creative managers, a divergence from BWC's usual autocratic management philosophy.

The Bureau of Workmen's Compensation

BWC is the government agency responsible for processing claims related to on-the-job injuries or illnesses. While this case concerns the central office, claims were first submitted by an injured worker to one of 30 Field Offices, located throughout the U.S. For simple cases, the Field Office executed the paperwork, processed the claim, and then sent the completed case to the Central Office for review. If a case called for actions beyond the authority delegated to the field office, it was forwarded to the Central Office for handling.

The Central Office was located in a large Department of Labor (DOL) complex in Alexandria, Virginia. Approximately 7,000 employees worked in Workmen's Compensation claims. Before the team experiment, workers were organized into divisions of several hundred employees according to the functions they performed in examining a claim. After visiting the large work areas of a functional division, the case writer described it as "impersonal, sleazy and depressing."

To start the process, when a case folder was received in the BWC mail room, it was classified

This case was prepared by Susan Forman under the supervision of Jon Brock, Lecturer at the John F. Kennedy School of Government, Harvard University. While the case is based upon field research, the identity of the agency and individuals are disguised and other information has been altered in the interest of confidentiality.

167

as either (1) the first for the particular claimant, (2) an adjustment to or addition to a prior claim, or (3) an appeal for reconsideration of an already processed claim. Once such a determination had been made, the case would be logged in and routed to one of the areas appropriate to the classification.

The case would then travel through a sequence of operations that were fairly similar for each of the three types of claims (see Exhibit 7-1). The first person to receive the case would be the "eligibility examiner," who would determine whether the person had a valid claim. If there were medical issues to be resolved, the "eligibility examiner" would get an opinion from the "medical advisor." If the claim was deemed valid, the case would be sent to the "benefit authorizer" who would determine the amount of benefit due the claimant. The case would be shipped next to the "payment section," where a worker would enter the request for payment into the computer record, to be checked by the "computer reviewer." Various support workers would also assist with the case, performing such functions as handling telephone inquiries, updating claimant information, or tracing lost benefit checks. Once the case action was completed, the case would be shipped to the enormous "hold room," where all of the case folders were stored.

A worker had virtually no control over the case flow that came to him. "Control clerks" in each functional area would receive batches of cases and distribute them to the workers of their section. When the workers completed their action, they would simply place the cases in their outbaskets to be picked up by the control clerk. An eligibility worker explained, "It was very important to develop a good relationship with the control clerk. They would make you or break you, depending on the type of cases they gave out."

The results of a BWC survey indicated that most workers had little idea of where a case was routed after they were finished working on it. Employees were generally rushed for time and therefore had little opportunity or reason to learn more about the total claims process or to correct errors made by other workers. There was a low probability of ever receiving the same case again.

Even though emphasis was placed on speed, case processing was extremely slow. It was not unusual to take 30 days for a folder to travel from one floor to the other. This made it extremely difficult to answer the many Congressional inquiries or field office questions concerning the status of a case. Since there were backlogs in each operation, a case could be delayed many times during the process, as well as in transit from operation to operation. As one director remarked, "It was like running a local train. We stopped at every station."

Management viewed the claims processing operation at BWC as huge and impersonal. Actual results did not come close to the Bureau's mission of providing timely and accurate response to persons submitting Workmen's Compensation claims. Management believed that this was partly due to the poor attitude of the work force, often exhibited by sloppy casework, high absenteeism, and disregard for rules and regulations. Public outcry about poor service was becoming louder, but efforts to "crack down" on the workers did not improve matters. Management essentially had their hands tied — they had little available in the way of effective rewards or punishments. Workers were aware that despite management's pleas or threats, there would be little difference in the rewards, promotions, or salary increases they received.

Experimenting with the Team Concept

The team concept that BWC decided to explore was based on the much-publicized experiment at the Volvo plant in Kalmar, Sweden. "Semi-Autonomous Task Teams" were established by Volvo, where employees were given collective responsibility for a specific portion of the production process. Ten to fifteen workers were put in charge of the entire set of tasks needed to produce their part of the automobile. This group of workers was responsible for maintenance, minor equipment repairs and quality control, as well as the actual production. Employees were encouraged to participate in the shaping of the experiment and in developing new methods of production. Indeed, Volvo management freely acknowledged the value of worker participation and noted that of the various experiments they tried, the most successful were worker-generated.

Results from the Volvo experiment and other similar studies were encouraging. Volvo found that by shifting from assembly line automobile production to small teams of specialists, cars were being produced quicker and more economically. Furthermore, it was reported that the Volvo plant was characterized by high morale; employees expressed pride in their work, satisfaction with the group process, and optimism about their career development.

In recent years, offices in several government agencies began experimenting with the task team idea. For these offices, the tasks did not lend themselves to Volvo's system of having all workers learn to perform all tasks. It was possible, however, to organize operations into small groups each of which could handle all the functions of the entire process. Follow-up studies of these experiments indicated success in terms of quality of work, speed of processing time, and the state of employee-management relations.

In May 1974, the Director of Operations of BWC, Martin Jones, became interested in this type of work organization, believing it could be successfully applied to BWC. He assigned Larry Harmon, his technical advisor, the job of investigating the feasibility of such an approach in BWC.

Harmon began his study by visiting offices elsewhere in the government that were using the team approach. He consulted with organiza-tional development specialists and carefully reviewed the existing literature. He then set out to form a task force with whom he could work to determine the feasibility of the project. If early results looked favorable, he would work with the Task Force to implement a team experiment.

For the Task Force, Harmon recruited 15 people from the various divisions of the functional organization. He chose mainly claims workers — people who were skilled technicians in their area of responsibility. He rounded out the group with two organizational analysts and three unit supervisors. These group members worked together on a full-time basis.

The group started out to develop a specific implementation plan. To do so, the task force had to determine the work flow of BWC in order to redesign the spatial and organizational arrangements (no flow charts existed at that time), assess the proper size of the new teams, the number of teams and the proper size of the team workload. They had to devise case control procedures, management information systems, and methods of evaluation for the teams.

"During the planning stage," Harmon recalled, "we could have used more assistance from top management and from the various specialists within the Bureau. We didn't have the total commitment of the rest of the organization. We got little help from the organizational people — they threw us a bone here and there, but we basically did it on our own. And, to make matters worse, we were operating on a shoe-string."

Establishing the First Teams

After eight months of study, planning and evaluating their plans, the Task Force decided that the team form of organization had great potential in BWC, and that they were ready to oversee the establishment of three experimental Teams. With the approval of top management, it was decided that the experiment would begin with three teams of about 60 persons each. Three teams would be grouped together in a coordinating group that would share certain support functions and technical experts. Eventually, they expected several coordinating groups would be grouped into a division for reporting purposes. (See Exhibit 7-2.)

In order to increase the quality of the output, the Task Force believed it essential to institute a system of accountability whereby certain types of cases "belonged" to certain teams. Therefore, the workload for the teams was to be assigned according to the first three digits of the claimant's Social Security number and a computerized version of their tracking system would be developed.

When the task force indicated that it was ready to begin the experiment, the Director of Operations sent a memo to the functional divisions in which he briefly described the study and asked for volunteers. Despite the fact that he gave no guarantees of status, rewards, or promise of career advancement, 30 percent of the claims workers volunteered to be transferred to the team.

No specific tests or ratings were used to select workers for the three experimental teams, although the Task Force did review the appraisals given by the current supervisors.

The workers selected to be part of the first three teams were then given a three-day orientation, where the team concept was explained in more detail and participants were given a chance to ask questions. These employees also attended a six-week cross-training course designed to develop an awareness of the tasks performed by their fellow workers. They were "loaned out" to other functional areas in order to gain actual experience with other jobs. Little of the training was addressed to the team concept itself, as the task force believed that such knowledge would best be gained from on-the-job experience.

Managers for the teams, who previously managed only single-function areas, were cho-

sen and briefed. They attended sessions in participative management in addition to the six-week cross-training. During management training, the task force stressed that the managers would have to do more than simply know the total work flow; they were going to have to manage people, not just papers. They would have to listen to and respect the substantive views of employees.

In order to ready the teams for operation, the control clerks were brought into the new areas two weeks prior to the rest of the teams.

Unlike the functional arrangement, the control clerks in the team arrangement would have to know, specifically, the proper order for routing a case through the team. Greater awareness of the process and more independent judgment were required of them. Similarly, the clerks' level of responsibility increased as they became the officials in charge of logging the specific whereabouts of each file as it traveled through the team. Previously, under the single-function form of organization, they simply delivered a case for one operation to be performed and picked it up, sending it to a central "switching" center which sent it on to the next necessary function for transmittal to the appropriate single-function control clerk. The control clerks spent the two-week period familiarizing themselves with the system and getting the cases ready for the arrival of claims workers. During this time, their future co-workers were encouraged to visit the site of the new teams and become familiar with the layout.

Along with the start-up of the teams, the BWC installed a computerized system of case tracking so that they could more easily know the whereabouts of each case. In order to set up the necessary computer files, and to physically locate the appropriate files in the team's area, the basic case files that the teams would be using had to be put into order to ensure a "clean" computer file and a clean start-up.

According to one of the medical advisors of Team I, operations proceeded smoothly from the beginning. "We spent the first day putting our manuals together, gathering supplies, etc. By day two we were doing our jobs."

A great deal of pre-planning went into the new physical arrangement, so that the teams could easily function as self-contained units with easy work flow and interaction among workers. The original plan was to locate all the files in the center of the team area, with the workers involved in two or more functions located around the files in clusters of six or eight desks. Managers and their assistants were to sit among the group, not in their traditional glass "cages."

Early in the planning stage the structure of the building caused a rearrangement of some of the physical plans. Because of their weight, files could only be placed over the girders, so they turned out to be arranged as "walls" between the teams, rather than forming the central area. Although there was still convenient access to the files, the physical arrangements were less "cozy" than the Task Force wished.

Reorganization of the Team

Within six months of the establishment of Teams I, II, and III, nine more teams were phased in. Due to space limitations, not all teams were located in the same area. There were teams in four different areas of the building.

Managers voiced complaints over the depth of coverage, saying that it was difficult to keep the work flowing smoothly when several workers who performed the same task were absent. They also found it difficult to get the necessary attention from the group of technical specialists who worked for each Coordinating Group. Some managers were pressing for the inclusion of such specialists in each team, but there were not enough specialists to staff such an arrangement. Furthermore, many workers and managers believed that the Civil Service Commission was putting pressure on BWC to reorganize the management structure. Although nothing had been said officially, rumor had it that Civil Service

was upset over the fact that there were managers now supervising fewer workers than they had as functional managers, but receiving the same pay and grade-level as before. The number of workers supervised is often an important determinant of a manager's grade level.

Martin Jones, the Director of Operations of BWC, studied the situation and decided to combine two teams into one and determine the effect on operations. Unfortunately, Jones's reasons were not explained well to the managers of the teams, according to Edward Brooks, a former manager of a team.

> The reasons for the change weren't communicated well to anyone. It was announced on Friday that on Monday morning Team II and III would be combined. Since I didn't know the full reason for the switch, I had trouble explaining it to my people. The workers took it hard: To them, it was just like building a house and then being told the bulldozers would be in on Monday to tear it down.

Brooks recalled that the workers signed a petition objecting to the change. The Division Director then came to speak to them, attempting to give a better explanation for the reorganization. "They didn't like it but they accepted it. People saw the team as a personal thing. For the first time they were having freedom in deciding and determining how they would work, and they resented such a high-handed change."

Despite the larger size, work progressed efficiently and management reported fewer problems with coverage and flexibility. Shortly after Teams II and III were combined, the rest of the Teams were also regrouped, resulting in six teams of 110 to 120 workers. (See Exhibit 7-3.)

Present Team Status

As of August 1978, there were six teams operating in BWC, comprising about 10 percent of the claims processing work force. Evaluation of the performance of the teams showed positive results. (See Exhibit 7-4.) An early study indicated that average case processing time had been reduced by about 10 days. Compared to the still existent functional organizations, one-third fewer folders were now out of the files being processed at any given time, and three times as many direct inquiries could be settled in the day an inquiry was received. Response time had decreased dramatically for critical cases.

A study conducted in February 1978 showed that the accuracy rate for the teams was greater than for like operations in the functional areas. Furthermore, processing time had decreased for most types of case actions. (See Exhibit 7-5.) Worker absences had also declined, according to recent personnel statistics.

In-depth interviews with employees were conducted during the first two months of 1978. Employees who were interviewed indicated that, for the most part, they were pleased with the change. They expressed satisfaction in being involved in the entire claims process. Judy Norman, a GS-7 Payments Worker, remarked, "My job in the functional area sometimes reminded me of an assembly line. I never understood the overall operation and I had no idea of what other people did. Now I know so much more — I understand the whole process. I know what types of jobs I might like to try for."

Judy Norman also commented that working in a team was a learning process for her. "If we encounter a problem situation, we can flag it as a test case. That way we'll get the case back and we can see if the action we took was acceptable. We'll know what to do next time."

Workers were in favor of the new system of accountability that had been instituted when the teams were established. Within a team, cases were divided among workers according to the last two digits of the claimant's Social Security number (terminal digits). Cases needing a particular type of authorization were automatically routed to the worker handling that particular task and set of terminal digits. Lisa Ford, an Eligibility Examiner, Grade 9, explained, "Now

there's a real incentive to do a good job. You know that if you don't straighten the case out now, you'll just get it back later. This also means that cases will get done faster because you'll be more familiar with them."

Team members explained that they liked the atmosphere in the teams much better than in the functional areas. Supervision, they said, was improved. A typical comment was that voiced by Peter Preston, a GS-4 Records Clerk, "Supervisors are more relaxed. They're too busy to be peering over our shoulders all the time. They don't get all upset if you talk to your neighbor."

When questioned about his dislikes, Peter Preston had little to say. He explained, "This is the first job I've liked in a long while. When I was in files I tried for a full year to get into the teams before I was finally picked. . . . It was so easy to become a part of the team. Now I know everyone in the team and I know I'm an important member of my team."

Managers, too, expressed approval of the change. They cited work improvements such as better control over folders, a reduction in lost case material, better service to Field Offices, and improved public relations. On a more personal basis, managers and assistant managers noted an improvement in the nature of their jobs. Carol Lindar, the Assistant Manager in Team I, explained,

In the functional organization I spent all my time checking on the progress of our work and yet I never felt like I had control over what we were doing. Now the work progresses smoothly and I have a chance to contribute to the development of the workers in my team. Yes, this is the only way to go.

Other managers said that they now felt like part of a management team, that they enjoyed the participative atmosphere, seeing the entire task through, and that they had more pride in their work.

When a Survey of Organizational Climate (SOC) was conducted in January 1978, some negative comments were also voiced. For the most part, morale had improved, but some workers felt that their contribution to an apparently successful experiment should entitle them to more pay. Some expressed the opinion that they did not like their expanded jobs and preferred to return to their functional units to work on a more predictable task. Disgruntled employees were suspicious of management's intentions, thinking that the teams might be a "trick" to get employees to work harder for the same salary.

Lewis York, a GS-5 Benefit Authorizer, returned to his former functional unit after one year in a team. When questioned, he explained that he did not see how the system would benefit the worker:

> If I like my team and decide to work harder, what will it get me? Not much. My manager may compliment me on my progress but then she'll get all the credit. Not only that, but next time she reviews my performance, she'll expect me to do more. I'll just have to keep working harder and harder just to look capable. If I got paid by the case I wouldn't mind so much.

Other workers approved of the team concept but felt that the situation was not as good as it had been in the beginning. When interviewed, Nel Albemarle, a medical advisor, stated,

> Team I has changed. We started as pioneers. It was fun — we were a small group. We had more meetings. The spirit has faded in the past few years. There's some disenchantment because no one's getting the special consideration or recognition they feel they deserve. In fact, it's widely believed that the best way to get a promotion is to go back to your old functional unit.

Some people felt that the team concept had changed for the worse when the teams were enlarged. It was an opinion shared by many that the team was no longer as personal or challenging. They explained that team meetings now were rarely held so there was less opportunity to pass along innovative ideas. Furthermore, it was getting harder to know everyone in the group.

Team workers reflected that at times they were treated as "step children." Technical information about a procedural change might filter down to their Team as much as 60 days after it was sent to the functional managers. "It's hard to remain an expert in your field under such conditions," commented Nel Albemarle.

Managers expressed some reservations as well. A few old-liners felt that participative management was "like giving away the shop." Others, like Carol Lindar, felt that the temporary nature of the teams was undermining morale. "We're all still technically on detail* here. My workers still report to a functional supervisor for yearly reviews, and they know they could be shipped back there at any time, without cause or explanation."

Despite some negative feedback, the majority of team members had reacted quite favorably to the team experiment. When Nel Albemarle was asked whether she was considering a return to her old office, she answered, "Absolutely not! The teams may have problems, but nothing that can't be worked out. Even right now they're a 100 percent improvement over where I came from."

Union leaders remained noncommittal during the experimentation stage. Although they had given their assent to the study, they were not heavily involved and they were said to see both good and bad in the plan. While they were in favor of increasing employee satisfaction and morale, they were worried that an improvement in productivity might result in the need for fewer

---

* A "detail" is a temporary assignment of an employee usually done for a short-term assignment or to fill a vacancy while a permanent replacement is being sought. Technically, the employee is assigned to his or her original work unit and all formal actions and paperwork flow through there.

workers. Further, it was their view that workers should benefit in dollars as a result of improved productivity. Management had reassured union representatives that any employee holding a job that was to be eliminated would be retrained and placed elsewhere in the Bureau. The unions had apparently decided to "wait and see."

Implementation Delays

Once the experiment appeared to be successful, it was decided that the entire organization would be converted to teams in a time-sequenced process that would take about 20 months. A detailed plan was completed in March 1978 for the formation of the remaining teams. Top management worked with the Task Force to prepare a schedule for employees and managers, which indicated where and when they would be trained and transferred.

Advanced preparations were begun. The workloads in many of the functional areas were reorganized according to terminal digits so that workers could remain with the same caseload after they moved into a team. Managers who were scheduled to enter the next several teams were given the training course, broadening their understanding of the work process. They attended seminars of management techniques and employee development as well.

Considering the large number of teams to be formed, the availability of physical facilities became a critical factor. Each time workers were reassigned to a new team, small pockets of space would have to be vacated throughout the functional areas. The problem became one of finding sufficiently large spaces in which to build new teams without repeatedly rearranging the remaining functional offices.

The Task Force determined that the least disruptive way to handle the reorganization was through the temporary leasing of "turnaround space." They proposed renting space in a nearby building for one or two years. Existing teams could be moved to this building and new teams

built in their former space. When all the Teams were formed, the leased space would be no longer needed and everyone could be consolidated back into the original building.

According to the U.S. General Services Administration (GSA), the BWC had authority to spend up to $625,000 per year for rent. Deducting what they were already spending for their present offices, the Bureau determined that they could afford to lease an additional 75,000 square feet. Although this was less than the 110,000 the Task Force considered optimal, it meant that no special Congressional approval would be required. Obtaining such approval would be problematic at best.

In April 1978, the Task Force received approval from top management for their leasing plan. Unfortunately, this occurred one week before the Secretary of Labor announced a reorganization of the entire Department. As part of this effort, the Secretary announced that the Occupational Safety and Health Administration (OSHA) would be moved to the Alexandria complex and would occupy 35,000 square feet of the space currently being used to process Workmen's Compensation claims. BWC was reassured that when a new BWC computer building was completed in late 1979, they could move into the space now occupied by the computers. Jones, the Director of Operations, attempted to convince the Secretary to keep OSHA in their present headquarters until the new space became available in 1979, but it was considered imperative to move OSHA within the next few months.

The Task Force began to work on a new plan to condense operations in their present building. They were consoled by the promise that as of May 1978 they would still acquire 35,000 square feet of turnaround space. Further plans for acquiring space were thwarted, however, by events beyond their control: The General Services Administration (GSA), the government agency in charge of obtaining the space, became the center of a nationwide scandal. The agency was accused of misuse of taxpayers' money through contract fraud and kickbacks. The GSA seemed to curtail many of its activities while FBI agents and U.S. Attorney's Office began looking into allegations of a $200 million fraud. There was nothing BWC could do to hasten the process. GSA was considered slow even in the best of times.

By August 1978 no turnaround space had been acquired for BWC, and they had still been obligated to give up some of their present building space to OSHA. Although GSA indicated that space might be available by October, the Task Force began to realize that further delays were quite possible.

Not only did this slow down the establishment of new teams, but, according to employees, it greatly damaged top management's credibility. Employees, who had been alerted by management to get ready to move to a team, now saw that nothing more was being done. They assumed that management had given up on the plan and expressed distress that they were not given an explanation.

Managers who were being prepared for the transition were also having difficulties adjusting to the delay. Although most did not doubt that the move would take place eventually, they were not happy to return to their old positions. Although these managers were often assigned to help out in the existing teams or put in charge of special projects, they were eager to begin their own teams. Amanda Rusello, scheduled to be an Assistant Manager in Team XI, explained, "Let's face it — what we're doing now is 'busy work.' Some of us are losing enthusiasm. We don't feel like we belong in our old units and we don't know when we'll be part of a team."

Acquisition of new space was not the only source of delay and frustration. BWC's present building was managed by a private contractor who required 2 months' notice for any repair or adjustment. All the structural changes required for the transition to the new teams had to be

planned in advance and handled solely by the owner. Minor adjustments, such as having telephones relocated, became logistical nightmares. Some workers in Teams V and VI had still not been moved near their co-workers; they had to sit near the existing phone hookups that were situated across the floor from the rest of their team.

Position Classification Difficulties

Problems were surfacing in areas other than physical planning, especially concerning position classification of workers in the teams. The Task Force had been working with the personnel office at BWC to establish position classifications for the jobs in the teams, so that workers could be taken off detail and be given permanent status in their new jobs. Although the Bureau had the authority to write position descriptions, the Civil Service Commission periodically audited job classifications to ensure conformance with the rules and regulations.

The Task Force had been pleased with the results of their classification work. They had been able to consolidate many positions, drastically reducing the confusing and often redundant number of classifications. They also had established a pattern of supervisory positions at Grades 7, 9, 11, 12, 13, 14, and 15. Since an employee could be promoted either one or two grades at a time, this sequence paved the way for management advancement from first-level supervision to management of an entire team.

Among other things, the Civil Service Commission objected to classification of the managerial position at level 9, saying it was only worth an 8. This broke the career ladder, since a capable GS-8 could not, according to regulations, be skipped three grades and promoted to GS-11. In order to advance, such a person would have to take a non-management position in the team, working in a technical spot as a GS-9. After putting in his or her time, the GS-9 could then advance to GS-10. When eligible, the worker would be able to take the test for the GS-11 management position, competing with all other GS-10s. The experience acquired in the technical position would have little in common with the skills needed to handle the GS-11 job and would have delayed a person's advancement to high-level management by several years. BWC feared that, during the hiatus, some of those who had developed supervisory experience might leave or would at least have impeded their development.

Another classification problem arose in regard to the Records Clerks. These workers entered the teams as GS-3s, which was the same level they held when working as file clerks in the functional units. The Civil Service Commission reclassified their positions to GS-4, citing the increased responsibilities and skills required. Although it would have been expedient to promote all of the deserving records clerks to GS-4, management noted that the union was poised to object. Since the union was responsible for all workers, they were prepared to object to the fact that workers still in the functional areas did not receive the same opportunity to be promoted.

Not only was classification a problem, but coordination between the teams was also becoming troublesome. Lacking formal operating procedures for the team method of processing claims, each team manager and staff had worked out ways to handle their work most efficiently. Some systems appeared to work better than others, but it was difficult to convince managers to share their innovations or change to better methods. The Task Force foresaw problems not only receiving information from the teams, but disseminating information to them as well.

Exhibit 7-1. Traditional work flow

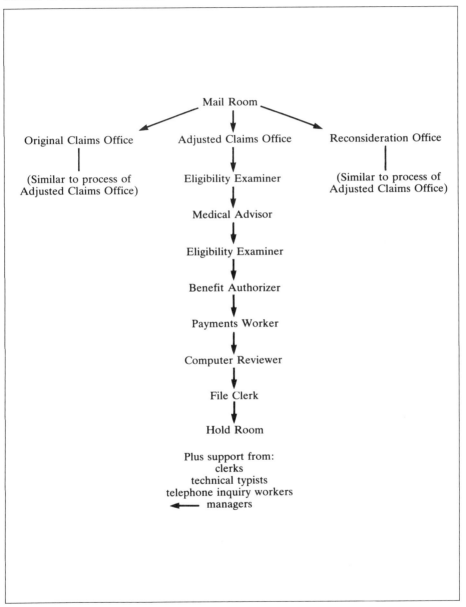

Exhibit 7-2. Typical team organization before reorganization

Coordinating Group Staff

1	Director
1	Deputy
2	Secretary
4	Benefits Technical Assistant
4	Reconsideration Technician
2	Equipment Operations Clerk

Team Staff

1	Team Manager
1	Secretary
6-7	Clerk-Typist
2	Assistant Manager
3-4	Reconsideration Eligibility Examiner
2-3	Medical Inquiries Specialist
6-8	Benefits Authorizer
2	Recovery Review Worker
5-6	Payments Worker
2	Telephone Inquiry Worker
3	Computer Reviewer
1	Claims Clerk
1	Lead Clerk
10-12	Records Clerk
1	Supply Clerk
1	Files Clerk

Team I

I
D
E
N
T
I
C
A
L

Team II

Exhibit 7-3. Typical team organization after reorganization

Coordinating Group Staff	
1	Director
2	Deputy
4	Secretary

Team Staff	
1	Team Manager
1	Secretary
10-12	Clerk-Typist
4	Assistant Manager
6-8	Reconsideration Eligibility Examiner
5-7	Medical Advisor
2	Benefits Technical Assistant
2	Reconsideration Technician
5-6	Medical Inquiries Specialist
12-14	Eligibility Examiner
12-14	Benefits Authorizer
2	Recovery Review Worker
10-12	Payments Worker
5	Telephone Inquiry Worker
6	Computer Reviewer
2	Claims Clerk
1	Lead Clerk
20-22	Records Clerk
1	Equipment Operation Clerk
1	Supply Clerk
2	Files Clerk

Exhibit 7-4. Excerpts from the BWC newsletter, January 1977

Ask Larry Harmon about the Teams in the Bureau of Workmen's Compensation, and he'll tell you only good things about them. He'll tell you how the entire work process is improved by the Team concept and how much happier and more satisfied employees are. He'll cite figures on how computer edit rates and use of leaves have gone down.

He just doesn't have anything bad to say about Teams.

However, Larry doesn't work in a Team. No, he was the BWC executive who led the planning for the Bureau's change-over from a "functional" organization to a "Team" organization.

When *The BWC Newsletter* decided to see how things were going in the Teams at the end of their second year in operation, we talked with Larry for only a few minutes. Then, armed with some basic information he supplied, we went out into the Teams and talked with the Records Clerks, Eligibility Examiners, and others whose efforts are needed to make the Teams work.

We asked them to describe what they do and how their jobs fit into the overall operation for their Team. But we also asked each person (promising them anonymity if they so desired): What do you or don't you like about being in a module? How do your co-workers feel about the setup? How would you improve the operation?

As it turned out, nobody had anything bad to say about the new system! Everyone thinks the Team organization is great.

The idea behind Teams is to package work in people-sized bundles and keep work components small enough so that each employee knows all of his or her co-workers, their duties, and how they fit into the whole work system.

Because of the way one position related to another in the Team setup, each employee is important — no, vital — to the Team's smooth operation. This, along with the increased job satisfaction brought about by the Team setup, is responsible for a noticeable drop in use of Leave Without Pay and sick leave by Team employees. . . .

People in the higher-grade positions become more appreciative of the importance of Records Clerks because they see what they do and become more aware of how vital they are to the whole claims process.

When Team employees talk about their jobs, they use words like teamwork, pride, personal approach, variety of work, and appreciation.

If the success of the Team experiment can be measured by employee enthusiasm, BWC has definitely come up with a winner.

Exhibit 7-5. Median processing times and accuracy rates for selected workloads

TYPE OF ACTIVITY

PROCESSING TIME (IN DAYS)

	November, 1977		December, 1977		January, 1978	
	Team	Functional	Team	Functional	Team	Functional
Field Office Inquiry	18	23	16	24	15	23
Congressional Inquiry	13	23	12	23	10	22
Critical Cases	9	16	8	16	6	17

TYPE OF WORKER

ACCURACY RATES (PERCENTAGES)

	Team	Functional	Team	Functional	Team	Functional
Eligibility Examiner	90	82	92	82	92	82
Benefit Authorizer	89	85	92	87	93	85
Payments Worker	94	85	94	86	95	87

CHAPTER 8

Motivating People in a Professional Task: The Use of What's Available

In addition to feedback in traditional forms like pay and performance evaluation, many potential tools for motivation exist in each job environment. As the previous case suggests, the content of the work, social conditions, changes in a person's status, and attention to various personal or professional needs can be used as feedback and will, if used well, have a positive effect on motivation. Because a public-sector manager may be constrained in the use of many formal feedback tools, such as promotions, salary, and bonuses, he or she must be especially attentive to the availability of other tools that can be formed from the work setting. To influence employees' job performance in the interests of accomplishing organizational goals, attention to these informal and often hidden motivational tools must be a conscious part of each manager's approach to human resources and day-to-day supervision.

As long as people are doing their jobs and coming to work, the many variables in the work setting will influence job performance whether or not the manager of the unit takes an active role. Whether part of the formal system or not, many of those variables may be influenced by outside actors, institutions, or processes.

The following case allows us to look at a situation in which characteristics of the work and surrounding institutional conditions would have a great impact on employees. This created a challenging management situation for each of the two managers in the case. "Motivation in the Office of Economic Integration" describes the efforts of these two conscientious managers in gathering and motivating a highly ambitious and well-educated group of economists, analysts, and administrative staff. The first manager operated in an unstructured environment characterized by involvement and consultation on high-level cabinet and subcabinet projects and decisions. Subsequently, political events caused the function of this small staff to be physically and organizationally downgraded as it became a part of a lower-level policy and research function. These changes brought certain alterations that the second manager had to respond to.

Since the case describes two successive managers of the same office, we can also consider the differences in management style between them and evaluate how well each style fits the circumstances. In contrast to the previous case, the managers in this situation have significant day-to-day interaction with all of the people in the work unit. Because of that interaction, the issue of management style becomes important to management and motivation.

The type of task is another difference between this case and the job enrichment case in Chapter 7. Here the task is more variable and less routine; it requires complex analytic skills, and the product is not measurable in the same fashion as are processed claims. Interestingly, the clerical employees in the Office of Economic Integration (the disguised site of this case) were treated in many of the same ways as were the analysts, and with good results for their satisfaction and productivity.

The case had its genesis in a request by Bob Irwin, the second manager, who asked for some consulting advice on how he should adapt his managerial approach to the circumstances at the end of the case. As we view the change in the organization's task and surroundings, we can observe how methods of supervision, intellectual challenge, sense of involvement, and status can be important motivators. We can also examine the manager's role in shaping and adjusting to this change and the variables and actions that can most help a manager adapt. Considering this case and the previous case together suggests the wide range of tools available to motivate people in varying circumstances, along with the use of different management styles.

STUDY QUESTIONS

1. What motivational tools existed for Jack Shelton's use and how did he use them?

2. What motivational tools exist for Bob Irwin and how should he use them?

3. What accounts for the differences in the type and affects the availability of motivational tools?

4. Bob Irwin would like some consulting advice on how best to manage and motivate his office under current circumstances.
   How would you evaluate his actions so far?
   What recommendation would you make to him?
   How did you arrive at those?

5. What lessons about where to obtain and how to use motivational tools could another manager learn from the advice you give Bob Irwin?
   What principles emerge?

RECOMMENDED READING

W. Earl Sasser and Wickham Skinner, "Managers With Impact: Versatile and Inconsistent," *Harvard Business Review*, 1979, No. 6.

SELECTED REFERENCES

Gene W. Dalton and Paul R. Lawrence, "Motivation and Control in Organizations," *Motivation and Control in Organizations* (Homewood: Richard D. Irwin, Inc. and The Dorsey Press, 1971), especially pp. 19–35.

Paul R. Lawrence and Jay W. Lorsch, "Organization and Environment Interface," in *Developing Organizations: Diagnosis and Actions* (Reading, Mass.: Addison-Wesley, 1969), pp. 23–30.

Motivation in the Office of Economic Integration

Dr. Robert Irwin was about to begin the daily staff meeting in his office at the Department of Health and Labor (H & L), one of the cabinet agencies in the U.S. government. One staff member, Harriet Ettinger, wouldn't be there. Irwin had worked out an arrangement whereby she could pursue her swimming avocation, arrive late for work, but stay a few hours later than normal. Ed Gralla, one of his economists, had not yet arrived. Irwin was awaiting the arrival of Greg Bozek, the officer above him in the hierarchy, who often co-presided at staff meetings. As he waited for Bozek, he looked around with some satisfaction. He reflected that things had changed here quite a lot and yet through the change and uncertainty, these people had managed to maintain high quality work.

Irwin's part of the agency was the Office of Economic Integration. It was an office within the purview of the Assistant Secretary for Research and Policy Formulation (RPF), who presided over a series of analysis and evaluation offices that corresponded to the six major organizational components of the overall Department of Health and Labor. Irwin reported through Bozek to the Assistant Secretary for Research and Policy Formulation, Jeff Stevens. Stevens in turn reported to the Secretary of Health and Labor. The Office of Economic Integration handled macroeconomic issues and other concerns that didn't fall under the purview of other por-

tions of Research and Policy Formulation. Also involved in macroeconomic policy for the Department of H & L was Harvey Baker, a former colleague of the Secretary of Health and Labor, Jerome Weir. Baker, a special assistant to the Secretary, was a Ph.D. economist.

Ed Gralla walked in, tossed a frisbee to one of the other staff members and sat down. A minute later Bozek came in and the meeting began. The meeting was short. Irwin went around the room asking each staff member about the status of his various projects and assigned a few new items. Bozek noted a few issues that he thought might come up requiring some studies by the office. Before closing the meeting, Irwin went around the room again asking each person if he had "anything else" to raise. Ira White, an economist, asked about the status of his promotion papers and Irwin agreed to get together later that morning to bring him up to date on the progress made with the personnel office, who had final say over such matters.

The meeting broke up after a total of about fifteen minutes. It had been informal and everyone contributed information or comments. The case writer remained in Irwin's office.

My job isn't just policy analysis. Each staff member has personal and professional needs and it's the largest part of my job to see that the work and work setting maximize the performance and satisfaction of the people involved. I have to manage these people. I never was trained as a manager, but what I've learned through observation and experience is that a manager ought to sit down every now and again and take inventory of his or her own performance. Are your professional goals being met? Are you helping the organization? Are you doing your best for your staff?

This case was prepared by Susan Forman under the supervision of Jon Brock, Lecturer at the John F. Kennedy School of Government, Harvard University. While the case is based upon field research, the identity of the agency and individuals are disguised and other information has been altered in the interest of confidentiality.

Copyright © 1980 by the President and Fellows of Harvard College. Reproduced with the permission of the John F. Kennedy School of Government.

History of the Office of Economic Integration

Bob Irwin had been a member of the OEI staff practically from its formation in June 1975, although he had not always been the head of the shop.

The idea for the OEI office came directly from Robert G. Manning, who at the time was Secretary of Health and Labor. Since Manning had wide experience in social and economic issues, Manning had insisted as a precondition for accepting the cabinet post that he be allowed to work within the government on issues outside the range of traditional H & L interests.

Since Manning's predecessor had little interest in issues outside H & L jurisdiction, the type of high-pressured, economic analysis required by Manning did not fall under the traditional constructs of the Department. There existed, however, an office of 35 people who technically might have been assigned this type of economic and political analysis. The primary objective of this office, the Research and Policy Formulation Office, was to evaluate departmental programs and decisions. Though RPF members possessed masters and doctorates in economics, they demonstrated an inability to handle the high-pressured, critical work dictated by the Economic Policy Committee — the President's cabinet-level economic advisors of which Manning was a member. When given such analytic projects, RPF became buried in paperwork, bogged down in academic trivia, and often the task was totally forgotten.

RPF's reputation among line managers was as poor as their ability to prepare quick, analytic presentations. Most line managers resented RPF's evaluation of departmental programs and decisions, noting that:

> These RPF analysts never worked with us to set up an evaluation system. They'd just impose one, usually ignoring some important realities of our program. In this and other areas they'd just send reports critical of our program to the Secretary or someone else. Half of the time we'd get a copy from the Secretary's office. Often they'd write a report or critique of our program without even visiting the facility or talking to the people who run it.

Manning felt that RPF could not serve the important function he had in mind. Although they aspired to it and welcomed Manning's arrival as a "rejuvenation," RPF did not seem able to become the wide-ranging analytic group, capable of displaying "instant expertise" on questions of major national consequence. The restrictions imposed by Civil Service rules created obstacles to the drastic reorganization and restaffing needed in the office.

The Hiring Begins

Manning's first contact was with Jack Shelton, a thirty-one-year-old man with whom he had worked at the Department of Commerce during an earlier sojourn in government. Shelton had a reputation for being an extremely bright, loyal, and hard-working lawyer with a degree in economics. He had often articulated a strong sense of public duty and was interested in promoting responsible government. Before coming to Washington, Shelton worked as a lawyer and actively participated in a number of political campaigns. He worked on some special projects for several cabinet officers and White House staff while he was at the Commerce Department and was rewarded for his efforts by extremely rapid promotions. The former Chief of Staff at the White House had written to Shelton describing him as "one of the most outstanding young men in government."

Manning offered Shelton a new position as director of a new function to be called the Office of Economic Integration. They would work together to determine the exact function of the office. Shelton had proven abilities as an analyst and a manager. He was demanding as a boss and was reputed to be hard-nosed in his dealings with other parts of an organization. Although he rewarded good performance and was loyal to his staff, Shelton also made it clear that he quickly became impatient with late, sloppy or unkept promises relating to work performance.

Shelton accepted enthusiastically and in turn contacted Mark Hoffman, a former colleague from the Department of Commerce. Hoffman had been a policy analyst there, working largely on economic issues. He was a recent graduate of a well-known eastern business school and had studied economics and psychology as an undergraduate. Shelton thought that they would make a good team both in managing their own staff and in dealing with other parts of the Department and with the bureaucracy in general. Hoffman was known as a good manager, especially in crisis situations. Moreover, he had demonstrated skill in mediating disputes between warring bureaucracies as well as in reviewing analytic work. Hoffman agreed to come on board as the ''number two'' person, even though he was technically too junior to occupy such a position. In recognition of Hoffman's worth to him Shelton agreed to seek a GS-15 rating for Hoffman, who had previously been a GS-13. Skipping the GS-14 level would require a special appeal to the Civil Service Commission, the government's central personnel agency. Since neither of them knew the probabilities for achieving this rating, Hoffman agreed to come on board based on the nature of the assignment with only Shelton's promise of ''doing his best'' on money.

In early 1975, Jack Shelton and Mark Hoffman began to contact some men and women with whom they had worked previously, and who were of high professional and personal caliber. Knowing that the job would be extremely demanding, they gave careful thought to the type of people they were interested in hiring. Hoffman explained, ''We were looking not just for competence, but for loyalty; people who were almost compulsive in their efforts; people who wouldn't have to be socialized into this milieu.''

Irwin Is Hired

Shelton and Hoffman hand-picked several economists and analysts, a lawyer and three secretaries. One of the economic analysts was Robert Irwin — an old colleague of Shelton and Hoffman at the Department of Commerce. Bob had recently completed his Ph.D. in Economics by attending night school while working in several government agencies during the day. Much of his work was at the third level of the Troika (Troika-III).* Irwin was unusual among these economic groups in that he not only had formal academic training in economics and knew the mechanics of the data, but he also had an interest in the political and bureaucratic nuances that often governed the interpretation and the use of the data. Through his experience he had developed a professional commitment to improving the quality of the data collected by the government and to maximize their use in economic policy analysis and decisions.

Shelton and Hoffman were anxious to recruit Irwin into the operation. Manning also knew his work and they expected that the requisite trust and rapport would immediately be established. Hoffman began to work out a package whereby Irwin could be hired quickly. Hoffman contacted Irwin and offered him a job as an economist; the Personnel Department would not permit a more prestigious title. Hoffman had, however, two options: He could hire Irwin as a GS-16 ''Schedule C'' employee, which was a ''political appointment'' and held no job security or Civil Service tenure; or could offer him a GS-15 appointment with Civil Service tenure. Government-wide restrictions on the number of

*Troika is a high-level interagency group which deals with various aspects of economic advice to the President.

tenured supergrades* made it virtually impossible to offer Irwin a GS-16 with tenure. The non-tenured, "Schedule C" slot would be easier to obtain, since traditionally the need for such positions were at the discretion of each cabinet officer. A more elaborate approval process was required for tenured, or "career," slots. A GS-16 would pay $36,338 and a GS-15 $31,309 in 1975.

It was expected that Irwin essentially would be the Secretary's chief analyst for macroeconomic and financial matters. He would have latitude to deal with his counterparts throughout the government, including the policy committee of the government which determined the nature and extent of the economic statistics collected. (This seat traditionally was reserved for senior Federal managers in the statistical and economic establishment.) Since he knew Shelton's penchant for being where the action was, and since he greatly respected Manning's stature as a professional economist and policy maker, Irwin expected the substance and impact of his work to exceed the potential of his current job in another agency, despite his loftier title there. He accepted the GS-15 and began to spend long hours on the job. He reasoned that the job security of the career GS-15 appointment would be important when Manning's term as Secretary ran out. Even though his role was not assured beyond Manning's administration, with basic employment security the short-term opportunities for significant involvement in important professional concerns were, in his view, clearly worth the professional risks.

Staffing OEI

Having filled the financial, international and macroeconomics part of what they perceived as their mission, Shelton and Hoffman had been

*"Supergrades" are those employees at grades 16–18 in the General Schedule.

thinking about other skills that would be necessary. Since Manning would often be called upon to testify before the Congress, make speeches and respond to a variety of inquiries, a capability for developing such statements would clearly be required. In addition, Manning often relied on Shelton for his assessment of the bureaucratic and partisan politics involved in particular issues or controversy and many times called upon Shelton to identify candidates for high-level assignments elsewhere in H & L. They also perceived the need for some additional analytic help in the economics area, particularly in the area of manpower programs which called for detailed statistical and econometric analysis. Irwin would need some assistance and they would all need someone to be sure that their analytic techniques were up to snuff. Since Manning had an interest in the reform of regulation, they would wish to have some capability to analyze from a legal, political and policy point of view some of the proposals emanating from various parts of the public and private sector.

Finally, the office would need clerical and administrative people possessed of the finest skills and dedication. The work environment would be fast-paced, with frequent and unexpected weekend work. Not an atypical task would have been to go through five drafts after normal hours and deliver 50 copies of a 40-page report to major officials in the executive and legislative branches of government — on 72 hours' notice. Good judgment, energy, and tact would be additional requirements of the clerical staff. Since this would be a small operation, the clerical staff would probably be asked to perform a variety of tasks often reserved for research assistants and more senior administrative types. Lastly, the need for confidentiality would be overriding in many of the matters that the office would be dealing with.

Five additional people were recruited to satisfy the personnel requirements. Robert King, a recent graduate of a prominent economics program was the first of those recruits. Though King had not yet completed his Ph.D., his reputation was one of a practical and skilled econometrician.

Barbara Reiner was the next hired. Her previous work as Shelton's personal secretary as well as her current employment at the White House had highlighted Reiner's ability to deal with high-level officials. Moreover, Barbara was knowledgeable of the protocol of working with cabinet officials, which would prove valuable in view of the contact OEI would have in this area. Though Shelton was unable to offer any financial incentive (she was already highly paid at a GS-10), Reiner enthusiastically came aboard. She had previously worked at the H & L Department and ". . . felt close to many of the people there. Besides, Jack and Mark have always been in interesting places and I really enjoy dealing with high-level people."

In trying to handle the political science, speech writing and political personnel functions, Shelton hit upon a gentleman he remembered from one of his projects at the White House. Jim Santee had graduated from Princeton a few years before with a major in English and Political Science. He had recently worked as an analyst in another government agency and most recently had worked in the part of the White House that recruited and screened Presidential appointees. Shelton recalled, "Jim has good instincts for unearthing quality job candidates. We made good use of his writing and editing skills and his ability in the space of an afternoon to go to a library and effectively research a topic and put it into a useful prose style."

While Shelton and Hoffman were waiting to bring the staff on board and begin operations, they were in particular need of some secretarial help during the interim. Carla Moody was assigned to them temporarily from elsewhere within the Department. Several months later Hoffman arranged to have her transferred permanently to their staff since she performed so well. Apart from her skills and good performance, Hoffman observed,

> She knew all of the internal procedures in the Department of Health and Labor and generally knew who to call to get things done administratively. She'd been there for six or seven years and surprised us with a great attitude, tremendous work output, and team spirit.

Mary Romano joined the staff a bit later, coming from a job in the Department of Transportation. Hoffman explained,

> Mary used to work for me at Commerce. She could handle more work and responsibility than any person I know. She didn't walk down the hall to deliver a memo. She ran. She was imaginative and very well organized and used to love to make order out of the chaos I created. We knew that the nature of work would provide plenty of chaos and she was tailor made. She'd just as soon fix a typewriter as type on it. No one could have been more loyal, but no one would tell you you were screwing up faster than Mary would. Long hours and crises were her thing, and she couldn't stand to be unoccupied. If she wasn't up to her ears in work, she'd be helping someone else do theirs.

Mary Romano stated:

> I was thrilled when they called me. They're great guys to work for. Even though the job security wasn't so great, I knew they'd do their best to take care of me and let me learn more and more sophisticated things.

All of the staff, except Irwin and Moody, were hired on various kinds of temporary or non-career Civil Service appointment authorities in order to eliminate the time and red tape usually associated with hiring civil servants. It also allowed them to choose their people rather than be subject to the list provided by the Civil Service Commission. While this left considerable job insecurity, the shop was able to get started quickly with hand-picked people.

Shelton's close contact with the Secretary facilitated the establishment of the office. The group's special status was confirmed by its office setting. They were housed in a large, plush office suite; just around the corner from the Secretary's personal staff. They had access to the Secretary's private dining room, conference room, and limousine service for official travel within the city. Frequently they would socialize with the senior staff of the Department and other members of the Secretary's personal staff, which provided a relaxed atmosphere for talking business and trading "war stories" and information.

Managing the Office
of Economic Integration
OEI's mission was generally to be a "fast turnaround" office able to analyze an issue quickly, draft concise memos to the President and other senior officials and prepare background information for cabinet-level meetings. Having a broad overview of U.S. policies, they also assessed proposed changes in H & L programs in the light of the economic environment. They had the opportunity to acquire pertinent knowledge which could influence in some way the policy and operations of significant social and economic programs in the U.S. government. Irwin, Hoffman, Shelton, Santee and King had access to senior experts and managers across the government. For young men with curiosity and ambition, it was, as one of them noted, "exhilarating to be able to tap these resources in an effort to support Manning's and the Department's role in the development and review of economic and social programs."

Consequently, by the end of 1975 OEI was an influential and integral part of the Department's input into the economic policymaking establishment of the government. OEI kept in close contact with Secretary Manning and various parts of H & L on a wide range of issues. For example, OEI and Irwin in particular had recently assessed the solvency of the Social Security System and was examining the economic impact of inflation on the cost of Supplemental Social Security benefits. The Administration was then considering major legislation designed to revise the financing and benefit calculations in the system, since it seemed that recent legislation contained a rather subtle but extensive error in the calculation of inflation-related changes in benefits.

As another example, while Congress and the Administration considered anti-recession steps during 1975, OEI worked on selection of the Administration's options for job creation and economic stimulus. Their staff work proved crucial to the ultimate arguments used by Manning to temper advocates of less cost-effective programs. Hoffman was the architect of most of the Secretary's Congressional testimony on economic policy.

Shelton as a Manager
As Hoffman explained, a great deal of the office's proficiency was due to Shelton and his attitude.

Jack was committed to excellence and professionalism and sought to provide us with a challenging and exciting environment even when things weren't exciting. The jobs *all* had to get done and since he had infected us with his spirit and attitude, we also responded to a "kick in the ass" on seemingly inconsequential assignments. He had earned our trust.

Shelton put a great deal of effort into acquiring interesting assignments by anticipating and responding to Manning's needs. Part of this came from careful listening to Manning and from the variety of social and professional interactions he had around the Department and town. His planning efforts paid off, as Manning expressed pleasure with the high-quality output of OEI and directed many challenging assignments Shelton's way. "The more timely and on-target we were with our work, the more trust Manning would have," said Shelton.

An important part of Shelton's management success could be attributed to his attitude toward his staff. Mary Romano, explained:

Although he had definite thoughts as to how he wanted things done, he was always willing to consider your ideas, and more often than not let you use them. He never made me feel like "just a secretary." I was as important as every other person in the office. That was a good feeling. Every morning, at 8:30 sharp, Mr. Shelton held a staff meeting. He made sure to include the entire staff, which was very important for morale. He listed what was to be done over the next few days and divided up the work. Since we knew what everyone else would be doing, we were able to see the big picture and understood where our task fit in and what the interim goals were. He always made sure to ask if anyone had anything else to contribute to the meeting.

Hoffman noted:

For about six months none of the secretaries ever said anything, then little by little they began to ask questions about processes and substance. There was another dimension: Since he had usually just come from a meeting with the Secretary or Secretary's other senior advisors, he was full of information that affected our tasks or which affected other issues of national significance. He shared these confidential matters with us, trusting us. We could read some of the Washington Post's biggest scoops and because of Shelton's input, we'd know that the newspaper was occasionally wrong! In Washington, that's sort of a kick. It was a way to feel a part of the larger universe of policymakers. These "tidbits" were not only fun to be in on, but often proved useful later when analyzing a problem or in setting our own work priorities. And there was never a leak or breach of confidence.

Hoffman observed that Shelton made careful effort to supply people with individually tailored task and benefits that would make their work interesting.

If you did the work in preparation for a meeting, he'd take you along or sometimes have you go by yourself to present your findings to the Secretary. He gave me a lot of leeway in negotiating bureaucratically with other offices in the government. He knew that I was inclined to mediate and generally let me perform on my own when mediation was called for. When a different approach was needed, one in which I was less comfortable, he gave me more support. He sent me to weekly senior staff meetings. Shelton felt that the meetings weren't all that significant, but he also knew I was extremely impressionable at that stage and got a charge out of going. It also gave me a chance to do some business with and get exposure to some of the line managers in the agency.

Bob King, the econometrician, observed:

I was there for the professional experience. If the work wasn't interesting, no amount of lunches within the Secretary's dining room would make up for it. But Jack had little problem providing challenging work, since the office was continually dealing with intellectually interesting and significant issues. It was obvious to us that our work was being used at the top echelons of the government so nobody minded xeroxing, collating and doing "data grubbing." My conversations with Jack suggested that he found it a challenge to keep people continually working at a fast pace, turning out top-quality work. We were all pretty ambitious and curious, so quality and relevance ranked high for us.

Bob Irwin reflected on other aspects of Shelton's method of motivating people:

He used a crisis to bring people together, getting us to work long hours. Lord knows there were enough crises! It hardly seemed necessary, but if it were necessary he would have invented a crisis. It kept us going. It's funny how comaraderie builds under pressure, when you're working as a team. It carries over to non-crisis periods.

"We were more than just co-workers, we were friends," Carla Moody related.

We often went out for drinks on a Friday evening or got together every few months on a weekend for a party, along with spouses, friends and other co-workers. Jack periodically had parties for us at his house, especially when we finished an important or grueling project.

Mary Romano recalled the atmosphere:

When assignments came in from Manning at the last minute, the entire office pulled together. No one would dream of leaving until all the work was completed, even if his or her part was done. That person would just help someone else. Sometimes we worked long hours, but we managed to have fun doing it. I guess that's because we all got along so well together. We enjoyed working together. We could speak in shorthand and professional differences or difficulties never became personal.

Uncertainties in OEI

The leadership and some members of the Office of the Assistant Secretary for Research and Policy Formation, the Department's old-line analytic shop, had in the meantime become resentful that OEI was growing in influence and getting the more current assignments. Thus, RPF got little opportunity to work directly with the Secretary's office or exert much impact on policy making, since Manning turned increasingly to OEI for those functions. In an effort to promote high esprit de corps in OEI, Shelton occasionally emphasized an elitism by belittling RPF's reputation. This was reinforced by the fact that his desire for excellence and results caused him to act impatiently toward RPF. The OEI staff tended

to take the lead from Shelton and although friendly on a personal basis, there was little professional interaction except for Irwin's occasional lunch conversations with some of his economist friends.

In the spring of 1976, attention began to focus on the upcoming Presidential election. It was difficult to predict whether President Gerald R. Ford would win reelection. If the Republicans stayed in office, it seemed likely that Manning would remain as Secretary of H & L and would continue to rely on OEI. However, if Administrations changed, it was not at all clear whether a new Secretary would wish to preserve his analytic and brainstorming capacity in the form of OEI.

During this period, Mark Hoffman left OEI to work in the Health Administration of H & L.

I had a sense that things were going to change politically and that our work, so dependent on Manning's stature and Jack's relationship with him, would become less interesting. While there was still some stability, I wanted to do something in a line program so that my experience wouldn't be all staff.

After the election, Shelton decided that he would be leaving the government to take a job in private industry. He planned to make his move in early December. Because Shelton felt that an operation like his was useful for providing advice of a high caliber, he sought to insure that the OEI office would survive and remain in the hands of competent leadership, hopefully with Bob Irwin in charge. He and Irwin discussed what should be done. As Irwin explained: "He called me in and said 'Bob, where do we go from here?' As he saw it, we had two main options: (1) dissolve the office; and (2) fight for survival. I decided to hang in there and fight. I thought it was important."

For starters, the two men decided to strengthen Irwin's chance of heading OEI. On August 28,

1976, they submitted a memo, as required, to the Assistant Secretary for Administration and Management to establish the position of Associate Deputy Under-Secretary for the Office of Economic Integration. The position was approved and thus the way was paved for Irwin to be in the line of succession to take over as head of the shop.

Shelton began consulting with Irwin on office matters and deliberately took long trips out of town so the staff could get accustomed to Irwin's style. He explained,

> I knew Bob was a sharp economist, but I didn't know how good a manager he could be. I wanted to give him a chance to step into the role gradually, beginning as my "number two" man. This interim time was a good training period for Bob and an important test of his abilities. He took to it quickly. He had good managerial instincts. He was willing to trust his people — let them go.

Transition

After Jimmy Carter was elected, both Shelton and Irwin shared the opinion that contact with the Carter transition team would increase the chance of a positive outcome for the OEI function. They drafted a highly personal transition memo for Manning to send to the new Secretary. This candid review of the need for analytic capacity, which underwent many careful revisions, discussed H & L's role in supporting the Secretary's role in national policy making. It went on to emphasize the usefulness of having an office available to deal quickly and broadly with economic and other issues. In addition, Manning volunteered to meet with Jerry Weir, the newly announced Secretary of H & L, to personally describe the usefulness of OEI.

During the transition process, Shelton and Irwin made sure to be open and honest with their staff. Irwin met with the office group and assessed the chances for survival at fifty-fifty. He

told them, "If you want to make a go of it, I'll make a commitment and I won't bail out. I'll be the last one to leave." The staff accepted it as a challenge and they all prepared to dig in for the fight.

Irwin as a Manager

Irwin acknowledged that he had been greatly influenced by Shelton. He made a conscious effort to implement these ideas, often putting people in charge of tasks outside the range of their normal job duties, a practice not condoned by Civil Service rules and often the subject of grievances in other organizations. Staff responded favorably to this treatment and demonstrated their approval by applying themselves to the tasks at hand. Mary Romano described her experience:

> Shelton realized that secretaries could think. He challenged me to do things I never did before. His giving me responsibility was motivating. I worked my tail off and learned a lot. It opened the door to future potential for me. I've gotten two promotions since I've been with OEI and thanks to Bob Irwin, no longer have a secretarial designation.

Irwin wished to continue Shelton's practices of socializing:

> If you like the people you're working with, you'll enjoy working a lot more. The social aspects of a work environment are pretty crucial parts of the job. I like getting together at my house with the staff, especially after we've accomplished something noteworthy.

Irwin felt the need to continue daily meetings:

> I was convinced that the staff meetings were very useful. I continued this process. It was a way to bring people together as friends and colleagues. It provided people with common information about the priorities of the work group. Also, by continuing a process that marked Shelton's reign, I promoted a sense of continuity as well. I worry about

the product, not people's hours or number of coffee breaks.

The comments of Carla Moody, a seven-year career employee, sum up the positive feeling of OEI:

> Morale in this office is great! A lot of offices envy us. I don't know why their bosses can't work this way. It's the boss. If the boss takes two hours for lunch and shows he doesn't care about the work, the secretary will do the same. I wouldn't move to another office in the Department for love or money.

However, despite the fact that Irwin had been successful in preserving the harmony of the office, there was still considerable uncertainty regarding the eventual fate of OEI. Since most of OEI had been hired on various sorts of temporary authorities, it would be relatively easy for a new Secretary to disband the office and create a new shop.

The Merger

In January and February of 1976, Jerome Weir, the new Secretary of H & L, had been working to install his own people into his chain of command. He offered the job of Assistant Secretary for RPF to a trusted professional colleague, Jeff Stevens. Stevens investigated the situation and told Weir that he would only take the job if he could be in charge of OEI as well. Stevens acknowledged that in order to exercise control over the Department's position in economic policy and avoid having another analytic group looking over his shoulder on all sorts of issues, it would be necessary to have OEI under his control.

By this time, Bob King had reached the conclusion that it was time for him to pick up his graduate studies once again and had returned to school in time for the new semester. Jim Santee had departed at about the same time to gain some business experience before beginning his graduate studies in business.

At this point, Irwin had the same three secretaries on board and had replaced King with a Ph.D. candidate from Georgetown University, Mitchell Daniels, who told the case writer: "I really enjoy analytic work and a number of my professors said that Bob was a solid economist to work with. I like to spend time working through a problem and come to a well-supported conclusion. I work well under pressure and find this to be a good combination of both."

Richard Danko, an attorney that Shelton hired to work on regulatory reform issues, was still on the staff with Irwin. He found himself increasingly assisting Irwin on coordination with other parts of the organization. "Bob has been very supportive and introduced me to a realm of bureaucratic interplay that is crucial to making the government work. Although it's not in the legal area, in which I am making my career, it's a worthwhile lesson. He's an awfully good manager."

The news of Stevens's appointment as Assistant Secretary over both RPF and OEI predictably threw the OEI office into turmoil. The staff was of the view that without an identity as a separate shop the interesting assignments would disappear.

Irwin did a great deal of anticipatory work for Stevens:

> I prepared a transition book, charted economic indicators, reviewed fiscal programs and much more. Everything was done neatly and written in layman's terms. There was careful attention to detail, down to drawing maps of the building. We wanted Stevens's early days to be comfortable. I didn't have to tell the others to do this. Everyone knew the office had to pull together. In this way OEI showed that it was useful, responsive, alive. As a result the comparison to RPF was pretty obvious.

The status of the office remained unchanged if uncertain during this transition period. During the middle of 1976, Irwin brought in another economist, Harriet Ettinger. She had previously been a sales representative of one of the computer services to which OEI subscribed.

> I was tired of running and trying to sell new systems and programs for economic analysis. I wanted a more regular routine and more stability. It does gall me when we bust our asses and the information doesn't get used.

As part of the uncertainty, OEI was moved out of its once-plush suite of offices and housed in a variety of makeshift sharing arrangements. Barbara Reiner's job was in jeopardy since Irwin was not at a high enough level to justify her civil service rating. Irwin ultimately was able to "engineer" her into an administrative position with Stevens, the new Assistant Secretary.

A New OEI

As of February 1977, the OEI staff consisted of five people. During most of 1977, Irwin made it known by his actions to Weir and Stevens that his group could tackle any assignment. Irwin continually demonstrated OEI's responsiveness and quality by accepting projects that may have fit better among the substantive responsibilities of another group in RPF, of which OEI was now a part.

Not only did Irwin seek to maintain quality work but he also worked on office morale. This, in part, was attempted through an emphasis on daily staff meetings:

> Since the group can't be together when we're working, it's especially important to interact as a unit at least once a day. We have to be aware of each other's assignments and progress. It's also crucial that we reinforce our group feeling.

The staff believed that Irwin was primarily responsible for keeping them intact during this period of disorientation. As stated by Harriet Ettinger: "If he wasn't here, I would have to quit. He sticks up for us all the time."

Though OEI had been split up spatially in late January, they did not receive an official word on their organizational fate until May. Jeff Stevens had been hesitant to relocate them permanently for several reasons. First, some RPF "veterans" had been trying to convince him to abolish OEI. Stevens, however, realized the usefulness and productivity of the OEI staff. No other office under his jurisdiction had the capability of producing top-quality projects in fast-turnaround situations. On the other hand, Stevens was concerned with OEI's established independence of RPF because he did not want OEI competing with him for the Secretary's or anyone else's attention.

Finally in May 1977, Stevens submitted a formal reorganization package. The plan included the creation of a new post, that of Deputy Assistant Secretary of RPF with responsibility for the Office of Economic Integration, to be filled by Greg Bozek. According to the organization plan, Irwin would report to Bozek, who would in turn report to Stevens. (See Exhibits 8-1 and 8-2 for the organizational charts before and after the reorganization.)

Irwin recalled:

> I met with Stevens and told him that I would be willing to continue running the day-to-day affairs of OEI. This would free up Bozek to work on research and policy formulation and thus save him from the administrative headaches. Stevens agreed with me. I figured that if Bozek was going to be part of the system, I'd prefer to have him in his own organizational box. Being so gracious earned me some points as well. Stevens began to agree with me that it was important to get my shop resettled as soon as possible.

Although this added another link to the chain of command, it was a clear sign that OEI would be allowed to survive intact. Spirit in the office picked up considerably.

The move to a new suite took place on June 9, 1977, more than four months after the original split-up. Although Irwin and his staff moved to a far less lavish suite than their original one, they were glad to be together. After being scattered over the fifth floor, it was gratifying to be in one, self-contained set of offices. Furthermore, they were still on the same floor as the Secretary's office.

Adding New Staff

The reorganization affected other offices in RPF and workers in RPF were encouraged to look around at the various new offices to decide where they might best fit. Stevens was aware of the poor reputation of RPF and sought to reorganize it in a manner that would be more responsive to the rest of the Department and to the Secretary. It was characterized as an "open season" giving RPF employees a chance to "start over." Several of them considered OEI, which worried Irwin. He was reluctant to take on anyone who had been socialized in RPF.

> I looked around at RPF and at first glance everyone looked lazy. But at the suggestion of one of my friends in RPF, I interviewed two people: Ed Gralla, an economist; and Debbie Lewis, a secretary. Although both had been socialized by RPF — essentially to work as little as possible — I saw a certain "spark" in each of them. I was worried, though. I knew that I was taking a big risk.

Once he brought on these new people, Irwin considered how to best integrate them into his staff. Since solidarity among the original group was so strong, Irwin had to make sure that Gralla and Lewis did not feel left out.

> I wanted to make sure that they were included on work projects as well as social events. Furthermore, I wanted them to understand and be glad that OEI was very different from RPF. The emphasis was on doing the work well, enjoying the work, and not on worrying about who was following the rules.

Irwin referred to Ed Gralla's progress as another "success story." Gralla had received a Ph.D. in economics from a large midwestern university, where he was an honors graduate. Since then he had been with RPF. He had some knowledge of the manpower area, although he had occasionally worked in other subject areas within H & L. He was known in RPF as a congenial, if not gregarious, sort. Gralla reflected on his progress and change of attitude and attributed his new-found job satisfaction to Irwin's style and interest in the work:

> Bob rescued me. I finally got a chance to use my talents. Bob has the ability to pick out the positive aspects of what I've done and I therefore seek to do more. He challenges me to think and go beyond the first draft or conceptualization.

Several other staffing changes also took place over the past year. At their urging Irwin was able to secure permanent career status for Mitch Daniels and Harriet Ettinger. Mary Romano left to become an Administrative Assistant at the Treasury Department. Although Irwin was delighted at her career advancement, he was unsure about how to proceed without her.

> She was the soul of the office — the office spirit. The day she left, I actually wondered if it was time to throw in the towel. But we all pulled together and managed. Luckily Carla was here. She stepped in and along with doing a spectacular job on Mary's formal duties, she took over much of Mary's informal role of keeping the workflow going. Two weeks ago Mitch Daniels left OEI to take a job as Jeff Stevens's Executive Assistant. He did a great job here, but it's time for him to move on. It's good for his career.

Most recently, Irwin took on two more economists: Karen Helfrich, new to the government service; and Ira White, a solid econometrician from another office of H & L. Karen Helfrich has a Masters in economics and was especially interested in productivity in the health care area. She had on several occasions lamented the lack of organization that characterized RPF and the government more generally. Ira White had, over the five years which he had been working elsewhere in H & L, developed a facility with the statistics used to analyze the labor force. Irwin spent a lot of time politicking to lure him away with the promise of more interesting and exciting work nearer to the top of the organization. White was at first unpersuaded, but Irwin promised him a promotion to the next grade and White was persuaded to join his staff. In Irwin's view, both of these economists turned out to be assets to the office and Irwin affirmed to the case writer his intention to promote them, which he had promised them as a condition of their coming to OEI, despite the laborious administrative procedures involved.

When it became difficult or impossible because of these problems to promote or reward an employee because of bureaucratic rules, Irwin shared the problems with the staff. He explained that a particular employee had done a superior job and deserved recognition. In one case, when he was having an especially difficult time promoting an employee, he drew out a chart to show everyone how complicated and time-consuming the procedure had been to date. When Manning was there, Shelton and Hoffman were able to more easily give formal rewards and recognition to the staff.

The Office as of July 1978

Irwin believed that the office was running smoothly once again. He explained with pride, "Stevens now realizes that we're the only effective office in RPF. He continually calls on us to bail out other offices when they've botched an assignment." He continued to challenge his staff, he told the case writer, and help them to develop new skills. Debbie Lewis explained her experience in OEI:

> I've changed. In RPF I got the work out, but I was bored. Now I'm relied on. Bob asked me to write a weekly progress report that he wanted to send to Stevens. I wasn't

sure how to begin, so I asked a few people for advice, and then I just dug in and wrote one. He went over it with me several times over coffee and let me work on it some more.

Ed Gralla said that Irwin looked out for his staff:

> Bob lets you know when you've done a good job. He gives out Performance Achievement Awards — only a couple of hundred dollars — something I had never heard of before I came to OEI. Not only that, but he allows for our personal needs. I recently decided I needed to clear my head and take a long vacation. Bob didn't even say "boo."
>
> This is my first experience working as part of a group and I like it. I used to keep my work to myself until it was in finished form. Bob taught me to get a draft on paper and show it to others for comments. Now I learn from everyone else.

The office was not without problems, however. Carla Moody expressed some concern over the nature of the work. Since she had been present in OEI throughout the various changes in the Department, she had noticed differences in the character of OEI's assignments.

> There's too much paperwork now and too many rules to worry about. I used to have much more direct contact with the support staff in the Secretary's office. We're not special people to this Secretary.

Harriet Ettinger also expressed frustration with the change in job content.

> Bob often sticks up for us when we get irrelevant assignments and we refuse to do them, or at least he apologizes to us for giving us these projects. We're doing too much number work and panic work. We should be doing macroeconomics and supporting the Secretary like we used to do. Many of the assignments we do actually belong to RPF but we all know they could never handle them properly. Sometimes it looks like Bob is just keeping us busy. I'm worried that we aren't

an essential part of H & L, the way we used to be. What happened to all our top-priority projects?

Irwin reflected on some similar matters:

In a sense I work for three people. I work for Bozek, Stevens gives me work independently and I get business from Baker, the Secretary's special assistant. He's the guy that Weir depends on for his Economic Policy Committee and special project stuff. He doesn't have a staff so he's happy to get the help. I've also got budget oversight responsibility for the statistics gathering parts of the Department among other things. RPF is set up a bit like the Office of Management and Budget or Congressional oversight committees so that each office in RPF uses its evaluation hat to look at the programs in each parallel operating area. RPF doesn't do it too well, but I've tried to use the role to pursue my desire to improve and make more compre-hensive the data gathered for economic analysis. Ira White has been helpful in watching over the area for me, as has Karen Helfrich.

To handle some of the work that comes from three "bosses" that isn't quite so interesting, I try to equitably distribute it among the entire staff. If I gave it to any one person they'd go crackers. But as it now stands there's enough interesting stuff going on so that we manage to maintain a sufficiently challenging environment. When the work is challenging people work harder and utilize more of their potential. Working within RPF has posed its problems culturally. Maintaining an identity and higher standards has taken some effort and some of the social things we do within the office or outside have been instrumental in maintaining the cohesion and sense of pride. It's funny how spatial arrangements and uncertainty regarding our organizational status took on a lot of symbolism. But now we are here and functioning.

Exhibit 8-1. RPF and OEI before reorganization

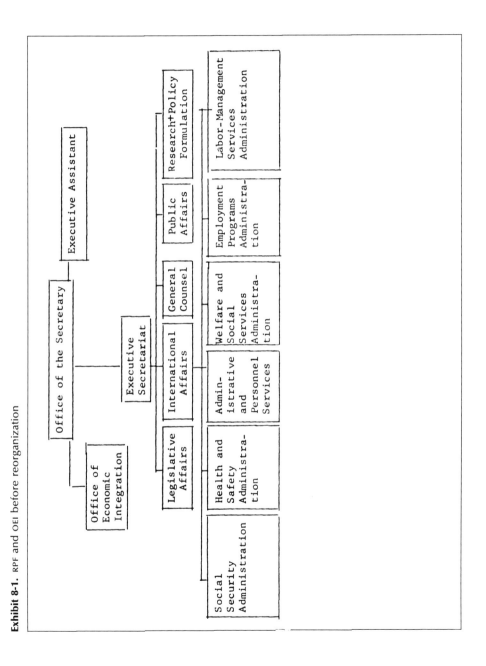

Exhibit 8-2. RPF and OEI after reorganization

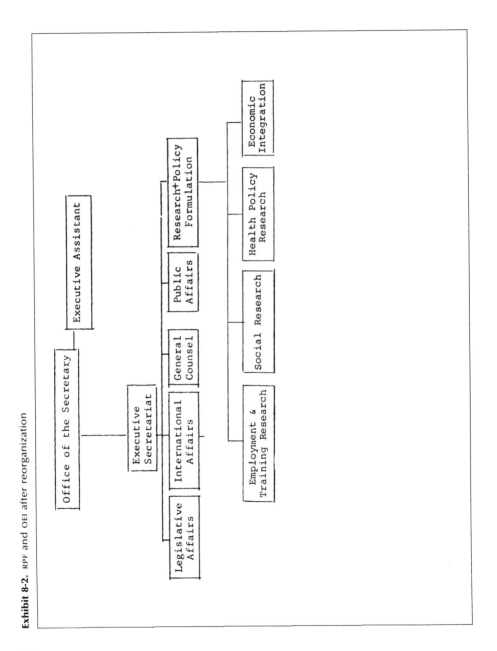

PART V

Feedback and Information

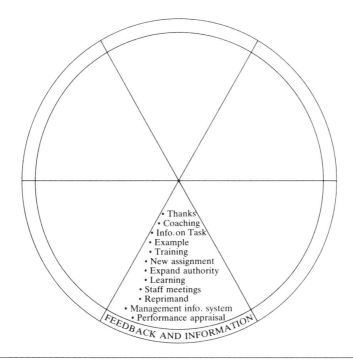

- Thanks
- Coaching
- Info. on Task
- Example
- Training
- New assignment
- Expand authority
- Learning
- Staff meetings
- Reprimand
- Management info. system
- Performance appraisal

FEEDBACK AND INFORMATION

As the cases in Part IV suggested, there are many sources of feedback and information in a job and work environment. This part provides some more explicit examples of feedback and information in a public sector workplace. In addition to providing formal orientation and training and seeing to a proper job structure and job match, most effective managers provide substantive guidance and feedback on a frequent basis. As one example of that role, two of the cases in this part of the book focus on aspects of performance appraisal, but, in fact, allow us to look far more broadly at the interaction among organizational purposes, a manager, and employees.

Analysis and design of performance evaluation systems contain or point out many of the most important features of a manager's role as the primary link between employees and organizational purposes and resources. By his or her activity in an evaluation system, a manager may fill this role well or poorly. Principles of work planning, job matching, delegation, feedback, and communication pervade the use or misuse of performance appraisal systems. These characteristics make the study of performance evaluation a useful way to sharpen our understanding of day-to-day management interaction and planning. The building blocks of a good appraisal system are nothing more than the principles of good management.

The cases on performance appraisals in this part are especially topical in view of the widespread interest by all levels of government in "pay-for-performance" or "merit pay." Many states and the federal government have adopted such systems, and others are studying adoption of them. Virtually all pay-for-performance systems require measurement of performance in order to determine an employee's pay differential for the year. Therefore, the form and features of a performance evaluation system become a common topic of debate whenever pay-for-performance is discussed.

An effective performance evaluation system is difficult to implement. The complexity of the system, the resources that must be devoted to it, and its possible unintended effects are rarely acknowledged or understood by actors and institutions who favor them. The case in Chapter 9 permits analysis of the major features and roles in a performance evaluation system in a public agency. The lessons of the case can be applied in designing or revising evaluation systems or in carrying out appraisals in most public settings.

The second case in this part examines executive development as a tool for strengthening organizational capacity. We examine executive development because of its importance as a form of training, as a reward, and as a means of developing a pool of talented managers. In Chapter 1 we discussed some of the deficiencies in management emphasis and development in the public sector. This is an area where more work has been done in private sector organizations and from which there might be some transferable lessons. Because of the General Electric Company's (GE) particular reputation for management development, a case based on that company is included.

Because of the implicit and explicit training that is part of management development, the GE case also provides a vehicle for thinking about the role and importance of training. Feedback and information can add greatly to the performance of a service organization. The formal evaluation process and implicit evaluation provided through such a training program in the GE management development program also suggest the use of such a program as a form of feedback and motivation.

In Chapter 11 we return to the site of the Chapter 9 case — the U.S. Patent and Trademark Office — to examine the use of bonuses as a management tool for providing employee feedback.

CHAPTER 9

Performance Evaluation: Structuring a System to Improve Performance

In order to influence the direction and performance of an organization, it is important that a top manager have the means to influence the managerial behavior of his or her subordinates. As in the previous case, personal style and organizational context can be important determinants of these means, but a number of more formal and systematic techniques can be used. One such technique is performance appraisal. The federal Civil Service Reform Act of 1978 explicitly acknowledged the usefulness of this tool by requiring its use in all federal executive agencies. Many other jurisdictions at state and local levels are following suit.

Apart from its attempt to improve the performance of managers and subordinates, part of the reform effort is aimed at making more specific the connection between rewards and performance. Many incentive pay and bonus programs are being considered or put in place requiring that some portion of compensation be determined by performance on the job. To do so generally requires that performance ratings or appraisals serve as the basis for awarding such pay. Therefore, in addition to examining the utility of performance appraisal as a tool for substantive feedback, it is important to anlayze performance appraisal as a means of providing financial reward.

The results of formal performance appraisals have been mixed in both public and private employment. Some organizations swear by their performance evaluation systems. Others find such large-scale formal systems to be a burden and to interfere with their basic management task and responsibilities. In addition to some success stories, there are many examples of appraisal systems that have done more harm than good, usually because of design and implementation problems.

Most performance appraisal systems are designed to have one or more of the following overall purposes:[1]

1. To motivate people toward common organizational objectives.
2. To provide employees with information on their performance or progress and identify strong or weak areas.
3. To evaluate people in an organization for monetary rewards.
4. To evaluate people in an organization for promotion, transfer, or separation.
5. To identify people of high potential for training and development.

Rarely can one system do all of these well; moreover, designing and carrying out a performance appraisal system becomes more complicated as the system's objectives become more ambitious.

To show how a performance appraisal system works and under what circumstances, the two cases on the Patent and Trademark Office examine several aspects of performance appraisal as a management technique, as an organizational control device, and as an information system. The cases raise the issues that are typically encountered in developing and carrying out appraisal systems. They should help you pick out the critical aspects of appraisal techniques and systems so that they can best be applied or avoided in varying organizational settings.

A study of performance appraisal illustrates some basic aspects of manager-employee interaction. It is commonly acknowledged that good managers provide frequent information and feedback to employees on expectations and on perceptions of employees' progress relative to their personal goals and those of the organization. In one sense a performance appraisal system is simply an attempt to systematize that manager-employee interaction.

The case in this chapter focuses on the initial design and implementation of a performance appraisal system in the U.S. Patent and Trademark Office. As the case opens, this agency was just putting into place a performance appraisal system as mandated by the Civil Service Reform Act of 1978. Thus, the system is examined in its early stages, where there is still an opportunity for adjustment.

STUDY QUESTIONS

1. By what criteria would you evaluate the new performance appraisal system in the Patent and Trademark Office?
2. For what purposes does the Patent and Trademark Office exist? Why is its work important to the country?
3. What has to be done well in each component of this organization in order for its mission to be fulfilled?

---

[1] This list is adapted from Paul H. Thompson and Gene W. Dalton, "Performance Appraisal: Managers Beware," *Harvard Business Review*, January–February, 1970.

4. How does the new performance appraisal system depart from that which was used in the past?
   What differences will it bring, therefore, in managerial behavior?
   Why do you think so?

5. What do you think will be the effects on individual performance of those in the system?
   What features of the system or environment will account for that?

6. What do you think the effects will be on organizational performance? What features of the system or environment will account for that?

7. Would you make any suggestions for alterations in the system or its implementation? If so, what would those suggestions be? What effect on performance and satisfaction would you expect from those changes?

RECOMMENDED READING

Herbert H. Meyer, Emanual Kay, and John R. P. French, Jr., "Split Roles in Performance Appraisal," *Harvard Business Review,* January-February, 1965.

SELECTED REFERENCES

Stephen J. Carrol, Jr. and Craig E. Schneir, *Performance Appraisal and Review Systems* (Glenview, Ill.: Scott, Foresman, 1982), Chapter 8, "The Analysis of Potential," pp. 217–248; Chapter 2, "Performance Appraisal Criteria: Choice and Utility," pp. 38–45; and Chapter 7, "Providing Feedback: The Performance Review," pp. 160–189.

U.S. Patent and Trademark Office (A)

Harley Borman, Assistant Commissioner for Administration at the U.S. Patent and Trademark Office, had just returned from an afternoon meeting at the Department of Business and Industry on September 13, 1979. The meeting concerned the implementation of the new Senior Executive Service (SES) performance appraisal system within the various departmental "operating units," including the Patent and Trademark Office (PTO). As part of the Civil Service Reform Act of 1978, the new procedures for evaluating performance and for eventually linking that performance to bonuses or incentive pay awards had to be operational by October 1, 1979.

In his capacity as Assistant Commissioner, Borman had been given lead responsibility for implementing the SES program in the PTO. After reviewing some notes and collecting his thoughts, Borman began preparing his presentation for tomorrow's training session during which the senior executives of the Patent and Trademark Office would be introduced for the first time to the specific provisions of the new performance appraisal system.

The U.S. Patent and Trademark Office

The U.S. Patent and Trademark Office is an agency steeped in history and tradition. So important was this particular governmental function deemed to be by the framers of the Constitution that they included a provision authorizing Congress

. . . to promote the progress of science and the useful arts, by securing for limited terms to . . . inventors the exclusive right to their . . . discoveries. (Article 1, Section 8, Clause 8)

Thomas Jefferson, himself an inventor, was instrumental in designing the Patent Office mandate and personally drafted the first patent law. Subsequently, the first American patent was issued in 1790 and was signed by the President, George Washington.

The first federal law providing for the recognition of trademarks was enacted nearly 100 years later in 1870. Since that time, patents and trademarks have been joined under one roof as a single governmental entity. Few federal agencies can boast of so long and continuous a service to the American public as the Patent and Trademark Office. This tradition and the time-honored practices that have evolved over the past two centuries set the tone for the PTO as it exists today.

The historical mission of the PTO grew from the concept that inventions as well as trademarks are intellectual property. A patent is a limited monopoly granted by the federal government in return for the disclosure of new and "non-obvious" contributions of useful technology. A trademark is a federal recognition of the right of an owner to use a word, name, symbol or device to distinguish goods and services from those manufactured by others. Unlike patents, which remain in force for seventeen years and cannot be extended, trademark registrations can be kept in force indefinitely.

Organization and Functions

The Patent and Trademark Office is one of a number of bureaus or operating units loosely organized under the Department of Business and

Industry (DBI) umbrella. Although the Commissioner of Patents and Trademarks technically reports to the Assistant Secretary of Business and Industry for Productivity, Technology and Innovation, PTO has established a measure of independence from the Department as a result of active lobbying efforts on the part of its outside constituencies, particularly the Patent, Trademark and Copyright Section of the American Bar Association. As one manager suggested:

> Every year we submit a budget through the Department, which they cut regardless of the justification we provide. Fortunately, the patent bar has enough power on Capitol Hill to restore whatever DBI takes away from us. . . . Naturally the Department resents our independence and takes every opportunity to bring us in line.

Numerous efforts to make PTO an independent agency have thus far proven unsuccessful.

Within the Patent and Trademark Office, Patent Examination and Trademark Examination are the two line functions. The rest of the organization, referred to as the Executive/Administration area, provides support to these functions (see Exhibit 9-1 for an organization chart).

Patent Examination. The patent examining function stands at the core of the entire PTO operation. Although a Presidential appointee, the Assistant Commissioner for Patents is traditionally selected from among those who have risen to the top of the Patent Examining Corps. To the best of anyone's recollection, no one has ever been appointed from the outside to this position.

Reporting to the Assistant Commissioner is a Deputy Assistant Commissioner, who is primarily responsible for supervising the Patent Examining Corps and Patent Documentation. Of the 1,600 employees under the Assistant Commissioner, some 900 to 950 are patent exam-

iners. At least 25 percent of the examiners are attorneys and all are trained in some area of technology.

The Patent Examining Corps is divided into three disciplines: chemical, electrical and mechanical. Each discipline is further subdivided into five major areas of technology. Supervising these fifteen subdivisions are Group Directors, who are in turn responsible for four to five "Art Units," each of which is staffed to examine patents in specific technologies. These technologies vary in complexity and sophistication ranging from paper clips to nuclear reactors. For example, a Group Director from the mechanical discipline might supervise one Art Unit responsible for inventions relating to automotive parts and a second Unit responsible for solar heat generators. It should be noted that of the 26 senior executive positions in the PTO, the Group Directors constitute a block of 15, with the Deputy Assistant Commissioner, the Special Assistant to the Deputy Assistant Commissioner and the Administrator of Patent Documentation holding three additional slots.

Defining the scope of an inventor's property rights is a complex process and may take up to two years (see Exhibit 9-2 for a flow diagram of the process). Of particular significance throughout is a time measure of the PTO's responsiveness, or "pendency." Essentially, pendency is that period of time between the filing of a patent application and the PTO processing of the application. Processing completion occurs when either the applicant abandons the application, the application is ultimately rejected, or the patent is granted. In the 1950s, patent pendency stood at about 42 months. In 1977, it dropped to just below 19 months. Most recently, however, it has begun to creep back up toward 22 months.

Each action on a pending application and the time taken to conclude it is tracked by a computer which provides information on examiner production, as well as aggregate data on patent operations. From these data, an intricate series of production standards has been devised which takes into account first actions (number of applications on which the examiner has forwarded to the applicant initial findings as to patentability), disposals (number of applications allowed for issue as patents plus the number of applications abandoned), and balanced disposals (an average of new actions and disposals). Also included are factors relating to the sophistication or difficulty of the art, the grade levels of examiners and various time factors having an impact on productivity (vacation, sick or training time). Using these factors in a complex formula, managers arrive at figures which indicate the productivity of individual examiners, Art Units, and Groups. This productivity information has traditionally been used to track performance and has been tied to promotions, adverse actions, and awards.

Trademarks. Reporting to the Assistant Commissioner for Trademarks, who is also a presidential appointee, are three subunits: Office of Trademark Programs, the Trademark Trial and Appeal Board, and Trademark Examining Operations. Each of these subunits is principally staffed by attorneys, and each is loosely organized into levels of supervision. Of the three subunits, only the Trademark Trial and Appeal Board and Trademark Examining Operations are supervised by managers at the senior executive level.

Much of the work of a trademark examiner is relatively routine and involves minimum use of legal skills. As a result, this group, representing 5 percent of the total PTO organization, experiences a tremendous turnover within the ranks of attorneys. Even the average stay of recent appointments to the position of the Assistant Commissioner for Trademarks has been no more than one year.

Trademarks administers the provisions of the Trademark Act by examining applications, reg-

istering those trademarks that meet statutory qualifications, providing trademark information to the public, and resolving legal disputes between private parties concerning registration rights. The trademark examiner must for each application research all registered or pending marks which are similar to the one for which registration is being sought. The examiner then applies a body of case law to determine whether or not the mark has ''confusing similarity'' to another or fails to meet other statutory requirements. The process concludes in one of three ways: the abandonment of the application; the registration of the mark; or an appeal of the examiner's final decision to the Trademark Trial and Appeal Board. (Refer to Exhibit 9-3 for a flow diagram of the trademark process.)

In trademark examination, pendency is measured as the period of time between the filing of a trademark application and the first examiner's action on the application. In 1975, pendency was less than three months. It now stands at about 13 months.

Standards have also been devised to measure the productivity of trademark examiners. They resemble those used by the Patent Examining Corps insofar as they utilize data pertaining to first actions and disposals. The trademark standards, however, are not nearly so complex and emphasize years of experience on the part of the examiner to determine productivity, rather than the intricate series of factors incorporated into the patent standards. A limited effort has been made to link the productivity information to promotions, awards, and adverse actions.

Executive/Administration. Apart from the patent and trademark functions, there are reporting to the Commissioner: the General Counsel's Office, the Board of Appeals, the Office of Information Services, the Board of Interferences, the Office of Legislation and International Affairs, and the Office of the Assistant Commissioner for Administration. The Commissioner's Office also includes an Executive Assistant and his staff. These have traditionally been considered together as the Executive/Administration grouping.

Although there is little that unifies this group outside of its general mission to provide services designed to meet the Commissioner's immediate needs, the range of responsibility can be reduced to three basic areas: Administration, the General Counsel's Office and the executive staff. The Assistant Commissioner for Administration, who is the one career appointee among the Assistant Commissioners, employs a staff of 750 and is responsible for providing a variety of support services. These include planning, budgeting and evaluation; management and organization; personnel; finance; general services; and automated data processing. The General Counsel's Office is more singular in purpose. Essentially, the General Counsel is responsible for providing representation before the courts in cases brought against the Commissioner. A deputy and ten attorneys assist the General Counsel and constitute the legal elite of the PTO. Finally, the remaining executive level offices provide a range of more "personal" services from Congressional liaison to general information and research required by the Commissioner. Of the PTO's 26 senior executives, six may be found in the Executive/Administration area.

With the exception of a measurement system implemented for his staff by the Assistant Commissioner for Administration, no effort has been made to quantify or track activities in these areas of the organization. The General Counsel's Office is responsible for meeting the highly unpredictable demands of the court system and relies upon direct feedback from either the Commissioner or the courts. The General Counsel must also work closely with the General Counsel's Office at the Department of Business and Industry and the Department of Justice in deciding policy and procedures. The Commissioner and his Deputy alone are responsible for making demands of the remaining executive staff and for insuring that the two appeals boards are responsive to the cases brought before them.

The Old System
of Performance Appraisal

Prior to the implementation of the Civil Service Reform Act of 1978, PTO performance appraisals were guided by the Performance Rating Act of 1950, the purpose of which was to insure that work performance of employees was appraised "fairly" in relation to performance ratings. Toward this end, employees were advised of individual summary ratings on a yearly basis. These ratings were limited to one of three adjectives: outstanding, satisfactory and unsatisfactory. In addition to the Performance Rating Act, the Salary Reform Act of 1962 provided for making an "acceptable level of competence" determination for purposes of awarding within-grade pay increases. Finally, awards and other forms of employee recognition were allocated in accordance with the provisions of Chapter 45, "Incentive Awards," of Title 5 of the U.S. Code. This section of the Civil Service Act provided for awards from medals to Quality Step Increases to Special Achievement Awards.

Above and beyond actual Civil Service requirements, performance appraisal in the Patent and Trademark Office was also governed by the terms of various labor-management agreements in effect within the organization. These contracts set performance standards and determined under what circumstances awards were to be made or adverse action to be taken. In addition, each of the three major functional areas was free to establish different mechanisms for evaluating performance and allocating awards, as long as they remained within the general guidelines of Civil Service rules and applicable labor contracts. The following is a brief description of how performance appraisal was conducted in each area.

Patents

Patent Examination has traditionally had the most exacting and comprehensive methods for measuring individual performance and for linking that performance to rewards. Based on the productivity standards described earlier, performance is tracked as a percentage of planned versus actual productivity. One Group Director described the process in the following manner:

Toward the beginning of the year, usually some time during the first quarter, we would be assigned "raw" goals. These goals would be based on a formula worked out from the Assistant Commissioner's budget and did not always correspond to the sum of the expectancies of the examiners in the Group to which you were assigned. For example, quite often in order to reach your goal as a Group Director, it was necessary for your examiners to exceed their goals or expectancies. Expectancies for examiners are negotiated by a union contract which says that anyone achieving better than 110 percent of expectancy has to receive an award. Group Directors never had such clearly established standards; they were more or less in competition with one another. Those who happened to fall above a certain cut-off line received an award; those below it did not. Although we never knew exactly where the line would be drawn, we did know that about 50% of us would receive awards of one kind or another and we knew generally what we had to do in terms of performance to win an award.

Under this system, the Deputy Assistant Commissioner for Patents, Sam Goldberg, was charged with complete responsibility for evaluating the Group Directors and for distributing the awards. He describes his part of the appraisal process as follows:

At the end of every fiscal year, I would do a post-audit review on each Director to determine who was outstanding. I spent hours going over the figures and ranking the Directors. Next I would decide on a reasonable break point for the awards. Then I would call each Director into the office and spend about two hours going over his performance for the year. At this meeting, I would advise him whether or not he was to receive an award. Where a Director would fail to meet his goal, I would listen to an explanation; but as the sign outside my door says, I expect results not excuses.

Goldberg goes on to add, "In the eight or nine years I have been doing this, I have never had to give anyone an unsatisfactory rating."

For the most part, Group Directors seemed to respond favorably to the old system. As one suggested,

There was never any reason to complain. We knew that Sam was scrupulously fair and that basically the same standards were being applied equally to all of us.

The patent examiner measurement system is believed by PTO management to have contributed significantly to the quantity of work produced. For example, the productivity of individual patent examiners in fiscal year 1979 measured against individual production goals resulted in the following statistics:

10.1% of all examiners produced below 90% of goal.

53.2% of all examiners produced between 90% and 109% of goal.

36.7% of all examiners produced at or above 110% of goal.

The Patent Examining Corps has made an effort over the years to employ additional measures of performance in order to evaluate other aspects of an examiner's job. Service to the public, personal conduct and attitude, as well as personnel development have recently been included in the evaluation factors. Also, an effort has been made to make some assessment of the *quality* of work performed, but because clear quantifiable documentation is not available to measure this element, it has often received only a cursory review by supervisors. As Goldberg suggests,

> We don't think we overemphasize goals. Production is important, but quality is also important. It's just hard to prove we are sincere in this area.

Trademarks

As in the Patent Corps, data are readily available to measure the productivity of trademark examiners, and productivity goals are assigned each year. However, as one supervisor remarked,

> Sure we count widgets, but we have not been enforcing the counts. Performance is evaluated on a yearly basis. If you meet your goals, fine. If you fall short, you get a pat on the head and are told to try harder next year. The net result is the same: Everyone gets a satisfactory rating.

The same supervisor goes on to describe an incident that took place under the old system.

> Once I was questioned by an employee about her satisfactory rating. She wanted to know why it wasn't outstanding. I responded by asking what she had done during the year that was outstanding. After some hesitation, she replied that she had met all of her deadlines. I suggested that that alone wasn't really what we could consider outstanding performance. She conceded that this was probably true and asked what she could do during the coming year to achieve an outstanding rating. I thought about it awhile and could not come up with an answer.

As outstanding performance ratings were required by the PTO to justify awards, few Quality Step Increases or Special Achievement Awards were made to individuals in the Trademark Office. As one manager suggests,

> Awards were made at the whim of the Assistant Commissioner. If he had the time, he awarded something. Usually, he did not. For example, only one award in ten years had

gone to an individual in my position — and that was a bone to get him to retire. You have to understand that Trademarks has more or less always been an orphan in the framework of the PTO. It's hard for us to get recognition of any sort.

Executive/Administration

Over the last two years, each of the senior executives reporting directly to the Commissioner has received some kind of performance award, as well as a cash bonus of $500. The system worked as follows:

> It was really a seat-of-the-pants sort of thing. Each year you would be called into the Commissioner's Office and would be told that you were doing an outstanding job. After that, a written justification would be put together and submitted for an appropriate award.

Formal performance monitoring systems in this area of the organization were nonexistent. According to one member of the Commissioner's staff,

> I have daily contact with the Commissioner. If I weren't doing a good job, he would certainly let me know in one way or another.

Over the years, the established routine has taken on an air of permanence. As one executive suggested,

> It will be a traumatic thing if I don't get my bonus. It's not the money so much as the status of being personally recognized by the Commissioner. At this point, if I don't get an award, I'll go elsewhere.

Along these lines, an executive outside of the Commissioner's immediate staff added, ". . . the golden boys always get."

Civil Service Reform and the Senior Executive Service

Hoping to "revolutionize" the workings of government at its highest levels and to adopt some of the more effective private sector management practices, the Carter Administration devised the concept of a Senior Executive Service and Congress incorporated it into the Civil Service Reform Act of 1978. Title IV of the Reform Act provides for the establishment of the Senior Executive Service "to ensure that the executive management of the Government of the United States is responsive to the needs, policies, and goals of the Nation and otherwise is of the highest quality." In pursuing this objective, the SES is to be administered so as to "provide for a compensation system, including salaries, benefits, and incentives . . . designed to attract and retain highly competent senior executives" and to "insure compensation, retention and tenure are contingent on executive success which is measured on the basis of individual and organizational performance."

Following from these broad mandates, the Reform Act provides for the development of comprehensive performance appraisal systems at the individual agency level. These systems are to be designed so as to motivate better performance and to serve as the basis for the distribution of various incentive pay awards as specified in the Act. Under the terms of the individual performance appraisal systems, each member of the Senior Executive Service is to negotiate an agreement with his or her superior and is to be objectively evaluated at least yearly on performance against that agreement. These appraisals are to be submitted for review and evaluation to an agency-wide Performance Review Board, composed of senior executives appointed for the purpose of ensuring consistency, stability and objectivity in performance appraisal. The recommendations of the Board are then forwarded to a designated "appointing authority" or the head of the agency or department. Final ratings are assigned by the appointing authority and may be based on one or more levels of fully successful performance, minimally satisfactory performance, and unsatisfactory performance. Any senior executive receiving a less than fully suc-

cessful performance rating is subject to removal from the SES as specified under conditions outlined in the Act. At the same time, any executive receiving a fully successful rating is eligible for incentive pay or bonus awards according to the criteria and procedures the agency develops. The agency appointing authority is responsible for the final distribution of such awards.

Finally, the Reform Act mandated that all agencies had to have operating SES performance appraisal systems for fiscal year 1980. The Office of Personnel Management was assigned responsibility for promulgating regulations and did so simultaneous to the implementation of the SES program in the Departments.

The Department of Business and Industry Model

Responsibility for implementing the SES within the Department of Business and Industry fell to the Assistant Secretary for Administration. A Task Force composed of senior executives from throughout the Department was formed to develop a "model" performance appraisal system that could provide the basic structure and requirements for developing individual operating unit systems.

After a series of meetings and considerable discussion, the Task Force made its recommendations. Following in the spirit of the law, operating units were largely left free to design systems to meet their individual needs. Every senior executive would be rated on the basis of a "collaboratively" developed performance agreement written prior to the beginning of the appraisal cycle (see Exhibit 9-4). The agreement would detail both the organizational and the individual "critical" elements on which the executive's performance would be rated, as well as indicate standards for each of those elements.

Under the DBI model, there could be one or more Performance Review Boards (PRBS) in each operating unit of the Department. There would also be a PRB at the departmental level which would be principally responsible for senior executives within the Secretary's Office. Each PRB would have to develop a written charter, approved by the Department, documenting required functions, delegated optional functions, appraisal review criteria, operating procedures, and membership requirements. Required functions paralleled those in the CSRA, that is, to review appraisals and make recommendations to the appointing authority. Optional functions included undertaking pre-appraisal audits of performance plans and assisting in the settlement of performance plan disputes. The PRBs had to consist of at least three members, one of whom had to be from outside of the agency.

The DBI Task Force initially recommended that the Secretary's office be allowed to retain 15 percent of the bonus funds allocated to the Department for purposes of recognizing those operating units and departmental offices achieving secretarial program and managerial objectives. This 15 percent set-aside was later increased to 25 percent by an executive level policy group within the Secretary's office. In addition, the same policy group subsequently elected to reduce the maximum number of bonuses to be awarded in each operating unit from the 50 percent allowed by law to 33⅓ percent. The remaining "slots" would be allocated in a manner similar to the Secretary's discretionary money. Six months into the process, specific criteria for distributing the Secretary's bonus cash allocation or slots had not been established.

The Patent and Trademark Office Plan

Hoping to minimize any disruption caused by the introduction of a new performance appraisal system, the PTO plan was designed so as to superimpose the SES requirements onto those systems that were already functioning within the agency. While requiring the negotiation of performance agreements, the PTO plan allows each area of the organization to proceed with the development of goals and objectives as well as performance standards according to whatever methodology is deemed appropriate or happens already to be in place. No effort has been made to set agency-wide standards or to impose a system for evaluating performance agreements before they go into effect. Hierarchies of review are to remain intact so that executives continue to receive initial ratings from the immediate supervisors who evaluated them in the past. Final ratings, however, are made by the appointing authority acting on recommendations made by both the immediate supervisor and the Performance Review Board. Bonuses and incentive pay awards are to be allocated in line with the final ratings and are to be limited by the number of slots and amount of money made available by the Department of Business and Industry.

The PTO plan was coauthored by two of the agency's senior executives. In describing how the system will operate, one of those responsible for its design suggests,

> Several features stand out as somewhat unique to our system. First is a bonus point scheme designed to rank senior executives achieving one of the five levels of fully successful performance. Supervisors will have to make recommendations for bonus points which hopefully will serve to differentiate between executives receiving fully successful ratings. In case more than 33⅓ percent of the senior executives receive ratings that would make them eligible for bonuses, the points will be used to rank the executives and to provide a cut-off line for the distribution of awards.

Continuing his description, he adds,

> Another unique element of the PTO system is a provision for the publication of reports advising the senior executives of who got how many bonus points and what awards. Basically, we wanted those individuals making decisions about our bonuses to know that we're all watching to make sure that there's no manipulation of the system. In addition, to avoid conflicts within the agency, we ar-

ranged for the executives reporting to the Commissioner to use the Department of Business and Industry PRB for their performance appraisal review. Following this procedure, the Assistant Secretary of Business and Industry for Productivity, Technology and Innovation will act as the appointing authority for these same people. Finally, in order to prevent unnecessary intrusions into a supervisor's right to set goals and standards for his employees, we stipulated that the PRBs would only "review" performance agreements at the end of the year and submit recommendations to the appointing authorities who will assign final ratings and award bonus points.

Taken altogether, the principal features of the PTO system may be summarized as follows:

• Supervisors will be primarily responsible for designating the elements and standards to be used in evaluating performance. Disputes between the supervisor and the senior executive relating to elements contained in the performance agreement will be resolved by the supervisor.

• Ratings will be based on seven levels of performance, five of which will be fully successful. (See Exhibit 9-5 for details.)

• For purposes of resolving disputes relating to individual performance ratings, the Commissioner shall designate three persons to act as higher level reviewers, none of whom may serve in this capacity for any employees under their supervision. Higher level reviewers may make recommendations to the Performance Review Board, but they may not change ratings or bonus point allocations.

• The Performance Review Board will receive initial ratings as well as the elements and standards used to conduct ratings. The PRB in turn shall forward the same materials along with the higher level review, if any, and the PRB's proposed rating and bonus point allocation to the appointing authority. The PRB will conduct no pre-appraisal audits of the performance agreements.

• Each career SES member rated at any fully successful level is eligible for the following bonus points to be initially recommended in conjunction with a performance rating by the employee's supervisor:

Fully successful level 1:	none
Fully successful level 2:	1-5
Fully successful level 3:	6-10
Fully successful level 4:	11-15
Fully successful level 5:	16-20

• If more than $33\frac{1}{3}$ percent of the senior executives receive bonus points, all Assistant Commissioners and officials who have career employees with six or more points will decide whether or not to provide increases in SES level or salary rather than a bonus for some employees. If the proportion of people with more than six points still remains over $33\frac{1}{3}$ percent, a cutoff line for awards will be drawn at that point.

• All executives reporting directly to the Commissioner will have their ratings reviewed by the Department of Business and Industry PRB. The Assistant Secretary for Productivity, Technology and Innovation will act as the appointing authority for this group. The remaining senior executives will use the PTO Performance Review Board and will have the Commissioner of Patents and Trademarks act as their appointing authority.

• At a minimum, all senior executives must receive a listing of:

1. All career members receiving bonus points and the number earned per member;

2. All SES members receiving an increase in ES pay and the number of steps earned;

3. All SES members receiving bonus or incentive awards and how much;

4. The bonus point cut-off.

On September 14, 1979, a two-hour training program highlighting the provisions of the Civil Service Reform Act and the new performance appraisal system was presented to all of the PTO senior executives. Having participated on the DBI Task Force and acting as one of the coauthors of the PTO plan, Harley Borman made his presentation. He carefully explained the bonus point system, suggested the differences between the two PRBs and appointing authorities, and enumerated the reports that would be provided to senior executives. At the conclusion of the session, Borman and his staff reminded the executives that their performance agreements would be due in the Personnel Office at the close of business Friday, September 28.

Exhibit 9-1. Patent and Trademark Office

Commissioner of Patents and Trademarks Deputy Commissioner

Office of Equal Employment Programs

Board of Appeals

Office of Information Service

Board of Patent Interferences

Office of Legislation and International Affairs

Assistant Commissioner for Patents Deputy Asst. Commissioner

- Patent Examination Deputy Asst. Commissioner
- Office of Patent Program Control
- Examining Groups
- Patent Documentation Admr. for Documentation
- Office of Documentation Planning Support and Control
- Office of International Patent Classification
- Office of Micrographic Systems
- Office of Search Systems
- Office of Technology Assessment & Forecast
- Scientific Library

Assistant Commissioner for Trademarks

- Office of Trademark Program Control
- Trademark Trial and Appeal Board
- Trademark Examining Operation

General Counsel Deputy GC

- Office of the GC
- Office of Government Employee Inventions

Assistant Commissioner for Administration Deputy Asst. Commissioner

- Office of Automated Data Processing Administration
- Office of Finance
- Office of General Services
- Office of Management and Organization
- Office of Patent and Trademark Services
- Office of Personnel
- Office of Planning, Budget and Evaluation
- Office of Publications

Exhibit 9-2. The patent process

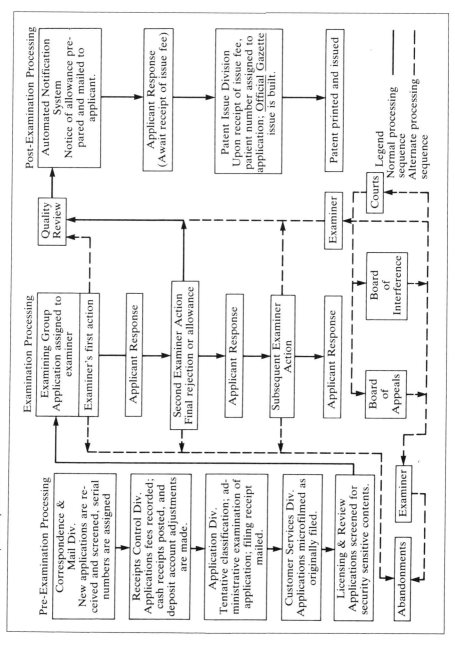

219

Exhibit 9-3. The trademark process

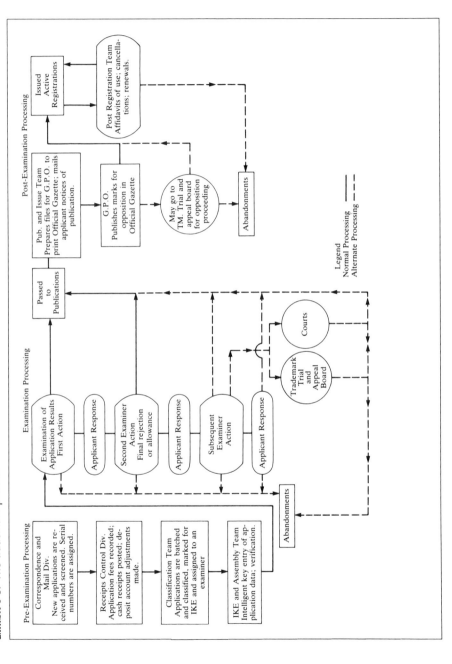

Exhibit 9-4. PTO performance appraisal process

APPRAISAL PERIOD
10/1 - 9/30

	Supervisor and Senior Executive	Higher Level Reviewer	Performance Review Board	Appointing Authority
September	Collaboratively develop performance plan.		Reviews performance plans (optional).	
October	Performance plan becomes effective (October 1).			
November ↓ February	Informal feedback, communication on plan accomplishments occurs.			
March 15 ↓ April 15	Formal progress review must occur (career development needs must be discussed).			
May ↓ August	Informal feedback, communication on plan accomplishments occurs.			
September	Hold preappraisal meeting. Collaboratively develop performance plan (next year's).		Reviews next year's performance plans (optional).	
October	Hold formal appraisal meeting. Performance plan becomes effective (October 1).	Reviews initial rating (when requested) and forwards comments and recommendations to PRB.		
November			Reviews appraisals and initial ratings; forwards recommendations to appointing auth.	
December				Considers PRB recommendations; assigns final ratings; takes other actions (bonus, pay, etc.).

Exhibit 9-5. Senior executive service levels of performance

All performance ratings are to be based on the following levels:

(A) *Unsatisfactory:* Unsatisfactory performance in any critical performance element

(B) *Minimally Satisfactory:*
   1. Less than fully satisfactory in any critical performance element, or
   2. Less than fully satisfactory in a majority of non-critical elements

(C) *Fully Successful:*
   1. Level 1: Fully satisfactory in all critical elements and a majority of non-critical elements
   2. Level 2:
      a. Outstanding performance in any critical elements and fully satisfactory performance in all remaining elements, or
      b. Fully satisfactory performance in all critical elements and outstanding performance in a majority of all remaining elements
   3. Level 3:
      a. Outstanding performance in a majority of critical elements and fully satisfactory performance in the remaining elements, or
      b. Outstanding performance in a majority of all elements and fully satisfactory performance in the remaining elements
   4. Level 4:
      a. Outstanding performance in all critical elements and fully satisfactory performance in the remaining elements, or
      b. Outstanding performance in a majority of critical elements and 90 percent of the non-critical performance elements, and fully satisfactory performance in the remaining elements
   5. Level 5: Outstanding performance in all performance elements

CHAPTER 10

Executive Development: Management as a Resource

One purpose of performance evaluation is to identify those with potential for top management. Moreover, one major goal of civil service reform has been to improve the quality of management. The use of performance evaluation and pay-for-performance in most recent reform efforts reflects this goal. When used appropriately, performance evaluation is intended as much to aid management in carrying out its supervisory function as it is to evaluate or motivate employees.

Some observers and participants have feared that the widespread use of performance evaluations at managerial levels would give undue control to politically appointed managers. Arguments based on this fear usually miss the point and ignore the facts.[1] The outcome depends on the design of the system, the culture, and the persons involved. There is little doubt that some aspect of evaluations will be subjective as long as humans are participating in governmental activities. Despite the fears of some, subjectivity has not prevented all organizations from usefully engaging in some type of evaluation system. Many private organizations and some public agencies — for example, the U.S. Forest Service, the Internal Revenue Service, the State of Minnesota, and several state revenue agencies — are known for their attention to executive selection and development.

The selection and promotion of managers is an area in which need for assessment and evaluation of performance and potential seems inevitable. Among other things, the following case on the General Electric Company's Executive Manpower Operation illustrates the use of a variety of evaluation tools — some not unlike performance appraisals — that are used to identify, develop, and place managers.

For a variety of historical, institutional, and political reasons, in public agencies management development and training has generally taken a back seat. Yet, since good leadership is essential to directing the efforts of government organizations, the development and effective placement of managerial talent is a function or a "tool" that can be used to improve the performance of a public organization.

---

[1] For an example of one such argument, see Fred C. Thayer, "Civil Service Reform and Performance Appraisal: A Policy Disaster," *Public Personnel Management Journal*, Vol. 10, No. 1, pp. 20–28.

Many organizations make little attempt to elevate management quality. They place little or no value on management quality, refuse to allocate the necessary resources, or shrink from making the judgments about who has the qualities to be a good manager. While many organizations seek to identify managerial talent informally, larger, more diverse organizations (or those for which equity or fairness concerns have special salience) often have more elaborate ways to identify and acknowledge executive potential.

Because private organizations have more experience with management development, I have selected a case about one noted for its success. The General Electric Company is highly regarded among the firms that have made a veritable ministry of executive development. It is known for development of management practices as well as managers, so we have also the chance to view their techniques as well as evaluate their results. While there are public agencies and jurisdictions that have emphasized and been successful at management development, this is the most useful case I have come across on the subject. In addition to being a detailed treatment of the practices and underlying philosophy of GE's brand of executive development, it permits a fairly ready comparison of GE's objectives and techniques to the kinds of public sector situations with which we are more familiar. Unlike most of the other cases in this book this case doesn't require a decision. Rather, comparison of GE's objectives and techniques to those of more familiar settings is intended to highlight the possibilities and impediments in viewing and developing managerial talent as a resource in public agencies. If people in public agencies are to be better managed, then managers must be up to the task. Since that is unlikely to happen at random, a look at purposeful techniques to strengthen the abilities of managers may be a step toward better management of public agencies.

STUDY QUESTIONS

1. General Electric has a reputation as a major developer of top managerial talent. Why is this so? From what you see in this case, is the reputation deserved?

2. How important is it in public agencies that managerial talent be identified and moved to positions of responsibility? Why or why is it not important?

3. Does the Executive Manpower Operation appear to be effective? What features of the system most account for the results you perceive?

4. How are General Electric's techniques in management development like those of public agencies with which you are familiar? How are they different?

5. Which, if any, of General Electric's managerial development techniques can be exported to public organizations?

6. If you were a commissioner or other department head, would you take any steps in the direction of management development? If so, would you do it department-wide? by division? or throughout the jurisdiction? Explain your choice.

RECOMMENDED READING

Herbert H. Meyer, Emanuel Kay, and John R. P. French, Jr., ''Split Roles in Performance Appraisal,'' *Harvard Business Review,* January-February, 1965, to get a flavor of General Electric's efforts in evaluation of employees.

Stephen J. Carrol, Jr. and Craig E. Schneir, *Performance Appraisal and Review Systems* (Glenview, Ill.: Scott, Foresman, 1982), Chapter 8, ''The Analysis of Potential,'' pp. 190–216.

General Electric Company: The Executive Manpower Operation — David Orselet

No action — such as interviewing a potential candidate, requesting such an interview, or "informally" discussing an opening with a potential candidate — may be taken prior to obtaining written approval of the candidate slate.

— GE Corporate Policy

The General Electric Company had established a Corporate Executive Manpower Staff in 1967 and charged it with the primary responsibility of ensuring the development and timely availability of broadly experienced, competent, and proven general managers for the Company's top positions, including that of CEO. With its charter formally based in corporate policy and informally based in corporate culture, the Staff reported directly to the Corporate Executive Office and consisted of three complementary Operations believed to be intimately connected: Executive Manpower, Organization Planning, and Executive Compensation.

A major responsibility of the Executive Manpower Operation was the preparation of candidate slates from which an executive was constrained to choose in making appointments to positions at the Department echelon and above. Slate development was an interactive process. It was supported by an elaborate annual manpower review and by a corporate management inventory; and it drew upon both the experience of line managers and the extensive, in-depth knowledge of the Executive Manpower Consultants (EMC).

David Orselet was one of five EMCs in 1979. Forty-nine and with 23 years of experience in GE's Relations function, Orselet was assigned to Sector Executive Jack Welch and the Consumer Products and Services Sector. As Welch said, "Successful management is having good people in key places where they can make things happen." * Orselet, with professional skills and a corporate-wide perspective, was deeply involved both in helping those "good people" to develop and in matching those "good people" with "key places." By all accounts, he brought a very high level of ability and interest to what was universally acknowledged to be a demanding and highly sensitive role.

General Electric Company

With 1978 sales of $20.1 billion, net earnings of $1.2 billion, and assets of $15 billion, General Electric was a major U.S. corporation. Headquartered in Fairfield, Connecticut, the Company's operations spanned the world. Products ranged from miniature light bulbs to huge turbine-generators, from household appliances to commercial jet engines. World-wide, employees totaled 401,000; domestically, they numbered 284,000, of whom the top 2 percent were the direct focus of the Executive Manpower Operation.

General Electric was highly decentralized, with 229 discrete units carrying P & L respon-

This case was prepared by David D. Rikert, under the supervision of Wickham Skinner, with the cooperation of General Electric and Executive Manpower Consultant David Orselet as a basis for class discussion rather than to illustrate either effective or ineffective handling of an administrative situation.

*See Harvard Business School Case #2-179-070 for a description of the Consumer Products and Services Sector and interviews with David Orselet and Jack Welch (from which this quote was drawn).

sibility. In the words of Ralph Cordiner, CEO in the fifties who had been the architect of the structure and articulator of the philosophy for which it stood:*

> In General Electric, decentralization is a way of preserving and enhancing the contributions of the large enterprise, and at the same time achieving the flexibility and the "human touch" that are popularly associated with — though not always attained by — small organizations.
>
> Under this concept, we have undertaken decentralization not only according to products, geography, and functional types of work. The most important aspect of the Company's philosophy is thorough decentralization of the responsibility and authority for making business decisions.

Structurally, GE's operating facilities such as plants were grouped by product or market into departments. Depending upon size, departments might be brought together into a division, and divisions might be combined into a group. For example, reporting to Sector Executive Welch were the general managers of the Lighting Business Group, the Air Conditioning Business Division, and the Television Business Department. The designation "business" in a component title indicated that it was a Strategic Business Unit (SBU), the "basic business entity" of GE within which strategic plans for a given market or market segment were developed and implemented. GE had designated 49 SBUS.

The philosophy of decentralization developed by Cordiner sought to place decision making authority as close to the point of action as feasible and to establish the concept of real delegation of both authority and responsibility. "A result," one executive noted, "is that we give people general management experience fairly low in the organization. And that underscores our

*New Frontiers for Professional Managers, Ralph J. Cordiner, McKinsey Foundation Lecture Series, p. 47.

need to identify those individuals who have real general management ability and help them to develop it."

A General Electric organization chart and summary financial and employee data are presented as Exhibits 10-1 and 10-2, respectively.

An Overview of the Relations Function in General Electric

The personnel function in GE was broadly known as Employee Relations (ER), or simply, Relations. Specific procedures and reporting relationships varied among the operating units, depending upon factors such as the style of the top executive, the culture of the unit, and the relative importance of hourly and professional people to the unit. For illustrative purposes, the Relations function within the Lighting Business Group and the Consumer Products and Services Sector is described in this case (see Exhibit 10-3).

At the plant (or section) level, a plant employee relations manager reported directly to the plant manager and, in a dotted-line fashion, to the department ER manager. Primarily an implementer, rather than conceiver, of Relations practices, the plant ER manager was responsible for all Relations activities in the plant community — "a crackerjack job, super for an individual's development," according to one Relations executive. As the operating unit became larger (department, division, group), this pattern of an ER manager reporting directly to a line manager, with a dotted-line relationship to a higher level Relations functional manager, continued. At the Group level, Jack Hamilton, ER Manager for the Lighting Business Group, said:

> In essence, I am the Vice President of Employee Relations for an independent company. The Corporate Relations Office develops basic guidelines — for example, policies on wage management plans, the standardized company exempt compensation

and benefit plans, basic parameters for union negotiations — but within these, I have a great deal of latitude. For example, we have developed a group incentive pay plan in one of our plants. We believe it is right for us and have fit it within the guidelines. We also have done a number of things on our own with training programs at all levels.

Within Hamilton's staff, there were two distinct groups. One, Employee Relations, was largely concerned with non-exempt and hourly employees (85 percent of the Group's 23,000 employees). Union relations, for example, were the responsibility of this group. The second, Organization & Manpower (O & M), focused on managerial and professional employees. Peter Mercer, Lighting O & M manager, explained:

O & M is growing in stature now. Ten years ago, the "best and brightest" went to union relations; now we have a better balance. Part of this arises because Jack Welch has used David Orselet a great deal and encourages his managers to use their O & M people. And those managers are finding us a very useful tool. For example, they are finding that salary decisions really can help discriminate among different levels of performance, that the candidate slate process does produce better appointments. We are increasingly assuming a counseling/advising role to the Group and Division executives, too. In all of this, the first interactions and appointments were critical, and our continuing role is very delicate. We have to be professional or we just won't have the credibility we need.

Mercer was responsible for candidate slate preparation for section level managers and was in frequent contact with Orselet and the relevant functional consultant on the Executive Manpower staff.* He was deeply involved in the

managerial manpower review process, and, as "human resource" issues increasingly became incorporated into the Group's strategic planning, was involved in them.† Four managers reported to Mercer; one assigned to each of the two major divisions within the Group (and responsible for "managerial staffing, manpower planning, organization planning and development, career counseling, and management consulting"), one assigned to professional relations, and one to exempt compensation.

When the sector organization level had been established in late 1977, it had been decided that the Sector Executive's direct-report staff should not include a Relations position. While an executive manpower consultant had been assigned to each Sector, the consultant continued to report to the Executive Manpower Staff to ensure the independence from the line and contact among the consultants upon which the truly corporate-wide perspective on executive talent was based. This decision was grounded in the belief that the overall relations function was best managed at the SBU level (group level and below with overall guidance from the Corporate Employee Relations Office). In addition, it was believed that there would not be sufficiently challenging work for such a sector level position, especially with the availability of the executive manpower consultant to act as a conduit for information among corporate, sector, and group levels. Orselet noted:

This leads to a grey area. Being accessible and visible, relations questions, as well as a wide variety of complaints received by the sector and executive officers, are frequently referred to me. I will usually try to find out what is going on, and then solicit

---

*The slate process was not mandated by corporate policy below the Department echelon. However, Executive Manpower Staff has the capability to respond if requested by operating management to slate requests for section-level functional positions.

†For example, with domestic unit sales of the Group forecast to be relatively flat, Mercer noted that two manpower issues had been explicitly raised: How can productivity be raised in an environment in which there is not a growing amount of unit volume? How can the sense of career opportunity for managers be kept alive?

advice from our relations experts or hand the matter over to them to handle. Of course, I have grown up with many of the executives in relations, and we have a good feel for the sensitivities involved in any given situation.

The Executive Manpower Staff

By the sixties, GE had developed a very strong Industrial Relations department under the leadership of Lem Boulware and Virg Day, "a real competitive advantage," one executive noted. At that time, Jack Parker, head of the Aerospace & Defense Group (which employed perhaps 50 percent of the engineering and other professional people in GE), hired a "talent scout" to work within the Group to identify promising managers. As Parker's program developed, CEO Fred Borch urged the other groups to look at it. As one executive said, "Borch was dissatisfied with management succession within GE. He felt general manager appointments were being made too much on a 'knowledge of the hiring manager' basis, and that GE would be stronger if this critical pool of executives were developed and utilized across the whole corporation." By 1967, the Corporate Executive Manpower Staff had been established. It reported directly to the Chairman.

Over the years, three primary activities have been consolidated under the Staff: the Executive Manpower Operation, responsible for managing the Company's upper level manpower system; the Organization Planning Operation, responsible for studying and recommending changes in the Company organization structure; and the Executive Compensation Operation, responsible for executive pay and benefit guidelines and plans. Ted LeVino, Vice President — Executive Manpower, explained that these three shared two characteristics that necessitated their independent-from-the-line and administered-by-one-staff status:

These are sensitive areas, requiring a high level of confidentiality, and an executive

MUST have a high degree of trust in the staff working with him. We believe that this organization can provide that professionalism. A second, and major, reason is that we often utilize organization structure and compensation in creative packages to provide developmental assignments for promising general managers. Thus these groups have to be in close contact.

Executive Development at GE

At the executive level within GE, training and development were believed to occur more through on-the-job experience than through formal course work. As one executive said, "At that level, an executive needs the more intangible attributes, such as judgment, a strategic sense, and interpersonal competence, that are hard to 'teach.' So we use job assignments to broaden and deepen an executive's experience, and we give him solid feedback on his performance."

Consistent with the decentralized organization and the emphasis upon on-the-job development, a strong "one-over-one" chain of command had developed. One executive explained:

Our managers have a great deal of authority to make decisions. These decisions will be reviewed by a manager's superior (the one-over-one principle), but will seldom be reversed. However, a manager is accountable — responsibility definitely accompanies authority.

Within GE, we have a strong culture, based on pride in the whole company, integrity, and very high standards. This has been established over the years by example, policy, reward, and audit. Managers who aren't comfortable operating within that culture usually end up leaving us. To tie this together, for example, if a manager deals with subordinates in a manner that doesn't fit our culture ("be tough on standards, not on people"), he may get by for a while, but more than likely will get scragged downstream.

GE maintains primarily a promote-from-within policy with 95 percent of the top 600 positions so filled. "We must," LeVino noted, "make GE a good place to work so that people will stay; and we must do all we can to help those people develop — for their own motivation and for competitive Company reasons."

The Executive Manpower Operation

The Executive Manpower Operation, headed by Ray Stumberger, drew its charter directly from corporate policy. This policy, one of only 35, mandated that appointments to Department echelon and higher positions be made from slates of candidates prepared by the Executive Manpower Staff (see Exhibit 10-4 for excerpts from the policy). Stumberger commented: "The hiring manager, of course, is deeply involved and makes the final selection, as he should, but the slate provides an element of formal, corporate control over a process that is key in our growth-occurs-on-the-job program of executive development, and that assures a corporate-wide look for the best person available."

Reporting to Stumberger were six executive manpower consultants (one assigned to each of the five sectors and one to corporate components), three management manpower consultants (assigned to the finance/strategic planning, engineering/manufacturing, and marketing functions), and the manager of the manpower data system. Stumberger noted:

> Working in the Sector yet reporting to Executive Manpower, the executive consultant position is one of the key Relations positions within GE. It is a challenging, high-risk job, demanding extraordinary sensitivity, integrity, and professionalism, as well as the ability to assess people well and to face difficult situations.

In addition to the preparation of candidate slates, the EMC's activities include participation in the annual manpower review, in-depth assessments of executives, assistance with salary planning, and various special projects. Some of this role is mandated, but much develops as the consultant becomes the "trusted sidekick" of the Sector Executive. Thus the actual role of the consultant will vary quite a bit from Sector to Sector, depending on the consultant, the executive, and other factors such as the nature of the business. For example, Consumer Products is growing rapidly so that there is a lot of change in the air, while Power Systems operates on a much longer time frame with less change.

I see about 80 percent of the work of the consultants and, of course, I talk with the Sector Executives. In evaluating a consultant, I ask questions such as: Is he good at assessing people? Has he shown courage in dealing with difficult situations? Were his slates both good and developmental?

The Executive Manpower Consultant — David Orselet

David Orselet had joined GE in 1956 with a college major in industrial relations. He had started in the corporate-wide Relations Training Program, and, over the years, had worked in a variety of relations jobs. In 1970, he had been appointed Manager of Professional Relations for the Switchgear Business Division; in 1972, Organization & Manpower Manager for the Consumer Products Group; and, in 1974, Executive Manpower Consultant.

In describing his job, Orselet said:

> Basically, I provide a professional input into the Sector's executive manpower activities, and work closely with Jack Welch. I spend about 25 percent of my time attending business review meetings, product assessments, manpower reviews, and so forth in order to watch the executives doing their thing in their own environments. I am actively involved with perhaps 50 or 60, and get to know

them well. My background in several of our businesses is helpful here too, since I have known some of them for a number of years and have seen them in a variety of positions. I also keep an eye out for younger people on the way up.

Another 20 percent of my time goes to the candidate slate development process, in which I work closely with Jack, the consultants responsible for the other Sectors, and Ray Stumberger. I spend about 15 percent of my time on salary and organization planning with Jack, and another 15 percent on special projects for him such as surveying the people side of an acquisition or working on some of the problems of a disposition. The remaining 25 percent of my time goes to interviewing and recruiting, both in-house and outside. For example, last year I talked with almost 50 managers from other Sectors or from lower down in Consumer Products who came to me to introduce and sell themselves, to find out how they stacked up or to seek career counseling. And, in another vein, I was up at Harvard talking with MBAs in February.

I'm on the road about 40 percent of the time and my weeks average 60–70 hours. I love the job. It is extremely important work because it is the process through which we develop the individuals who will lead this company in the coming years. It is exciting because I interact with people across the whole organization structure. It is meaningful to me because it gives me an opportunity to influence the direction of a business, through the selection process. I get a good deal of psychic income when both the individual and the business succeed. And I really enjoy the opportunity to talk about so much more than just manpower. For example, I participate freely in the discussion of business strategy or manufacturing problems, and am not just pigeon-holed in personnel.

Several aspects of Orselet's job as Executive Manpower Consultant are described in more detail in the following paragraphs.

Candidate Slates

Orselet was responsible for generating slates for level 19–21 positions and for providing input to higher level slates.* He typically worked on 40–50 slates per year. The process consisted of the following steps:

1. Orselet "spec'd" the job with the executive to whom the position reported to determine the skills and experiences needed at that point in time. It was explicitly recognized that a particular job might require different skills at different times.

2. Orselet gathered a list of possible candidates from his own knowledge of executives, from fellow consultants, from line managers, and from the corporate management inventory.† He noted that the practice of an executive (or an EMC) "keeping a good person in his pocket" was minimized since the EMCs were measured in part on the amount of movement across division/group/sector lines.

3. He pared that list down to the formal slate, usually from two to five people, with no check for their availability. It was at this stage that the business needs of the organization and the development needs of the individual were balanced. This process was interactive, and detailed personal knowledge of

---

*All GE exempt jobs were classified by position level (PL), with PL1 the lowest and PL29 the highest (CEO). PL19 was Department echelon, PL23 Division, PL25 Group, and PL27 Sector.

†Experience, skill, and performance data on "promotable" managers from PL13-14 and from all managers from PL15+ were carried in a corporate management inventory. Included in 1978 were (approximately) 3,450 PL13 and 14s, 2,150 PL15-18s, and 600 PL19+'s. In addition, the executive manpower staff maintained a Finance manpower inventory of all exempt PL10+ managers (5,000), and a Relations manpower inventory of all exempt PL5+ managers (1,400). Orselet noted that the inventory was most useful for PL18 and below managers since, above that level, the consultant knew most all of the executives in the sector personally.

candidates, based on direct observation, discussion, and reference, supplemented the written reviews of the formal record.

4. The slate was presented to the appropriate executives for written approval, as specified in the policy.

5. When the slate had been approved, Orselet tested the availability of the candidates, with the rule of thumb being that an executive was "fair game" after two years in a position (and occasionally after one or one and one-half). If a manager did not want to let a subordinate go, the decision was referred up the chain of command, to the chairman if necessary. One executive noted that availability was seldom a problem and that blocking a subordinate's move, except for very specific reasons, was rarely done.

6. The executive with the position to fill interviewed the candidates and selected one. Orselet was often asked by the executive to interview a candidate at this point, especially one from another Sector that he did not personally know. If the hiring manager found none of the candidates to be acceptable, the slate was refused, and the process began again. Orselet noted that few slates were, in fact, rejected: "The process is really very interactive, within executive manpower and with the line executives, so that problems are identified and resolved earlier in the process. But that option exists."

LeVino estimated that 25 percent of the appointments were made from outside the sector, and noted the importance of this movement to the development of broadly experienced executives. He also estimated that 60 percent of the hiring managers would say that candidate slates helped the selection process. "A conflict can arise," he noted, "if a manager tends to have his mind set on one person, especially when that person is not on the slate. It is in such situations that the judicious use of power all around is needed."

As an example of the impact of the candidate slate process, several executives cited a change within the Lighting Business Group. Historically, it had been a very independent Group within General Electric, with Lighting executives all grown within the Group. In the early seventies, as a position within the Group opened up, slates had been presented with no internal candidates on them. Executives reported initial heavy resistance to the outsiders, but by 1979, with a series of very successful appointments, the resistance had faded and the Group was in the mainstream of management talent flow across the Company.

The Annual Manpower Review Process

In the words of one executive, the annual manpower review, known as Session C, was "the process by which the Company takes a regular, organized look at executive staffing." The review had evolved in the late sixties under the leadership of Cordiner, although it had not been formalized in corporate policy as the candidate slate procedures had. It was explicitly kept separate from the annual performance review, which a manager held with each subordinate, and from the annual salary review.

A five-month process when completed, the review began with the subordinates of a Department echelon manager filling out one side of the *Evaluation and Development Summary* form (Exhibits 10-5 through 10-9), which had sections entitled "career interests," "self-evaluation," and "development actions and plans." The manager then completed the other side (see below),* which had sections entitled "evaluation of performance and qualifications" and

---

*Exhibits 10-5 through 10-9 contain these forms for five different managers.

"development and career recommendations." The manager and subordinate then met face to face to discuss their responses — "an important and distinctively General Electric process," one executive noted.

As the next step, the manager completed the *Individual Career Forecast* form (Exhibit 10-10) in which he/she rated these subordinates on a scale ranging from "high potential — can move to the next higher organization layer with potential to move at least another organization layer later" to "unsatisfactory performance" and estimated when they would be ready for promotion. In addition, the manager completed the *Organization and Staffing Plan* (Exhibit 10-11) in which the three best replacements for each subordinate, and the manager, had to be identified — in essence, a succession plan.

At that point, the manager presented the evaluations, career forecasts, and succession plan to his/her superior in a formal review meeting. Discussion focused on individuals rated "high potential" and "unsatisfactory," upon the succession plan (with at least forty percent of the meeting devoted to it), and upon special concerns such as the identification of able minorities. This process was repeated at each organization layer up to the Chairman. At appropriate levels, o & m managers such as Mercer and EMCs such as Orselet sat in on the review presentations. Orselet explained:

> I take a very active role in these meetings, sometimes as advocate, sometimes as adversary. They are a great opportunity to bring several viewpoints to bear on how an executive is doing, and they can be quite lively.

> Of course, many managers fall somewhere between "high potential" and "unsatisfactory," and many have reached a level of responsibility at which they would like to remain. While this process doesn't focus on these managers, we do very much expect them to actively keep up with their field from year

to year as well as, of course, to do the job well.

Data from the *Evaluations* and *Career Forecasts*, as well as from *Individual Experience* forms, were placed in the corporate management inventory. This file was maintained by the Executive Manpower Staff and utilized by the consultants and by o & m managers to help identify prospective candidates for positions.

The Accomplishment Analysis

This was an in-depth look at the strengths and weaknesses of a manager 10-15 years down a career track (and so in a reasonably stable pattern) along dimensions such as knowledge, strategy, decision making, leadership, and relationships. Orselet gathered data from long interviews with the manager and his/her superiors and from the annual reviews. He discussed his analysis thoroughly with the manager, who could suggest changes. The analysis was used for developmental purposes by the company and the individual. Stumberger noted that, "It is really quite intensive and generates enriched data that goes well beyond an operating manager's annual performance review." An accomplishment analysis was very time-consuming; each consultant was given an ongoing objective of completing six per year.

Perspectives

As Orselet reflected upon his job, he questioned:

> Are we "kingmakers" in executive manpower? While some in the company may occasionally see us this way, I believe that there are sufficient checks and balances to minimize that role, for us or for anyone, really. In any organization, certain values and skills will be rewarded and certain groups or individuals will do the rewarding. At GE, we have

chosen to make this process quite explicit and above-board, with line management and executive manpower both interactively involved.

A key, and difficult, element in this process is talking straight, or negative feedback. And a good deal of this falls in my lap, or in the lap of a Pete Mercer or Jack Hamilton, for line managers often find it hard to do. When someone isn't selected from a slate, or doesn't make a slate, or isn't getting good reviews, we try to let them know the major things that, in other people's as well as our own perspective, are holding them back, and to work with them on identifying ways to improve. If a manager is not meeting his numbers, he knows that and it is easy to address. But it is much more difficult to explain to a manager, who may be meeting his numbers, that he is perceived by the people evaluating him as weak in the softer areas of management, such as style, leadership or interpersonal relations. This feedback is important; and so too are opportunities, such as the movement of individuals into new units to which they will have to adapt, for managers to gain experience in these softer yet essential aspects of successful management.

I think that most criticisms of executive manpower boil down to a feeling that we infringe upon what a manager may have blocked out as his territory, such as a completely free hand in the selection of his own people and building his own organization. A manager he wants to promote, for example, may be a good manager, yet, when compared across the whole Company, he might only be the fifth best for that position. We try to provide that corporate-wide perspective.

Lighting Business Group Executive Ralph Ketchum had worked in Parker's Aerospace Group in the sixties and had been one of the early "outsiders" in the Lighting Group. Having compiled an excellent record there, he had been appointed Group Executive in 1979. He discussed the executive manpower operation from his perspective:

I am excited by the work we are doing to develop executives within GE as a whole and here in Lighting. We're providing great opportunities for promising managers and, as I view the progress here in this Group, doing good things for the Company. I am so excited by the annual manpower review process, for example, that I plan to take it down another layer or two in my organization this coming year, and will personally sit in on all the presentations, about five or six days of my time.

Besides the corporate-wide exposure and movement the candidate slates provide, I think they generate fairer and more objective assessments of managers. I've heard some people question the fact that Orselet is involved: "How does he know me and the work that I'm doing? He's not a line manager," and so forth. But I believe that David does have a good basis for judgment. He actively participates in the Session C meetings, continually observes managers in their own settings, constantly talks with me, for example, about how people are doing; he's a real professional.

The annual manpower review is very effective, but hard, for it forces us to evaluate and make judgments. That is easy with a top-notch subordinate, but harder with someone who isn't doing well, particularly in the face-to-face meeting. One of David's roles is to filter through the protective praise (and unfair criticism) that sometimes results. In a sense, he is a part of a system of checks and balances on executives. He has a key role, with respect and confidentiality critical.

While these processes are implemented corporate-wide now, I think there is still quite a difference in *how* they are used. In one group, for example, their use is still quite perfunctory and I'd guess we are three years ahead of them. I want to keep working the process hard here to get good people — in no way are we yet inundated with good general managers. But I wonder about the future. As I look through our officer ranks now, there are many of us who came through Parker's group and moved on to find new challenges. As we now grow good managers across the company, will we continue to have the positions and challenges for these people?

Exhibit 10-1. Organization chart 6/1/73

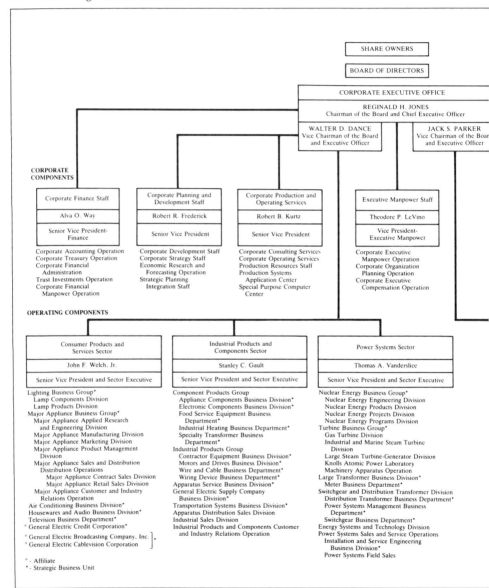

Exhibit 10-1. Continued

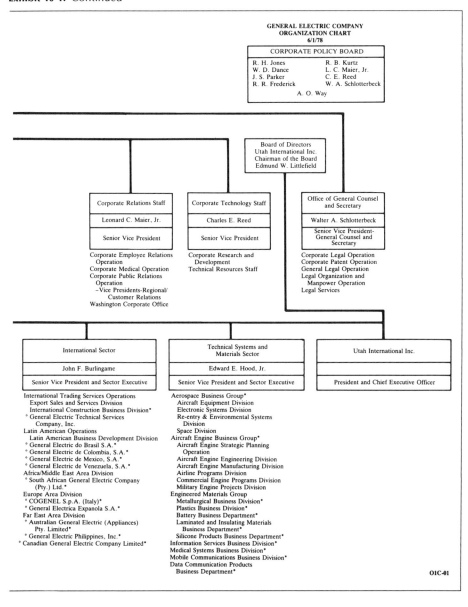

GENERAL ELECTRIC COMPANY
ORGANIZATION CHART
6/1/78

CORPORATE POLICY BOARD

R. H. Jones	R. B. Kurtz
W. D. Dance	L. C. Maier, Jr.
J. S. Parker	C. E. Reed
R. R. Frederick	W. A. Schlotterbeck
	A. O. Way

Board of Directors
Utah International Inc.
Chairman of the Board
Edmund W. Littlefield

Corporate Relations Staff

Leonard C. Maier, Jr.

Senior Vice President

Corporate Employee Relations
Operation
Corporate Medical Operation
Corporate Public Relations
Operation
–Vice Presidents-Regional/
Customer Relations
Washington Corporate Office

Corporate Technology Staff

Charles E. Reed

Senior Vice President

Corporate Research and
Development
Technical Resources Staff

**Office of General Counsel
and Secretary**

Walter A. Schlotterbeck

Senior Vice President-
General Counsel and
Secretary

Corporate Legal Operation
Corporate Patent Operation
General Legal Operation
Legal Organization and
Manpower Operation
Legal Services

International Sector

John F. Burlingame

Senior Vice President and Sector Executive

International Trading Services Operations
  Export Sales and Services Division
  International Construction Business Division*
  ° General Electric Technical Services
    Company, Inc.
Latin American Operations
  Latin American Business Development Division
  ° General Electric do Brasil S.A.*
  ° General Electric de Colombia, S.A.*
  ° General Electric de Mexico, S.A.*
  ° General Electric de Venezuela, S.A.*
Africa/Middle East Area Division
  ° South African General Electric Company
    (Pty.) Ltd.*
Europe Area Division
  ° COGENEL S.p.A. (Italy)*
  ° General Electrica Expanola S.A.*
Far East Area Division
  ° Australian General Electric (Appliances)
    Pty. Limited*
  ° General Electric Philippines, Inc.*
  ° Canadian General Electric Company Limited*

**Technical Systems and
Materials Sector**

Edward E. Hood, Jr.

Senior Vice President and Sector Executive

Aerospace Business Group*
  Aircraft Equipment Division
  Electronic Systems Division
  Re-entry & Environmental Systems
    Division
  Space Division
Aircraft Engine Business Group*
  Aircraft Engine Strategic Planning
    Operation
  Aircraft Engine Engineering Division
  Aircraft Engine Manufacturing Division
  Airline Programs Division
  Commercial Engine Programs Division
  Military Engine Projects Division
Engineered Materials Group
  Metallurgical Business Division*
  Plastics Business Division*
  Battery Business Department*
  Laminated and Insulating Materials
    Business Department*
  Silicone Products Business Department*
Information Services Business Division*
Medical Systems Business Division*
Mobile Communications Business Division*
Data Communication Products
  Business Department*

Utah International Inc.

President and Chief Executive Officer

O1C-01

Exhibit 10-2. Summary financial and employee data

General Electric Company					
	1978	1977	1976	1975	1974
Revenue	$20,073	$17,909	$15,972	$14,279	$14,125
Net earnings	$ 1,230	$ 1,088	$ 931	$ 689	$ 705
Assets	$15,036	$13,697	$12,050	$ 9,764	$ 9,369
Total capital invested	$ 8,692	$ 8,131	$ 7,305	$ 6,628	$ 6,317
World-wide employees	401,000	384,000	380,000	380,000	409,000

Consumer Products & Services Sector (% of Company totals)			
	1978	1977	1976
Revenue	$ 4,788 (23.8%)	$4,148 (23.2%)	$3,453 (21.6%)
Net earnings	$ 300 (24.4%)	$ 256 (23.5%)	$ 204 (21.9%)
Assets	$ 2,019 (13.4%)	$1,792 (13.1%)	$1,644 (13.6%)
Employees	110,849 (27.6%)	99,609 (25.9%)	91,795 (24.2%)

[Dollar figures in millions]

Source: General Electric Annual Reports and Company personnel.

Exhibit 10-3. Overview of relations function

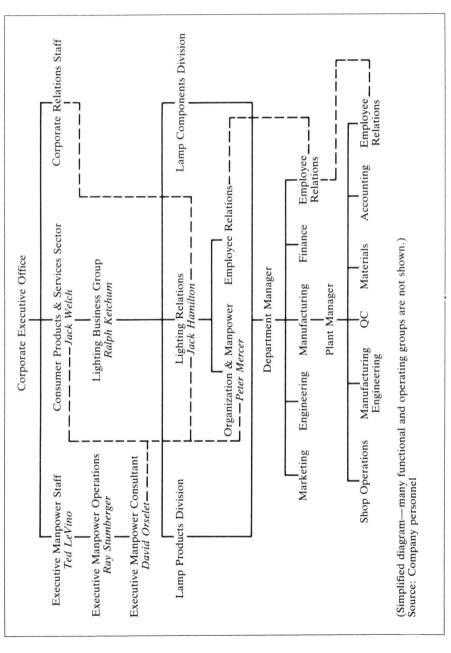

(Simplified diagram—many functional and operating groups are not shown.)
Source: Company personnel

Exhibit 10-4. Excerpt from corporate policy

COMPANY PROCEDURE FOR APPROVAL OF STAFFING CHANGES

A consistent procedure for approving high-level changes in staffing can realize the greatest positive impact from such changes, and also help prevent misunderstandings. To achieve these benefits, the procedures outlined on the next pages are to be followed in presenting and securing approval for staffing changes in positions at the echelons indicated.

Corporate Officers, General Managers and managers authorized to initiate and approve the changes described in the Procedure are responsible for seeing that those individuals in their components who are directly concerned both understand and follow these procedures.

Candidate Slates

Procedures and responsibilities for developing and obtaining approval of candidate slates for Department-echelon and higher positions are shown in Table 2. The necessary requests, recommendations and approvals must be documented. No action — such as interviewing a potential candidate, requesting such an interview, or "informally" discussing an opening with a potential candidate — may be taken prior to obtaining written approval of the candidate slate.

TABLE 2
CANDIDATE SLATES

1. General rule for approval of candidate slates is "one-over-one" (e.g., the echelon above the Manager to whom the position being filled reports). Exceptions to this general rule are:

Position Being Filled	Candidate Slate Approved by
Vice President — Regional Relations; Group Executive	Chairman (after review by CEO)
Division General Manager; intermediate-echelon General Manager reporting to Group Executive	Vice Chairman (after review by CEO)
Department General Manager; intermediate-echelon General Manager reporting to Division General Manager	Vice Chairman
Positions reporting to Senior Vice President in Corporate Staff; or to Officer who reports to the Chairman	Vice Chairman or Chairman (after review by CEO)

2. Department-echelon positions and higher: Executive Manpower Staff recommends/concurs on all candidate slates.

(Exhibit continues on following page.)

Exhibit 10-4. Continued

---

3. Additional concurrence on certain candidate slates is required as follows:

Position	*Additional Required Concurrence*
Manager — Finance	Senior Vice President — Finance
Counsel — Sector/Group/Division	Senior Vice President — General Counsel and Secretary
Manager — Strategic Planning and/or Review	Senior Vice President — Corporate Planning and Development
Manager — Employee Relations (Section level and higher)	Manager — Corporate Employee Relations
Manager — Organization and Manpower (Sector/Group/Division)	Vice President — Executive Manpower

Source: Company document

Exhibit 10-5. Evaluation and development summary: marketing section manager

---

GENERAL ⊛ ELECTRIC

EVALUATION AND DEVELOPMENT SUMMARY
(This side to be completed by employee)

Strictly Private

NAME <u>Marketing Section Manager</u>   SOCIAL SECURITY NO. _____
<small>(last)   (first)   (initial)</small>

I. CAREER INTERESTS (show your specific preferences and alternatives including position title, type business, product or service industry, etc. plus desired timing)

A. NEXT

- Manager of product department
- Manager of new business venture
- Staff position - strategic planning

B. LONGER RANGE

- P&L responsibility of multi-function organization with broad product scope (general management)

II. SELF EVALUATION (describe technical, interpersonal, managerial qualifications, etc. and comment on the areas in which you feel you need further development)

A. STRENGTHS

- Business acumen
- Cross-functional integration ability
- People management - team coordination
- Broad perspective, handling great variety of multi-function activities

- Profit orientation
- Intelligent
- Versatile
- Goal oriented
- Risk-decision making

B. DEVELOPMENT NEEDS

- "Rounding out" in Marketing Manager position
- Continued attention to developing the Marketing interface with related organization of Sales, Product Service and International

III. DEVELOPMENT ACTIONS AND PLANS

A. ACTIONS (taken in last 12-18 months to enhance skills, knowledge, experience, etc.)

- Attended Executive Development Course
- Increased interface with sales and key dealer personnel getting closer to the pulse of the market
- Increased interface with sister organization to broaden perspective to Division level considerations

B. PLANS

- Continue actions in A above
- Offshore trips to broaden total market knowledge and plant interface
- Work closely with other organizations in Division to strengthen strategic positioning and broaden personal contribution
- Increase activities to better understand our ultimate customer--the consumer

SIGNED _____   DATE FORWARDED
                                        TO MANAGER _____

CMMD-3 Rev. 12/70

(Exhibit continues on following page.)

Exhibit 10-5. Continued

EVALUATION AND DEVELOPMENT SUMMARY
(This side to be completed by immediate manager)   *Strictly Private*

IV. EVALUATION OF PERFORMANCE AND QUALIFICATIONS

A. PERFORMANCE (Describe individual's overall performance on present assignment in terms of major objectives. Describe special accomplishments. Indicate performance trend.)

Continues as the strong leader providing Marketing direction to this business. His business breadth utilizing our modified matrix structure enables him to become involved and a contributor in many non-Marketing aspects of our business. He has directed three considerable different businesses very effectively and has been a significant contributor to the great 1978 business results of the Department.

B. QUALIFICATIONS (Describe technical, interpersonal, managerial qualifications, etc.)

1. STRENGTHS

- Strong manager/team leader
- Strong balanced business judgment
- Integrates well with other business functions
- Handles many tasks/large volumes of work well

- Intelligent
- Analytical
- Logical
- Persistent
- Work-a-holic

2. DEVELOPMENT NEEDS

- Should become a "student" of push vs. pull Marketing strategies
- Should continue to maximize his exposure to sales and distribution and key customers.
- Care should be taken not to let his persistent quality come through as "dogmatic"

V. DEVELOPMENT AND CAREER RECOMMENDATIONS

A. DEVELOPMENT RECOMMENDATIONS (Specify development plans for the next 12 months which are responsive to identified needs.)

- Accelerate involvement/exposure to Marketing both for assisting and personal education purposes

- Press BBD&O in the areas of "pull" evaluations/tests/alternatives, etc.

B. NEXT ASSIGNMENT (Consider alternatives)

Position Title	Organization Layer	Timing
General Manager	Product Department	Now
General Manager	Functional Department (Marketing)	Now
Manager, Oper./Strategic Planning	Department	Now

C. CAREER ROUTE AND GOALS (How realistic are the individual's career goals and are they compatible with your views? Make a clear statement with respect to long-range development needs and recommendations for future positions and training.)

A strong, dedicated individual. He is ready now for a General Manager challenge but an added year in his current position would not be time wasted.

Completed by _____ Date _____ Date Discussed with Reviewing Manager _____

CMMD-3 Rev 12/79   Date Discussed with Employee _____

Exhibit 10-6. Evaluation and development summary: multi-functional general manager

---

GENERAL ⊛ ELECTRIC

Strictly Private

EVALUATION AND DEVELOPMENT SUMMARY
(This side to be completed by employee)

NAME Multi-functional General Manager   SOCIAL SECURITY NO. _____
         (last)   (first)   (initial)

I. CAREER INTERESTS (show your specific preferences and alternatives including position title, type business, product or service industry, etc. plus desired timing)

A. NEXT

Division General Manager - Multi-functional business - e.g., ACBD -- 1 year

B. LONGER RANGE

Group Executive

II. SELF EVALUATION (describe technical, interpersonal, managerial qualifications, etc. and comment on the areas in which you feel you need further development)

A. STRENGTHS

Experienced in managing diverse, multi-functional business. Profit oriented. Analytical, conceptual and independent thinker. Able to deal with complex business problems and make difficult decisions. Competent in selection, training and motivation of employees. Effective at goal setting, planning, meeting deadlines and implementation. Able to work with people whether employees, peers, managers or outside the Company.

B. DEVELOPMENT NEEDS

Continuing experience as multi-functional general manager. Exposure to Sector and Corporate issues through task force assignment or similar experience.

III. DEVELOPMENT ACTIONS AND PLANS

A. ACTIONS (taken in last 12-18 months to enhance skills, knowledge, experience, etc.)

Have gained significant experience and new knowledge serving in two multi-functional, general manager assignments. Both businesses were in turn-around situations. Developed long-term strategies while maximizing current period operating results.

B. PLANS

Continue in present assignment leading the final development and initial implementation of a new strategy for my current business.

SIGNED _____   DATE FORWARDED
                                             TO MANAGER _____

CMMD-3 Rev. 12/79

(Exhibit continues on following page.)

Exhibit 10-6. Continued

EVALUATION AND DEVELOPMENT SUMMARY
(This side to be completed by immediate manager)   *Strictly Private*

IV. EVALUATION OF PERFORMANCE AND QUALIFICATIONS

A. PERFORMANCE (Describe individual's overall performance on present assignment in terms of major objectives. Describe special accomplishments. Indicate performance trend.)

Moved into his current position with the specific assignment to develop an overall business strategy focusing especially on product-line fixes. With his team, a new strategy has been developed and outstanding new product concepts have been developed, approved and put into motion. Has developed a "win" spirit not seen in years. Through excellent merchandising plans, share has improved dramatically. Margin, however, has eroded and represents a real challenge.

B. QUALIFICATIONS (Describe technical, interpersonal, managerial qualifications, etc.)

1. STRENGTHS

Decisive, results-oriented	Intelligent, adaptable and resourceful
Strategic thinker	Broad business interests and talent
Well organized	Sets high standards
"Take charge" leader	Can create team spirit and effort

2. DEVELOPMENT NEEDS

Must monitor his personal needs to be sure not in conflict with business needs. Must increase support of Group while being an advocate for his business.

V. DEVELOPMENT AND CAREER RECOMMENDATIONS

A. DEVELOPMENT RECOMMENDATIONS (Specify development plans for the next 12 months which are responsive to identified needs.)

Concentrate on maintaining a "win" team attitude. More participation in Group issues.

B. NEXT ASSIGNMENT (Consider alternatives)

Position Title	Organization Layer	Timing
General Manager	Division	1 year

C. CAREER ROUTE AND GOALS (How realistic are the individual's career goals and are they compatible with your views? Make a clear statement with respect to long-range development needs and recommendations for future positions and training.)

Goal to become a Division Manager is clearly realistic. His longer term goal to become a Group Executive will depend on successfully broadening himself in a Division assignment.

Completed by _____ Date _____ Date Discussed with Reviewing Manager _____

CMMD-3 Rev 12 79   Date Discussed with Employee _____

Exhibit 10-7. Evaluation and development summary: functional general manager

GENERAL ⬤ ELECTRIC

Strictly Private

EVALUATION AND DEVELOPMENT SUMMARY
(This side to be completed by employee)

NAME <u>Functional General Manager</u>   SOCIAL SECURITY NO. _____
(last)   (first)   (initial)

I. CAREER INTERESTS (show your specific preferences and alternatives including position title, type business, product or service industry, etc. plus desired timing)

A. NEXT (1) In current position, contribute effectively as Product Board member and through leadership of the Manufacturing Department to the planning and decisioning required to successfully reach important and challenging productivity and quality improvement goals a new level of profitability in our several product lines, plus identifying the priority issues facing the business and applying broad business thinking and bringing resolution; (2) Move to General Manager position in a larger manufacturing department or expand the scope of the current assignment by adding component plant(s) to this department.
B. LONGER RANGE

Manager--Manufacturing Management and Quality Control Consulting, CCS

II. SELF EVALUATION (describe technical, interpersonal, managerial qualifications, etc. and comment on the areas in which you feel you need further development)

A. STRENGTHS
Ability to conduct objective and constructive evaluations of operations and programs/projects, and generate alternative plans. Ability to recognize and foster development of potential in personnel. Ability to organize and integrate multi-functional effort to achieve complex business objectives. Ability to provide logical and useful counsel on functional, organizational and personnel matters.

B. DEVELOPMENT NEEDS

Assist in Product Board issue identification and resolution by bringing concepts and alternatives into Product Board deliberations which extend well beyond functional perspectives. Support alternatives with sound feasibility determinations.

III. DEVELOPMENT ACTIONS AND PLANS

A. ACTIONS (taken in last 12-18 months to enhance skills, knowledge, experience, etc.)
Updated personal knowledge of state of the art in process technology, CAM and automation in areas where productivity and quality improvement is critical to meeting business objectives. Visits have been made to four European manufacturing plants, two auto manufacturing plants, GE Brockport housewares plant plus CCS and CR&D and Pemco among other actions to accomplish this update. Continued as Chairman of Board of Trustees of 6th class city.

B. PLANS

Continue extension of personal knowledge of new technology and alternate methods and sources that hold potential for significant improvements in product cost, process yield levels, employee productivity, more productive investment expenditures and improvement in prioritization of resource application.

SIGNED _____   DATE FORWARDED
                                                TO MANAGER _____

CMMD-3 Rev. 12/79

(Exhibit continues on following page.)

Exhibit 10-7. Continued

EVALUATION AND DEVELOPMENT SUMMARY
(This side to be completed by immediate manager)   *Strictly Private*

IV. EVALUATION OF PERFORMANCE AND QUALIFICATIONS

A. PERFORMANCE (Describe individual's overall performance on present assignment in terms of major objectives. Describe special accomplishments. Indicate performance trend.)

Performed in a fully satisfactory manner in 1978. He continues to do well in balancing his role as a Board member and functional Department manager. He has picked up on the technology thrust and is actively pushing this area in a number of significant projects. His performance trend continues to be favorable. He has built an excellent manufacturing organization staffed with high caliber people. He can improve his contribution to this business by continuing his work on differentiating his approach to problem analysis. He has a large capacity for detail and on occasion can get overly involved. He needs to also continue to drive himself and his people to aggressively pursue key areas of cost and productivity.

B. QUALIFICATIONS (Describe technical, interpersonal, managerial qualifications, etc.)

1. STRENGTHS

Excellent problem analysis skills, logical thinker, good coach and counselor. Good and interested listener. High level of integrity. Appropriately flexible. Tenacious and thorough. Always considers alternates.

2. DEVELOPMENT NEEDS

Needs to continue to work on differentiating between problems which can be scoped and those requiring detailed analysis so as to better utilize his time. He needs to speed up his decision-making process; needs to pursue critical evaluation of some of the manufacturing related business problems; should work at more aggressive questioning of alternates.

V. DEVELOPMENT AND CAREER RECOMMENDATIONS

A. DEVELOPMENT RECOMMENDATIONS (Specify development plans for the next 12 months which are responsive to identified needs.)

I intend to assign one of the pooled plants to him. Also, any swap of General Managers among business would involve him.

B. NEXT ASSIGNMENT (Consider alternatives)

Position Title	Organization Layer	Timing
Mfg. & Eng. Consulting, CCS	Department	1979

C. CAREER ROUTE AND GOALS (How realistic are the individual's career goals and are they compatible with your views? Make a clear statement with respect to long-range development needs and recommendations for future positions and training.)

Goals are realistic. He can perform quite well on a higher level Manufacturing Department assignment and would be excellent in a role in CCS. I consider him as a viable Purchasing back-up. He would be outstanding in a role in Corporate Production and Operating Services.

Completed by _____ Date _____ Date Discussed with Reviewing Manager _____

CMMD-3 Rev 12/79   Date Discussed with Employee _____

Exhibit 10-8. Evaluation and development summary: manufacturing section manager

---

GENERAL ⊕ ELECTRIC

Strictly Private

EVALUATION AND DEVELOPMENT SUMMARY
(This side to be completed by employee)

NAME <u>Manufacturing Section Manager</u>   SOCIAL SECURITY NO. _____
    (last)   (first)   (initial)

I. CAREER INTERESTS (show your specific preferences and alternatives including position title, type business, product or service industry, etc. plus desired timing)

A. NEXT In the next one to three years, I would like to become a multifunctional Department General Manager. Specific options to achieve this goal that are of interest to me would include:
- Manager of a business section with multifunctional responsibilities
- Manager of manufacturing in a business which is closer to the consumer market place
- Manager of Strategic or Operational Planning
- General Manager of multifunctional department

B. LONGER RANGE
My longer range goal is to progress to higher levels of operating responsibility. For example, a Division General Manager of a business where my strengths in manufacturing management and materials processing would be of value. Alternatives along this career path for strategic planning and other staff assignments would be considered to round out my experience base.

II. SELF EVALUATION (describe technical, interpersonal, managerial qualifications, etc. and comment on the areas in which you feel you need further development)

A. STRENGTHS
I am highly achievement motivated with a healthy disrespect for the status quo. I'm a strong believer in and user of goals and measurement systems to insure optimum use of resources. I have an extensive background in materials and materials processing with a good understanding of business finance and strategy. I have good oral and written communication skills. I enjoy working with people and helping them reach their full
B. DEVELOPMENT NEEDS potential as employees.

In order to reach my career objectives, I need to develop a better understanding of market/customer/business interfaces and to become more familiar with marketing strategies and concepts. I need more non-GE customer contact and exposure. I also need to continue to gain experience with multifunctional business and operational planning activities.

III. DEVELOPMENT ACTIONS AND PLANS

A. ACTIONS (taken in last 12-18 months to enhance skills, knowledge, experience, etc.)

- Attended Business Management Course, Crotonville, February 1978
- Led Explorer Scout Sales Team
- Attended Product/Market Strategy Development Seminar

B. PLANS

- Attend Advanced Marketing Manpower Seminar during 1979
- Continue to demonstrate performance in my current job while gaining more customer exposure
- Seek job opportunities which would provide more market/customer exposure

SIGNED _____   DATE FORWARDED
                                     TO MANAGER   _____

CMMD-3 Rev. 12/79

(Exhibit continues on following page.)

Exhibit 10-8. Continued

EVALUATION AND DEVELOPMENT SUMMARY
(This side to be completed by immediate manager)   *Strictly Private*

IV. EVALUATION OF PERFORMANCE AND QUALIFICATIONS

A. PERFORMANCE (Describe individual's overall performance on present assignment in terms of major objectives. Describe special accomplishments. Indicate performance trend.)

Improved % plant margin by 2.1% over 1977. Exceeded P&E budget by 4.8%, Versus sales increase of 20.2% (3% price), reduced exempt employment by 3.8% and non-exempt by 7.6% versus 1977. In spite of extensive overtime, held absenteeism to 2.4%. Overall accident rate dropped to 5.4 from 5.8. Maintained excellent quality record with customer returns under 0.8% of sales. Supported Syn-Cronamics cost reduction study with target of $860K savings. Savings verified and Chemical Products to be accomplished in 1979. Overall, achieved a tighter control of operations and improved rate of accomplishment over 1977.

B. QUALIFICATIONS (Describe technical, interpersonal, managerial qualifications, etc.)

1. STRENGTHS

Detail planning, technical comprehension, interpersonal relationships, communication, team player, responsive, paternalistic.

2. DEVELOPMENT NEEDS
Greater knowledge of total business and planning for given financial result. Customer exposure. Harder line with subordinates over failures/non-responsiveness. Challenge by numerically larger organization where scope of work requires greater delegation. Challenge by an assignment outside of manufacturing.

V. DEVELOPMENT AND CAREER RECOMMENDATIONS

A. DEVELOPMENT RECOMMENDATIONS (Specify development plans for the next 12 months which are responsive to identified needs.)

Attend AMMS. Involve in customer relations. Involve more in total department financial planning. Assign leadership in total business planning. Actively pursue a promotional assignment to address development needs identified above.

B. NEXT ASSIGNMENT (Consider alternatives)

Position Title.	Organization Layer	Timing
Business Section or Venture Mgr.	Section	Now
Manufacturing Mgr. (large dept.)	Section	Now
Strategic Planner	Division	Now

C. CAREER ROUTE AND GOALS (How realistic are the individual's career goals and are they compatible with your views? Make a clear statement with respect to long-range development needs and recommendations for future positions and training.)
Expectation of Dept. General Manager is probably realistic and a Manufacturing General Manager would be most readily achieved. To achieve this, an assignment such as a strategic planner or a venture manager would be helpful. A longer term division manager goal is contingent mostly on getting a department manager position and demonstrating really superior performance and achievements.

Completed by _____ Date _____ Date Discussed with Reviewing Manager _____

CMMQr-3-Rev.2(79/.   Date Discussed with Employee _____

Exhibit 10-9. Evaluation and development summary: staff section manager

---

GENERAL ⚙ ELECTRIC

EVALUATION AND DEVELOPMENT SUMMARY
(This side to be completed by employee)

Strictly Private

NAME <u>Staff Section Manager</u>   **SOCIAL SECURITY NO.** _____
        (last)   (first)   (initial)

I. CAREER INTERESTS (show your specific preferences and alternatives including position title, type business, product or service industry, etc. plus desired timing)

A. NEXT

By mid-1980, general manager of a small, off-shore affiliate operation to demonstrate business and people management skills, to leverage successful prior experience in foreign environments and cultures and to parlay prior training and preparation for operating in the international business arena.

B. LONGER RANGE

Line general management in domestic and international organizations of increasing size, scope and complexity in GEs consumer, durable-goods based businesses. At least one significant corporate staff assignment in the area of strategic planning probably around sixth or seventh year of service. Goal: Division-level executive in 10 years.

II. SELF EVALUATION (describe technical, interpersonal, managerial qualifications, etc. and comment on the areas in which you feel you need further development)

A. STRENGTHS
- Record of successful management of human and financial resources toward agreed-upon goals and objectives; a highly motivated team player
- Strong interpersonal skills; ability to build confidence and to get commitment from others
- Sound judgment; fact-based/analytical orientation; broad business perspective
- Strong oral and written communication skills

B. DEVELOPMENT NEEDS
Greater tolerance of individual differences in skill, motivation and ability to deliver results; must learn to work with the best each has to offer rather than always gravitating to the "super stars" who will deliver. Become less matter-of-fact/rigid when others don't see things my way. Could be more flexible without fear of compromising desired results. Learn to say "no" rather than overcommit (but difficult with high-task completion needs).

III. DEVELOPMENT ACTIONS AND PLANS

A. ACTIONS (taken in last 12-18 months to enhance skills, knowledge, experience, etc.)
- Engagement Management Training Program. One-week workshop in Switzerland (5/77) to reinforce approaches to managing people and ideas.
- Video Communications Workshop. Three-day workshop in NYC (10/77) to fine-tune oral presentation skills.
- Business Development (10/78) and Strategic Planning (11/78) Workshops to enhance overall effectiveness in current planning position

B. PLANS
- Through Strategic Planning/LRF cycle, develop deeper understanding of this business, its opportunities, vulnerabilities and economics to validate hypothesis of where I can make greatest personal and professional contribution to the short term
- Attend BMC - 9/79

SIGNED _____

DATE FORWARDED
TO MANAGER _____ _____

CMMD-3 Rev 12/79

(Exhibit continues on following page.)

Exhibit 10-9. Continued

EVALUATION AND DEVELOPMENT SUMMARY
(This side to be completed by immediate manager)   *Strictly Private*

IV. EVALUATION OF PERFORMANCE AND QUALIFICATIONS

A. PERFORMANCE (Describe individual's overall performance on present assignment in terms of major objectives Describe special accomplishments. Indicate performance trend.)

He has done an outstanding job in raising the level of planning for the Division. He has dramatically improved the level of strategic thinking in all of the Division's depart-ments. In addition, he has contributed to the strategic planning effort of the Group by providing analyses of competitors and their strategic thrust as well as those Division portions of the Group strategic plan. The unsolicited demand for his services by the Division Departments is growing daily to the point where in just six months on the job significant priority setting is required. He is off to an excellent start in the General Electric Company.

B. QUALIFICATIONS (Describe technical, interpersonal, managerial qualifications, etc.)

1. STRENGTHS

Good analyst. Goal-oriented. Good with people. Good communicator.

2. DEVELOPMENT NEEDS

Needs to establish a General Electric track record by obtaining an opportunity to manage a GE line organization of some type. A product section or a foreign affiliate might fill this bill.

V. DEVELOPMENT AND CAREER RECOMMENDATIONS

A. DEVELOPMENT RECOMMENDATIONS (Specify development plans for the next 12 months which are responsive to identified needs.)

Enroll in appropriate Company courses to get broader experience and exposure in the Company, e.g., he is attending BMC in 1979. Try to find Group and/or Company task force or study assignments which would accomplish a similar end.

B. NEXT ASSIGNMENT (Consider alternatives)

Position Title	Organization Layer	Timing
Manager, Marketing	Section	1 year
Manager, Product Section or Affiliate	Section	1 year

C. CAREER ROUTE AND GOALS (How realistic are the individual's career goals and are they compatible with your views?. Make a clear statement with respect to long-range development needs and recommendations for future positions and training.)

His objective of managing a product section or a small affiliate some time in the next 12 to 24 months is realistic and probably an excellent way for him to demonstrate his longer range potential. Assuming a satisfactory performance in such a position, he appears to have the tools to function as a line General Manager in the Company. It is too early to comment on his long-term goal of Division level within 10 years.

Completed by _____ Date _____ Date Discussed with Reviewing Manager _____

CMMD-3 Rev 12/79   Date Discussed with Employee _____

Exhibit 10-10. Individual career forecast

GENERAL ● ELECTRIC

Strictly Private

INDIVIDUAL CAREER FORECAST

1979
Year

(Identify Component and Parent Organizations through Group Layer)

NAME			Position Level	Position Title	Months in Position	FORECAST*		
Last	First	Initial				Code	Timing	Comments
			14	Manager, Accounting Operations	23	3	Now	Accounting Operations or Administration
			15	Manager, Operations Analysis and Financial Planning	15	1	2-3 yrs.	Division Management -- Information Systems
			14	Manager, Information Systems	24	2	Now	
			12	Manager, Auditing	17	3	2-3 yrs.	Finance Section or Division
			15	Manager, Manufacturing and Engineering Oper. Analysis	37	2	Now	Cost Operation
			13	Manager, Marketing Operations Analysis	22	2	2 yrs.	
			15	Manager, Financial Operations Component Products Section	32	2	Now	Capable of full finance operation

* FORECAST INSTRUCTIONS

List *all* employees reporting to the Manager of the Component and indicate for each a current career forecast using *one* of the codes below.
Also <u>forecast</u> timing (now or number of years) for next move.

1. *High Potential* Can move to the next higher organization layer with potential to move at least another organization layer later.

2. *Promotable* to the next higher organization layer.

3. *Advanceable* to a higher position level within current organization layer.

4. *More time needed* before designation as promotable or advanceable.

5. *Not advanceable* but has satisfactory performance.

6. <u>*Unsatisfactory*</u> performance.

(Submitted By) _____   _____ Date

CMMD-1 Rev. 11-74

252

Exhibit 10-11. Organization and staffing plans

GENERAL 🄶🄴 ELECTRIC

ORGANIZATION
AND
STAFFING PLANS

Strictly Private

COMPONENT

INCUMBENT MANAGER

(NAME)   (AGE)(PL)

★

(NAME)   (AGE)(PL)   (NAME)   (AGE)(PL)   (NAME)   (AGE)(PL)   (NAME)   (AGE)(PL)   (NAME)   (AGE)(PL)   (NAME)   (AGE)(PL)

★★

★

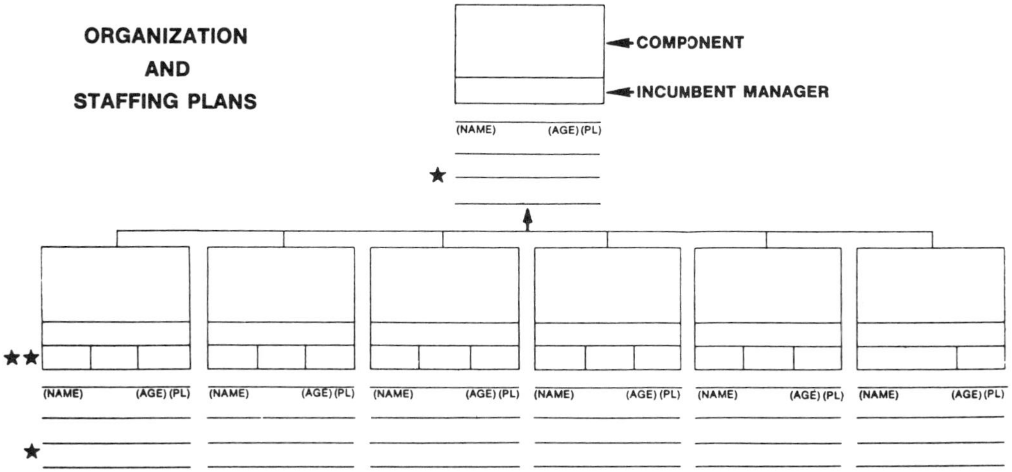

★ **BEST REPLACEMENTS (LIST IN ORDER OF PREFERENCE SHOWING NAME, THIS YEAR'S AGE, POSITION LEVEL)**

★★ **THIS YEAR'S AGE | POSITION LEVEL | MOS. IN POSITION**

Casewriter's note: The form presented here has been excerpted from the larger and more detailed Company form.

PREPARED BY _____ DATE

REVIEWED BY _____ DATE

CHAPTER 11

Bonuses for Performance: Equity or Excellence?

This case follows from the case in Chapter 9 on performance appraisal. As that chapter suggested, many public agencies are becoming interested in using performance evaluation as a means of determining certain aspects of pay. In the system we have studied in the Patent Office, performance evaluations were to be the basis for giving out bonuses. If necessary, you can refresh your memory on the details of the appraisal and bonus system by glancing over the Patent and Trademark case in Chapter 9. For some data on the effects of compensation on employees you might also wish to recall the case and readings in Chapter 6.

As the case in this chapter opens, some changes have been made in the number of bonuses available to managers subject to the performance appraisal system. The Secretary of the Department of Labor and Industry (a disguised name for a real department) must decide how bonuses will be distributed under the new arrangements. The several hundred managers who have been evaluated during the past year have considerable interest in the outcome of this decision since it will affect bonus availability, bonus amounts, and bonus distribution within the agency.

In the literature and in practical discussions on the subject of monetary rewards there is a lot of uncertainty, if not controversy, over distribution of dollars. The idea, of course, is to provide rewards so that employees are motivated to do things that will help the organization. In attempting to do so it is important to avoid unintended negative affects on employees or the organization. All too often a poorly designed method of giving rewards can cause more harm than good.

The decision maker in this case has a complex problem on her hands. Since the research, literature, and conventional wisdom provide no easy answers, this decision is going to have to be made in the context of the circumstances at hand and a consideration of its possible positive and negative effects on employees and on organizational health and direction.

Many good managers would rather avoid judgments on distributing bonuses or evaluating performance for the purpose of determining pay. They prefer to rely on other tools to motivate and provide feedback. However, even where managers eschew the use of variable financial rewards, given the current interest in the technique, they may find it thrust upon them by legislative or departmental action.

Under such circumstances, the sensitivity of employees to variations in compensation — their own or someone else's — behooves managers, nevertheless, to try to minimize the harm, if not try to improve organizational performance, through the use of evaluation and reward systems.

Since decisions on bonuses come at the end of a performance appraisal process, review of this case provides a certain perspective on the other parts of the appraisal system. As we see how the bonus decision is affected by the structure and handling of the system, there is an opportunity to review the workings of the other parts of the appraisal system. Since this is their first year using the system, there may be some adjustments worth recommending.

By putting ourselves in the decision maker's shoes, we can see what factors may be most important in designing a reward system that can perhaps obtain positive results and at least avoid negative results from performance-based reward systems. Whether in a small agency or a large, complex department, this requires careful analysis and creative thought. Reflecting on this, you may find this case to be especially challenging.

STUDY QUESTIONS

1. What policy for allocating bonuses would you adopt?

2. With that choice, what will be the likely effect, for example, on the senior executives in the Patent and Trademark Office?

3. In particular, what kinds of managerial and subordinate behavior are likely to result? Why?

4. What are the objectives of the secretary of the department? How might a bonus system further those?

5. Taking the viewpoint of the secretary of the department, what decision would you make? What will be the likely response of managers throughout the department? How will that affect the secretary's objectives? Departmental performance? Are there ways to accentuate the positive aspects of this system and minimize the negative?

6. How would you set up the system for next year? Would you choose a different option? Which one? Why? What principles or criteria would govern? How would they relate to organizational performance? To concerns about fairness?

7. Would you make any recommendations to alter other aspects of the appraisal system?

RECOMMENDED READING

Paul H. Thompson and Gene W. Dalton, "Performance Appraisal: Managers Beware," *Harvard Business Review*, January-February 1970.

U.S. Patent and Trademark Office (D)

On July 21, 1980, Helen Corcoran, Assistant Secretary of Business and Industry for Administration, received notification from the Office of Personnel Management (OPM) that significant changes had been made in the Senior Executive Service bonus award program. As a result of the Civil Service Reform Act of 1978, the Department of Business and Industry (DBI) had recently implemented new procedures for evaluating the performance of Senior Executive Service (SES) members and for linking performance to bonuses or incentive pay awards. According to the OPM memo, the Department would have to revise the bonus portion of the policy it had established and communicate these changes to all departmental "operating units," including the Patent and Trademark Office. Assistant Secretary Corcoran and her staff would be responsible for insuring that these tasks were completed in time for implementation prior to the end of the fiscal year.

Bonus Awards

In January of 1980, following implementation of the performance appraisal program, DBI began issuing formal guidelines for operating units to follow in the distribution of bonus or incentive pay awards to members of the Senior Executive Service. Essentially, the Department authorized each operating unit to award bonuses up to 33⅓ percent of the total number of career executives within the unit. Out of the Depart-

ment's total allocation of bonus funds, 75 percent was to be distributed to operating units on a per capita basis. Undistributed bonus funds (25 percent) and allocable positions (up to the 50 percent allowed by law) were to be reserved for the Secretary to recognize units and offices achieving Secretarial program and management objectives and to reward those SES career members primarily responsible for the success of these programs.

In June of 1980, the U.S. House of Representatives began consideration of a number of revisions to the SES program. One of these changes would have placed a "cap" on the dollar amount of bonuses to be awarded under individual programs such as the one being operated by the Department of Business and Industry. Although the Civil Service Reform Act (CSRA) provided for possible bonuses of up to $20,000 per year, the House proposal, by establishing a maximum combination of salary and bonuses, would have effectively limited the bonus payments to no more than $2,500 in most cases.

After considerable public debate (see Exhibit 11-1), the House Appropriations Committee agreed to a compromise. Instead of placing a ceiling on the *amount* of the bonuses to be received, the Congress elected to reduce the *number* of bonuses distributed to senior executives. Under the new Congressional guidelines, bonuses could be awarded to no more than 25 percent of the career SES members in an agency, instead of the 50 percent originally allowed by the CSRA. As part of a supplemental appropriations bill for FY 1980, this provision would be binding through September 30, 1980.

In its interpretation of the new restriction, the Office of Personnel Management insisted that the 25 percent figure was an absolute limit, not a norm. To enforce the limit, OPM issued a pol-

This case was prepared by Nancy Griesemer, under the general supervision of Jon Brock, Lecturer, Kennedy School of Government. While based on field research, some of the facts and names of persons and organizational units have been altered in the interest of confidentiality.

icy memo on July 21, 1980, which advised agencies to reduce the number of bonuses to be awarded to no more than 20 percent of the eligible career executives. Any awards in excess of this percentage would have to receive prior OPM approval. In addition, OPM restricted the payment of the maximum bonus (20 percent of salary) to no more than 5 percent of those receiving awards and limited bonuses in excess of 12 percent of salary to a maximum of one quarter of all recipients (see Exhibit 11-2).

Incentive Awards

Prior to the Civil Service Reform Act, agencies had been free to grant "incentive awards" for suggestions, inventions, superior accomplishment or other personal efforts which contributed to the efficiency, economy or other improvements in government operations. On March 21, 1980, the Department of Business and Industry issued a statement to operating units encouraging the use of incentive awards in the SES ". . . to reinforce the link between achievement and rewards." It was suggested that unused funds initially allocated to the operating units for awarding SES bonuses should be used for the payment of incentive awards to senior executives.

On July 24, 1980, the Office of Personnel Management issued a memorandum to heads of departments and agencies revoking the authority to grant incentive awards for sustained superior performance to SES members. Referring to recent actions on the part of the Congress to restrict the total number of bonuses awarded to senior executives, OPM justified the policy change in terms of "Congressional intent" (see Exhibit 11-3).

The DBI Model

On August 20, 1980, Assistant Secretary Corcoran convened a staff meeting to discuss the various policy options that had been developed in light of the recent changes handed down by the Office of Personnel Management. In an attempt to design enduring procedures for operating units to follow, an effort was made to forecast future Congressional action with regard to SES bonus awards. A number of possible outcomes were suggested which ranged from a continuation of existing controls to the imposition of new controls such as the pay cap that had been considered previously. There was also the possibility that bonuses could be entirely eliminated or that no cap or controls would be enforced beyond those contained in the CSRA. Any one of these options would have an impact on future DBI policy.

Applying the July 21st guidelines, the Department found that 20 percent of the 400 career eligibles in Business and Industry amounted to approximately 80 awards. Using the OPM formula, the bonus distribution would be as in Table 11-1. Out of the total number of bonuses to be awarded, this meant that an operating unit such as the Patent and Trademark Office, with

Table 11-1. Bonus distribution

Bonus Percent of Salary	Percent Receiving Bonuses	Number Receiving Bonuses	Cumulative Awards
20%	5%	4	4
17–19%	5%	4	8
12–16%	15%	12	20
up to 11%	75%	60	80

23 filled SES positions, would be allowed to award a total of 5 bonuses.

Given this information, the Department was forced to reconsider its entire bonus scheme. Accordingly, three options were drawn up by Assistant Secretary Corcoran's staff:

A. *Centralization of the Entire Approval Process at the Department of Business and Industry Level:* Operating unit Performance Review Boards would prepare a prioritized listing of proposed bonus recipients with recommended amounts for each. The list would be transmitted by the appointing authority to DBI for disposition, and the Department would select the top executives and assign bonus awards as per OPM guidelines.

B. *Partial Delegation of the Approval Process to Operating Units:* Appointing authorities would approve the selection of bonus recipients and the Department would determine the size of individual bonuses.

C. *Extensive Delegation of the Approval Process to the Operating Units:* Appointing authorities would approve the selection of all bonus recipients and would grant individual bonus amounts for 11 percent or less with the approval of bonuses between 12 percent and 20 percent reserved to the Department.

Also considered was the possibility of "clustering" certain of the operating units which fell under the responsibility of an individual Assistant Secretary. For example, the Assistant Secretary for Productivity, Innovation and Technology would make decisions with regard to the distribution of bonuses to the 134 career executives in the National Bureau of Standards (106), the Patent and Trademark Office (23), and in the Office of Productivity, Technology and Innovation (5). If implemented, such a consolidation would help ease the problems posed by the application of percentages in bonus distribution.

As Assistant Secretary Corcoran began the meeting to decide on a policy for the Department, she advised her staff that the final decision would be made by an executive level policy group, and that it would probably be based on recommendations from her office. In any event, it was hoped that the final policy could be communicated to the operating units no later than the first week in September, as the bonus year for the FY 1980 SES performance appraisal program would be ending on September 30th.

Exhibit 11-1. Editorial from *The Washington Post,* June 20, 1980

Doing wrong by civil servants

After years of general hand-wringing about the civil service system, some fairly major reforms were enacted in 1978. For top-level federal managers, the new Senior Executive Service offered the chance of large pay bonuses in return for outstanding effort and an increased risk of penalties for inadequate work. The new rules for these 7,000 or so senior career officials have been getting arranged for nearly two years now, and the first decisions on who deserves a bonus are just being made. Enter the House of Representatives, which threatens to undo the whole system by eliminating almost all of the bonus money.

This is a truly stupid thing to do. Senior career executives are working right now for considerably less money than their colleagues in the private sector, and one purpose of the bonus provision was to provide the genuinely exceptional among them a reason to stick with the government. For years, federal salaries have been artificially restrained by a congressionally imposed ceiling, which now stands at $50,112. Eighty-six percent of the senior executives are at that ceiling. Some 80 percent would, if paid at the level their jobs draw in private industry, earn more than the $52,750 the House has set as its limit on the combination of pay and bonus.

This issue is an easy prey for demagogues, because not many people in the country make $50,000. But it should be remembered that the size of some of these jobs is staggering. We are talking about some of the most responsible executives in the country.

In addition to keeping some of the best people from leaving, the penalty-and-reward structure of the reform was also intended to encourage those who had not been working very hard or very effectively to get with it. Actions like those of the House committee are likely to incline them, instead, only to dig in their heels.

There is, inevitably, a tension in government between the political people — legislative and executive — and the career civil servants. Success in running the government requires taking positive advantage of that tension, with career staff providing the analytic work, the institutional background and continuing management capacity, and the political officials providing the judgment of how to get things done and which things to try to do. The senior career executives are the bridge between the political staff and the vast operational apparatus. They have seen administrations come and go, and are like the legendary British civil servants who, it is said, serve all political masters with equal loyalty and disdain. It makes no sense to tip the balance further toward disdain and cynicism by reneging on an agreed-upon change in the terms of employment after they have given up their security and before they have had a chance to reap any benefit. The funds should be restored.

Exhibit 11-2. Memorandum to heads of departments and agencies

---

United States of America
Office of
Personnel Management   Washington, D.C. 20415

In Reply Refer To   July 21, 1980   Your Reference

MEMORANDUM TO HEADS OF DEPARTMENTS AND AGENCIES

The Office of Personnel Management, with the advice of other agencies, has
prepared the following guidance in respect to awarding Senior Executive Service
performance awards (bonuses). In part, this guidance reflects the appropriation
act limitation restricting the proportion of SES members who may receive bonuses
to no more than 25 percent of the number of SES positions in the agency. In
addition, we are responding to strong Congressional concern that the 25 percent
be viewed as a ceiling. We are therefore enunciating guidance on the number and
distribution of awards which we strongly recommend agencies to follow. GAO in
cooperation with OPM has been directed by the Congress to do a thorough study of
bonus payments. Any agency which chooses to award bonuses in excess of the
number or distribution recommended below must consult in advance with the Director
of OPM.

1. Number of Awards

Agencies are limited in payment of bonuses to a maximum of 25 percent of SES
positions. The Congress has made it clear that the 25 percent figure is to be
a limit, not the norm. Agencies should generally limit bonuses to 20 percent
of the eligible career employees. If the agency head feels a higher proportion
is essential, he or she must consult with the Director of OPM.

2. Distribution of Awards

In deciding the amount of bonus to be paid, agencies with 100 or more career Senior
Executives should not exceed the limitations shown below. These limits cannot be
rigidly applied in small agencies, but should be considered as general guidelines.

   (a) Bonuses of 20% should be limited to no more than 5% of those
       receiving bonuses.

   (b) Bonuses of 17-20% should, in total, be limited to no more
       than 10% of those receiving bonuses.

   (c) Bonuses of 12-20% should, in total, be limited to no more
       than 25% of those receiving bonuses.

(Exhibit continues on following page.)

Exhibit 11-2. Continued

3. General Procedural Recommendations

(a) One area about which a number of legislators were concerned was the perception that members of Performance Review Boards would be taking care of themselves and their friends in the awarding of bonuses. We do not believe that this concern has substance, but to further add to the objectivity of the review process, an agency may wish to include on its PRB panel one or more members from another Federal agency. OPM will maintain a list of experienced career Senior Executives who could serve on PRB's across agency lines if the agency so requests. This same procedure might well be useful in the future in passing on proposed nominations for Meritorious and Distinguished Presidential Rank within an agency.

(b) Each agency should publish a notice in the Federal Register of the agency's schedule for awarding bonuses at least 14 days prior to the date on which the awards will be paid.

(c) Career Senior Executives are eligible for both bonus and rank awards. In general, agencies should avoid giving multiple awards to a single SES member in a year.

The SES system provides agency management with an unprecedented level of discretion. It is vital that this discretion be used responsibly to establish a sound foundation for the future.

Alan K. Campbell
Director

cc: Director of Personnel
    Assistant Secretary
    Executive Administrative Directors' Group

Exhibit 11-3. Memorandum to heads of departments and agencies

United States
Office of
Personnel Management   Washington, D.C. 20415

In Reply Refer To   Your Reference

July 24, 1980

MEMORANDUM TO HEADS OF DEPARTMENTS AND AGENCIES

The purpose of this memorandum is to bring you up to date on recent events concerning SES bonuses and to inform you of the requirements that OPM is placing on incentive awards made to senior executives. These requirements are necessitated by the overlapping purpose of the two types of payments and by congressional concerns about the number of SES members who receive monetary awards based on performance. Agency heads must consult with the Director of OPM before making an incentive award to an SES member that would not be in accordance with these requirements.

I. RECENT EVENTS

The FY '81 Legislative Appropriations Bill, as reported out of Committee, would have capped SES pay plus bonuses at $52,750. On July 21, 1980, the House adopted an amendment which allows agency payment of SES performance awards to no more than 25 percent of the number of Senior Executive Service positions in the agency. This provision is identical to the one contained in the FY '80 Supplemental Appropriations Act. The Senate has not acted on the FY '81 bill as yet.

Throughout the process, it has been evident that many Members of Congress were extremely concerned that any performance award be limited to those senior executives whose work was truly outstanding, and that agencies rigorously comply with both the letter and spirit of the statutory provisions. I urge you to continue to monitor these awards carefully and to comply fully with OPM's July 21, 1980 guidance on the number and distribution of these awards.

II. INCENTIVE AWARDS

To carry out the congressional intent, agencies must not use incentive awards to circumvent either the statutory language or OPM's guidance of July 21, 1980, concerning the number and distribution of awards. An incentive award for sustained superior performance under 5 U.S.C. Chapter 45 is analogous to an SES performance bonus under 5 U.S.C. Chapter 54. Thus, agencies may not use incentive awards to reward sustained superior performance by SES members.

(Exhibit continues on following page.)

Exhibit 11-3. Continued

Agencies, however, may continue to use incentive awards to recognize a specific one-time accomplishment, a suggestion, an invention or a scientific achievement made by a senior executive. Agency heads should review personally all awards to ensure that the type of award is appropriate and that the individual SES member is deserving of recognition.

These requirements are essential to the success of the pay-for-performance provisions of the Civil Service Reform Act. I appreciate your cooperation in their implementation.

Alan K. Campbell
Director

PART VI

Resolving and Avoiding Conflict

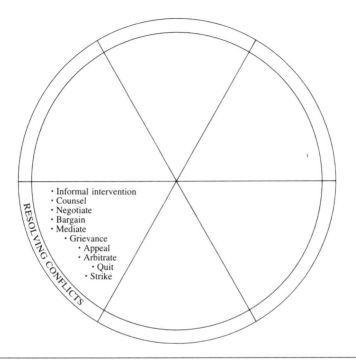

- Informal intervention
- Counsel
- Negotiate
- Bargain
- Mediate
  - Grievance
    - Appeal
    - Arbitrate
      - Quit
      - Strike

RESOLVING CONFLICTS

Analysis of the cases in this section draw on many of the principles, skills, and actors encountered in earlier cases and then goes on to explore some new conceptual and cultural elements of an extended personnel system. The cases that follow portray conflicts or controversies of several sorts, ranging from labor-management disputes to a perplexing case of employee misconduct that brought an entire work unit nearly to a standstill.

Conflicts can arise from many sources, often from difficulties in some of the other five elements in the extended personnel system. For example, in the Equal Employment Opportunity case in Chapter 3, there is a conflict over a promotion. In the hiring case in Chapter 4, the agency and the Civil Service Commission are having a conflict over their respective powers in employee selection. In this part, the first two cases involve conflicts arising from differences between labor and management. In Chapter 12, the parties are at loggerheads over a reorganization. Even though a contract defined certain rights and procedures, there was considerable confusion over just how to resolve matters. A more classic labor-management conflict over wages and working conditions is depicted in the "Police Negotiations" case in Chapter 13. In that case the use of mediation and arbitration are examined.

The last two cases in this part deal with conflicts of the sort that arise in connection with human resource flows, the subject of an earlier part of the book. In these and in many other conflict situations, the means for resolving the problem are not as well defined as they tend to be in labor-management situations. In these latter two cases, the ability of management to resolve the situation is affected by technical features of civil service rules, by the priorities of other actors, by the culture, and by expectations of employees in each of the organizations. Ethical and operational considerations seem to conflict as the needs of the affected individuals and the needs of the organization are weighed.

It is often said that conflicts are healthy since they point out problems requiring solutions. While serving as a mechanism that identifies problems, conflicts can be a costly way to find out about them. Conflicts can escalate, causing damage to the parties, to the future relationship of the parties, and to the organization. The value of a conflict as a warning signal and indicator can be realized only if there is a way to resolve it. To mitigate the risks and to take advantage of conflict as a warning, it is important to have in place a working channel to resolve the dispute and to identify its causes. Where there is a channel available through which to resolve a dispute expeditiously, the dangers of a festering sore or an uncontrolled conflict are reduced. A speedy grievance procedure may be capable of resolving individual disputes, but if a policy or personality is causing the conflict, it will continue to affect employees and the smooth working of the organization. There should also be a way to get at the *source* of the dispute.

One of the problems that conflicts often point out is the need to have a better way of resolving conflicts. This is especially obvious when a small issue has major repercussions or takes an especially long and convoluted route to solution. If, for example, a personal disagreement between employees leads one of them to quit, the odds are that finding a better way to resolve such conflicts would be in order. Conflicts may also suggest the need for better mechanisms to *anticipate* problems that can lead to conflict. If the underlying problem can be avoided or removed without conflict, unpleasantness and risks can be avoided.

Unnecessary or unnecessarily virulent conflicts sap valuable time and energy from managers and employees. The pressure conflicts can generate may encourage decisions that are not in the interest of the people involved or in the interest of the long-term health and stability of the organization. Yet the pressures generated by disputes and conflicts are many and often unanticipated; the temptation to make expedient or tension-reducing decisions can be great.

A manager will be less likely to be a victim of short-sighted decisions or festering discontent if he or she conscientiously seeks to influence the variables in the extended personnel system. Such a manager — one who thinks carefully about his or her actions in the workplace — is less likely to be caught unawares by conflict-producing forces, issues or decisions. Many conflicts can be seen a mile away, if only a manager will take the time to look over the organization, gather information informally and use his or her diagnostic ability. Often, conscious planning or other processes that recognize the potential for dissatisfaction or conflict can be used to avoid or dampen disputes that might otherwise erupt. Even if a conflict can't be prevented through anticipation and preventive management practices, at least a manager can be prepared to see its implications, solve it, and contain its negative effects.

Finally, if caught in a conflict that requires a decision under pressure, a better decision — in the interest of the organization — can be made by keeping well in mind the probable affect of the decision on the organization's purposes. The best defenses against these pressures and temptations are probably anticipation and orderly resolution of conflicts and a decision-maker who regularly and in the midst of a crisis considers longer-term consequences to the organization's central purposes.

CHAPTER 12

Bargaining for Conditions: Labor-Management Relations in the Federal Government

Few things promise to be so critical in the next decade as the nature and impact of labor relations in the public sector. Public sector unionization has grown rather suddenly to the point where nearly 60 percent of federal workers are members of unions. In state and local government nearly 50 percent are members.

In this age of fiscal constraint, the citizenry seems to be demanding more from government at less cost. To the extent that a manager's primary production resource is people, that manager can get greater or better production only by affecting the way people do their jobs. In the event that the pursuit of productivity involves a reduction in the work force or changes in work practices or contract provisions, unions will surely be interested and be present to greet such actions. In most instances they will have a statutory right to exercise their interest. Although the quality of labor and management leadership will vary, the relationship a manager forms with the union is likely to make a great difference in the flexibility a manager has to respond under resource-scarce conditions.

Apart from fiscal difficulties affecting collective bargaining, labor-management relations in the public sector have several other problems. Formal labor-management relations are newer to the public sector than to the private sector. In public employment, union recognition and formal collective bargaining began only during the 1960s and came to many jurisdictions only in the mid to late 1970s. Many jurisdictions still do not permit collective bargaining by public employees. Because of its recent development, the labor relations environment in many public agencies may be confused and may lack structure, maturity, and experience. Frequently, both labor and management have a lot to learn about their roles. Because of the impact of labor-management relations and the features of labor contracts on the work environment, work practices, productivity, costs, and employee satisfaction, any time taken to improve management's handling of this area will be time well spent.

This case begins an examination of handling labor relations that continues for two chapters. It focuses on the nature of the labor-management relationship and the technical and cultural features that often affect that relationship in public agencies. The example chosen for this case concerns labor relations in a federal department.

In the federal sector and in some states, collective bargaining is permitted over terms and conditions of employment, but management and labor are not permitted to bargain over compensation issues. In private employment — and in other states and most local jurisdictions where there is collective bargaining — compensation is on the table. Where there is no bargaining over pay, but where a bargaining relationship exists, the union frequently concentrates its effort to win influence over other aspects of the workplace. Under such circumstances, two areas that commonly get attention are matters related to (1) hiring and other aspects of human resource flows and (2) working conditions and work rules. These are areas that in other settings have more usually been left as management prerogatives, or have been ''bought'' or traded off by management in exchange for compensation or other considerations. This concentration in the public sector on human resource flows or working conditions can erode management flexibility for managers who feel that they have already significant restraints on their prerogatives: Civil service rigidities and the influence of other outside factors already restrict their influence over personnel matters. Thus, where the handling of the labor-management relationship is not especially productive or skillful, a public union's heightened interest in influencing these non-wage matters and the manager's interest in preserving those as prerogatives can cause a great deal of conflict. Some skills that can improve the outcome of bargaining and otherwise handle day-to-day labor relations will be important both where there is and where there is not wage bargaining.

The present case, ''Labor Relations in the United States Employment Service Reorganization,'' in describing a reorganization that resulted in unfair labor practice charges, examines a variety of issues in public labor-management relations. It contains examples of peculiarities that make government labor-management relations especially difficult to carry out. While the Labor Department has some unusual characteristics in connection with their labor relations, the circumstances described in the case are common in many public bargaining situations.

The case suggests (1) the effects of the lack of an established bargaining structure, including the nature of the bargaining unit and structure for handling labor-management disputes; (2) the role of responsible union and management leadership; (3) the effect of a negotiating strategy; (4) the need for management knowledge and training in the labor relations aspects of their job; and (5) the influence of personalities and informal communications on the outcome of a dispute. The case also provides background on some of the less formal or tangible aspects of formal personnel authority and the impact of a few new external actors on man aging people.

It is a long case with many actors and events, but one that captures some of the subtleties and difficulties in government labor-management relations.

STUDY QUESTIONS

1. What are the factors that caused this dispute to become so contentious?
2. Could those factors have been anticipated?
3. Under whose influence or control were those factors and how might they have been influenced?
4. Would you attribute the confrontation and impasse to personalities? Politics? Structure? Rules? Other things? Which were the primary causes?
5. If you were briefing the incoming Secretary of Labor, Bill Usery, what would you tell him about the situation? Preparatory to a decision, what would he need to know?
6. What is at stake for Secretary Usery?
7. What should Secretary Usery decide?
8. How should he implement his decision?

SELECTED REFERENCES

Milton Derber, "Management Organization for Collective Bargaining," in Benjamin Aaron, Joseph R. Grodin, James L. Stern, eds. *Public Sector Bargaining,* Industrial Relations Research Association Series (Washington, D.C.: The Bureau of National Affairs, 1979) pp. 80-117.

Richard Martin, "Note on Federal Labor-Management Policy," HBS Case Services, Harvard University (9-482-500), 1981. [This note describes federal labor relations after the Civil Service Reform Act of 1978.]

James L. Stern, "Unionism in the Public Sector," in Benjamin Aaron, Joseph R. Grodin, James L. Stern, eds., *Public Sector Bargaining,* Industrial Relations Research Association Series (Washington, D.C.: The Bureau of National Affairs, 1979) pp. 44–62.

Labor Relations in the
United States Employment Service Reorganization (A)

It was February 9, 1976, and W. J. (Bill) Usery, Jr. had just been sworn in as Secretary of Labor. Born in Hardwick, Georgia, he had come up the hard way, and had subsequently enjoyed a successful career in the trade union movement before entering Federal service in 1969 as Assistant Secretary of Labor for Labor Management Services. He went from there to a distinguished sojourn as Assistant to the President for Labor-Management Relations and Director of the Federal Mediation and Conciliation Service. He had been elevated to the Cabinet level by President Gerald R. Ford. Highly regarded by management and labor for his skills as a mediator and a neutral, Bill Usery was considered a friend of the worker.

In his first days on the job he was, among other things, confronted with a controversial decision on an internal labor relations problem within the Department of Labor itself: The internal union was strongly opposed to a reorganization of one of the Department's subunits. After a year of careful organizational analysis and planning, objections of the local union affiliate of the American Federation of Government Employees (AFL-CIO) had so critically affected the implementation status of the reorganization that Usery's predecessor was compelled to stop the reorganization at the 11th

This case was prepared by Jon Brock, Lecturer at the John F. Kennedy School of Government, Harvard University. The author wishes to point out that, while based upon a factual situation, the names of the individuals are disguised and other information has been altered in the interest of confidentiality.

hour and order a review of the reorganization. As a result, implementation was stalled for months after its announcement. During that period, the hallways were replete with rumors about political intentions to punish Democrats and employees were uncertain of their status in the new organizational alignment. Much work time was taken up with discussion of the latest rumors.

Kensington (Kent) Smith, the Director of the United States Employment Service (USES) had been receiving calls from interested and angry congressmen and their staffs, and his own management team was beginning to wonder whether or not it was all worth it. Smith feared that the delay, brought on by the Secretary of Labor's response to highly publicized charges of unfair labor practices and political influence, would cause confusion and distrust among employees that would detract from the organization's ability to perform its tasks. Smith was also fearful that prolonged delay would cause non-management influences and judgments to dilute the form and substance of the changes he was seeking to institute.

The United States Employment Service

The USES is one of the oldest of the agencies in the United States Government concerned with social welfare programs. Its functions were inaugurated and its predecessor agency established in 1933 with the passage of the Wagner-Peyser Act. The Act specified a Federal-State system of employment and employment security services. While in 1976 some 22 laws and 17 Presidential Executive Orders specified the activities to be performed by the Employment

Service, it was probably best known for its activities in the area of job matching, where employers are encouraged, and required by law in some cases, to list job openings with the state or local employment service office for the purpose of creating central "job banks" in local labor markets. These services are provided by state-run agencies.

During the 1960s, economists and manpower specialists pinned high hopes on these job matching mechanisms to reduce frictional unemployment in local and in national labor markets. Relative to these expectations, the results were disappointing, even with the introduction in recent years of computerized job matching services: Only about 10 percent of all job placements in the domestic economy had been made via the Employment Service and many of the jobs so listed were low-skill, low-paying jobs, and thus fell short of the prerequisites for broad, economy-wide job matching.

During the late 60s and early 70s the romance with job matching and related notions came to an end and resource commitments to federally controlled manpower programs began to dwindle. This was particularly true as revenue sharing programs allowed the states and localities to decide where and how their employment and training dollars should be spent. Along with this freedom, the states and localities — not the Federal government — were responsible for creating, setting policy for, and running the administrative mechanism that would deliver the services they chose to offer. Under the new scheme, Federal activity was largely restricted to policy guidance, approval of grant applications, technical assistance and audit and oversight responsibilities; the excitement and sense of Federal power in solving social ills — which in the 60s drew many people to Washington and motivated their energies — came to a bumping end in the early 70s. New hiring in the USES and its sister agencies came essentially to

an end and cutbacks were required in response to budgetary and legislative pressures.

Organizational Setting

The National Office of the Employment Service is an organization within the Employment and Training Administration of the Department of Labor. The Employment and Training Administration was one of the six major agencies in 1975 which comprised the Department of Labor (see Exhibits 12-1 and 12-2). The Employment and Training Administration also was responsible for administering the Federal-State system of unemployment insurance and overseeing the decentralized manpower training programs that, with Federal grants, were operated under the Comprehensive Employment and Training Act of 1973, as amended.

In 1975, the Labor Department was under the stewardship of John T. Dunlop, former Dean of the Faculty of Arts and Sciences at Harvard University and a prominent labor economist and mediator. The Employment and Training Administration was headed by a Presidential appointee, Assistant Secretary of Labor Michael H. Lambert. His experience included an earlier stint at the Employment and Training Administration and several years at the Office of Management and Budget (OMB) as a senior official with responsibility for human resources funding and policy. He was well regarded in the Congress on both sides of the aisle and by organized labor and by employers. Lambert consistently worked to build a responsible and responsive management team. He tended to delegate thoroughly to his managers but held them accountable for results.

The Need for Reorganization

In early 1974 Kent Smith returned to the Labor Department and prepared to take over as Director of the USES. Smith had recently spent a year in the private sector after serving from 1971 to

1973 as the Executive Secretary of the Cost of Living Council, the temporary agency responsible for the Federal wage and price controls program of 1971–1974. Smith had previously worked in the Employment and Training Administration as Regional Administrator in two of its ten regional offices. He arrived at the USES in the midst of staff and budget cuts and immediately noted the demoralization, disorganization and lack of direction that characterized the USES during this period. Because of further cutbacks to staff and resources that were mandated by the Office of Management and Budget (OMB), the Labor Department — ordered by the Under Secretary of Labor — began a comprehensive set of manpower utilization studies in all of the employment and training programs in the department. Generally, these studies were designed to eliminate excessive personnel. The National Office of the Employment Service was chosen as the first agency within the Employment Training Administration to be studied. The study was conducted by a five-person team from the yeoman-like Office of Organization and Manpower Utilization, a sort of Department-wide internal management analysis group. Although Smith was not the originator of the study, he noted later that he:

> . . . was glad to have it done. I was new, the study was just getting underway, and I had to face some tough cutbacks coming down from above. I encouraged a candid study and opened the doors to them.

They finished the study in late 1974. Their findings were appalling. They were so amazed at what they found that they went beyond their original charter. In addition to sloppy utilization of manpower, there were serious operational problems. The organization clearly wasn't responsive enough to the field offices or to the states. That's where they place people into jobs. We were trying to improve the number of placements performed by the USES system but it wasn't at all clear how we could

do it. I couldn't get any policy analysis or program evaluation done unless it was done by the program office who had responsibility for the program. That's like having the production foreman doing quality control. To make matters worse, the study said that middle management was weak, morale was terrible and there was little or no work product control.

I took these findings, along with my own observations, and discussed it all with my deputy, John Chandler, who had been here about three months before I arrived, and with a few other key people. The only prescription was to perform a massive overhaul with no quick fixes and no patching, just a careful and thorough job.

Chandler recalled:

> We knew that our operating arm — the state agencies — weren't happy and we knew that the program was undergoing a lot of other external criticism. The organizational structure that we were using was established years ago, when the organization was twice its existing size. The thrust of the program was different in those days. Consequently, you had people running around here trying vainly to recapture past glories and influence by laying large reporting burdens on states, writing all sorts of field directives, and editing — none of which were useful to managing or accomplishing our tasks.
>
> We decided to stop this needless writing, editing and reviewing and seek to have the national office help the managers of the state operations measure the performance of the system, get more out of the system and to review on a broad national scale important elements of the program.
>
> Once we got the concepts and the organizational design together, we then had the problem of putting the best available people into what ultimately was going to be a reduced number of positions. Many of the managers were good technicians but were poor managers. Unfortunately, the classification

and seniority rules of the Federal personnel system tend to put good technicians — or poor technicians, but technicians — into managerial jobs. It also put into key positions individuals who were trying to relive the good old days rather than pay attention to our narrower mission. We were trying to select the best people we had for those senior managerial jobs, maybe get some new blood and to try and project a new image to our own organization and to our clients who had become severely disenchanted with us.

Deputy Assistant Secretary Ron Scabatini, a long-time career official of the Department was the next up in the chain of command, and it was him that Smith went to next in early 1975 to seek general approval. Scabatini said:

> Kent worked hard on his study and the subsequent plan to reorganize. He had been a good soldier and had implemented the cutbacks imposed to date and had convinced us to allow the cutbacks to take place by attrition and repositioning people, so as to avoid firings and RIFs.* I told him to proceed.

In the spring of 1975 Smith asked the team that had just completed the organization and manpower study to participate in planning the reorganization of USES, since they were familiar, in detail, with the problems of the organization. Smith, Chandler, and a number of special assistants began to work with the study team to develop the new organizational plan.

Deputy Assistant Secretary Scabatini reported:

> He came back to us in the early summer of 1975 with a plan that looked to all of us like it made sense organizationally and it took into account the objectives of the agency with

---

*RIF is an acronym for "Reduction in Force" wherein personnel resources can be reduced, but only according to specified procedures involving seniority and job classification. Typically, more senior employees or those with other employment preferences — such as veterans — "bump" less senior employees in like job classifications until the reduced resource level is reached.

sensitivity for the people in the organization. There were a number of overgraded people in the agency, especially at a high level, and a real hard-nosed reorganization could have put their jobs in jeopardy. To maintain those jobs and provide some important services, Kent had established a special projects group of 6-8 senior — GS-14 or -15 — people to handle these sorts of problems.† Unfortunately, this group was later dubbed the "turkey farm." It's too bad; some of those guys were very knowledgeable about the program — although others were simply overpaid, but none of them were strong managers. Putting them in this sort of an operation was an ideal solution to a lot of problems.

Smith talked about the special projects group:

> It was a hell of a good way to provide senior technical assistance to the field and to the states, who had been screaming for help. We were concerned about the Commission's predisposition to downgrade such arrangements, so we checked that out pretty carefully ahead of time with the Assistant Secretary for Administration and Management and with the Commission and the preliminary signals came out "go."

The Protocol of Reorganization

In accordance with personnel management procedures set up by the Department, any reorganizations involving alterations in duties and responsibilities required approval from two portions of the Office of the Assistant Secretary for Administration and Management: (1) The general structure of the organization had to be approved by the Office of Organization and Manpower Utilization, which was generally concerned with lines of authority, resource utilization, and non-duplication of functions within or among agencies of the department. (2) Job descriptions and related salary levels for all GS-14 through GS-18 job classifications were subject to review

---

†In late 1975, GS-14 meant a minimum annual salary of $26,861 and GS-15 meant $31,309.

by the Office of Personnel. The Employment and Training Administration itself had been delegated the authority to classify positions below the level of GS-14 (as had the other major portions of the Labor Department). This classification review determined whether or not the organization and its functions could actually "support" a given job and its pay level, i.e., whether a specific individual was eligible for a given job and what the pay level would be.

There is, typically, much informal interaction between the agency undergoing reorganization and these agents of the Assistant Secretary for Administration and Management (OASAM).

In a series of letters written back and forth between union and management during this period, the union sought access to management planning drafts. Management refused to share such documents with the union until the proper administrative approvals for the reorganization from the Assistant Secretary for Administration and Management had been secured. One management official, who generally expressed sympathy for union views and rights, explained:

> How can you consult with the union until you have made relatively final decisions, which have been approved by the personnel people? People and organizational structure are very interdependent, and talking about specifics before approvals are nailed down can jeopardize management's prerogative to make alterations. Unfortunately, by the time we get the approvals back and sit down with the union, there's not much to negotiate that wouldn't unhinge significant parts of the plan. Thus management, by the end of the process, isn't interested in negotiating very much. But, if you bring the union in earlier, you may violate confidentiality, or may have options construed as promises.

Another manager observed:

> As a general matter, management should communicate with the union as early as pos-

sible at every stage in the process — but that assumes you have the luxury of dealing with responsible union stewards, who you can deal with, be candid with and not be afraid that everything you do or say is going to come back to haunt you.

The first official noted that meaningful and responsive negotiations are further restricted because so much flexibility is circumscribed by the rigid, government-wide personnel rules (found in the Federal Personnel Manual) and by the additional requirements of getting approval of the Office of the Assistant Secretary for Administration and Management for most aspects of major organizational change.

The USES followed all of the normal procedures, and its structure and position classifications were approved by the Assistant Secretary of Labor for Administration and Management in the late fall of 1975. Management reported that one GS-15 job they had sought was ultimately classified as a GS-14 despite formal appeals for reconsideration. Otherwise, the Assistant Secretary formally and informally endorsed the structure of the reorganization.

Labor-Management Relations in the U.S. Employment Service

Since 1973 the department had operated under a labor-management agreement between Local 12 of the American Federation of Government Employees — an AFL-CIO affiliate — and the department. Local 12 had won by election the exclusive right to represent Department of Labor employees. The contract specified union and employee rights in a number of areas and outlined several methods by which labor union and management officials would interact. It also listed union and employee rights in a number of areas and specified grievance procedures. There were, of course, other avenues of appeal open to employees including the "administrative" type, provided for by normal Federal personnel procedures, and those which charged unlawful discrimination.

The agreement also sought to define the bargaining unit, i.e., that group of employees for which the union was the bargaining agent. Employees outside of the bargaining unit were not entitled to union representation. There was significant disagreement on who was a part of the bargaining unit and, therefore, afforded exclusive union representation. The agreement states that "the unit includes all employees in the National Office, except supervisors, management officials and guards . . . (non-clerical) employees engaged in Federal personnel work. . . ." However, the definition of management officials and supervisors was constantly disputed among the parties, despite wording in the Executive Order (see excerpts in Exhibit 12-3) which sought to define these terms for the whole of Federal labor-management relations. Development of a traditional or well-accepted line of demarcation has been impeded by the lack of a white collar/blue collar distinction in Federal executive departments and by the fact that many Federal employees were in the "bargaining unit" for a long time prior to becoming supervisors. Neither of the parties was especially happy with the existing agreement and when it expired in July 1975, a protracted set of discussions was begun to come up with a new agreement.

Included in the contract (excerpts in Exhibit 12-4a and 12-4b) was a formal requirement to provide the union with details of proposed organizational changes and it further required that "Local 12 will be provided a minimum of five (5) days to respond to management's proposal before implementation." The contract also requires that labor and management enter into ". . . meaningful consultation between them on organizational changes." Finally, the agreement recognizes Local 12 "as the exclusive representative of all employees in the bargaining unit," and requires negotiation, at the option of the local, in connection with any employees (within the bargaining unit) who are "adversely" affected by reorganization. Local 12 assiduously protected its right to be the conduit of such information, believing that any bypass of the union institution was a symbol of management nonrecognition.

Both management and labor officials agreed that labor-management relations were strained within the department. Local 12 issued a newsletter (12NOW) about once per week, more often than not denouncing management.

By all accounts the labor-relations atmosphere in the National Office of the USES was terrible. In addition to the findings of the management study, the USES was widely reputed to have had a higher grievance rate than any other comparable portion of the Department. (The USES national office in 1975 consisted of some 175 persons.) Some managers said that a number of grievances — usually from a predictable group of people — could be expected to greet nearly any management action. Conscious of this, the Director of Personnel for the Employment and Training Administration, Stephen Cardarelli and others counseled Kent Smith to be sure that both the substance and process of the reorganization adhered to established Federal regulations and the provisions of the departmental labor-management agreement regarding reorganizations and related personnel actions.

Management's View

Stephen Cardarelli was Director of Personnel for the Employment and Training Administration at the time of the USES reorganization and was therefore involved in the formal preparations, job analysis and submissions to the office of the Assistant Secretary for Administration and Management regarding the reorganization.

> The new structure — which Kent and John worked hard and long to design — really stood to help us get better. It was a solid organization, with one possible weak spot: The so-called "turkey farm."

Smith tried his damndest to get communications going with the union stewards. He had Chandler doing a lot of legwork with the union. It seemed like the USES steward started from a negative posture, just on general principles, and really never looked at it from the standpoint of employee welfare. In contrast, when Smith brought me into the matter as the personnel expert, he told me that he wanted to accomplish this without hurting anyone.

At the time, the Civil Service Commission was in the Employment and Training Administration performing a comprehensive job audit.* We knew damn well that we had a series of jobs that were unsupportable. We managed to get the Commission to stay out of USES on the assumption that the reorganization would alter things such that responsibility/grade level comparisons would then be more to their liking.

Several management officials noted that many of those occupying high level management positions had been there for many years — and effectively had become "technologically obsolete." The program content and the scope of the national office activity was different than it was even five years before. Therefore, some new mid-level leadership was seen as necessary. However, had the USES been unable to reorganize in a way that found jobs for its high-graded people, there would have been, according to one official, expert in such matters, a RIF, which would have permitted displaced USES employees to "bump" employees with less seniority from jobs in USES and other parts of the Employment and Training Administration. When the consequences were analyzed, management found that women and minorities would have

* A job audit involves comparison, by Civil Service Commission staff, of duties performed to duties described in a job description. Audits often result in demotions for employees and in formal reprimands to managers for abuse of the personnel system.

lost out and, were a RIF to occur, no new people could have been brought in.

Smith recalled:

The union had reason to distrust us. Our predecessors had left behind horrible personnel relations and had been very sloppy. There were at least 30, maybe 40 people who had lodged complaints regarding their positions and related things. These complaints had been left unattended for years. Chandler went to work on each and every one. But, until the returns were in from the reorganization, they had every reason still to be suspicious.

There was general agreement among managers that Smith was genuinely committed to both protecting employees' security and to following proper procedures, but there was also agreement that he was one of the more hard-nosed managers in the department; he was not interested in a lot of "mickey-mouse." One management official said:

Kent would not acknowledge the institutional authority of the unions — even apart from his personal distaste for the behavior of some of the union representatives. Like many managers, Smith wants to deal directly with employees. He sees it as his right, but such is *not* the nature of union operations or the way management is required to operate under a formal labor-management agreement. You can't do it. You have to go through the employee representatives on issues of this sort.

The Union's Position

The union's representatives were informally notified of the intent to reorganize and were asked to provide comments in May 1975, the same time that USES senior management and Department of Labor senior management were informed of the outlines of the plan. (Exhibit 12-5 contains a chronology of these events.)

In July, when the USES formally asked the Assistant Secretary for Administration and Management for approval of the proposed reorganization, the USES formally notified Local 12 that the reorganization was being planned and, at the same time, solicited comments from the union. As required under the contract, Local 12 proceeded to designate employee representatives to consult and negotiate with management on the reorganization. The notification from management was passed from the president of Local 12 to Gary Jones, chief steward for the Employment and Training Administration, the parent agency of the USES.

Jones recalled:

I received documents noting the proposal and an outline of the substance of a reorganization of the USES national office. I appointed a union negotiator to deal with USES management on the matter. In accordance with our usual practice, I appointed Carl Beck, who was the chief steward for USES.

As nearly as I can remember, no meetings took place between Beck and management, just a lot of letters going back and forth. Management surely was unresponsive and uncooperative, but had it been anyone other than Beck I think Smith would have been more responsive and would have talked during that period.

Carl Beck, the USES steward, had the following observations:

The Employment Service has a history of being run by manipulation, not for the good of the organization. During the 1960s, problems were masked because the organization was growing, and the manipulators could be worked around. Now, terrible things happen to employees. The plan was to get Nixon operatives into the bowels of the organization so they could carry out the goal of getting rid of social programs. Of course, the USES is the key to almost all social programs: It administers the work test, which applies to welfare, unemployment insurance, training programs, you name it. If they got us, they got the social programs. So, they sent in the wrecking crew. They brought in Smith from a political outfit, and he immediately insu-

lated the regional offices from Washington so that they'd be out from under the influences of the Democratic Congress and of the national union headquarters.

Smith had a couple of meetings with union stewards after he came on. I was willing to try and work things out. Previous to Smith, when Chandler was acting as the head of the agency, we were able to work things out. Not that Chandler was so great, but you ought to know that people could be reasonable around here.

We were made aware of the impending reorganization in the summer of 1975. It was not intended to make the organization better but rather to deal with personalities. Unfortunately, Smith had, in his earlier days in the agency, formed opinions about personalities, and his opinions were wrong. The political motive, of course, was to make the USES an ineffective, paper organization. The next time we heard from management was in December when they showed us the official paperwork and expected us to rubber stamp the thing.

Hey, this place needs a reorganization, but not by manipulation. A good example is the "turkey farm." Some people who landed in the "turkey farm" had to be dealt with, no doubt about it. We could have worked things out on those, if management would have been straightforward, but they weren't, so we encouraged the grievances and filed an unfair labor practice against them.

A lot of people said that the "turkey farm" was Democrat-Republican stuff, but it wasn't that kind of politics, it was the in-house kind. We began to get into some negotiations with the management people in December and January and we thought we had some agreement on the unfair labor practice, but that went to hell: Dunlop wouldn't sign it even after his reps said he would. That's another thing! We were dealing with errand boys, not the people who had authority to deal.

Gary Jones, the steward for the Employment and Training Administration had the following observations:

The underlying problem in this situation was one we've had with the Employment and Training Administration in general. It goes back to 1972 when they tried a general reorganization of ETA under Lambert, who was sent directly by the White House.

Carl and others saw the 1975 USES reorganization as a part of a continuing attempt to weed out some of the high-graded people.

What really precipitated things and put it all out of management's control was the fact that management [in December 1975] started meeting individually with people we represent, prior to any union-management consultations taking place. They sent notices to people's homes, also prior to consultation. That's just blanket disregard for our role as the employee's representative. From our point of view, the December 1975 version of the reorganization was substantially changed from the plan they showed us in July, so they were obligated to give us time to study the new documents. One thing that really stood out was the special projects staff. The people that were slated to go into that were known to be out of favor with Chandler and Smith. There was unquestionably a need for consultation, both procedurally and substantively.

Trouble Begins

On December 8, 1975, when the bulk of the necessary approvals had been received from the Department's Assistant Secretary for Administration and Management, Sy Krimkowitz, a long time career manager in the Employment and Training Administration, and its Director of Administration, contacted the union to arrange a consultation meeting regarding the reorganization. The meeting was set for Friday December 12 to accommodate Local 12 President Leonard Telman since his presence was considered important to such matters. Telman later noted that he ordinarily does not get involved in such "local" matters, but thought his presence would be stabilizing in view of poor labor relations in the USES.

In the meantime, Kent Smith, unbeknownst to Krimkowitz, called a meeting for the afternoon of Friday, December 12, of all National Office employees of USES.

The Friday morning meeting with management and union representatives was largely confined to providing to the union representatives a copy of the materials describing the new and old organization, including listings of staff assignments and organization charts. These materials were required under the labor-management agreement. (The "old" and "new" organization charts are reproduced in Exhibits 12-6 and 12-7, respectively.)

In the process of receiving the paperwork, Telman noted that management was obligated formally to invite union officers to the all-employee meeting. (A letter of invitation was sent to him within several hours.) He also reminded management that they could not discuss specifics of the organization, particularly employee assignments, at the all-employee meeting or otherwise hold such discussions directly with employees: Such discussion, according to the contract, was considered the exclusive domain of the employees' elected representatives.

Management noted in retrospect that, although they were anxious to get the union view so that they could press ahead, they mistakenly had left rather fuzzy the union response date, but they generally expected that the union would respond in a timely fashion. According to Telman, no sense of urgency was transmitted.

Gary Jones described some of the union discussions which followed receipt of the detailed documents on the morning of December 12:

There was some disagreement among us on how to proceed: I tried to get the USES representatives to put in writing our concerns and send it to Smith as soon as possible. Included with our submission should have been recommendations on how to alleviate the problems we had identified. Those guys never put anything to paper. What I got out of my conversations with them was that they were just opposed to any change at all.

I would have put things in writing and made constructive recommendations. Even though the contract gives us the right to consultation and negotiation, they still have, according to the contract, ultimate authority over organizational structure. But the fact that they did have to sit down with us gave us a lever — prior to implementation — to get some things changed. In this reorganization there were some real problems where some of the people we represent could have been hurt.

Management may think that unfinished job descriptions are just a matter of getting it done later; we've seen too many temporary assignments that never got changed or, often, the managers who promised that they would personally take care of a particular situation were gone or promoted to a different job. We like to see all of that nailed down — officially and in writing — ahead of time.

Maybe everything was fine, but in the absence of discussions, we couldn't find out. In the absence of constructive recommendations on our part, we were going to be stuck with management's version of things, and that wasn't in the interests of the employees who elect us. As far as I know, we never did respond to or discuss substantively the reorganization plan.

On December 12, the meeting of all USES employees was held. Management discussed in general terms the structure of the proposed new organization. The meeting was tape-recorded by a union representative, but was otherwise uneventful. A few days later, another meeting with Local 12 officials took place where additional copies of the reorganization plan were provided to them.

One management official noted:

> To avoid mistrust, it's important to tell employees as soon as possible what it is you are doing. But, if you don't have good communications and relationships with responsible and mature union leaders, the message to employees almost always gets garbled. Then employees don't trust management.

During the December 8-11 period, John Chandler, Smith's deputy, individually counseled some 26 employees, only one of whom was — in management's view — a member of the bargaining unit, to inform them of their probable assignments in the new organization and discussed with them the recourse available to them via appeals, other jobs, retirement options, etc. Chandler later described the discussions as part of a conscious attempt by management to equitably and compassionately communicate with individuals who would be affected by management's decisions regarding changes in the organization.

In the union's view, these counseling sessions were wholly inappropriate. The parties, of course, disagreed on whether or not certain of these employees were members of the bargaining unit and therefore entitled to union representation.

Many of those assigned to the special projects group felt that there was a change in status conferred upon them, since they would no longer be managers. They apparently became especially convinced of this when their prospective assignment became known as the "turkey farm." Some of these people reportedly had been dissatisfied with the outcomes of previous reorganizations and other management actions and were said to have reached the end of their patience. They retained Joseph Rauh, a well-known Washington attorney.

Over the next few days, tension increased and the pace of events quickened. On December 16, Local 12 called a meeting of its USES membership to discuss the reorganization. According to a chronology supplied by management, approximately 35 people attended. At about the same time, management provided official notification to the individuals previously counseled of the actions — formally described as "adverse actions" — affecting their status. This was the first official movement toward implementing the reorganization and it came prior to formal comment from or consultation with Local 12.

In the meantime, following a common practice, John Chandler met with Marvin Barkerman, the General Counsel of the Senate Labor and Public Welfare Committee, the Committee which has primary Congressional oversight jurisdiction over most Labor Department programs, for the purpose of informing him, and thereby the Committee, of the reorganization.

By the end of the following week, USES had not yet heard from the union. Sy Krimkowitz called Len Telman to find out when the union would respond. Mr. Telman left word via his secretary to say that he was going on leave for the Christmas holidays and that he would be prepared to discuss the matter upon his return. Smith, in the meantime, began to sense employee unrest and uncertainty and was champing at the bit to put things in motion. Also, news of the reorganization began to leak out to interest groups, Congressmen, and to individual employees, so Smith wanted to exercise his prerogatives before too many extraneous pressures came to bear. A variety of Congressional and farm labor groups had already begun to call Smith to question or complain about the reorganization.

At Smith's request, Krimkowitz sought to accelerate the process of gaining union comments. Having heard that Telman was still in the building, Krimkowitz tried to reach him. Failing at informal contacts, USES management sent Local 12 a letter dated December 22, saying that in the absence of comments from or discussion with the union, the reorganization would proceed.

Unfair Labor Practices

On December 22, the union formally filed an unfair labor practice (ULP) charge against the USES for failing to consult and negotiate, and requested a delay in implementation of the reorganization. Management agreed to the request for delay, postponing the effective date to January 4. During this period, some discussions took place in an effort to resolve the ULP. It was

the view of the USES stewards that filing of the ULP effectively barred implementation of the reorganization.

Anticipating implementation on January 4, management sent to the union a memo on December 30 for comment, which it intended to distribute to all USES employees, that both announced the effective date and specified new employee assignments. In the subsequent, expanded ULP filings, the union referred to this request for comments as a "sham," alleging that the memo was being duplicated and envelopes addressed and stuffed for distribution even while they were meeting with management on December 31 to discuss the memo.

Attorneys and the Press

On January 9 and January 24, 1976, the *Washington Star* published stories by their government employee columnist, Mike Causey, characterizing the USES reorganization as a politically-motivated shakeup by Republicans to "get" Democrats. His column went on to say that a "turkey farm" was being established to serve as a receptacle for these Democrats.

Prior to that, several of the employees who were going to be assigned to the "turkey farm" and lose their managerial status decided to file administrative grievances charging adverse action on the part of the USES. While many management officials dismissed these people as "professional grievers," their attorney, Joseph Rauh personally got in touch with Secretary of Labor John T. Dunlop and strongly protested the reorganization, highlighting the allegations of unfair labor practices and politicization.

According to union and management sources, the union was active in supplying information to journalists. It was reputed that some union officials were able to use their friendship with Mr. Causey to get the story into the *Washington Star*. Columnists for several other papers apparently declined to run a story.

The union also utilized its channels via the national American Federation of Government

Employees, AFL-CIO, to inform Congressmen and their staffs. Similarly, Local 12 provided information and material to Rauh in the hopes that his involvement would benefit the union more generally.

Finally, the union's house organ, *12NOW*, provided the entire Department of Labor with a running summary of the union view of the situation. (See Exhibit 12-8.)

A prominent union member said:

> If nothing else we did during that period did any real service to the employees, the publicity certainly helped. It generated enough heat so that management was forced to back off a few things, most notably the two managers who were reinstated when they appealed officially. The publicity is what got the Secretary and senior department staff interested and gave us a shot at further dragging out discussions, until the atmosphere changed in our favor.

The Secretary Intervenes

In late December 1975, the press and general scuttlebutt in Washington were full of speculation regarding Secretary Dunlop's possible resignation. Several weeks earlier, President Ford vetoed the Collective Bargaining in Construction Act of 1975, known as the "common situs picketing bill." Dunlop was regarded as the architect of the bill and earlier had been led to believe that the President would sign the bill. Although Dunlop subsequently resigned (effective February 1, 1976) his intentions were unknown at this time.

Before the press account hit the streets, the Secretary had, on January 2, decided to put a hold on the reorganization until he had independently looked into the issue. As the chief executive of an organization with 13,000 employees and a budget of around $20 billion, ordinarily the Secretary did not personally get involved in such matters.

Appealing to the Secretary of Labor

Smith, who in 1973 had worked under Dunlop at the Cost of Living Council,* called Dunlop at home, appealing the Secretary's decision to review the reorganization. Smith voiced his view that the reorganization was both managerially sound and that it had been developed in accordance with all relevant procedures. The union, he said, was simply stalling. Dunlop was sympathetic to the manager's predicament but, with long experience as a "neutral" in labor-management relations he saw it as necessary to review the matter.

Significant publicity had been generated and the state of labor-management relations was no small matter at the Labor Department. One person observed: "Dunlop knew how much trouble Rauh could cause publicity-wise and through the national union if things weren't Kosher. He wanted to be sure everything was clean before telling Rauh to pack it in." Employees of USES were informed on January 5 — one day after the announced implementation date — that the Secretary was personally reviewing the reorganization.

The Secretary's Review

The group appointed by the Secretary to review the matter was led by Joseph Berberian, Deputy Assistant Secretary for Labor Management Services (second in command in the portion of the Department that presided over private sector labor relations matters.) Also involved were several of Berberian's staff, other senior attorneys, a member of the Labor Department's Policy Analysis Office and Allen Bane, the only full-time person in the Department for internal labor-management relations.

The group came back to the Secretary — orally — three weeks later with their findings:

---

*The Cost of Living Council, of which Dunlop was Director during 1973 and 1974, administered the Federal wage and price controls program of 1971–1974.

First, they found *no* evidence of political motivation. Second, the organizational structure and concept were sound and they saw no need to substitute their judgment for that of USES management. Third, with respect to the proper conduct of labor-management relations, it was problematic as to whether or not management had properly met its obligations to consult and negotiate with the union.

In reaching this third conclusion, the group noted actions such as (1) directly counseling employees — some possibly outside of the unit, prior to consultation; (2) an all-employee meeting without significant lead time for consultation with union leadership; (3) the timing and form of consultation efforts surrounding the December 31 memo, and (4) the simple fact that to date *no* consultation actually had occurred. A complicating factor was the Christmas holidays and perceptions of fairness in expecting timely comments during this period.

Based on this report, the Secretary approved the reorganization subject to completion of consultation and negotiations.

In the course of the three-week hiatus — which to Smith seemed like an eternity — Allen Bane negotiated an agreement under which the union would have withdrawn the ULP charge, thereby breaking the impasse caused by the union's refusal to negotiate on questions related to the reorganization until the ULP was resolved. (ULP procedure mandates 30 days for the parties to seek their own accommodation before it can go through formal ajudication.) Believing that he had a priority mandate from the Under Secretary and others to resolve the ULP, a memorandum of agreement was drawn up (Exhibit 12-9).

One manager said: "When Kent saw that memo, he went bullshit and called Dunlop immediately." Dunlop had already seen the document — handed to him walking down the hall — and found it unacceptable and so informed his agents. Bane returned to the table

the next day (January 20) and said management wouldn't accept it. Smith was pleased, but a member of the union team said, "Allen came back to negotiate some more. We told him we didn't want to negotiate with him: We wanted to negotiate with the decision makers."

Consultation and Negotiations Begin

Shortly after Dunlop received the report a management negotiating team was established. The management team was headed by Allen Bane and included Tom Cuillo, an assistant to Berberian, Sy Krimkowitz, John Chandler and Dave Kiley, a Labor Department attorney specializing in employee rights. Management also formed a management policy group, which was given authority, as the Secretary's agent, to approve or reject agreements reached by the negotiating team. The policy group consisted of Berberian, Tony Pero (Counselor and Executive Assistant to the Secretary of Labor), Deputy Assistant Secretary Scabatini, Smith and Stanton Melbane (Deputy Assistant Secretary for Administration and Management).

The negotiating team for Local 12 included Len Telman, president of Local 12, Gary Jones, chief steward for the Employment and Training Administration, and Carl Beck.

The management policy team (by letter dated January 27, signed by Assistant Secretary for Administration and Management, Paul Spiro) contacted the president of Local 12, Mr. Telman and officially informed him that the negotiating team was prepared to meet as the Executive Order required on matters related to the USES reorganization. The union refused, partly as a tactic and partly miffed at what seemed like an "order" to appear the next day. The management group, who knew Mr. Telman well, reminded him informally that the contract requires that management provide an opportunity to consult and negotiate: If the union continued to refuse the opportunity, then the Secretary would simply allow the reorganization. It was management's feeling that the union ultimately came to the table because they perceived that their ability to prevail on the ULP would be weakened if they did not demonstrate interest in good faith bargaining.

The two groups met the next day and nothing of substance was discussed. The union maintained that it would not discuss the reorganization until the unfair labor practice was resolved. A compromise was worked out whereby the teams would spend half of their time discussing the unfair labor practice and half of their time on ground rules regarding negotiations over the reorganization. These discussions went on daily until about February 9. One member of the management team later remarked: "This was a ridiculous solution, but it allowed us to meet. We had to have some sort of discussions in order to demonstrate, on the record, our willingness to sit down with them."

The initial emphasis on "ground rules" grew out of a long-standing disagreement between the two parties concerning the contractual requirements pertaining to consultation and negotiations over reorganization. It was management's position that they were only required to negotiate on personnel actions that would have a specific adverse effect on individual employees and that consultation on design aspects were advisory only, with no obligation to accept or agree to union views; management retained all rights to determine the shape and functions of the organization. The union, on the other hand, asserted that they were entitled to significant influence over the form and functions of the organization. The "ground rules" discussions centered on this difference of opinion.

Management was interested in discussing the substance of the reorganization and related personnel implications while Local 12's priorities seemed to center on the ULP settlement, next on development of ground rules and only then to consult or negotiate. This set of priorities was perceived by management as a stalling tactic.

One union official explained:

Part of our strategy in insisting on resolution of the ULP was to try and drag the process out. As long as we were actively negotiating on the ULP as a precondition to discussion, it was unlikely that the reorganization would be implemented. They were concerned that substantive discussions take place and as long as the ULP was perceived as a removable barrier, they would keep talking. But we didn't want to block things forever. We simply wanted to keep things going until Dunlop was gone since we figured that Usery would bring in some new folks who would take a fresher and more favorable look at the situation. We had talked to some of Usery's people and became convinced that we would have a different reception from them.

After nearly two weeks of those "interminable" discussions, the management negotiating team concluded that the ULP had to be moved out of the way before any sort of consultation could take place. Thus, the two negotiating groups agreed, on the morning of February 6, to a memorandum they felt would defuse the ULP issue and finally move the discussions along. The memorandum was essentially the same as the previously rejected memorandum. The management group, led by Allen Bane, went back to the management policy group for approval of the memorandum. Having been embarrassed once, the negotiating team argued strongly for acceptance of the document. The USES management still objected, but in the absence of some of the more offensive language, their colleagues overrode them in order to move the discussions. One member of the management team recalled, "The Department was, in essence, selling out the USES."

The document was brought back to the bargaining table that afternoon. The union president, Mr. Telman, was not present that afternoon and the other union representatives refused to sign the document.

"Somehow, Len wasn't aware of the afternoon meeting where they offered us the agreement," Jones said.

They made a mistake trying to get that signed without Len there. Beck wasn't about to let it by. Now, to be honest, we really didn't think that management would go along with our proposal, since it was so much like the last memorandum, which they rejected. I would have signed it. Len had said we'd sign it. In reality, it was exactly what we had been negotiating for, but Beck just wouldn't sign it. Neither I nor management had any idea *what* he wanted them to do. After they agreed in principle to sign the thing and went to get approval and to get it typed, we went back to our union headquarters to discuss it. Beck said that Len had attached conditions to it, such as agreement on ground rules. I tried like hell to find Len to get it straight from him, but I couldn't locate him. I was disappointed. I know what I heard and what we had been negotiating for. It was hypocritical to refuse to sign it. It wasn't in keeping with our responsibility to the union members and the rest of the USES employees.

Getting them to admit wrongdoing in settling the ULP was damned important to us. If they were sufficiently embarrassed, they — or their colleagues — wouldn't do it again and would be more conscious of employee rights. Also, it would force them to acknowledge that Local 12 was indeed the employees' representative and was doing its job in that capacity. This was also an important part of our strategy, as Len will tell you.

Anyway when we came back in the afternoon and Beck started talking about conditions, the management guys blew up. They started yelling and screaming and then left the room to caucus. When they came back, they told us that they absolutely would not talk about the ULP any further and they walked out.

Members of the management group also noted that no additional conditions previously had surfaced and observed that demands for conditions after the fact was "bad faith" bargaining. Allen Bane personally had gone out on a limb with his management colleagues in the interest of progress, to gain approval of a distasteful position. It was Bane who angrily led the management team out of the room on the afternoon of February 6. He went to the management policy group that afternoon with his recommendations that consultation and negotiations be terminated and the reorganization be implemented.

Negotiations Break Down

On the following Monday, February 9, both teams showed up at the usual place. The union president was present for that session and offered to sign Friday's version of the ULP agreement. He was surprised by the management response: "It's no longer for sale. You guys added a new condition to a previously negotiated agreement. That's not simply bad faith; you are just stalling." The union walked out.

The management policy group was to meet the next day and make its recommendation to the new Secretary of Labor.

Exhibit 12-1. Department of Labor organization chart: 1975

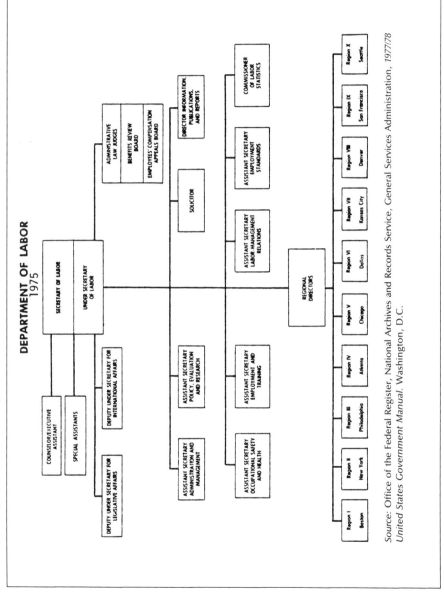

DEPARTMENT OF LABOR
1975

Source: Office of the Federal Register, National Archives and Records Service, General Services Administration, *1977/78 United States Government Manual.* Washington, D.C.

Exhibit 12-2. Employment and Training Administration organization chart: 1975

EMPLOYMENT AND TRAINING ADMINISTRATION ORGANIZATION CHART

1975

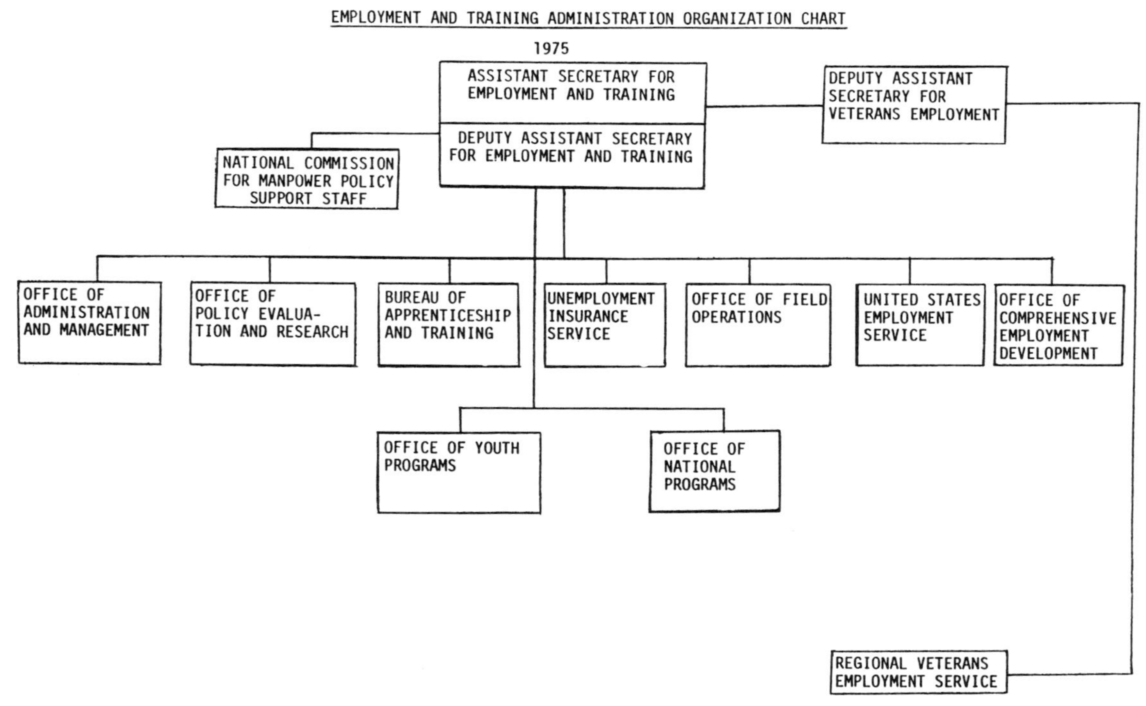

Source: United States Department of Labor.

Exhibit 12-3. Excerpts from Executive Order 11491, as amended

Excerpts from:

EXECUTIVE ORDER 11491
AS AMENDED

LABOR-MANAGEMENT RELATIONS IN THE FEDERAL SERVICE

Sec. 2. *Definitions.* When used in this Order, the term—

(a) "Agency" means an executive department, a Government corporation, and an independent establishment as defined in section 104 of title 5, United States Code, except the General Accounting Office;

(b) "Employee" means an employee of an agency and an employee of a nonappropriated fund instrumentality of the United States but does not include, for the purpose of exclusive recognition or national consultation rights, a supervisor, except as provided in section 24 of this Order; _

(c) "Supervisor" means an employee having authority, in the interest of an agency. to hire, transfer, suspend, lay off, recall, promote, discharge, assign, reward, or discipline other employees, or responsibility to direct them, or to adjust their grievances, or effectively to recommend such action, if in connection with the foregoing the exercise of authority is not of a merely routine or clerical nature, but requires the use of independent judgment; _

Sec. 10. *Exclusive recognition.* (a) An agency shall accord exclusive recognition to a labor organization when the organization has been selected, in a secret ballot election, by a majority of the employees in an appropriate unit as their representative; provided that this section shall not preclude an agency from according exclusive recognition to a labor organization, without an election, where the appropriate unit is established through the consolidation of existing exclusively recognized units represented by that organization.

(b) A unit may be established on a plant or installation. craft. functional, or other basis which will ensure a clear and identifiable community of interest among the employees concerned and will promote effective dealings and efficiency of agency operations. A unit shall not be established solely on the basis of the extent to which employees in the proposed unit have organized, nor shall a unit be established if it includes—

(1) any management official or supervisor, except as provided in section 24;

(2) an employee engaged in Federal personnel work in other than a purely clerical capacity; or

(3) [Revoked.]

(4) both professional and nonprofessional employees, unless a majority of the professional employees vote for inclusion in the unit.

Questions as to the appropriate unit and related issues may be referred to the Assistant Secretary for decision.

(c) [Revoked.]

(d) All elections shall be conducted under the supervision of the Assistant Secretary, or persons designated by him, and shall be by secret ballot. Each employee eligible to vote shall be provided the opportunity to choose the labor organization he wishes to represent him, from among those on the ballot, or "no union", except as provided in subpraragraph (4) of this paragraph. Elections may be held to determine whether—

(1) a labor organization should be recognized as the exclusive representative of em ployees in a unit;

(2) a labor organization should replace another labor organization as the exclusive representative;

(Exhibit continues on following page.)

Exhibit 12-3. Continued

(3) a labor organization should cease to be the exclusive representative; or

(4) a labor organization should be recognized as the exclusive representative of employees in a unit composed of employees in units currently represented by that labor organization or continue to be recognized in the existing separate units.

(e) When a labor organization has been accorded exclusive recognition, it is the exclusive representative of employees in the unit and is entitled to act for and negotiate agreements covering all employees in the unit. It is responsible for representing the interests of all employees in the unit without discrimination and without regard to labor organization membership. The labor organization shall be given the opportunity to be represented at formal discussions between management and employees or employee representatives concerning grievances, personnel policies and practices, or other matters affecting general working conditions of employees in the unit.

AGREEMENTS

Sec. 11. *Negotiation of agreements.* (a) An agency and a labor organization that has been accorded exclusive recognition, through appropriate representatives, shall meet at reasonable times and confer in good faith with respect to personnel policies and practices and matters affecting working conditions, so far as may be appropriate under applicable laws and regulations, including policies set forth in the Federal Personnel Manual; published agency policies and regulations for which a compelling need exists under criteria established by the Federal Labor Relations Council and which are issued at the agency headquarters level or at the level of a primary national subdivision; a national or other controlling agreement at a higher level in the agency; and this Order. They may negotiate an agreement, or any question arising thereunder; determine appropriate techniques, consistent with section 17 of this Order, to assist in such negotiation; and execute a written agreement or memorandum of understanding.

(b) In prescribing regulations relating to personnel policies and practices and working conditions, an agency shall have due regard for the obligation imposed by paragraph (a) of this section. However, the obligation to meet and confer does not include matters with respect to the mission of an agency; its budget; its organization; the number of employees; and the numbers, types, and grades of positions or employees assigned to an organizational unit, work project or tour of duty; the technology of performing its work; or its internal security practices. This does not preclude the parties from negotiating agreements providing appropriate arrangements for employees adversely affected by the impact of realignment of work forces or technological change.

(c) If, in connection with negotiations, an issue develops as to whether a proposal is contrary to law, regulation, controlling agreement, or this Order and therefore not negotiable, it shall be resolved as follows:

(1) An issue which involves interpretation of a controlling agreement at a higher agency level is resolved under the procedures of the controlling agreement, or, if none, under agency regulations;

(2) An issue other than as described in subparagraph (1) of this paragraph which arises at a local level may be referred by either party to the head of the agency for determination;

(3) An agency head's determination as to the interpretation of the agency's regulations with respect to a proposal is final;

(4) A labor organization may appeal to the Council for a decision when—

(i) it disagrees with an agency head's determination that a proposal would violate applicable law, regulation of appropriate authority outside the agency, or this Order, or

(ii) it believes that an agency's regulations, as interpreted by the agency head, violate applicable law, regulation of appropriate authority outside the agency, or this Order, or are not otherwise applicable to bar negotiations under paragraph (a) of this section.

(Exhibit continues on following page.)

Exhibit 12-3. Continued

(d) If, as the result of an alleged unilateral change in, or addition to, personnel policies and practices or matters affecting working conditions, the acting party is charged with a refusal to consult, confer or negotiate as required under this Order, the Assistant Secretary may, in the exercise of his authority under section 6(a)(4) of the Order, make those determinations of negotiability as may be necessary to resolve the merits of the alleged unfair labor practice. In such cases the party subject to an adverse ruling may appeal the Assistant Secretary's negotiability determination to the Council.

Sec. 12. *Basic provisions of agreements.* Each agreement between an agency and a labor organization is subject to the following requirements—

(a) in the administration of all matters covered by the agreement, officials and employees are governed by existing or future laws and the regulations of appropriate authorities, including policies set forth in the Federal Personnel Manual; by published agency policies and regulations in existence at the time the agreement was approved; and by subsequently published agency policies and regulations required by law or by the regulations of appropriate authorities, or authorized by the terms of a controlling agreement at a higher agency level;

(b) management officials of the agency retain the right, in accordance with applicable laws and regulations—

(1) to direct employees of the agency;

(2) to hire, promote, transfer, assign, and retain employees in positions within the agency, and to suspend, demote, discharge, or take other disciplinary action against employees;

(3) to relieve employees from duties because of lack of work or for other legitimate reasons;

(4) to maintain the efficiency of the Government operations entrusted to them;

(5) to determine the methods, means, and personnel by which such operations are to be conducted; and

(6) to take whatever actions may be necessary to carry out the mission of the agency in situations of emergency; and

(c) nothing in the agreement shall require an employee to become or to remain a member of a labor organization, or to pay money to the organization except pursuant to a voluntary, written authorization by a member for the payment of dues through payroll deductions.

The requirements of this section shall be expressly stated in the initial or basic agreement and apply to all supplemental, implementing, subsidiary, or informal agreements between the agency and the organization.

- -

CONDUCT OF LABOR ORGANIZATIONS AND MANAGEMENT

Sec. 18. *Standards of conduct for labor organizations.* (a) An agency shall accord recognition only to a labor organization that is free from corrupt influences and influences opposed to basic democratic principles. Except as provided in paragraph (b) of this section, an organization is not required to prove that it has the required freedom when it is subject to governing requirements adopted by the organization or by a national or international labor organization or federation of labor organizations with which it is affiliated or in which it participates, containing explicit and detailed provisions to which it subscribes calling for—

(1) the maintenance of democratic procedures and practices, including provisions for periodic elections to be conducted subject to recognized safeguards and provisions defining and securing the right of individual members to participation in the affairs of the organization, to fair and equal treatment under the governing rules of the organization, and to fair process in disciplinary proceedings;

(Exhibit continues on following page.)

Exhibit 12-3. Continued

(2) the exclusion from office in the organization of persons affiliated with Communist or other totalitarian movements and persons identified with corrupt influences;

(3) the prohibition of business or financial interests on the part of organization officers and agents which conflict with their duty to the organization and its members; and

(4) the maintenance of fiscal integrity in the conduct of the affairs of the organization, including provision for accounting and financial controls and regular financial reports or summaries to be made available to members.

(b) Notwithstanding the fact that a labor organization has adopted or subscribed to standards of conduct as provided in paragraph (a) of this section, the organization is required to furnish evidence of its freedom from corrupt influences or influences opposed to basic democratic principles when there is reasonable cause to believe that—

(1) the organization has been suspended or expelled from or is subject to other sanction by a parent labor organization or federation of organizations with which it had been affiliated because it has demonstrated an unwillingness or inability to comply with governing requirements comparable in purpose to those required by paragraph (a) of this section; or

(2) the organization is in fact subject to influences that would preclude recognition under this Order.

(c) A labor organization which has or seeks recognition as a representative of employees under this Order shall file financial and other reports, provide for bonding of officials and employees of the organization, and comply with trusteeship and election standards.

(d) The Assistant Secretary shall prescribe the regulations needed to effectuate this section. These regulations shall conform generally to the principles applied to unions in the private sector. Complaints of violations of this section shall be filed with the Assistant Secretary.

Sec. 19. *Unfair labor practices.* (a) Agency management shall not—

(1) interfere with, restrain, or coerce an employee in the exercise of the rights assured by this Order;

(2) encourage or discourage membership in a labor organization by discrimination in regard to hiring, tenure, promotion, or other conditions of employment;

(3) sponsor, control, or otherwise assist a labor organization, except that an agency may furnish customary and routine services and facilities under section 23 of this Order when consistent with the best interests of the agency, its employees, and the organization, and when the services and facilities are furnished, if requested, on an impartial basis to organizations having equivalent status;

(4) discipline or otherwise discriminate against an employee because he has filed a complaint or given testimony under this Order;

(5) refuse to accord appropriate recognition to a labor organization qualified for such recognition; or

(6) refuse to consult, confer, or negotiate with a labor organization as required by this Order.

(b) A labor organization shall not—

(1) interfere with, restrain, or coerce an employee in the exercise of his rights assured by this Order;

(2) attempt to induce agency management to coerce an employee in the exercise of his rights under this Order;

(3) coerce, attempt to coerce, or discipline, fine, or take other economic sanction against a member of the organization as punishment or reprisal for, or for the purpose of hindering or impeding his work performance, his productivity, or the discharge of his duties owed as an officer or employee of the United States;

(4) call or engage in a strike, work stoppage, or slowdown; picket an agency in a labor-management dispute; or condone any such activity by failing to take affirmative action to prevent or stop it;

(5) discriminate against an employee with regard to the terms or conditions of membership because of race, color, creed, sex, age, or national origin; or

(6) refuse to consult, confer, or negotiate with an agency as required by this Order.

(Exhibit continues on following page.)

Exhibit 12-3. Continued

(c) A labor organization which is accorded exclusive recognition shall not deny membership to any employee in the appropriate unit except for failure to meet reasonable occupational standards uniformly required for admission, or for failure to tender initiation fees and dues uniformly required as a condition of acquiring and retaining membership. This paragraph does not preclude a labor organization from enforcing discipline in accordance with procedures under its constitution or by-laws which conform to the requirements of this Order.

(d) Issues which can properly be raised under an appeals procedure may not be raised under this section. Issues which can be raised under a grievance procedure may, in the discretion of the aggrieved party, be raised under that procedure or the complaint procedure under this section, but not under both procedures. Appeals or grievance decisions shall not be construed as unfair labor practice decisions under this Order nor as precedent for such decisions. All complaints under this section that cannot be resolved by the parties shall be filed with the Assistant Secretary.

- -

Sec. 26. *Effective date.* This Order is effective on January 1, 1970, except sections 7(f) and 8 which are effective immediately. Effective January 1, 1970, Executive Order No. 10988 and the President's Memorandum of May 21, 1963, entitled Standards of Conduct for Employee Organizations and Code of Fair Labor Practices are revoked.

RICHARD NIXON

THE WHITE HOUSE
October 29, 1969

Exhibit 12-4a. Excerpts from agreements between U.S. Department of
Labor and American Federation of Government Employees, Local 12

EXCERPTS FROM: AGREEMENTS BETWEEN U.S. DEPARTMENT OF LABOR AND AMERICAN
                FEDERATION OF GOVERNMENT EMPLOYEES, LOCAL 12

Article V Structure of Union-Management Relations:

E. In mutual recognition of the obligations and responsibilities imposed
on the parties by section 11 of Executive Order 11491, as amended, the
Department and Local 12 agree that there shall be meaningful consultation
between them on organizational changes.

    1. Major Organizational Changes:

        a. When the change is of the magnitude defined in the Manual
of Administration as a "major" organizational change, consultation will
not take place until the change has been approved at the OASA level.

        b. The appropriate agency head shall notify the President of
Local 12 of the impending change and the President shall identify the
appropriate union representatives to be consulted.

        c. During the consultation sessions management shall discuss
and, to the extent that they have been developed, present to Local 12
representatives copies of the following:

        (1) Organizational charts (old and new)
        (2) Mission and function statements
        (3) Staffing patterns (old and new)

        d. Local 12 will be provided a minimum of five (5) days to
respond to management's proposal before implementation.

        e. In response to orders from authorities outside the Department,
or in order to meet an emergency situation that exists in the Department,
it may be necessary to effect an organizational change before the documentation listed in c. immediately above becomes available, or before OASA
approval is received. In such a case, consultation shall occur prior to
the date of implementation but only with such information and documentation
as it is possible to provide at that time.

    When such circumstances occur further consultation shall take place
as the information and documentation are developed.

    2. Other Organizational Changes:

        a. The management official responsible for the organizational
entity being changed shall notify the President of Local 12 of an organization change.

        b. The Local 12 President shall designate the appropriate union
representative to be consulted.

(Exhibit continues on following page.)

Exhibit 12-4a. Continued

c. During the consultation session management shall discuss and to the entent that they have developed provide documents on:

    (1) Nature of the change
    (2) Reason for the change
    (3) How the change shall be effected

3. Nothing in this article shall be construed as precluding the parties from negotiating appropriate arrangement for employees adversely affected by such changes.

Exhibit 12-4b. Excerpts from agreements between U.S. Department of
Labor and American Federation of Government Employees, Local 12

EXCERPTS FROM: AGREEMENTS BETWEEN U.S. DEPARTMENT OF LABOR AND AMERICAN
                FEDERATION OF GOVERNMENT EMPLOYEES, LOCAL 12

Article III   Recognition:

A. The Department acknowledges that each employee of the Department has the
right, freely and without fear of penalty or reprisal, to form, join, and
assist a labor organization or to refrain from any such activity, and that
each employee shall be protected in the exercise of this right as provided
in the controlling Executive Order, rules and regulations. To interfere with,
restrain, or coerce an employee in the exercise of this right is an unfair
labor practice.

B. In recognition of the fact that a majority of the employees in the bargaining unit have indicated that they wish to be represented by Local 12,
and a majority of the professional employees in the unit have indicated that
they wish to be included in the same bargaining unit, therefore, Local 12
continues to be recognized as the exclusive representative of all employees
in the Department in the unit described in section C below which conforms to
the requirements of Executive Order 11491, as amended.

C. The unit includes all employees in the National Office, except supervisors,
management officials and guards as defined in Executive Order 11491, as amended;
employees engaged in Federal personnel work in other than a purely clerical
capacity; and employees to which Section 3 of Executive Order 11491, as amended,
applies.

D. The provisions of this Agreement may be extended to, and become applicable
to, any group of employees which meets the prerequisites specified in Executive
Order 11491, as amended, and are appropriately added to the bargaining unit.
The method of this extension will be determined through consultation and
agreement by the parties concerned.

E. As the exclusive representative of all employees in the bargaining unit,
Local 12 shall be entitled to act for, and to negotiate agreements covering,
all employees in the unit. It shall be responsible for representing the
interests of all employees in the unit without discrimination and without
regard to labor organization membership. Local 12 shall be given the opportunity to be represented at formal discussions between management and employees
or employee representatives concerning grievances, personnel policies and
practices, or other matters affecting general working conditions of employees
in the unit.

F. As the exclusive representative of employees in the unit, Local 12 shall
have the right to consult with management at any stage of a grievance and to
be represented at grievance proceedings.

G. The Department and Local 12, through appropriate officials and representatives, shall meet at reasonable times and confer with respect to personnel
policies and practices and matters affecting working conditions, so far as
may be appropriate subject to law and policy requirements. This extends to
the negotiation of supplementary agreements on any question arising under this

(Exhibit continues on following page.)

Exhibit 12-4b. Continued

(Article III)

Agreement, to the determination of appropriate techniques, consistent with the terms and purposes of Executive Order 11491, as amended, to assist in such negotiations, and to the execution of written supplementary agreements or understandings incorporating any agreement reached by the parties. In exercising authority to make rules and regulations relating to personnel policies and practices and working conditions, the Department shall have due regard for the obligation imposed by this section, but such obligation shall not be construed to extend to such areas of discretion and policy as the mission of the Department; its budget; its organization; the number of employees; and the numbers, types, and grades of positions of employees assigned to an organizational unit, work project, or tour of duty; the technology of performing its work; or its internal security practices; however, the management of the Department agrees to discuss with Local 12, insofar as possible, changes contemplated or foreseen as they affect employees in the unit in such matters.

Exhibit 12-5. Key events in the development of the United States Employment Service reorganization

Date	Development of Reorganization	Labor-Management Contacts	USES Staff Contacts	Contacts With Groups or Individuals Outside DOL
August 6, 1974	Under Secretary informs Assistant Secretary (A/S) Lambert that OASAM will conduct a manpower utilization study of USES[2]			
August thru November 1974	Survey team on-site conducting manpower utilization study			
December 1974	Survey team prepares report of findings			
	Briefing provided to USES Executive Staff on study results			
January 7, 1975	Formal report submitted to A/S Lambert			
January 1975	ETA[3] Personnel Office commences classification review of USES positions (not connected with OASAM Study)			
February 26, 1975	Meeting – Smith & Chandler with OASAM Organization & Manpower Utilization Staff to discuss major USES organizational problems & methods of correcting			

(Exhibit continues on following page.)

Exhibit 12-5. Continued

Date	Development of Reorganization	Labor-Management Contacts	USES Staff Contacts	Contacts with Groups or Individuals Outside DOL
March 14, 1975	Further discussion between OASAM & USES staff regarding organizational problems			
March 1975	Classification review halted pending outcome of resolution of organizational problems			
April 8, 1975	Lambert, Scabatini, Krimkowitz, Smith & Chandler meet to discuss USES organizational problem and methods for addressing such problems			
Mid-April thru early May	OASAM & ETA staff develop staff utilization proposal which will serve as the basis for USES organizational modification			
May 6, 1975	Scabatini & Smith meet with Paul Spiro, Assistant Secretary, OASAM, to present proposal to improve USES staff utilization	Initial contact with Local 12 officials regarding organizational restructuring of USES. Local 12 officials requested to provide comments.		USES senior staff (Office Directors & Division Chiefs) informed of organizational restructuring & requested to provide comments

298

Date	Development of Reorganization	Labor-Management Contacts	USES Staff Contacts	Contacts with Groups or Individuals Outside DOL
Mid-May thru early June	USES staff and ETA Organization & Management staff continue to develop organizational structure & functional distribution of duties and responsibilities			
June 6, 1975		USES and Local 12 officials engage in further discussion regarding reorganization		
Mid-June thru June 30	Work on organizational structure & revised Mission & Functions Statements completed			
June 30, 1975 July 3, 1975	Proposal to reorganize USES sent to A/S Spiro			
July 7, 1975	USES staff selected to develop position descriptions. Staff selected on basis of knowledge of a given functional area.			John Chandler briefs representatives of the National Association of Agricultural Employers on the USES reorganization & its effect on agricultural activities.

(Exhibit continues on following page.)

Exhibit 12-5. Continued

Date	Development of Reorganization	Labor-Management Contacts	USES Staff Contacts	Contacts with Groups or Individuals Outside DOL
July 14, 1975				Smith & Chandler brief representatives of the Interstate Conference of Employment Security Agencies on the USES Reorganization
July 15, 1975	USES & OASAM staff meet to discuss proposal submitted to A/S Spiro			
July 17, 1975				Smith & Chandler brief Rural Congressional Caucus on the USES Reorganization - rural concerns addressed regarding the planned abolishment of the Rural Manpower Service
July 21, 1975	USES & OASAM staff meet to discuss proposal submitted to A/S Spiro			
July 21, 1975				Kent Smith testifies before the Subcommittee on Rural Development of the Senate Agriculture and Forrestry Committee on S. 1807. Questions were directed to Mr. Smith regarding reorganization. Subcommittee state objections to reorganization with respect to impact on rural America.

Date	Development of Reorganization	Labor-Management Contacts	USES Staff Contacts	Contacts with Groups or Individuals Outside DOL
July 30, 1975		Letter from Local 12 requesting to meet & negotiate the proposed reorganization		
August 1, 1975		Response from Smith to Local 12 regarding request of July 30.		
August 4, 1975	Smith & Krimkowitz meet with Deputy Assistant Secretary Melbane (OASAM) to discuss USES staffing			
August 5, 1975		Letter from Local 12 to A/S Lambert stating USES refusal to negotiate and requesting a meeting to negotiate reorganization		
		Letter from Local 12 to Sy Krimkowitz naming Carl Beck as union representative who will represent Local 12 at consultation sessions with ETA management		
August 15, 1975		Response to Local 12 letter to A/S Lambert with offer to consult on September 8, 1975		

(Exhibit continues on following page.)

Exhibit 12-5. Continued

Date	Development of Reorganization	Labor-Management Contacts	USES Staff Contacts	Contacts with Groups or Individuals Outside DOL
August 27, 1975		Letter to A/S Lambert from Local 12 regarding response of August 15		
August 29, 1975	USES GS 14 and GS 15 position descriptions sent to OASAM for classification			
September 5, 1975		Local 12 letter to Secretary Dunlop stating ETA has not consulted with union; request a meeting with Secretary		
September 12, 1975		A/S Lambert response to Local 12 letter of August 27		
		Separately, ETA attempts to arrange a meeting to discuss reorganization		
October 28, 1975	Classification approval received from A/S Spiro for majority of positions at requested grade levels			
November 7, 1975	ETA staff meet with OASAM staff to appeal grade levels of several positions			
November 19, 1975	Written appeal sent to OASAM			
December 4, 1975	OASAM response to appeal received.			

Date	Development of Reorganization	Labor-Management Contacts	USES Staff Contacts	Contacts with Groups or Individuals Outside DOL
December 8, 1975		Sy Krimkowitz contacted President of Local 12 to arrange consultation meeting regarding reorganization		
		Letter from Local 12 to A/S Lambert requesting meeting. This letter was apparently an outcome of a Local 12 meeting held with Secretary's representatives who contacted Local 12 as a result of the September 5, 1975 letter to the Secretary		
			Memos sent to all USES staff advising them of a meeting to be held December 12 to inform them of the status of the reorganization	
December 11, 1975		Scabatini response to Local 12 letter of December 8.		
December 8 thru 11			Courtesy meetings held with individual USES staff regarding proposed assignments in planned organization	

(Exhibit continues on following page.)

Exhibit 12-5. Continued

Date	Development of Reorganization	Labor-Management Contacts	USES Staff Contacts	Contacts with Groups or Individuals Outside DOL
December 12, 1975		Consultation meeting with Local 12; organizational materials provided	All employee meeting - general changes in missions, functions, structure discussed; no discussion of employee assignments	
December 15, 1975		Certain USES staff learn of proposed assignments from documents provided Local 12		
December 16, 1975		ETA meets with Local 12 officials & provides additional copies of materials presented to them on December 12.	Local 12 invites USES membership to meeting to discuss reorganization; approximately 35 people attended. Membership informed that copies of assignment roster available from USES stewards and that by grieving, membership could stop reorganization	
December 18, 1975			Two Adverse Action letters & one RIF notice presented to employees	

Date	Development of Reorganization	Labor-Management Contacts	USES Staff Contacts	Contacts with Groups or Individuals Outside DOL
				Chandler meets with Marvin Barkerman General Counsel of the Senate Labor and Public Welfare Committee re-garding reorganization.
December 19, 1975			Four Adverse Action letters presented	
December 22, 1975		Sy Krimkowitz letter to Local 12 President advising him that in event further consulta-tion does not take place, reorganization effective December 28, 1975		
		Local 12 files Unfair Labor Practice complaint (ULP)		
December 24, 1975		Letter to Sy Krimkowitz from Local 12 suggesting delay in implementation of reorganization		

(Exhibit continues on following page.)

Exhibit 12-5. Continued

Date	Development of Reorganization	Labor-Management Contacts	USES Staff Contacts	Contacts with Groups or Individuals Outside DOL
		Letter from Sy Krimkowitz to Local 12 to request comments regarding reorganization and informing Local 12 that January 4 to be effective date of reorganization		
December 30, 1975		Meeting with and memo sent to Local 12 official requesting comments concerning all employee memo announcing effective date of reorganization, describing employee assignments and announcing January 5 meeting.		
December 31, 1975		Meeting with Local 12 official to discuss content of memo.		
		Memo mailed to staff.		
January 2, 1976		Secretary decides to stay implementation pending review.		
January 5, 1976			USES All-Employee meeting held; staff informed that the Secretary was personally reviewing reorganization; therefore, reorganization not effective January 4	

Date	Development of Reorganization	Labor-Management Contacts	USES Staff Contacts	Contacts with Groups or Individuals Outside DOL
January 9, 1976				Newspaper stories appear describing "turkey farm" and alleging political motives in reorganization
Early January thru January 20		Bane & Krimkowitz meet with Local 12 negotiating team to resolve ULP complaint		
January 20, 1976		Discussions cease. Management would not agree to memorandum of agreement previously negotiated.		
January 25, 1976		Secretary receives Berberian's report. OK's structure, but requires further negotiation and consultation.		
January 27, 1976		Letter to Local 12 stating Secretary's position & requesting meeting on January 28.		
January 28, 1976		Meeting held.		
January 29, 1976		Meeting held.		
January 30, 1976		Meeting held.		
February 2, 1976		Meeting held.		

(Exhibit continues on following page.)

Exhibit 12-5. Continued

Date	Development of Reorganization	Labor-Management Contacts	USES Staff Contacts	Contacts with Groups or Individuals Outside DOL
February 4, 1976		Meeting held.		
February 5, 1976		Meeting held.		
February 6, 1976		Meeting held; tentative agreement reached on ULP in a.m. - Union refuses to sign at p.m. meeting unless conditions were attached. Management team walks out.		
February 9, 1976		Short meeting held. Union offers to sign agreement. Management refuses. Union walks out.		
		Letter from Bane to Telman stating that Department would consider its obligation to consult and negotiate fulfilled unless "meaningful" discussions took place.		
February 9, 1976		Secretary Usery agrees to meet with Telman.		

Exhibit 12-6. USES organizational structure: 1974

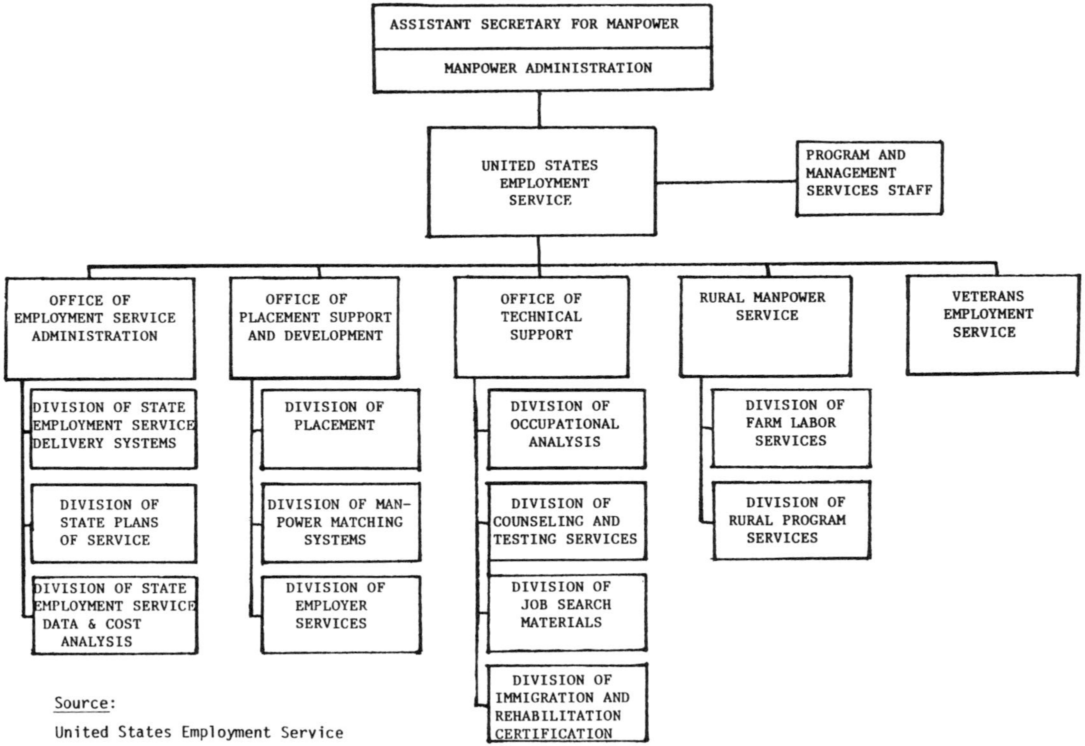

ASSISTANT SECRETARY FOR MANPOWER
MANPOWER ADMINISTRATION

PROGRAM AND MANAGEMENT SERVICES STAFF

UNITED STATES EMPLOYMENT SERVICE

VETERANS EMPLOYMENT SERVICE

RURAL MANPOWER SERVICE
- DIVISION OF FARM LABOR SERVICES
- DIVISION OF RURAL PROGRAM SERVICES

OFFICE OF TECHNICAL SUPPORT
- DIVISION OF OCCUPATIONAL ANALYSIS
- DIVISION OF COUNSELING AND TESTING SERVICES
- DIVISION OF JOB SEARCH MATERIALS
- DIVISION OF IMMIGRATION AND REHABILITATION CERTIFICATION

OFFICE OF PLACEMENT SUPPORT AND DEVELOPMENT
- DIVISION OF PLACEMENT
- DIVISION OF MAN-POWER MATCHING SYSTEMS
- DIVISION OF EMPLOYER SERVICES

OFFICE OF EMPLOYMENT SERVICE ADMINISTRATION
- DIVISION OF STATE EMPLOYMENT SERVICE DELIVERY SYSTEMS
- DIVISION OF STATE PLANS OF SERVICE
- DIVISION OF STATE EMPLOYMENT SERVICE DATA & COST ANALYSIS

Source:
United States Employment Service

309

Exhibit 12-7. USES organizational chart: proposed reorganization

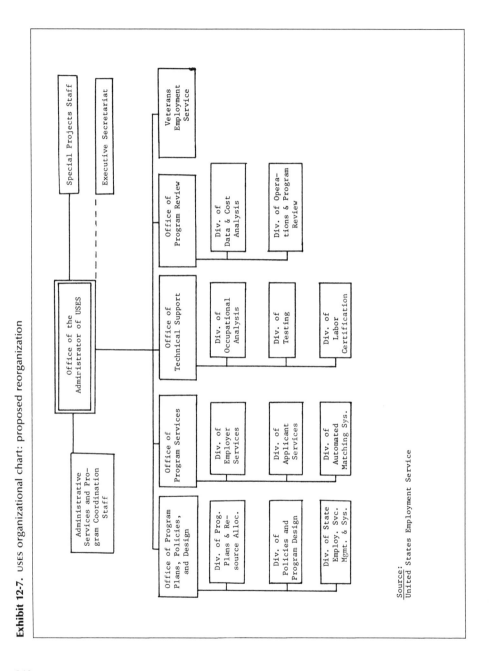

Source:
United States Employment Service

Exhibit 12-8. Newsletter from Local 12

12NOW

TUESDAY
27
JAN. 1976

Local 12 American Federation of Government Employees

GSA
Siege

Last week a state of siege came to the New Labor Building. DOL employees and Stouffer's employees were "the enemy".

On Monday 3 GSA police came to the OASA audit department on the fifth floor of the South Building to arrest an employee they said stole a Parking Sticker. After dumping the contents of her purse on the supervisor's desk, it was established that the sticker on the car was her own. Not satisfied, the police took her to their of-fices and held her from 9:30 am to 2 pm. GSA would not release her until she wrote a statement that she had stolen a sticker. 12NOW spoke to Captain Rutherford in charge of GSA police in the building, and he refused to comment.

After the cafeteria strike began, Stouffer's employees were barred from the building. It was necessary for Local 12 officers to accompany them into the building although they had been regularly entering and leaving the building prior to the strike. Meanwhile hundreds of visitors entered the building without this procedure, many without signature (including a few pickpockets).

By Thursday, the Washington Star described the situation at DOL as "wilder and wilder". GSA Building Manager Harvey attempted to suppress Local 12's leaflets. Extra police appeared at all entrances and DOL employees were checked for passes. At 4:30 pm Thursday the two central banks of elevators were turned off, forcing employees to leave work by the stairways. (What did the handicapped do?) A DOL official said the elevator shutdown was to "keep pickets out of the building". A NBC reporter was roughed up by GSA police on Thursday afternoon. Local 12 wrote to GSA administrator Jack Eckerd asking his help in changing the "landlord" approach of the GSA building management. . . .

(Exhibit continues on following page.)

Exhibit 12-8. Continued

Cafeteria Boycott

Last Thursday, 30 Stouffer's employees decided they needed a union. They joined Local 25 of the Hotel Restaurant Workers AFL-CIO, asked their employer for union recognition and sat down in the cafeteria to await the answer. The employees, who earn an average of $2.60 per hour, came to the end of the road on hard work for no money and unreasonable supervision.

Although a clear majority (90%) of the employees have voted with their feet, Stouffer's maintains it is not sure and wants an election. The union is not filing for an election and has filed unfair labor practice charges against Stouffer's for firing employees engaged in concerted action.

The cafeteria workers ask that all DOL employees support their strike by not patronizing Stouffer's. (Information on area cafeterias appears on back side.)

———

12NOW dropped into the Secretary's office the other morning and found it was flapjack time. On a piece of the new china at each person's desk were a few flapjacks, butter, and syrup. Yum yum. It left us wondering who pays?

WHY I JOINED THE UNION

Cafeteria workers speak:

• I joined the union because I was fired and it showed me that we need someone to protect our rights. We are being overworked, not enough pay, respect is not shown, or appreciation, for that matter. I don't want this to happen again to me or anyone else. Who needs this?

• I was tired of not being respected, not appreciated.

• I joined the union because if you are by yourself you lose all your rights. When you have a group then you have power.

• I joined the union because it shows unity and togetherness the way people should be.

———

$2,000 worth of videotape equipment was stolen from OSHA this month. It was taken on a week night with no marks of breaking and entering.

Exhibit 12-9. Memorandum of understanding regarding unfair labor practice charge

MEMORANDUM OF UNDERSTANDING
REGARDING UNFAIR LABOR PRACTICE CHARGE, JAN. 21, 1976

The Department of Labor and Local 12, AFGE, AFL-CIO, hereinafter referred to as the parties, agree to the following as a resolution to the unfair labor practice charges filed against the Department by Local 12 on December 22, 1975. In veiw of the fact that the Department did not engage in proper consultation and negotiation with Local 12 prior to taking steps to implement the presently proposed reorganization of the USES, the parties agree to the following:

1. No action will be taken to implement the proposed reorganization of USES, including modifications, until the obligations and requirements of the Agreement and the Executive Order, as amended, are fulfilled.

2. The Employment and Training Administration will within three (3) workdays of the signing of this memorandum, issue a memorandum to all USES employees at their home addresses rescinding all memoranda to USES employees on the subject of the reorganization, including the December 31, 1975 memorandum.

3. The memorandum mentioned in Item 2 above will provide an explanation of the recision.

4. Management will refrain from any consultation and negotiation concerning the impact of the reorganization (which consultation and negotiation should appropriately be with Local 12) with bargaining unit members for for which Local 12 is the exclusive representative.

5. The unfair labor practice charge is withdrawn upon the execution of the agreement, issuance of memorandum to all USES employees referred to in Item 2 above, and the withdrawal of any adverse action proposals or reduction-in-force notices issued to unit employees, or other employees, which notices or proposals the Department determines or agrees adversely impact employees in the unit.

6. The parties agree to sign a memorandum of understanding concluding consultations and negotiations as required by the Agreement and Executive Order, as amended, on the reorganization of USES.

Agreed to and signed this _____ day of _____, 1976.

C.B. 1/20/76

_____   _____
FOR LOCAL 12   FOR THE DEPARTMENT

CHAPTER 13

Bargaining for Pay:
Labor Relations, Mediation,
and Arbitration
in Local Government

Where collective bargaining exists in state and local jurisdictions, it commonly involves pay issues. This case provides an opportunity to observe, in addition to observing pay bargaining, some common problems in carrying out public sector bargaining and labor relations. Here, elected town officials and the police union in a small municipality reach a bargaining impasse over the issues that separate them and which are, therefore, preventing agreement on a labor-management contract. In addition to the usual problems between the parties in a dispute, the characteristics of local government and the frequency of elections also affect the nature of the labor-management interaction.

The case is suggestive of strategic and tactical issues in public sector bargaining. It also demonstrates the use of two common techniques of dispute resolution: mediation and arbitration. Face-to-face negotiations between the parties is ordinarily the preferred means by which to resolve labor disputes since the parties themselves resolve the issues. Mediation is a means that introduces a neutral third party (in this case two "third" parties) to facilitate negotiations and, thereby, agreement. Although this case doesn't use "fact-finding," it is common practice to provide for it in many state labor relations statutes should mediation fail. Fact-finding involves appointment of yet another neutral third party who is empowered to investigate the situation and issue a set of recommendations for settlement. The parties ordinarily are not bound by the fact-finder's report, although the purpose of the exercise is to try and effect a settlement based on that report. In many states and occupations where it exists, fact-finding is the last step provided to settle a labor-management dispute. Where it is the last step, if the parties don't accept the fact-finder's recommendation there *may* be more bargaining, but otherwise there is no formal channel to resolve the conflict. More than occasionally, in the absence of another statutory mechanism, there may be a strike — illegal in most public sector jurisdictions and occupations.

Beginning in the late 1960s, primarily in public safety (police and firefighters), a further step was added beyond mediation and fact-finding to try to obtain closure and avoid strikes in contract disputes. It is now used in nearly two dozen states to resolve bargaining impasses, restricted largely to public safety occupations. This technique, "compulsory and binding arbitration," is considered a final step in that the parties must, by law, comply with the decision of the arbitrator.

In arbitration a neutral third party acceptable to both sides is appointed, usually by a state labor relations agency, and empowered to decide the issues still in dispute. This form of arbitration over "interest" disputes (i.e., disputes over contract terms) is rarely used in U.S. private sector labor relations. In private sector situations the threat or undertaking of a strike or lock-out — legal in the private sector but not in most public employment — acts as the spur to final settlement of an impasse. In private employment, arbitration had been widely used, however, to settle grievance disputes (i.e., disputes over *application* of a contract provision). Public jurisdictions also use grievance arbitration, but mandatory interest arbitration is exclusively a public sector phenomenon. There are variations in the form of interest arbitration among the states that use it and in the conditions under which it may be invoked to settle public employee contract disputes.

Where interest arbitration is used, some states permit the arbitrator to fashion a settlement that he or she deems appropriate. Others require the parties to submit their "final offers" on the issues in dispute and the arbitrator must choose from among their proposals on each issue. Elsewhere, the arbitrator may only choose the entire submission of one party or the other. Under some statutes, a "med-arb" process can take place in which the neutral party is appointed with an understanding that mediation is the preferred method of resolution, but where the same neutral party has the power to arbitrate should mediation fail.

Although binding and compulsory interest arbitration is usually limited to police and firefighters, there is considerable controversy over its application to public safety in jurisdictions where it does not now exist and to its application in other occupations as well. The technique is not without its difficulties, and the labor-management and political communities are still in a state of flux on the question of how best to resolve public sector labor disputes in the context of politics and government. Interest arbitration is by no means the accepted route for closure of contract disputes, but where there is a route, it is the most common. The "Barkfield" case shows the use of arbitration, but in a more flexible context and in a way that is more closely connected to mediation than is usually the norm.

Because public labor-management relations have characteristics distinguishing them from those in private sector employment, finding and using techniques that best fit public employment has been elusive. Politics, the separation of powers, and other factors make public labor relations rather different than in the private sector.

What with the slippage between the better-established and accepted private sector model of labor relations and the conditions of public sector bargaining, the search goes on for better means of practicing labor relations in the public sector.

Some of the problems arise from lack of experience and tradition in public sector labor relations; others arise more from the separation of powers and the role of politics. These features of the public management environment often make face-to-face bargaining and settlement difficult. Still, to be able to resolve labor disputes and otherwise to carry on constructive labor-management relations in an agency, it is important for public managers to understand the special circumstances under which public bargaining takes place. With that understanding it is possible to take steps to prevent these enduring features from unduly interfering with day-to-day management and governance. This case suggests those special circumstances and some methods for getting around the difficulties inherent in public bargaining.

The Barkfield case is about to be decided by an arbitrator, and the case problem is to recommend to the arbitrator a decision that will resolve the dispute.

STUDY QUESTIONS

1. If you were advising the chairman of the arbitration panel, how would you suggest that he decide each of the issues outstanding at the end of the case?
2. What factors in the situation led you to that decision?
3. Do you think that the arbitration award you propose will be satisfactory to both parties? Why or why not?
4. Is that arbitration award in the "public interest?"
5. How will this bargaining impasse and arbitration settlement affect the parties' day-to-day working relationship and future bargaining?
6. What factors caused the Barkfield situation to be so difficult to settle through direct bargaining and through mediation? How might these factors be ameliorated in future bargaining?

RECOMMENDED READING

Jonathan Brock, "The Need for New Approaches to Public Sector Dispute Settlement," in *Bargaining Beyond Impasse: Joint Resolution of Public Sector Disputes Labor* (Boston: Auburn House Publishing Company, 1982), Chapter 1, pp. 1-21.

SELECTED REFERENCES

B.V.H. Schneider, "Public Sector Labor Legislation, An Evolutionary Analysis," in Benjamin Aaron, Joseph R. Grodin, James L. Stern, eds. *Public Sector Bargaining*, Industrial Relations Research Association Series (Washington, D.C.: The Bureau of National Affairs, 1979).

Derek C. Bok and John T. Dunlop, "Collective Bargaining and the Public Sector," in *Labor and the American Community* (New York: Simon and Schuster, 1970), Chapter 11.

William E. Simkin, "What is Mediation?" in Simkin, *Mediation and the Dynamics of Collective Bargaining* (Washington, D.C.: The Bureau of National Affairs, 1971).

Police Negotiations in Barkfield, Massachusetts (A,r)

Introduction

The Joint Labor Management Committee had begun operations beginning in January, 1978 as a legislatively established mechanism to handle labor-management contract disputes between police and firefighters and their respective municipalities. Municipal management — their views represented by the Massachusetts League of Cities and Towns — had been dissatisfied with the results of the last-best-offer compulsory binding arbitration statute that had been in existence since 1973. Management disliked the fact that a third party with no responsibility to the electorate and without intimate knowledge of other municipal priorities could force a municipality to fund a decision by the arbitrator. Further, management had lost by a 2:1 margin in the decisions rendered since the statute began operation. The public safety labor movement in the state favored compulsory and binding arbitration and, led by the Massachusetts Firefighters Association, had lobbied strongly for it. The union position was that, in the absence of any other mechanism to do so, compulsory and binding arbitration forced the settlement of contract disputes, a matter of significant importance to organized police and firefighters; without the right to strike, these two groups of public safety employees were anxious to have a way to ensure that contract disputes would not simply drag on. A bitter political battle between these

This case was prepared by Jon Brock, Lecturer at the John F. Kennedy School of Government, Harvard University. This case is based on field research, although most names and locations are disguised to protect confidences. The author wishes to thank John T. Dunlop for his cooperation in the preparation of the case.

labor and management groups took place when legislation governing the arbitration process came up for renewal in 1977. A political compromise between the municipal leaders and the union was passed by the legislature. The result was a Joint Labor Management Committee, with six representatives from cities and towns and three representatives each from the police and firefighter unions. This committee was empowered to intervene or provide assistance in resolving any contract dispute that arose between public safety officials and municipalities.

In December of 1978, the Chairman of the Joint Labor Management Committee for Police and Firefighters was discussing a forthcoming arbitration award with two members of his staff and two of his committee colleagues. They had just heard the case, a contract dispute between the Police Alliance and the Board of Selectment of Barkfield, Massachusetts, and were reviewing the history of the case before issuing the award.

In addition to the specifics of the Barkfield case, the Committee members and staff were musing about the evolution of the Committee and its practices. They wondered whether or not it was a mechanism that was useful in the Commonwealth of Massachusetts and further, whether or not it might be useful for other state or occupational groups to study the mechanism for possible adaptation.

Barkfield, Massachusetts

Barkfield, Massachusetts is a town of about 10,000 people resting just to the southeast of Worcester, Massachusetts. Worcester is the largest city in the state other than Boston. Barkfield had recently settled a contract with its highway workers and was trying to wind up contract discussions with the police local. The police contract was more elusive and six months had elapsed since the old contract expired. The Joint Labor Management Committee was trying to settle the dispute and expected soon to issue an arbitration award on the remaining issues.

The town government is a "selectman" form of government, in which a five-member Board of Selectmen, elected every two years, carries out the town's business. Annual town meetings are held at which the budget and major organizational items are discussed and voted upon.

The police department, although small at ten full-time officers, was regarded in the Commonwealth as well trained in all aspects of police work, including emergency medical training, finger printing, crime prevention, photography, and firearms. One difficulty, however, with this highly trained work force was that turnover among Barkfield police was high; surrounding communities hired Barkfield officers away.

The five-person board of selectmen had been negotiating with the two representatives of the Barkfield Police Alliance since late November, 1977. Although the contract would not expire until July 1978, the negotiations began early since the contract then in effect specified that the parties would begin negotiations at least 60 days before the budget was slated to be approved. This would be voted upon at the March town meeting.

By June 1978, both sides were frustrated with the course of negotiations. Union leaders, selectmen, and the chief all reported that the negotiations were leading nowhere and virtually no agreement could be reached. They reported that relationships between the board and the police force were strained, and the chief claimed that his relationship with his department was deteriorating. A member of the Board later recalled: "Negotiations became very complex, all the issues intertwined. We were really swinging at one another."

The Issues in Dispute

The lack of agreement centered around three major issues and one minor one: (1) wages, (2) work schedule, (3) provision of ambulance service, and (4) Blue Cross/Blue Shield benefits. The first three had been certified for arbitration.

Wages

All parties acknowledged that the Barkfield Police Department was underpaid relative to comparable departments, and Police Chief Richard Dives reported losing six officers in the previous three years to nearby towns that paid higher salaries. According to figures on patrolman's pay obtained from the Massachusetts League of Cities and Towns by the Board of Selectmen, Barkfield was fourteenth out of 24 towns of comparable size located primarily in the rural Berkshire Mountains area. The police union disputed these data and, noting that they were also a year behind suggested that a more appropriate comparison would be to the towns with which Barkfield was in "competition" for officers and whose police work and cost of living were more like Barkfield, that is to say, those towns surrounding Worcester.

The Police Alliance made their own survey seeking up-to-date data from nine towns to which they believed Barkfield was comparable. This survey found that in only two were the police paid less than in Barkfield. By the police chief's estimate, Barkfield patrolmen's salaries were about 40 percent lower than those of comparable police forces in the area, and yet the Barkfield patrolmen were, in his view, "better trained, offering more services."

In their initial proposals the Police Alliance sought $265 per week plus cost-of-living adjustments each year for the remaining two years of the contract. The town offered $240 per week and 4 percent increases each of the next two years.

The union president said, "The selectmen initially agreed with us on the appropriateness of the comparison; they know we're doing the same job as the cops in those communities. Our brawls are just as big.''

Generally, the board members favored granting additional wages and other benefits to their police force, but as one of them noted: ''I'm for it, but not all at once. They'd been so underpaid and overworked that lots of improvements were in order.'' Another selectman recalled: ''The police deserve a healthy raise, but that was an awfully large percentage increase they sought in the first year. It doesn't look good to the townspeople. The police wanted an increase on wages alone that would have been better than 20 percent, never mind the extra holidays and everything else we gave them.''

''We only wanted average pay, not the top,'' one union leader said, ''so we just averaged everything out. At the end of the old contract our base patrolman's pay was $221 a week. We have to pay for the same loaf of bread as the other towns in the area, who were making about $260, and by the time our contract went into effect, even more than that. After the selectmen agreed that these 9 towns made the right comparison, we made 35 phone calls to police chiefs and union leaders and compiled a lot of information on the full range of pay and benefits. We put it into a booklet and later presented it to the Joint Labor Management Committee when we went to Boston for a hearing on the issues.''

Barkfield, in June, had just settled with Local 495 of the Service Employee's International Union who represented the employees of the Barkfield Highway Department. The town had agreed to a full cost-of-living adjustment. One observer reported: ''The town had just been run through by Local 495 and their professional negotiator, and had given away this uncapped cost-of-living adjustment. It was a little difficult to cry poverty to the police.''

Work Schedule

The police officer in Barkfield worked a ''5-and-2'' schedule — five days working and two days off in a seven-day period. Usually, an officer worked the same shift, all seven days, either 8:00 a.m. to 4:00 p.m., 4:00 p.m. to midnight or midnight to 8:00 a.m. This was unsatisfactory to the officers. They preferred a 4-and-2 schedule. As the union president explained: ''Compared to most of the towns in our survey — all of which had either a 4-and-2 schedule, received educational benefits, or received longevity pay — we were in a lousy position. Most of the other towns had both 4-and-2 plus either education or longevity. We couldn't get all three so we decided to go for one this time. We had a lousy schedule and schedule improvement would benefit all of our members, not just the old, not just the young: Educational incentive would help the younger guys get a few extra dollars; longevity pay would help the older guys, who were less likely to go to school. As it was, only one guy had a bachelor's degree, so educational pay wasn't going to help much. Under the operation of our 5-and-2 schedule some of us ended up working seven, eight or nine days in a row — without overtime — since the time was worked without working over forty hours in any one week and officers without seniority always ended up working nights and weekends.''

Bob Batley described the scheduling problem. He was a police officer in another town, who as an alternate member of the Joint Labor Management Committee, served as one of the mediators later sent by the Committee. ''There was no fixed schedule. It was at the whim of the Chief, who put up a new schedule every week or so. The shifts seemed to be built around the convenience of part-time officers. The overtime was offered first to part-time people rather than full-time officers. The part-timers seemed to be the protected species rather than the full-time officers. Part of the problem was the contract; it was poorly written and didn't specify the operating schedule, seniority for overtime, and related things. The Chief could do it any way he wished. It seemed as if he was trying to save money without regard for the welfare of the men.''

The union contended that the change to a 4-and-2 schedule would not require more full-time patrolmen and would not itself cost the town additional money. However, the head of the union noted that under the contract they were seeking to negotiate, there would, in fact, be increased costs related to manning the new schedule: Currently, overshift hours were worked largely by part-timers who were paid straight time. By the requirement in other parts of the union proposal that full-time officers get preference for overtime assignments and be paid time-and-a-half, costs of manning a shift would increase by virtue of the higher hourly cost of full-timers. The union contended that no additional full-time officers would be needed, if the existing complement of full-time officers were used first, based on seniority, and part-timers used as necessary to fill in.

Another feature of the 4-and-2 schedule that appealed to the union was the fact that it would rotate the days of the week that an officer would have off. Under the 5-and-2 schedule, days off tended to fall always on the same day of the week; if an officer began his or her work week on Wednesday, he or she would work through Sunday and have each Monday and Tuesday off, week after week. Although officers would work their shift based on seniority, under a 4-and-2 schedule, days off would rotate automatically such that junior officers would not always work on weekends as they currently did. Finally, the officers contended that the practice of working an officer seven or eight days in a row would cease to provide a cost advantage if the 4-and-2 schedule were adopted with overtime and other language designed to prevent the practice. Overall, the union felt that the 4-and-2 would be less demanding and would disrupt family life less than the current 5-and-2 schedule. The union made this one of its key demands.

The chief had a somewhat different view of the costs of the 4-and-2 work schedule. ''It cuts the work week by 3.5 hours per man. With ten men, that's two and a half man days for which we would have to pay time and a half. That's about $24,000 a year. Hire another man for less? Sure, but that would put the department over the limit for the 'ratio law.' That law specifies that when the force is up to twelve men, they have to pay me 1.8 times the salary of the highest paid officer rather than 1.5 if it's under twelve.''

State law also defines the powers of the chief relative to the other town authorities. Under one application of this law, the Barkfield police chief was, formally, a ''strong chief,'' which gave him rather more latitude and independence with respect to controlling the department. If he were not a ''strong chief,'' he would have to share more managerial authority with the Board.

''I run a pretty tight ship, have for 15 years as chief. There's been a lot of bitching about the shifts and the overtime. I was guilty and my sergeant was guilty about making those assignments. On the other hand, we rarely have enough overtime in the budget and often go back for supplemental money. The old contract was too vague and didn't specify the way overtime was to be handled so we did it in expedient ways.''

Joe DeCata, who acted as one of the two Committee mediators, recalled that during mediation, he had noted among the police a lot of bitterness concerning scheduling. He and Batley urged the selectmen to influence the chief to be more orderly and fair about it. Although the selectmen promised to speak to the chief about the practice, there was no change during the negotiation period.

Ambulance Service

The Town of Barkfield had provided an ambulance service to surrounding communities for the past 30 years. The service always had been operated by the police department. Emergency medical training had been a part of a patrolman's job description as long as anyone could remember (see Exhibit 13-1) and all members of the force had been certified as emergency medical technicians (EMTS).

Robert Tucker, president of the Police Alliance, was a qualified instructor for EMT and carried on most of Barkfield's training. He recalled: "We were getting a lot of complaints for being on the ambulance. We only run three men on a shift. One is at the desk in the stationhouse and the other two are out in cruisers. When an ambulance call comes in, one of the cruisers goes to the scene and the other goes to get the ambulance. One of us drives the ambulance to the hospital and the other administers emergency care in the back. The town is left with no police protection on the streets while we're on ambulance duty."

"Someone else should take the time to go to the hospital and otherwise administer aid. We are police officers first, although we are first responders on anything and everything. The selectmen wanted us to stay in the ambulance business but weren't willing to pay us for the training and skills. We're all qualified technicians and periodically have to retrain to stay certified. We wanted the town to pay us for our efforts to keep our skills and for performing this service. Initially we asked for $2,000 per certified officer. It would have cost them a grand total of $20,000."

The chief described the ambulance service: "The ambulance service has been offered free of charge for over 30 years and the cops here have always been qualified EMTS. It's the only thing the department does that every citizen appreciates. Everything else you do, you make at least one enemy and maybe one friend. If you help an accident victim, bandage him, save him, everyone remembers the good police officer, remembers that the police officer is your friend, like they used to tell you in grade school. The ambulance service has built a lot of good will for us. For example, when we wanted civil service protection and the issue was coming up for a town vote, we took out the old ambulance lists

and wrote letters explaining our position. Those people felt good about us and supported us.

"It's certainly true that the ambulance service left us without police protection periodically. While continuing to be untenable in the short term, the goodwill and support it bought for the department would, it seems to me have paid off in a few years. My guess is that the way the town is changing, we would double the size of the department in two years, leaving us plenty of coverage. Without the service and with some of the bitterness that this contract negotiation caused, I don't know. . . .

"Some of the men were against the ambulance service for personal reasons. It's difficult for some people to deal with a dying person; they often feel they could have done more to save him."

In January of 1975 the Massachusetts Police Institute had submitted a manpower study to Chief Dives which analyzed the services and operations of the Department. It noted the heavy manpower demands and the consequent lack of police protection caused by the ambulance service, and suggested that a citizen's committee collaborate with the police department in seeking a solution. (See Exhibit 13-2 for an excerpt from this study.)

The ambulance service/EMT issue had been a dominant subject of discussion throughout the negotiations in late 1977 and during 1978. Just before negotiations began, when the Board refused to provide overtime funds, the chief suspended all EMT training. Later, in the Spring, the head of the union was removed from his EMT training duties and the officers formally served notice that they would not serve as EMTs after the end of 1978.

"At that point," Tucker recalled, "they threatened to fire us and we said, 'Go ahead.' If you believe in something like that, you get ready to take the consequences." The EMT work, however, was in the patrolman's job description. It was the chief's view that a patrolman who refused to carry out those duties could and would be dismissed, and he intimated so in a subsequent letter to the Board.

Blue Cross/Blue Shield

An important side issue concerned disagreement over the percentage of Blue Cross coverage that the town would pay. Several years before, the Highway Department's employees failed to negotiate an increase in the town's contribution to health insurance. The town had been paying 50 percent and the highway department workers wanted 90 percent. Failing to win it through negotiations, the local representative of the highway workers circulated a petition to put the matter to a town meeting vote. After some questioning of the petitioning procedure, the town meeting voted to increase the proportion to 90 percent effective for all town employees in February of 1977. The Board of Selectmen filed a prohibited practice complaint over technicalities regarding the petitioning procedure. The Massachusetts Labor Relations Commission found for the union. The issue was still a source of friction as the town sought in its various 1978 contract negotiations to negotiate back down to 50 percent. The police were willing to settle for 75 percent as had the other unions but insisted that the town live up to its voted-upon commitment to pay 90 percent for the period from February 1977 until a new police agreement was signed. An appeal by the town to the Labor Relations Commission ruling was pending.

The Board of Selectmen

This was the second labor negotiation for most of the members of the Board. The first had been the negotiations with the highway department workers, part of which had overlapped the beginning of the police negotiations. The highway department settled in June 1978. In that instance, the Board negotiated as a committee with Selectman John Borghese as their chairman. Ordinarily, Robert Castman was chairman of the Board of Selectmen. However, in his job in the Worcester Highway Department, he was a member of the same union that represented the highway department in Barkfield. He, therefore, would have been in a conflict of interest situation had he chaired the Board during those negotiations.

At first, the Board negotiated as a "headless" committee, but a chairman was chosen after the Board had several times confused the facts of the two negotiations that were being conducted concurrently. Borghese noted later that as the person in the chair, he "prepared for two weeks at a time prior to negotiation meetings."

One of the Committee mediators recalled: "There was a lack of unity and communication among the selectmen. I could see problems on the Board. Borghese was a strong, articulate guy, who wanted to be chairman. Castman is the chairman and seems to be seeking a higher office. He recently ran for County Commissioner. The lack of communication between them made it very difficult to settle the dispute since agreements among the selectmen were even more difficult to achieve than between the parties. They didn't spend a lot of time together and had different views of the politics and propriety of small items. There was little disagreement, however, that the cops deserved more money."

Negotiations were time-consuming. One Board member pointed out: "We're only part-timers. Besides, we have other town business to perform. These negotiations had gotten so complex and time-consuming that we began to schedule bargaining sessions for evenings that were not regular Board meeting nights. We had to do other business and it seemed important that the police negotiations get more continuous attention and be held in private. Board meetings are open meetings, although the state's collective bargaining laws permit closed meetings during negotiations. The union requested closed meetings, although such a practice was rare for us in Barkfield."

The Board's meetings take place in the basement of the Town Hall every Tuesday at 7:30, where candid and open discussions are held on issues ranging from rules of conduct for teenagers in a town park, to expenditures and construction specifications on a dam, or sewage system, or a high school track.

There was a lack of expertise regarding police work and collective bargaining, one selectman admitted, and he attributed this to the turnover that inevitably occurs when the Board's seats are filled every two years.

The police chief, Richard Dives, noted that "The police officers had done their homework and had all the facts and figures. The selectmen were less prepared." Two members of the Board of Selectmen composed a police subcommittee of the Board who met with the chief once per month. According to Dives, they "rarely got into great detail" and were especially wary of getting involved with the financial statistics, which were divided up into some 42 line items. "No one comes down to see how things work," the chief said.

One observer reported: "It's not the ideal Board for conducting police labor negotiations. There were two brand-new members and the others didn't have much experience with these sorts of things. Only one member has a college education, some don't have a high school education, and only one owns a business where he has to meet a payroll and calculate true operating expenses. The average Board member makes less than a cop. One of them is our mail carrier. One is a member of another union and all of them do this on a volunteer basis. The town has just established a personnel board to handle a variety of employee-related issues, so perhaps that body will begin to be involved with labor negotiations."

Since the selectmen had their own jobs and businesses to attend to, a full-time "municipal assistant" acted as a staff to the board, and carried on communications and monitoring functions on its behalf. He was well regarded by all of the parties and townsfolk, although by the nature of his position his policy influence was minimal. An astute observer, he viewed himself as an honest broker and rarely was identified with a particular faction on any issue or in any controversy.

The Police Alliance

The Barkfield Police Alliance was represented by two officers, Robert Tucker and Bruce Angelli. The Alliance represented only those officers who were full-time, and, in fact, the Alliance had only registered as a bargaining agent some three years before; previously, it has been a loose gathering of police workers, including the chief and part-timers. It dealt with community activities, improvement of law enforcement and the like. In previous negotiations the Alliance had been represented by another officer, but recent elections were won by Tucker and Angelli as the tenor of the organization changed toward that of a labor union, responding to the economic position of the Barkfield officers.

It was their first negotiation. In preparation, they consulted with their members and began to gather facts and information that would guide them in their negotiations. Examples of their preparation include the survey of nine nearby communities that they carried out to determine key features of other police contracts. Early in the negotiations the union leaders often asked the police chief for facts and figures as they analyzed and developed advocated their bargaining position. Similarly, the chief provided figures to the selectmen. The chief, of course, was not in the bargaining unit and was part of management.

In the 1977-1978 negotiations the union president reported, "We never argued about the number of men or any of the things that were up to management, we only wanted to be paid and treated fairly for our efforts." On several occasions, these union representatives went to Boston to represent their interests in formal and informal hearings before the Joint Labor Management Committee.

The Chief

Richard Dives had been an officer in Barkfield since 1946 and chief since 1963. An observer from the Joint Labor Management Committee for Police and Firefighters remembers his impressions of the chief's role: "The chief — we never met him. He seemed to be trying to save money by avoiding overtime, running that brutal schedule and using part-timers. He showed no regard for full-time officers. He wanted the ambulance service kept intact. He liked it so much that he's spent thousands on the ambulance and EMT equipment, but wouldn't seek equivalent funds for regular departmental vehicles. There was some sort of antagonism between him and the Board. Why, for example, were the selectmen so bent on keeping the department below 12 men? It was just to keep the chief from getting paid more. So what? They'll pay out the money in overtime. Still, Dives is a pretty expert politician. The selectmen were buffaloed by him. They're very deferential to him in his presence, but recently they overruled him on selection of an officer."

The chief of police recalled that in negotiations neither party seemed to know what they were doing, that there was lots of posturing among the Board members, and often a difference between what they said in public meetings and what they said in caucuses or with only the two parties present. "For a time I was regularly present and a part of management's caucuses. I was also the source of statistics for both sides. I finally walked out; I was the fall guy. After that I'd get a letter every now and then on some question or another."

In his own view: "I'm a 'strong chief' as far as the law goes, but I'm not hard to get along with. Every now and again the selectmen will

get some political heat to put on a special detail or cover some shift, without regard for cost or anything. I just smile. Often I just ignore it and generally they don't care. Just the same, I think that they'd like to get the department out from under the provisions of '97a' [the strong chief law] so they'd have more control. On the other hand, these negotiations educated them a bit about what it takes to run a department, and maybe they'd just as soon leave it to me. I'm not sure why they're so concerned about the ratio law. I had already been technically over the manpower limit for a year and a half and didn't put in for the money due me. As a matter of fact, I've waived my right to it. I guess as part-timers, they don't know the law well."

Some selectmen observed: "The chief is a tough nut," and, "He was pretty arbitrary."

Negotiations

In September the decision from the Massachusetts Labor Relations Commission had mandated that the town pay 90 percent of the cost of Blue Cross/Blue Shield benefits. In November the chief went to the Board with his supplemental request for overtime money. The overtime allocation in the town budget, passed just six months before, was exhausted. "I told them it wasn't enough," the chief said. "We needed about $24,000 and they voted $9,900." Subsequently, when the money ran out, the selectmen voted against the increment requested by the chief. He responded by suspending all EMT training (see Exhibit 13-3), since the regular recertification of all ten officers took place in off-duty hours, which were compensable at time-and-a-half. EMT training was a large consumer of overtime dollars. The officers responded with a grievance.

In late November, the Police Alliance wrote to the Board of Selectmen, seeking to open contract talks. Opening proposals were requested by the Board and submitted on December 7, 1977, in advance of a scheduled December 12 meeting of the Board. In that communication, the Alliance requested a closed meeting and laid out some 19 items: the Blue Cross issue, clothing allowances and pay for court time to vacations, wages, education and longevity pay as well as EMT pay of $2,000 per year. Particular attention was paid to the work schedule and to overtime. A few negotiating sessions took place after the Christmas holidays and the Board made some counter offers.

By February some agreement and change in position had occurred. The Police Alliance had backed off a bit on their wage demands and insurance proposals. However, the wage question was far from settled, the scheduling demands had barely been discussed and the EMT pay, training time, and other issues had yet to be agreed to. Bargaining took place on February 1 and February 10, and then paused as the Board began to prepare the town budget for submission to the March town meeting. No provisions for altered police costs were included.

Negotiations continued following the budget "season" and in mid-April some additional progress was made. The selectmen had offered $240, based on a calculated average of $236 for comparably sized towns in the state. The union, whose representatives had started their demands at $275 per week, effective July 1, 1978, were now willing to accept the town's offer of $240, with the proviso that on January 1, 1979, a survey of police wages in the Worcester area would be taken and the average paid to the Barkfield officers. The Alliance noted that the current average for the relevant surrounding towns was already above $260, but they reasoned that with the January 1 adjustment, they would come out in an acceptable position. For the next two years of the contract, the officers sought a cost-of-living adjustment based on the Consumer Price Index for Boston, the same adjustment won by the highway workers. If this wage adjustment package was accepted, the union would drop demands for longevity and educational pay. They

had backed off on part of their demand for an increased clothing allowance and were willing to accept the 4-and-2 schedule in the second year of the contract rather than immediately, as originally proposed.

On April 27, Officer Tucker was removed from his duties as a training officer for EMT certification. The chief noted in his letter (Exhibit 13-4) to the Board of Selectmen that this was done so that certification training could begin outside of the normal channels. The ambulance service soon would be jeopardized since certification of a number of officers was about to expire. The EMT controversy raged during the month of May with the board seeking to reestablish certification without increasing costs. Through Anslow, the administrative assistant, the board wrote to the Alliance asking if they would train for EMT during working hours. The union responded with a grievance and a succinct statement of their position:

"We are willing to take EMT training as part of our regular 40-hour tour of duty or take compensatory time off on the basis of one and a half hours for every hour of EMT training done on our own time. . . . Our willingness to cooperate in this respect, however, shall not constitute a change of our job description so as to include the requirement for EMT training and ambulance service. We shall continue to perform first responder duties and CPR duties. We are agreeable to continue EMT duties through December 31, 1978 or until other arrangements are made. . . . If it becomes necessary to perform EMT duties beyond (that date) we would expect that we would receive compensation as outlined in our collective bargaining discussions."

The chief reviewed the letter and responded angrily to the board when they asked him to work up the cost implications of the officers' statement. He referred to the officers' "ultimatum" and suggested strongly that the Board not be led around by the officers.

The Joint Labor Management Committee Gets Involved

In late May, Bob Batley, an alternate labor member of the Joint Labor Management Committee (JLMC) and a police union president himself, heard through the police grapevine that Barkfield's negotiations were running into difficulty. At around the same time, a Committee member who hailed from that part of the state communicated to Batley what he had learned of the Barkfield situation. Since the JLMC was a new and not a well-known institution, Batley had made it a practice to "prospect" for situations where the JLMC might lend a hand in bargaining. To maintain a neutral posture in accordance with the JLMC normal practice, Batley kept the senior management staff member informed of such contacts. When out near Barkfield working on another case, Batley called Robert Tucker to introduce himself and talk about the bargaining situation. On June 20, he stopped by Tucker's home for a cup of coffee and a description of the bargaining situation. On the same trip he "touched base" with half a dozen or so other police departments in the state.

The Barkfield contract expired on July 1, 1978 and Batley and Tucker had kept in touch until then. Later, in July, Batley, accompanied by Joe DeCata, the senior management staff member of the JLMC, spent a day in Worcester seeking to resolve some collective bargaining problems in that part of the state and to acquaint jointly some union people with the mediation and other services offered by the Committee. A handful of police union people stopped in and talked informally about their situations, received some information on the Committee, and generally received guidance on collective bargaining matters.

Several members of the Barkfield Police Alliance stopped in and told their "tales of woe," as Batley put it, this time to Batley, of union background and DeCata, with a management background. Since Batley and Tucker had last talked, the Barkfield Police Alliance on July 11 had written a letter outlining their position. They sent the letter to their attorney for transmittal to the board. There had been no bargaining since April and their letter was intended to restate their position in a hopeful attempt to restart negotiations, hopefully at the July 18 meeting of the Board. They had received no reply to the letter and as the July 18 meeting of the Board went past, the Police Alliance wrote to the Joint Labor Management Committee asking that it take jurisdiction of the case.

The Committee considered the petition, but, as was their practice, asked Joe DeCata, the management senior staff representative, to get some input from the management side, the selectmen, before any official Committee involvement would take place. DeCata called Larry Anslow, the municipal assistant, to learn about the situation from management's point of view. Anslow confirmed the issues and communications problems that Batley had gleaned from his contacts with the police. He agreed to check with the Board to see how they would react to JLMC involvement. Although the Committee could simply exercise jurisdiction, they sought the agreement of the parties to their involvement. The Board didn't demonstrate much knowledge of the Committee, but agreed to the Committee's staff coming out if it could serve as a "lubricant" to negotiation.

Mediation at the Staff Level

Arrangements were subsequently made for DeCata and Batley to meet on August 15 first with the police union and then with the Board. After a "productive" meeting with the police, DeCata and Batley walked across the street to the Board's meeting and began to explain their presence and function as mediators and problem solvers. Batley reported, "We got a bad reception. They didn't trust who Joe was and they didn't even want me in the room." (Batley is president of a local police officers' union else-where in the state and therefore was suspect to them. DeCata, a knowledgeable labor relations specialist, with years of municipal experience, was often mistaken for a union leader because of his physical appearance.)

At the next selectmen's meeting Batley and DeCata returned and brought along Dick Horne, an appointed member of the Joint Labor Management Committee and recent past President of the Massachusetts Selectmen's Association. Most of the Barkfield selectmen knew Horne or knew of him. He explained the Committee's role and functions: to save time and money and promote settlements that the parties could live with. The Committee provided mediative and other assistance and was composed jointly of individuals with management experience and people with labor backgrounds. Their assistance was free and expert and he urged them to accept the help. Help would come first in the form of mediation. If the parties could not agree, other types of assistance were possible and binding arbitration under committee auspices could still take place, and at less cost, with less time elapsed than under the normal state procedures. Horne suggested that through mediation, a significant degree of agreement probably could be reached before arbitration might be invoked on any outstanding issues. Much of the time that evening was spent "selling" the Committee, as one observer put it.

Horne began his remarks by referring to Batley in his folksy and casual brogue, "By the way, gents, do you mind if Mr. Batley here remains with us in this little management session? We consider him one of us. . . ." The selectmen agreed to Batley's presence. The police, based on Batley's introduction and the meeting in Worcester, had already agreed to DeCata's presence in their caucuses. Batley, however, later passed a remark on the way the ambulance service in his own town was run. John Borghese, sitting as chairman of the Board that evening,

attacked Batley for his "biased, police views," although their relationship improved as time went on.

Mediation under Committee auspices began at that meeting. To get a sense of the status of each side's position, Batley met with the police separately and DeCata and Horne met with the Board. Afterward DeCata, Batley and Horne caucused and compared notes, confidentially, and decided to bring the parties together into the same room, an event that hadn't occurred in the past four months.

The police, among other things, outlined their problems with the work schedule: They were working more than a forty-hour week, receiving no overtime pay and receiving their assignments on short notice, which disrupted their family lives. The selectmen listened sympathetically and promised to try to get the situation changed. That evening the union also noted that they had sent a letter via their attorney outlining their latest position and seeking to meet with the Board during the regularly scheduled July 18 meeting. Why hadn't the Board responded? Apparently, they had never seen the letter and had not learned of the union's renewed interest in negotiating. It seemed that the union's attorney and the Board's attorney had communicated, but the letter or its contents had not yet been forwarded. Somehow, the attorneys representing the parties had not completed the communication. This realization broke some of the tension and distrust, and the two mediators began, with the parties now sitting across the table from one another, to list on paper all of the contract issues under discussion, separating them into agreed-upon and open issues.

Mediation Techniques

DeCata recalled the mediation process: "Bob and I had worked together in the Framingham case, where we also got to know Al Erskine, a management member of the Committee from that area. The Framingham case came early in the Committee's existence and our tools and procedures weren't fully developed. We somehow fell upon the tandem, or joint, mediation technique and it worked very well. We had a lot of trust between us, so we decided to try joint mediation in Barkfield, where the mistrust between the parties was rampant and the parties' bargaining experience limited. Sometimes we met together with one or both parties, sometimes separately with our respective sides, but we were in constant communication. By reducing the issues to a written list, going over the list at each session and by going back and forth, probing for give-and-take, the neutrals can keep control over the process so that old enmities and side issues don't flare up. The two sides are kept honest and their feet held to the fire, or to the issues, if you will.''

"The list of items," Batley observed, "forced them to focus on the substance, leave out extraneous stuff and personalities. By going over it each time, we narrowed the differences step by step. We would listen and then try to capture the issues and then see if the parties would agree that those were indeed the issues. Otherwise, we'd redefine them so there was agreement on the formulation of the issues. You need to know what the issue is if you're ever to resolve a dispute on it.''

In a few sessions after the August 15 meeting, the police came back with new proposals in time for a meeting on August 22. The mediators were able to clear away such issues as death benefits and funeral expenses because of the mediators' familiarity with practices in other communities and applicable state laws. Vacations and pay for court time were susceptible to similar handling. The overtime issue was a bit more difficult. While there was a law requiring overtime pay over 40 hours of work in a week, the chief ran the schedule so that rarely did an officer work more than 40 hours in a calendar week but worked six to eight days in a row,

over two separate weeks. The change had to come in management practice, but this change was related in the officers' minds to the 5-and-2, 4-and-2 controversy. Batley gave DeCata a quick tutorial on 4-and-2 and 5-and-2 in the Barkfield context.

In the course of mediation, the Committee mediators learned about the substance of the issues that separated the parties and became aware of the emotions on both sides. They also discovered the strong resistance of the selectmen to a larger force level, and their sensitivity to the public's reaction to cost increases.

By late August, the sides had agreed on all but five issues: wages, including educational incentive and longevity pay; clothing allowance; retroactivity in Blue Cross/Blue Shield; the work schedule; and the ambulance service. At the end of a mediation session on August 30 that lasted until 2:30 in the morning, DeCata and Batley left the two sides in a room together. They were closer together on the remaining issues, and the mediators, exhausted but hopeful, left them there to resolve the rest of the issues. "Do your best, call us tomorrow." As they walked out the door they said to each other, "If this doesn't settle it, there's nothing else we can do." They began the three-hour drive home.

The second- and third-year wages had yet to be worked out and there was $25 difference between the union and the town in the second-year clothing allowances. There was also disagreement on the number of credits that would have to be earned to qualify for educational incentive pay. The Blue Cross issue was a matter of getting the town to drop its appeal to the Labor Relations Commission and ironing out the dates for retroactivity, which DeCata essentially had worked out with the Board a few days before. The town had agreed to try a 4-and-2 schedule in the third year of the contract, assuming that a citizen's committee found it feasible, but sought a proviso that the number of full-time officers required would remain constant and that overtime costs wouldn't be excessive. Finally, there was the ambulance issue.

To the mediators and the parties it all looked close, but old animosities emerged, the discussion reverted to name calling, recrimination, "Look what I've already given up," and ended the discussion. The mediators returned on September 20 to try to resolve these questions (see list of items, Exhibit 13-5), but couldn't bring the parties any closer.

A Hearing on the Issues

DeCata and Batley reported at one of the JLMC's weekly meetings in early October that mediation efforts could bring the parties no closer. Another of the Committee's tools would be required. It was decided to invite the two sides for a hearing, hoping that something would shake loose, or that in a different forum a new mediative approach might prove fruitful. "It lent the process some additional legitimacy," DeCata suggested, "at a point where things had stalled."

A hearing on the issues was scheduled for October 6 in Boston but was canceled because the selectmen were unable to attend. The next date was October 18, and John Borghese and Thomas Mullen of the Board showed up along with Larry Anslow, the administrative assistant. DeCata and Batley sat as "assessors," advising the Committee's chairman, Professor John T. Dunlop, a prominent labor economist and mediator from Harvard University and a former Secretary of Labor. The chairman opened the hearing by discussing possibilities for future mediation or other ways to resolve the dispute. They hoped to find agreement on a process that might lead to resolution of the issues in dispute. Barkfield's Board of Selectmen had not authorized Borghese and Mullen to negotiate, so no additional progress was made that day and no subsequent negotiations took place back in Barkfield. It was simply agreed that another date would be set.

It was hoped that at the next hearing appropriate representation from the Board would permit some further negotiations under the chairman's auspices. Ordinarily, some additional negotiations took place at these hearings or subsequent to them. At a minimum, a new approach to negotiations was usually fashioned.

The Committee held another hearing on November 10, hoping to carry on some further mediation, but only one selectman showed up, again with orders not to negotiate. Chairman Castman and Selectman Borghese, who had been active in the negotiations, at the last minute were not able to attend. In the time between the October 18 hearing and the November 10 hearing the parties had no formal or informal communication.

The assessors at the hearing — who had served as mediators in the case — recommended to Dunlop in a caucus that the case be handled by arbitration of the outstanding issues. They discussed this with their respective sides and then with both parties together. The union and management, weary of the dispute, agreed to conventional arbitration by the Committee as the preferred method of resolution. According to its procedural rules, before the Committee could actually take the case for arbitration the full Committee had to vote on a motion to do so. At the next Committee meeting, DeCata raised the issue and Al Erskine moved that the Committee take the staff recommendation to arbitrate. The Committee voted unanimously to take the case for arbitration.

Arbitration

DeCata and Batley were disappointed that they couldn't resolve the dispute through mediation, but later expressed the view that their mediation had narrowed the gap on the outstanding issues and had resolved many of the others. Indeed, when, on December 5, the case was certified for aribitration, three issues remained and all others were found to be in agreement as a result of the summer and fall mediation. The arbitration panel would have to decide on wages, the work schedule and the EMT ambulance problems. DeCata had in the meantime persuaded the town to agree to the union's Blue Cross proposal and Batley had convinced the sides to agree on the clothing allowance.

On December 19 an arbitration hearing was held where chairman Dunlop presided and the Committee members, Al Erskine, a leading town finance committee officer in the Commonwealth, and Dave Morley, a police officer and member of the Committee, sat as members of the panel. DeCata and Batley had briefly explained the issues to the panel members and the chairman and had outlined the current and candid positions of the parties. The police union made a presentation that included the wage and benefit comparisons they had surveyed and listed their positions on the issues. The town's administrative assistant, representing the town, had brought with him the town's "last" offer (see Exhibit 13-6). The parties' real positions had changed little since the September 20 meeting, but, in fact, some hardening in their stated position was evident as they outlined it to the arbitration panel that day.

After the final hearing DeCata and Batley discussed their views with the arbitration panel members (John T. Dunlop as neutral chairman, Dave Morley on the police union side, and Al Erskine for management). DeCata and Batley gave the labor (Morley) and management (Erskine) panelists further background and history on the situation, and their views of the parties' most important priorities and concerns. [Exhibit 13-7 provides a chronology of the Barkfield police negotiations.]

Exhibit 13-1. Patrolman's job description

DEPARTMENT OF POLICE

BARKFIELD, MASSACHUSETTS

Richard Dives, Chief

(617) 894-1212
(617) 894-5661

September 27, 1977

DUTIES OF A PATROLMAN

Immediately after reporting for duty, each officer going out on duty relieves the officer, as assigned, whose tour of duty has expired. He con-
fines his Patrol within the limits of his route, except in the case of
Fire, Arrest of a prisoner, or other cause of necessary absence until he
is regularly relieved, unless sooner ordered elsewhere by a superior.

Because he serves his entire Town, and not merely a particular place or
route, it is his duty to give proper attention to violations of law committed in his sight anywhere within his Town, especially such as involve
injury, or the risk of injury to person or property.

When a Patrolman becomes sick during his tour of duty, he reports at
once to his Station House or to his Sergeant.

He especially avoids giving cause for gossip, or scandal by conversing
with women in the streets at night when he is in uniform, whether on his
route or not. He constantly patrols his route except for his halts necessary to the proper performance of his duties. He does not sit down, lean
against walls, posts or trees, or conduct himself in any respect other
than as a responsible official exposed to public observation and criticism, with important work to do.

When assigned to crossings, he will give his entire attention to such
duties, avoiding all unnecessary conversation.

He renders such aid as may be consistent with his duties to persons requesting it. He keeps his number in sight, and gives his name and number
to all who request it.

He directs strangers and others, when requested, by the nearest and the
safest way to their destination. If he hears a call for assistance, he
proceeds to render aid with all dispatch, taking every practicable pre-
caution for his protection of his route when he leaves it for this or for
other purpose.

When any Way becomes blocked by vehicles, he, using his best judgment,
aids in disentangling the same. When the stream of travel is continuous,
he opens a way for foot travelers, attending especially to women, children and the aged wishing to cross.

When a Disturbance occurs, he instantly proceeds to the spot and uses
his best efforts to restore quiet.

He also notes during the night all vehicles which in any manner excite
suspicion.

So far as possible, he attends at School Buildings on his route before

(Exhibit continues on following page.)

Exhibit 13-1. Continued

and after sessions for the purpose of preserving order and protecting the
children from injury.

Insofar as he can, without intruding on the privacy of individuals, the
Patrolman notes all movements into, and removing from the limits of his
route. He acquires sufficient knowledge of the residents as will enable
him to recognize them. He makes himself thoroughly acquainted with all
parts of his route, and with the streets, private ways, house, buildings,
stores, and business concerns included in it.

He constantly observes the conduct of all persons of known bad character. He notes their movements and the premises they enter. He learns
their names, residences, and occupations. He reports to his Commanding
Officer any useful information he may obtain concerning them. He fixes in
his mind all characteristics necessary to identify them.

He takes particular note of all places where intoxicating liquors are
sold. He reports all unlicensed places, and all places where the terms of
the License under which the liquors are sold are not fully met.

He notes all street lamps out of repair, not lighted at proper times,
or extinguished too late or too early. He notes all buildings erected, or
in the process of being erected contrary to Law, or defectively built or
which have become unsafe, or in which any noisy, dangerous, or unwhole-
some trade is carried on. He reports all this to his Commanding Officer
without delay.

At night and during the time that business buildings are closed he exercises the greatest vigilance, giving particular attention to vacant or
unoccupied buildings and dwellings. Once each night shift he examines and
tries accessible doors, windows, gratings of such places and investigates
all suspicious and unusual circumstances, such as open doors, lights out
over safes, and open safes. In the daytime he examines in the same manner
all vacant or unoccupied buildings and dwellings in his patrol area. When
a door or window is found open under suspicious or unusual circumstances
on any tour of duty, he makes a thorough investigation and determines, if
possible, whether burglary or any other crime has been committed, and
whether the door or window can be secured. He notifies the dispatcher to
inform, if possible, the owner or person having control of the premises.
He gives special attention to all vacant dwellings to prevent depreda-
tions. He is vigilant to prevent fires, waste of water, and to see that
fire escapes are not obstructed. He calls to the attention of the abut-
ters the state of the sidewalk and roofs, where, by snow, ice or other
cause, they are rendered dangerous, or when obstructed with goods, or
where ashes, or garbage, dead animals, or other offensive matter are
thrown in the streets. If the law, ordinances, by-laws, orders, rules, or
regulations that govern such cases, upon notice given, are not forthwith
obeyed, he ascertains the names of the offending parties and reports same
for complaint and prosecution.

He takes care that the sidewalks are not obstructed by persons loiter-
ing thereon to the inconvenience of other pedestrians.

He carefully preserves any property which comes into his possession in
his official capacity, and marks and delivers it to his Commanding Officer.

He strictly complies with the requirements that he should not have in
his possession a key to any premises, not his own, on or near his route,
except with the knowledge and consent of his commanding officer.

He will not leave the boundaries of the Town of Barkfield except in
compliance with standing general orders.

(Exhibit continues on following page.)

Exhibit 13-1. Continued

He will keep abreast of all changes in Mass. General Laws as well as Town by-laws within his jurisdiction and enforce them to the best of his ability.

He shall hold a current E.M.T. card certified by the national registry and also a CPR certification.

He shall attend all schools, courses, classes as required to keep both certifications current.

He shall also be required to attend all courses, classes, seminars as is required to keep abreast of laws and by-laws.

He shall be required to perform any and all duties related to his work as a Police Officer. (The word ''He'' as stated shall be interpreted to signify either ''He'' or ''She.'')

Exhibit 13-2. Excerpt from Massachusetts Police Institute Manpower Survey

Ambulance Service

Another major factor concerning the utilization of police personnel in Barkfield involves the police ambulance service. The extent to which the Barkfield Police Department is a virtual prisoner of its ambulance service tradition is seen when one considers the extent to which personnel are committed to provide this service. The following chart indicates the ambulance run activity for 1972 and 1974. Due to non-availability of accurate figures for 1973, that year was not computed.

CHART #8
AMBULANCE CALLS

	# FOR 1972	# POLICE PERSONNEL INVOLVED	# FOR 1974	# POLICE PERSONNEL INVOLVED
January	26	47	30	45
February	28	49	33	51
March	23	40	33	44–
April	31	36	28	44
May	28	39	51	77
June	29	47	36	52
July	20	34	33	52
August	29	44	38	55
September	27	44	26	42
October	23	43	30	44
November	21	25	—	
December	30	53	—	—
	315	461	338	456

It should be pointed out that for every man-hour spent providing the community with ambulance service, there is an equal amount of time where police protection within the community has decreased by one-half and oftentimes, totally.

Chart #8 shows that for the year 1972, there were a total of 315 ambulance service runs, and from January to October 1974 there were 338 runs. From 1972 to 1974 the actual number of runs has increased as well as the total man hours required to provide this *free* service.

The average cost computed by the survey team for each ambulance run, irrespective of equipment costs, came to ($20.00) twenty dollars. Applying this figure to the total number of ambulance runs up to October 1974 yields a total cost of $6760.00.

(Exhibit continues on following page.)

Exhibit 13-2. Continued

The ambulance function on an *ad hoc* basis is certainly an important part of the total police service provided in some communities. On the basis of the reaction created by such a service in Barkfield, ambulance service is an important ingredient in terms of the positive rapport of the Police Department with Barkfield residents. Yet the routinized provision of such a service as provided by the Barkfield Police Department detracts from the ability of the Department to fulfill its main mission.

Under the recently proposed "Ambulance Regulations," the Department of Mental Health has outlined some provisions which should be of particular interest to the Town of Barkfield. The provisions are as follows:

1. Written policies and procedures on the operation and maintenance of ambulances must be prepared by each department.

2. Each department must have a heated garage large enough to house all ambulances (including all cruiser ambulances).

3. Twenty-four-hour-a-day phone coverage and ambulance service is required.

4. Ambulances must be cleaned, washed and disinfected inside after each use.

5. Station wagon ambulances can be used to transport sick or injured persons until July 1, 1977. After that date, only communities that have a fully-equipped Class I vehicle as a primary transport vehicle may use station wagon ambulances, and then only as a backup.

6. Even communities which have traditional full-sized ambulances will be required to use these only as a backup to Class I vehicles.

7. The amount of medical supplies required for dual purpose vehicles, although less than that required for other vehicles, may well exceed the space available in a station wagon ambulance.

8. One third of all employees who may be called upon to be ambulance drivers or attendants must be EMT-A trained (81 hour course) by July 1, 1975, another third by July 1, 1976, and all trained by July 1, 1977.

9. All ambulance operators (drivers) and attendants must attend refresher courses each year.

10. All operators and attendants, while waiting to comply with July 1, 1977 EMT-A requirements, must have Red Cross standard or advanced first aid certificates. In the interim, the person with the higher level of training shall be the attendant, riding in the patient compartment.

Based upon the above possible provisions, it is recommended that the Town of Barkfield establish a Task Force of local citizens for the expressed purpose of investigating the current ambulance service rendered by the town in relation to the proposed new ambulance regulations and also in relation to the present nonavailability of sufficient police manpower to provide this service.

(Exhibit continues on following page.)

Exhibit 13-2. Continued

Police Vehicles

The Town of Barkfield established a policy whereby the Chief of Police was authorized to request purchase of a replacement cruiser every nine months. Currently the department operates a fleet of three cruisers which are identified as follows:

1973 Chevrolet (Wagon)—80,000 miles

1974 Chevrolet (Wagon)—70,000 miles

1974 Chevrolet (Wagon)—50,000 miles

The two 1974 cruisers are presently used on a daily basis to provide for two mobile patrol sectors in the town. The 1973 cruiser, with 80,000 miles, is held in reserve for spot use. Clearly, from the mileage figures on two of the three cruisers, now is the time to buy a new one. However, the chief indicated that the 1975 budget does not provide for a replacement cruiser.

During the course of the survey, the MPI Technical Specialists were given a complete ride-along tour of the town that covered virtually 90 miles of roads and took four hours. This ride-along revealed that much of the present roadways patrolled by the Barkfield Police are dirt roads or extremely limited access. Patrolling these roads results in detrimental physical abuse of the patrol vehicles. Consequently, the excessive wear and tear caused by poor road conditions along with the fact that two of the vehicles already have over 70,000 miles, necessitates immediate replacement of these two vehicles. In addition, it is recommended that the previously established policy of vehicle replacement be adhered to in the future.

Exhibit 13-3. Police chief's suspension of EMT training

DEPARTMENT OF POLICE

BARKFIELD, MASSACHUSETTS

(617) 894-1212
(617) 894-5661

Richard Dives, Chief

25 Nov 77

To: All Full-time Police Personnel
From: Chief of Police Richard Dives
Subject: E.M.T. Training and Personnel Shortage

As of this date 11/25/77 there will be no further E.M.T. Training, unless approved by the Chief of Police for the following reasons:

1. The Board of Selectmen have voted not to pay any overtime (time-and-one-half) for E.M.T. Training, and that officers involved in this training be given time off during the week the E.M.T. Training is to take place. That the full-time personnel involved in E.M.T. Training hours be no more than 40 (forty) hours, E.M.T. Training time included in one week.

2. The full-time officers have filed a grievance with the Chief of Police on this matter, as set forth in the present contract between the Town of Barkfield and the Police Association of Barkfield. Step 1 and Step 2 have been completed and Step 3 is pending.

3. The Board of Selectmen by a vote of 3 to 2 have refused to request a list to fill the position now held by Dick Harries on a permanent basis. This will cause Dick Harries to revert back to Permanent Intermittent as of 1/3/78. This was done even after the Chief of Police signed a waiver of increase in compensation that the addition of another full-time officer may entitle the Chief of Police to. This waiver involved only officers Moruzzolini and Harries.

4. At the time the waiver was signed the Chief of Police was already entitled to an increase in the amount of $3,447.60 annually, he has not pursued or intends to pursue the matter any further, and orally stated this to the Board of Selectmen. The Board of Selectmen had been informed officially by the Town Counsel Darren L. Byne, that the Chief of Police was entitled to the additional salary increase.

5. It would seem that certain members of the Board of Selectmen are not at this time willing to provide adequate personnel on a full-time basis, for reasons that they have not stated. They have officially voted to reduce the full-time force even further. The manpower of the police department will be at a critical point. Therefore I as Chief of Police must control the working force with a careful displacement of officers

(Exhibit continues on following page.)

Exhibit 13-3. Continued

and the hours worked. I do this at this time of the year with regrets,
it is a situation over which I have no control, and have tried to the
best of my ability to correct. Should this matter change, I will advise you. As I am sure you can see this will have an adverse effect on
planned vacations, but it is a matter that I have talked over with the
Selectmen and they have moved not to help with this situation. Again I
will state this is not the Board as a whole, but only certain members.
The records are open to the public, you may want to read them, as all
of this is a matter of record.

Richard Dives

Richard Dives
Chief of Police

Exhibit 13-4. Police chief removes EMT officer

DEPARTMENT OF POLICE

BARKFIELD, MASSACHUSETTS

(617) 894-1212
(617) 894-5661

Richard Dives, Chief   1 May 78

Board of Selectmen
Town Hall
Barkfield, Massachusetts

Gentlemen:

This is to advise you that on April 27, 1978, after having a conversation with Patrolman Robert Tucker, in my office at the Barkfield Police
Station, I have removed him as training officer for E.M.T.

The reason for this was not in any way related to his ability to perform this assigned duty, or in any way a disciplinary action.

As I am sure you are aware of this matter is very much involved in the
present contract negotiations between the Barkfield Police Alliance and
the Town of Barkfield (i.e., your Board).

As there has been no training conducted of any type since collective
bargaining commenced, I am of the opinion that the total ambulance service of the Town of Barkfield would indeed suffer if immediate action is
not taken to start a recertification training program. With this in mind
and a deep concern for the future status of the ambulance service of the
Town, I intend to meet with several qualified persons in the area who
carry on continuing recertification programs. After this is done, I will
meet with your Board so that we can resolve the current problem of recertification to the satisfaction of your Board.

I feel that your Board should be aware of the following: Of the eight
full-time officers and one temporary full-time officer, there may be a
question of E.M.T. status requirement of six officers. They are:

Sgt. Derek Frost

Sgt. William Donovan

Ptlmn. Fevyer   *

Ptlmn. Cardillo*

Ptlmn. Stevens *

Ptlmn. Bornot *

Ptlmn. Tucker

(Exhibit continues on following page.)

Exhibit 13-4. Continued

```
    *One of these officers will be appointed Sergeant. More than likely he
will be an E.M.T. as it is in his job description, this will leave six
officers, of the six remaining the final answer to their being required
to be E.M.T.'s will be settled in the Courts. As I am sure you are aware
that I will take immediate action, should an officer refuse to continue
his training or duties as an E.M.T. I will suspend him and request that
he be dismissed permanently at a hearing held by your Board.
    As I have stated, as has our previous Town Counsel, that ambulance work
and duties have been a part of the duties and responsibilities of a Ser-
geant or Patrolman of the Barkfield Police Department for about the past
thirty years. This was of course prior to the department becoming full-
time in 1955. There are many more facts to be brought forward in this
matter but they are best to be held until they may be needed.
    All of the part-time officers that are active must be E.M.T. with the
exception of James William, and he has kept his E.M.T. status current on
his own through various courses available.
    The following is for your information on the E.M.T. status of the Town
of Barkfield.

    +   Must maintain E.M.T. status

    *   They may question if they are required to be E.M.T.s

    -   E.M.T. status at present


                                        ''Full-time''

     1.  Sgt. Derek Frost                  * -
     2.  Sgt. William Donovan              * -
     3.  Ptlmn. John Fevyer               * -
     4.  Ptlmn. Jack Cardillo             * -
     5.  Ptlmn. Reginald Stevens          * -
     6.  Ptlmn. Robert Tucker             * -
     7.  Ptlmn. Paul Bornot               * -
     8.  Ptlmn. Dick Harries              * -
     9.  Ptlmn. Harry Pady                * -


                                        ''Part-time''

    10.  Ptlmn. George Mabon              + -
    11.  Ptlmn. Kevin Hale                + -
    12.  Ptlmn. Rachel Gordon             +    in training
    13.  Ptlmn. Gwyn Davies               +    will train soon
    14.  Ptlmn. Thomas Mullen             + -
    15.  Ptlmn. David Muir                +    will train soon
    16.  Ptlmn. Kevin Lucas               +    will train soon
    17.  Ptlmn. Marcus Kent               +    will train soon


                                        ''Special Police''

    18.  Ptlmn. Pamela Miller             + -
    19.  Ptlmn. Victor Hills              + -
    20.  Ptlmn. Bernie McPhee             + -
```

(Exhibit continues on following page.)

Exhibit 13-4. Continued

```
                                      ''Other E.M.T.s''
21.  C.D. Director Graham Brown        —
22.  F.M. Matthew Carse                —
23.  Nurse Graham Nelson               —
```

                         Very truly yours,

                         Richard Dives

                         Richard Dives
                         Chief of Police
                         Barkfield, Massachusetts

Exhibit 13-5. Mediator's worksheet

ITEMS IN NEGOTIATION

ISSUES	PRESENT	UNION	MANAGEMENT
1. Wages	$221.00/wk	$240.00/wk now Avg. pay after 1/1/78 plus C.L.A.** for 2nd and 3rd year per B.C.P.I.***	$240.00/wk 4% — 2nd year 4% — 3rd year
2. Clothing Allowance	$250.00/yr	$250.00 — 1st yr. $275.00 — 2nd & 3rd drop holster & gun	$250.00/yr and revolver and holster for new man
3. Educational Incentive	Own Plan	$250.00 — 30 Cr. $500.00 — 60 Cr. Or Longevity: 1% — 5 yrs. 2% — 10 yrs. 3% — 15 yrs.	$250.00 — A.S. $500.00 — B.S. And Longevity: 1% — 5 yrs. 2% — 10 yrs. 3% — 15 yrs.
4. BC/BS	In Litigation	75/25 — 90% Retro from 2/1/77 to present.	75/25; Split 90/10 2/1/77 to 6/30/77.
5. Work Schedule	No Fixed Schedule	5-&-2 4-&-2 — 3rd yr.	5-&-2 (one year trial schedule) 4-&-2 possible in third year.*

*Study Committee for 3rd year implementation
**C.L.A. — Cost of Living Adjustment.   ***B.C.P.I. — Boston Consumer Price Index.
9/20/78

Exhibit 13-6. Town's final offer

TOWN OF BARKFIELD
MASSACHUSETTS
BOARD OF SELECTMEN

SELECTMEN

MUNICIPAL ASSISTANT

CLERK

Telephone
894-1377

December 19, 1978

Commonwealth of Massachusetts
Department of Labor and Industries
Joint—Labor—Management Committee
Attention: Chairman, John T. Dunlop
Room 408 — 130 Bowdoin Street
Boston, Massachusetts 02108

Gentlemen:

Attached is a copy of the last offer of the Barkfield Board of Selectmen to the Barkfield Police Alliance in the matter of contract negotiations for the period beginning July 1, 1978.

It is the feeling of the Selectmen that the offers they have made are
reasonable and equitable and they do not propose to make any increase in
their offer.

It should be noted that the value of the offer, expressed in terms of
the average patrolman per week is 15.26% more than the Fiscal 1978.

Sincerely yours,

Lawrence Anslow

Lawrence Anslow
Municipal Assistant

LA/mkd
Enclosure

(Exhibit continues on following page.)

Exhibit 13-6. Continued

SELECTMEN'S LAST OFFER — POLICE

Article 6 — Court Time — 4 hours straight time minimus time ½ over 4 hours.

Article 7 — Patrolman Base $240.00 1st year, 4% 2nd year, and 4% 3rd year.

Article 8 — Vacations 1 — 1, 2 — 2, 7 — 3, & 12 — 4

Article 9 — Clothing $250.00 Per Year

Article 10 — Holidays — Same as existing contract but change the wording.

Article 11 — Bereavement

A. 3 days for immediate family (mother, father, son, daughter, spouse, brother, and sister)

B. 1 day for grandparents of either spouse, brother or sister-in-law.

C. Personal Day — 1 per year

Article 12 — Work Schedule & Overtime

A. 5+2 — 40 hour schedule

B. Overtime in accordance with Chapter 147, Section 17E accepted by the Town March 13, 1971 (time ½ over 40 hours)

C. Willing to discuss 4+2 week provided that manpower is not increased and budget does not require more for part time.

Article 13 — Blue Cross/Blue Shield

A. 75/25 from July 1, 1977 on thru the contract

B. Life Insurance — $6,000

C. False Arrest — 100,000/300,000 limits

Article 14 — Sick Leave 1¼ days per month accumulated to 90 days

Article 15 — Education Incentives Article 22 — Longevity Combined

A. (Same as old contract) Town pay for materials required for courses.

B. $250.00 Cash Bonus for Associates Degree payable once a year. $500.00 Cash Bonus for Bachelors Degree payable once a year.

C. Longevity — 1% for 5 years; 2% for 10 years; 3% for 15 years on base pay

Article 16 — Mileage — Per Town Vote 10¢ per mile.

Article 22 — Longevity (see Article 15)

(Exhibit continues on following page.)

Exhibit 13-6. Continued

Article 24 — Funeral Expense Agreed to place article for acceptance of Chapter 41, Section 100G. (Duty related death, Funeral payment) on Town Meeting Warrant.

Article 25 — No Strike Clause — Agreed in principle

Article 26 — Training

A. Overtime if mandatory training is off duty and beyond 40 hours per week

B. Ambulance — willing to discuss variation if Police keep service in Dept.

Exhibit 13-7. Chronology: Barkfield police negotiations

September 2, 1977	Decision by Massachusetts Labor Relations Commission re: prohibited practice on health insurance. Decision against town.
November 25, 1977	EMT training halted by chief in response to overtime deficit.
December 7, 1977	Opening collective bargaining proposal presented by Barkfield Police Alliance.
February 1, 1978	Meeting — Board and union
February 10	Meeting — Board and union.
April 22	Unfair labor practice charge.
April 25	Tucker removed as EMT training officer.
April 27	Batley first hears of Barkfield negotiation problem.
June 20	Batley goes west and touches base with several police departments. Meets Tucker, president of Police Alliance.
July 1	Contract expires.
July 11	Letter sent by union to attorneys seeking to restart discussion on July 18.
July 25	DeCata and Batley go to Worcester, meet with various unions, talk about their role, union problems. Barkfield police come in and tell "tales of woe."
August 1	Union requests JLMC jurisdiction.
August 15 7:30 p.m.	Batley, DeCata go to meeting with Alliance.
	Batley, DeCata go to Selectmen's meeting 8:00 p.m.
August 16 5:30 p.m.	Batley and DeCata and Dick Horne go to selectmen's meeting — Horne explains Committee's purposes. Selectmen agree to talk to chief about schedule.
August 22 7:00 p.m.	Mediation session.
August 30 7:30 p.m.	Mediation and negotiation
October 2	Grievance withdrawn
October 6	Hearing scheduled, canceled.
October 18 1:30 p.m.	Hearing on the issues
October 18 until mid-December	Phone calls with parties re contract language, lawsuits, grievances.
October 19	DeCata discusses case with Horne.
November 10	Hearing — Only Anslow appears on town's behalf.
December 5	Case certified for arbitration.
December 19	Batley and DeCata meet with Morley and Erskine, prior to arbitration hearing.
January 3, 1979	DeCata and Batley discuss case. Blue Cross suit dropped. Grievance dropped.

CHAPTER 14

Compassionate Layoffs in an Era of Fiscal Stringency

The next two cases focus on the questions that arise when a manager considers the possibility that an employee has to be let go and in some sense has to look him or her in the eye. In the case in this chapter, "Surplus Employees in the Claims Division," looking workers in the eye is a bit difficult: There are nearly three thousand to look at. The reasons for the removal of these employees are not related to any individual's job performance. Rather, the major issues here concern the way the organization should handle what amounts to a mass layoff that has come about in response to external and operational exigencies.[1]

The effects of recession, shortfalls in tax revenues, and efforts to reduce the size and scope of government has made cutback management a primary occupation — or preoccupation — for public managers of the early eighties. Shrinking the size or scope of an organization is difficult and in public agencies the problem may be magnified: Because few public agencies had, until recently, experienced major reductions in activities and resources, public managers and employees are notably unprepared for this period in terms of either expectations or experience. Managers are responsible for developing and implementing an institutional response, a response that must consider the needs and perceptions of the people involved, and that helps the institution to weather the transition, to serve its clients, and to meet its other obligations.

Some Sources of Stress. As in the following case, organizational stress and change can be generated either by external circumstances over which the organization exercises little influence or by internal management decisions, sometimes in response to external factors. In either circumstance, lack of work or activity can be either a very important source — or a symptom — of stress and anxiety: Diminution of certain work activities frequently accompanies cutbacks, and at the same time major cutbacks or uncertainty over mission of the organization can cause

---

[1] Much of the following discussion first appeared in *Washington Public Policy Notes,* a publication of the Institute for Public Policy and Management, University of Washington, in the Spring 1982 edition. I am grateful to the Institute and to the editor, Susie Anschell for permission to adapt it in this volume and for expert editorial help in the initial development of the piece.

managers and employees to deal primarily with stress symptoms rather than the work of the organization. Stress may also arise from the inability, due to cutbacks in resources, of an individual or task unit to serve clients or meet certain organizational goals or requirements; dedicated professionals will find this inability glaringly frustrating and debilitating.

In public agencies, small issues such as changes in carpool arrangements have caused no end of anxiety and diversion — even while job tenure or security were not in question; now, with job security no longer well assured, the degree of anxiety and stress attendant to change or uncertainty is likely to be even greater.

Under stressful organizational circumstances, behaviors are often triggered that are ultimately of little value to individuals, their colleagues or the organization. Anticipation of these triggers, and some action aimed at their sources, would seem to be in the interest of continuing organizational effectiveness and individual well-being.

Some Human Dimensions. One way to sort out the change/stress problem is to think of a person's job and environment in terms of possibilities for job satisfaction. A well-functioning, busy organization provides many opportunities for satisfaction. During periods of uncertainty or actual change, there may be a loss or perceived loss of control over things and that's the stuff of which stress and neurosis are made. Typical managerial reactions generally exacerbate the problem by focusing attention away from those activities that could promote at least some continued job satisfaction; energies are more usually diverted to less constructive activities that provide little real help for direct satisfaction of personal and professional needs. Typical consequences include a good deal of underlying or overt conflict, a lot of time spent expressing anger to oneself or one's peers, and time spent checking the latest rumors — or time spent in a wondering or depressed state. None of these responses are likely to contribute very much to anyone's need satisfaction or, for that matter, to the work or stability of the organization.

Uncertainty is a central cause of behavior that blocks satisfaction of higher-level needs. Uncertainty can breed great insecurity, a psychological state that leads the individual to concentrate on simply trying to protect basic physiological and financial integrity; this leaves little psychic energy for considering organizational purposes, work activity, or patience with clients.[2]

Uncertainty activates the imagination to fill the information gap. It breeds imaginings about management intentions and about one's own abilities and future — imaginings that not only can lead to incorrect and damaging assumptions about the organization and its intentions or about one's own lifelong career prospects, but also take up time as people seek information to fill the gaps and release the anger that is bred by what they imagine. What they imagine is usually much worse than anything that could actually occur under the circumstances; after all,

---

[2]For a discussion of the concept of human need satisfaction, see Abraham Maslow, "A Theory of Human Motivation," *Psychological Review 50* (1943) 370–396.

imagination and fantasies are intended to take us beyond reality. The negative effect of uncertainty in activating the imagination underscores the importance of eliminating unnecessary uncertainty.

A Typical Organizational Response to Change. Uncertainty prevails under conditions of change partly because of the way organizations typically handle such conditions. Perhaps the most characteristic response is failure of management to tell employees very much very soon. Although no one likes to be the purveyor of bad news — and managers are no exception — the failure of managers to provide information is not entirely their fault. In the public sector, hard information on probable cutbacks or alterations in services is frequently unavailable in a timely fashion. The political process is not quick to plan for or recognize bad news, so difficult decisions and those that are likely to be unpopular are frequently made at the last minute. In many public jurisdictions the budget — often the object of considerable dispute and the more so when dollars are scarce — is passed in the final hours of the session. Until the budget is passed, managers do not have hard information to act on or pass along. Public managers are generally without any particular experience or perspective from which to make judgments or predictions on the probable depth or impact of cutbacks. The upshot is that uncertainty and rumors prevail and little is done by way of preparation.

A second typical response is to put the personnel department primarily in charge of handling the cutback situation. That pattern probably has its origins in a period of time when such cutbacks and layoffs as arose were minor and technical in nature and did not affect the fundamental operations of the agency. Moreover, where there is major organizational trauma, counseling skills and outplacement skills are necessary, and generally we have not staffed our public personnel agencies to include this class of skills. There simply hasn't been the need. Moreover, major cutbacks require major change and significant and central involvement of policymakers and managers to link substantive decision making to organizational structure and personnel policy; this degree of change is too broad to be carried out by one functional area, not centrally involved in program or policy, and often without high-level clout across the organization.

Third, although someone usually draws up an action plan and a timetable, rarely is there any sort of an infrastructure available to deliver on the plan; consequently it falls into disarray. Because the cutback situation is unusual, the usual organizational structures and relationships are not always appropriate to carrying out the tasks and communication that are necessary. Without an infrastructure that matches the task and its substantive and communication needs, the plan is not well implemented, even if the ideas were good to begin with.

The effects of these organizational responses tend to have some of the following characteristics. First, the work of the agency languishes to some degree — depending on the level of uncertainty that prevails and the skill with which the transition is handled. As a result, the mission, quality of work, and reputation of the organization can be harmed. Second, people in the organization are not prepared for the outcome as it affects them: There is no lead time to look for jobs and a sort of panic may set in. Third, such outplacement systems as may have been created become overloaded and there is no time for the job-search process to work. Fourth, if the organizational change and the cutback becomes a rout, managers can lose control over communications with employees, who get their information instead from the press, their contacts in other institutions, or from one another's imagination. The loss of trust in management as a source of information not only has consequences for any managerial help in dealing with personal and professional anxieties but also harms management's ability to run the organization during and after the period of change.

A Preferable Response: Concentrating on Substance. The organization's first concern should be to alleviate uncertainty — to provide whatever certainty is possible on any point possible. In many state or federal agencies, it is not difficult to predict that cutbacks are likely. Talking to employees about this sort of probability may seem contributory to panic, but they will be thinking about it anyway; they read the same newspapers as managers and have their own information networks. By assuming responsibility for conveying that information early and regularly, management can establish a channel *and* credibility, providing the possibilities for greater control and order later on, and reducing the risk that rumors will swallow up productive activity. At the same time, there is a need to create an environment in which people understand the seriousness of the issue and in which they can minimize uncertainty and perceptions of lack of control in their personal and professional lives. To maintain trust, it is important that commitments be made only when they can realistically be kept. That means that management must have already in place the infrastructure to carry out commitments. One example: A promised placement effort can only be executed if the parts are in place.

One central principle that can go a long way toward creating an environment with information, understanding, and individual and managerial control is to choose a strategy that deals with the source of the problems and issues involved in the cutbacks. Dealing with program-related issues has important advantages for the organization and for the individual. First, in most instances the agency will continue as an entity and provide some type and level of services. However, it will require changes in organizational alignments and practices to operate at the reduced level of resources. Maintenance of effective service with reduced resources will require considerable application of professional knowledge and abilities; thus, involving staff in restructuring the organization and its practices can help it continue to fulfill its mission and serve its clients.

Second, by revealing the substantive aspects of the problem, a collective focus on real problems and issues can help individuals to understand personnel decisions arising from the resource shortfall, perhaps defusing feelings of being personally singled out — feelings that may otherwise result from an unexplained termination or removal. Third, work on restructuring can provide something of importance to do that focuses employees' skills and energies during a period when rumors or other negative nonfulfilling activities would otherwise dominate. By being set to work on productive organizational tasks solving significant task-related problems, a sense of competence, usefulness, and importance can persist even in a time of great change.

Fourth, management channels established to work on these tasks can displace the rumor mill as the dominant information channel. Management can become an information source in which the work force has confidence. There are some risks, of course, that change options under discussion could trigger unnecessary rumors. On the other hand, there are likely to be equal risks in the opposite managerial behavior: A closely held planning process is just as likely to result in rumors and attendant lack of work-focused activity.

Other Aspects of Response. Involvement in developing and operating a process for outplacement can be another constructive activity with multiple advantages. Again, it focuses on usefulness and competence as the outplacement system is created and as it finds people jobs. People who have assisted in outplacement efforts of this sort report a great deal of personal gratification — and frequently develop job contacts themselves.

Also critical to implementation of a cutback or changed organizational structure is that the implementation be perceived as fair and orderly. Technical errors or mistakes, such as improper calculations of seniority, may erode trust in management. This means, among other things, having a smoothly running personnel function handling the technical issues and having in place some central source where people can get information on their status and otherwise remain informed of their personal options.

Many kinds of controversy and conflict can be anticipated by looking at the history and traditions of the organization. The odds are high that seniority and affirmative-action types of questions will arise during this period; other issues will be more specific to the organization in question. Machinery should be in place for handling conflicts before they get outside of the organization and subject to external influences.

There is also the necessity and desirability of dealing as constructively as possible with any bargaining unit representation and the provisions of labor-management contracts. There are many examples of productive labor-management interaction during periods of change, including modifications in work practices and contract revisions. Joint committees of labor and management have produced some impressive changes.

Any impact on personnel will be of interest to representatives of the bargaining unit, and their capacity to help or hinder should be understood fully and factored into any process or substantive strategies that evolve. Accommodation, if possible, is far preferable if it can be attained. Apart from bargaining rights, public unions frequently have too much savvy and political muscle to be ignored during such periods, lest they use channels outside the organization to get their way. Relationship building well in advance of crisis is likely to minimize labor strife.

Secrecy or grandstanding are unlikely to help; they will only divert energy from the major tasks.

It is important to remember that some people will be frustrated, especially in a slow economy and will not be as successful in getting a new job. Even with the best-managed adjustment and alteration mechanisms, the organization must counsel realistically and be prepared to deal with residual stress. In addition to leadership within the organization, instruction may be obtained in what are commonly called "stress management" techniques. Available resources range from organizations that teach breathing exercises to those that help people eliminate stress by identifying its sources, taking personal inventories, and fashioning personal strategies to move beyond the stress. Many organizations in the public and private sector have made good use of such seminars and skills and find that the results flow over into more normal periods of activity. And by discovering that there is something they can do about it, people can help to reduce the levels of stress and uncertainty for themselves, with benefit also to the organization.

During periods of change and uncertainty, organizations and individuals each have certain responsibilities. The organization is responsible for providing information and at least a modicum of services and leadership to help individuals weather the period. The organization's most critical responsibility, however, is to consider its mission. Inevitably in considering the mission, the welfare of the individuals in the organization must be considered, since it is those individuals who will help to redefine and then carry out the altered mission of the agency.

In the Claims Division case that follows, many of these issues arise for the agency head. A combination of reorganization, computerization, and legislation that changed the nature of a claims processing operation has made 2,800 employees unnecessary to the workings of a large governmental function. The situation is complicated by affirmative action considerations, since most of the employees in jeopardy are black and female. Because of the juxtaposition of operational and personnel considerations, questions of efficiency versus equity pervade the case, and the possibilities for internal and external conflict abound.

In reviewing the situation, we observe some of the retraining and outplacement options that the agency was attempting to carry out. In addition to more compassionate considerations, there are management, budgetary, and administrative forces that are important in the decision process. Discussion of options for dealing with the situation transmits also some important knowledge about seldom-used parts of the personnel system including the arcane procedure known as "reduction in force" or "RIF."

Another form of cultural knowledge concerns the sort of pressure that actors outside the formal organizational structure can exert on what would seem to be an internal management decision. The need to influence the many actors in this process demonstrates the complexities in solving major personnel problems in a manner consistent with organizational *and* individual interests. In this case some of the actors and restrictions we have met reemerge, and new actors come to the fore.

STUDY QUESTIONS

1. How would you evaluate the various components of the Claims Division's effort to handle this surplus problem? What are its strengths and weaknesses and how would you account for those?

2. What are the most important considerations for the manager in this case? What's at stake for him?

3. Identify the major actors and institutions he must deal with to solve this problem. Why are they important?

4. If you were Phil Johnston, what would you decide?

5. How would you carry out your decision so that its intentions were fulfilled?

6. What management techniques would you use?

RECOMMENDED READING

"Personnel Placement at the End of the Economic Stabilization Program: Finding 1008 Jobs," Joseph L. Kirk in *Historical Working Papers on the Economic Stabilization Program, August 15, 1971 to April 30, 1974,* Part II (U.S. Government Printing Office, 1974).

Surplus Employees in the Claims Division

Phil Johnston, Administrator of the Claims Division, U.S. Department of Internal Affairs (DIA), looked out his window to see the five o'clock traffic scurrying past. Most of the office personnel had left. A few were around but he was in relative isolation for the moment. As he gazed at the traffic it brought his thoughts back to the problem he had been wrestling with throughout most of the day. He imagined that some of the very individuals he was thinking of — most of the personnel of the Electronic Data Processing branch (EDP) of the Claims Division — were at this moment driving past and heading for home. Johnston's office was in the main DIA building and he reported to the Secretary of DIA.

It was July 1978. About a year had elapsed since Johnston had decided to avoid a reduction in force (RIF)* in EDP, despite the fact that problems in paring down surplus staff threatened to grow larger. The surplus had not been significantly reduced and both external pressures, in-cluding Congressional inquiries (see Exhibit 14-2), and his own conscience led him to review the situation. Following his review he wished to discuss it with his senior staff people in the Claims Division. Among other things it was important to evaluate the effectiveness of current efforts at retraining and placement. In view of the pressures on him to reduce the surplus and in light of what had been done to remedy the situation, was a RIF now an important option or was it simply unrealistic to even consider? The DIA, which numbered over 150,000 employees, had never had a RIF and prided itself on loyalty to its employees and the resultant good morale, despite its often monotonous tasks.

The Electronic Data Processing Branch

The Electronic Data Processing Branch (EDP) is one of the four branches within the Operations Administration of the Claims Division (CD), a large subdivision of the Department of Internal

---

This case was prepared by Phillip Sharpless under the supervision of Jon Brock, Lecturer at the John F. Kennedy School of Government, Harvard University. While the case is based upon field research, the identity of the agency and individuals are disguised and other information has been altered in the interest of confidentiality.

Copyright © 1980 by the President and Fellows of Harvard College. Reproduced by permission of the John F. Kennedy School of Government.

*A "RIF" is a systematic way of reducing the number of employees in an organization. It is typically carried out according to seniority — with some preference given to veterans — within specified job categories, organizational components or even commuting areas. A manual used in the Bureau of Training, Civil Service Commission, describes a RIF:

"A reduction in force occurs when an agency is obliged to demote, separate, or furlough one or more employees because of lack of work, shortage of funds or reorganization. The cause of reduction in force may come from action

of Congress, the President or the Office of Management and Budget, or from decisions of the head of the agency or some official who has been authorized to make such decisions.

"Whatever the source of the requirement for reduction in force, officials of the agency must decide how to distribute the remaining resources and what parts and programs of the agency to cut, and how much. This may require the balancing of priorities so as to cause the least necessary delay in completing the work that remains to be done after the reduction in force."

A RIF is an administratively cumbersome process, requiring a lot of judgment among many individuals and organizations including the Civil Service Commission, the agency head, the Office of Management and Budget, and sometimes political leaders. Even after general agreement is reached among the parties, success of implementation is still complex and subject to appeal by individual employees.

See Exhibit 14-1 for an explanation provided to employees by the Civil Service Commission.

Affairs, a U.S. government cabinet agency. (See Exhibit 14-3.) The Claims Division employs about fifty thousand. Of these, approximately eight thousand work in EDP. An organization chart for the Claims Division appears in Exhibit 14-4.

EDP occupies several large buildings in downtown Arlington. Each floor is a spacious, wide-open, columned area covered with hundreds of desks and massive piles of paperwork. Hundreds of clerks sit at these desks where they file, code or type while surveying the open room and observing others doing the same. These file clerks and keypunch operators perform most of the day-to-day operational work within the EDP branch of the Claims Division.

The work of the EDP consists of receiving and examining employee/employer claim statements and converting this information into a form for use by the computer. Any changes or additions to the master file* are registered and each entry is verified. Most of the clerical operations are rote and are therefore relatively easy to master. The work is routine and repetitive: first-level line work, somewhat analogous to an assembly line or production task.

EDP works with the Internal Revenue Service and several other agencies on a major portion of its tasks, which necessitates scheduling of work to ensure coordination between the agencies. For example, after EDP processes claim statements they are then forwarded to IRS, which uses them for income tax purposes.

The workers in EDP are typically unskilled and few, if any, are educated beyond high school. In addition, the majority of the work force is minority and female with most paid at either the GS-3 or GS-4 level (between $8,000 and $10,000 per year). Exhibit 14-5 describes demographically the employees with EDP.

_____
*The master file is a massive record system containing CD information for 40-odd million individuals who file claims with the agency.

Automation at EDP

EDP, like many government organizations, had steadily increased in size over the years to handle a growing work load. Certain changes, however, had recently created an employee surplus within EDP. This surplus resulted from a combination of factors, some internal to EDP operations, others external to it.

With its task of processing millions of bits of information yearly it was inevitable that the Claims Division would change over to computerized operation.

As Fred Clough, a line manager with EDP observed:

This thing (computerization) has been delayed for 22 or 23 years. I saw it coming as early as 1955. We all feared technological unemployment even then, but the workload here in EDP has grown such that we haven't had any problems until recently.

A major turning point in the automation process was the AC-5 project. The AC-5 project involved converting 100,000 feet of paper data files into computer-usable magnetic tape. The project had been initiated in 1975 and was completed late in 1978. While the paper-to-tape conversion was essential for the changeover to automated information and processing storage, the fact that it was near completion created several problems: First, with AC-5† near completion, what would those people on the project do? Second, with an automated process now in operation, workers on the old manual system would soon become surplus. Employment ceilings, which defined the number of persons an agency could employ each budget year, were imposed by the Office of Management and Budget (OMB) and by the financial and administrative bureaucracy of the Department of Internal

_____
†The AC-5 conversion represented about 10 percent of the previous year's total EDP work load.

Affairs.* The employment ceilings effective for fiscal 1979, which took into account the end of AC-5 and automation of part of the process, made these people officially surplus and put DIA over their allowable full-time personnel ceiling.†

Fred Clough disagreed with these personnel ceilings and felt that there was really no over-staffing problem. He stated:

> The Administrator, OMB — they are insu-lated from the problem here. We really need these people. Sure, maybe we have a few surplus individuals today, but what about next month? I feel that there will be plenty of work coming along in the near future and it just doesn't make sense to consider them surplus and farm them out. It will just make us go out and hire more people later; then those we are redeploying now will really be surplus.

Changing Standards

Apart from automation and AC-5 completion, standards for input quality control were changed within EDP. This change served to reduce fur-ther the agency's work force needs. Data pre-viously sent to CD by claimants are checked for

*The Office of Management and Budget (OMB) is the President's financial and managerial watchdog over the var-ious Executive Branch agencies. Among other things, it is charged with aiding the President in budget preparation and administration. OMB works with the department and agency heads in establishing departmental budgets, personnel ceil-ings, etc. and acts as the President's agent in doing so. OMB also works with the Congress as the Congress considers the budget of the United States government. The budget, of course, is subject to Congressional approval. Usually, ma-jor agencies can exercise some latitude in administering in-ternally their budgets and personnel ceilings but by law they must adhere to the agreed-upon totals for the department.

† Under federal budget procedures agencies generally have limits or "ceilings" on the number of personnel they may have on board during any fiscal year. Often agencies are permitted to hire part-time, temporary, or intermittent workers which do not count against the full-time authorized ceiling, but which may count against a separate, but often more flexible "other-than-full-time ceiling."

accuracy and then must be matched to and merged with the proper segment of the master file. Usually data are added by first matching the code numbers. If there is a discrepancy be-tween the identifiers in the new information and the information on the master file, this discrep-ancy has to be reconciled, usually by contacting the individual submitting the information.

If standards are loosened, a larger number of discrepancies can be dismissed or overlooked. If the master file shows a person to be 70 years old and the new information describes the per-son as 75 years old, then under a five-year stan-dard it is assumed that this is the same individ-ual and that the information is essentially correct. Had the old standard of three years been in ef-fect, additional work would have been required to resolve the inconsistency as phone calls, rec-ord checks and corrections would have been made. The loosened standard, therefore, reduced the work load and speeded processing.

There were other system changes, such as the use of optical character recognition equipment which also reduced manpower needs.

Change in Legislated Procedures

External causes were also affecting the work force needs at Claims. Congress had passed leg-islation in December 1976 which would reduce further the number of people required in EDP operations. What had previously been a quar-terly submittal of claim statements would be-come simply an annual requirement. This not only reduced the total work load at EDP but more importantly it altered the nature of the needed work force. A relatively constant work force level was maintained to handle the quarterly submit-tal and subsequent processing. Now, however, the job would occur at the beginning of each year only, and a seasonal work force would be more appropriate. Most of the current work force were full-time permanent employees.

At the end of fiscal year 1978, with all of

these changes and pressures, approximately 950 of 8,000 employees (12 percent) would be surplus. This would leap to 2,800 of 8,000 (35 percent) in 1979 assuming no further changes in 1978–1979. Exhibit 14-6 illustrates in more detail the magnitude of the overstaffing relative to employment ceilings by fiscal year.

Reclassification and Downgrade

Other pressures complicated the problems at the Claims Division. To police for abuse of the personnel system, the Civil Service Commission periodically reviews or audits job classifications within the various departments of the Executive Branch. In 1975, officials in CSC and DIA's central personnel office performed such a "job audit," primarily on GS-3, GS-4, and GS-5 positions in several regional CD offices. They found that many of the jobs sampled, according to application of CSC qualifications standards, were overclassified. In effect, these employees were deemed overpaid relative to the CSC's assessment of the work they performed. CSC and DIA issued an order to EDP requiring that they review all clerical jobs within CD. The review and reclassification was to be completed over three years — from 1976 to 1979. After the reclassification review was begun, a preliminary screening indicated that 80 percent of the employees in EDP might be overclassified, therefore requiring downgrade.

According to a variety of officials, the overclassification problems had evolved gradually. In the late 1950s and early 1960s there was much sentiment that federal employees, particularly those at the lower grade levels, were underpaid in comparison to equivalent private sector positions. Since the salary scale at that time was altered only periodically by act of Congress, one of the few options for raising salaries was by raising the classification of a job or class of jobs to higher grade levels. Since the early 1960s, however, federal pay had been raised yearly in

accordance with a "comparability" survey of pay levels in a sample of roughly equivalent private sector jobs, obviating the "underpayment" problem.

Since federal salaries are now regularly adjusted upward, there is apparently less tolerance of "grade creep" that previously may have been overlooked and, indeed, the government estimated that prior grade creep was in 1978 costing the government a half-billion dollars. In the opinion of some officials, the emphasis on affirmative action in federal employment and the related desire to provide better pay and status to minority employees may have led to another "round" of grade creep.

In 1978, when EDP's internal adjustments resulted in a large surplus problem, the Claims Division through the central personnel office of the Department of Internal Affairs requested from the Civil Service Commission a moratorium on the reclassification review in Electronic Data Processing. Ben Paden of Human Resources and Personnel explained:

> We couldn't possibly start downgrading people in the present climate. It's difficult enough to move people about, but when you start downgrading it gets tougher. Would you want someone transferred to your department who has just been demoted? And that's just part of the problem. What about morale in EDP? I don't think the people working in EDP could handle both of those things at once. It's bad enough to figure you're going to be moved out, but to be demoted at the same time —this would really shake up some people.

Handling the Surplus

Once the decision was made to avoid a RIF, the situation in EDP became one which required a creative program of personnel resource management within the non-insignificant constraints of the Federal bureaucracy. The Office of Human Resources was assigned by Administrator

Johnston the major responsibility for solving the problem.

Human Resources developed an action plan to handle the situation which is shown in Exhibit 14-7. They regarded this as a comprehensive attempt to consider the problem in detail and to develop courses of action which, if simultaneously pursued, would rectify the overstaffing.

Among the options, early-out* retirement for those eligible was proposed and later approved by the Civil Service Commission. (See Exhibit 14-8 for a description of this procedure.) A special mini-computer was set up to give instant information to potential retirees. The computer could determine pension benefit availability based on number of years in service, salary and other factors particular to an employee. This way the individual could consider the impact of alternate retirement dates on his or her pension plan. To qualify an employee had to be over 50 with 20-plus years of service. About 35 individuals qualified.

Seasonal or part-time employment was offered to all who wanted it, since employees who did not work full time did not count against the full-time employment ceiling imposed on the agency by the Office of Management and Budget. This option was chosen by about 100 persons.

A large portion of EDP personnel was being surveyed regarding reassignment to the Disability Branch, which had need for clerical employees at the time. Human Resources also planned to identify other branches with employee needs that could possibly be filled with surplus EDP people, perhaps after some training.

In addition to studying the transfer of people to jobs in other parts of Internal Affairs or other departments, the Human Resources office studied the many tasks performed within the Claims Division and began identifying work that could possibly be transferred to EDP from other parts of the Division. They felt this would increase the work load within EDP, justifying existing personnel levels, and reduce redeployment requirements.

In another activity, employees were "detailed" to other jobs. This is a process of assigning individuals to vacant or specially created jobs for periods of 30 to 120 days. The mechanism is generally used to fill vacancies on a temporary basis while the incumbent is absent or while a permanent employee is being sought. It is also used to try out employees in new jobs. This procedure provides flexibility to move staff around on a short-term basis without going through an elaborate set of qualifying criteria and paperwork. The process is, however, watched closely by the Civil Service Commission and employee unions, since the normally rigid job assignment and job qualification procedures, in essence, are temporarily ignored. The union prefers the more restrictive CSC guidelines, which limit discretion on decisions regarding movement of employees. Detailing is only temporary, however, and the jobs eventually must be filled by individuals who have met all of the procedural requirements. Further, the detailed person still counts against the employment ceiling in the original agency.

An excerpt from an official interagency letter describes another device used to absorb some of the surplus employees:

> One major step has been to reach agreement with the Internal Revenue Service. For the first two years of annual claim reporting, we can elongate the processing cycle for wage statements to 12 months. This would facilitate using nearly 1000 of the otherwise excess full-time permanent employees rather than hiring seasonal employees. This, in effect, provides a two-year respite for dealing with a major portion of the overstaffing problem.

---

*Under current law there are provisions in Civil Service rules providing employees with the option of early retirement or early-out. These provisions are only applicable when an agency is faced with an impending major reduction in force.

Training

Training was viewed as essential to the redeployment effort. Gloria Simpson of Human Resources related to the case writer how the training program was focused:

> EDP has a surplus of clerks — you know, the people who file and push paper. Yet at the same time there is a shortage of good typists. It was felt that the initial training effort should focus on this problem. The goal is to certify a large number of the surplus clerks as typists.

She stated how the training was initiated:

> First, we made an announcement through the Central Office bulletin (a weekly publication distributed to all employees) that any CD employee was eligible to take the CSC typing exam, although we planned to select only EDP people.
>
> The results so far haven't been bad. Of 300 tests, 124 persons passed the exam and are now certified typists. Another 55 individuals came close to passing, so we felt a refresher course would help them get over the 40-words-per-minute hurdle.*
>
> We have also solicited 698 applications from individuals who have no typing experience. We have selected 100 of the most promising and intend to train them from scratch.

Sandra Beasley, who was in charge of administering the training, spoke of logistical problems that had been hampering efforts to begin training the 100 individuals selected for typing training:

> As you know, we have nice training facilities all set up but we just can't get things rolling. We have had all these new typewriters for over a year now and we can't use them. We are waiting for programmed typing texts. Supposedly they are on the way — have been

for months. We are having problems with requisitions through DIA's central supply bureaucracy.

> We plan to expend 75 hours per person for training. This is typically required according to the secretarial colleges we have checked with. I feel this is sufficient but, if the past is any indication, some of the people will not want to leave class after reaching 40 words per minute. They will want to type at higher rates so that they will have the best chance of qualifying for the new jobs and performing well, perhaps even for higher pay. Of course, we don't object to their remaining if they first get it cleared through their supervisors.

Waiver of Qualifications for Current Vacancies

Civil Service regulations for job selection limit the potential for permanent transfer to higher or more broadly skilled jobs of most individuals within EDP, where most of the jobs (and thus qualifications) are narrow and unskilled. Civil Service rules, however, will permit organizations undergoing a RIF to waive qualification requirements on a temporary basis. If implemented, this measure would provide EDP more latitude in immediately relocating persons into vacancies, avoiding the possibility that the vacancies might be filled by the time training was completed.

The Civil Service Commission stipulates qualifications for jobs in the federal service by the use of "classification standards" to which the various departments and agencies within its purview must adhere in filling jobs. Classification standards are guidelines that stipulate individual skills required to successfully perform a job and are used to determine the grade and salary for the position. Human Resources felt that in this case, with so many persons involved, it would be beneficial to approach CSC and ask for a waiver of qualification requirements for transferred EDP personnel. In the request, CSC was promised that these individuals would eventu-

---

*Forty words per minute is a representative goal for one semester of high school instruction. A skilled secretary usually types 60 words per minute or more. A top executive secretary may reach 90 words per minute.

ally be trained and certified for their new positions.

Management Attitudes

As in most complex situations there was some variance of management opinion as to what the problems really were and what solutions would be most effective.

The existence of surplus staff was questioned by a minority of line managers within EDP. More fundamentally, there was a difference of opinion across other branches about the quality and desirability of individuals who might be transferred.

Gloria Simpson stated that:

In some cases the recipient branches felt abused. Their ability to hire was frozen. They felt like EDP has been sending them the loafers. EDP disagrees, of course, so we in personnel have to referee these things. In one case we had to show the Disability Branch the leave records* of proposed transferees before they were willing to consider them.

Line-staff frictions developed as the redeployment effort progressed. EDP line managers indicated that the personnel staff often let their own priorities dominate rather than providing a service to the branches. On the other hand, the personnel staff complained that the branch managers hampered reassignment effort because of their reluctance to accept people.

Fred Clough noted:

I think personnel is really attempting to help us solve this problem. It just seems that sometimes they are a bit too procedural. They sometimes lose sight of the objective — in this case to reassign people — and become tied up in administrative procedures, slowing the process. I view personnel as a service function and hope that it will operate that way.

Gloria Simpson responded:

*Leave records indicate the amount of sick leave or vacation time available to the employee.

We are a service function. But we also have to be directive at times if we are to coordinate things. When we transfer a person across branches, we must consider the needs of both branches. We are caught in the middle and we expect some compromise between branches or the problem will never be solved.

Regarding procedures, in the federal environment you can't escape them. We have rules from DIA, OMB and CSC. These structures cannot be ignored — it's just a matter of working within the constraints of red tape the best way you can.

Attitude toward training varied, generally depending on how high or low the individual was in the organizational hierarchy. Usually, lower-middle level managers felt that the training efforts in EDP were meaningful and effective. At higher levels, there was more pessimism about the efficacy and worth of training programs. Sandra Beasley, training administrator, remarked:

In the late '60s and early '70s the top management at DIA was all for training. We did most of the training in-house then.

Things have changed now. DIA doesn't want to mix training in with CD business. If training is needed, DIA would rather contract out for it — they don't want to deal with in-house programs.

But, I think the contractors are a ripoff and I know we could have saved money in many cases, had we done the training ourselves. We are handling the EDP situation, though, and plan to get going once we receive the programmed typing manuals.

There was general agreement that the decision making process throughout this crisis at CD was one of consensus, i.e., general agreement among all relevant parties before decision implementation. This meant that regular meetings were vital for discussion and decision implementation. Fred Clough commented on the importance of good communication during the redeployment effort:

In the beginning of the redeployment effort staff meetings were held daily among all concerned EDP persons — the managers, the personnel staff, and the training staff. These were crucial to get the involvement and commitment of all affected parties. We had one meeting where five levels of EDP management were represented. That's consensus decision making. This way, no one can say, "Fred, you goofed this up." Blame and praise are shared together.

The Union

The Human Resources Office had attempted to remain in contact with the union leadership. Discussions had been held with the union to enlist its support of the proposed actions to handle the general redeployment effort, although they had displayed little overt enthusiasm.

There had been resistance to several portions of the Redeployment Action Plan (Exhibit 14-7), however. According to Ben Paden, part-timers were less likely than full-time employees to join and support the union. Hence, opposition had been expressed to this part of the proposal. As indicated earlier, the union was also concerned about the use of detailing.

Ben Paden related his opinions of the union and redeployment:

They get bogged down in minutia. It seems the big, overriding issues aren't discussed — just the details.

Gloria Simpson commented further:

It seems there is a misunderstanding about the whole issue of redeployment. We were just completing a reorganization before all of these other things happened. The unions seem to think that these people have become displaced because of reorganization which has nothing to do with the surplus problem. Either we're not clear on this or they're refusing to listen. I feel it's the latter.

The personnel office just simply doesn't know what the union wants. All we ever get in reactions to our proposals is criticism, never constructive suggestions.

The case writer had been unable to talk to union representatives.

Employee Morale

According to Gloria Simpson of Human Resources:

I spoke with a number of the affected employees to discover their concerns. There wasn't really that much fear of outright job loss as you might think. I feel that the way we handled things had a lot to do with this. We were open and frank with the employees and explained the situation. We reassured them that every attempt was being made to avoid a RIF. I think they believed us and this reassured them.

She explained further:

The real concerns were, I feel, minor in nature even though I'm sure the employees felt that they were important. Employees expressed concern about leaving their old buddies and about the disruption in their commuting patterns and car pools. They were concerned about having to relocate to other buildings.

Frequently the case writer overheard the following sentiment pass between EDP employees:

That would be fine, but I just wish they would let us know something. I'm tired of not knowing.

Even though morale seemed to have suffered somewhat in management's view, most managers felt that the work output had not declined appreciably. Fred Clough attributed this to the nature of the work. "The work is easy. If a person can count he should be able to do the job."

Present Situation

Phil Johnston pulled the staffing level chart (see Exhibit 14-6) out of a file and tried to mentally sum up the situation. EDP presently had something like 950 surplus employees. This would increase to almost 3,000 by the end of the next year unless some movement occurred rapidly.

Exhibit 14-1. "Fed Facts" 13 on reductions in force in federal agencies: U.S. Civil Service Commission pamphlet

Changes in program, lack of funds, decrease in work, reorganization, or the need to place a returning employee with reemployment rights may require a Federal agency to make a reduction in force. This means the agency would lay off, furlough for more than 30 days, reassign, or demote some of its employees. Standard reduction-in-force (RIF) procedures are set up by regulations so that these actions will be carried out in a fair and orderly way.

Under this system employees compete for retention on the basis of four factors specified by law: type of appointment (tenure), veteran preference, total length of civilian and creditable military service, and performance ratings. Generally, veterans with "Satisfactory" performance ratings are given higher retention standing than nonveterans. For certain retired members of the uniformed services, however, another provision of the law withholds veteran preference in RIF's and limits their credit for military service.

HOW THE SYSTEM WORKS

Reduction in force does not begin or end with layoff notices to employees. The agency must (1) decide the jobs to be affected (The agency decision to abolish one kind of job instead of another is not subject to review by the Civil Service Commission.); (2) determine, according to an equitable formula, which employees will lose their jobs or change jobs, (3) determine whether employees about to lose their own jobs have rights to other positions; (4) issue notices to the affected employees at least 30 days before the reduction is scheduled to take place, and (5) help career and career-conditional employees who are, or will be, displaced find other jobs. (The Civil Service Commission has special programs to help.)

DECIDING WHICH EMPLOYEES LOSE OR CHANGE JOBS

Competitive Area — First the agency fixes the competitive area (the geographical and organizational limits within which employees will compete for retention). A stenographer in one city, for example, would not ordinarily compete with a stenographer in another city. Each competitive area usually consists of a single office or installation in the field service, or a bureau or similar organization at headquarters.

Competitive Level — Next the agency groups positions by competitive level (by type and grade of work). An accountant, for example, would not compete with a stenographer, since each could not ordinarily do the other's job. Instead, similar jobs at the same level — jobs that are interchangeable — are grouped together in a competitive level to show clearly which employees are in competition: GS-9 accountants are listed with other GS-9 accountants, GS-2 typists with other GS-2 typists, etc.

Retention Registers — At this point the formula combining the four factors — type of appointment (tenure), veteran preference, length of service, and performance rating — comes into play.

Employees in the kinds of jobs to be affected (for example, GS-3 stenographers) are ranked on a retention register in three groups according to type of appointment (tenure):

Group I — With a few exceptions, career employees who are not serving probation.

Group II — Career employees who are serving probationary periods, the ex-

(Exhibit continues on following page.)

Exhibit 14-1. Continued

ceptions from Group I, and career-conditional employees.

Group III — Indefinite employees, term employees, status quo employees, and employees serving under temporary appointments pending establishment of registers.

Each of these groups is divided into two subgroups — A for veterans and B for nonveterans.

Three types of employees are not placed in groups and subgroups but are listed apart from the retention register: (1) employees with temporary appointments limited to a year or less, (2) employees with temporary promotions to the positions affected, and (3) employees with "Unsatisfactory" performance ratings. They do not compete for retention in the competitive level. They must be released from the level before any employee in Group I, II or III is released. The release of an employee with a temporary promotion would be accomplished in a normal situation by returning that employee to his or her regular job.

Within each subgroup employees are ranked by "service dates" which reflect their total Federal service (civilian and creditable military). An employee with a current "Outstanding" performance rating receives 4 additional years of service credit.

Selection of employees to be released from the competitive level begins at the bottom of the retention register, that is, with the employee in the lowest subgroup who has the latest service date. Using the example of GS-9 accountants, Group III accountants are released first, then Group II, then Group I. Nonveterans are released before veterans in each group.

Except under certain specified conditions, the normal retention-register order must be followed when employees are to be released from their competitive levels by separation, furlough, or demotion. Per-

sons to be released out of regular order must be notified of the reasons and of their right to appeal the action to the Commission.

DETERMINING RIGHTS TO OTHER POSITIONS

Employees in Group III have no right to another job. When they are reached for layoff, they can be separated.

When employees are in Group I or Group II and are released from their own job, they are entitled to a "reasonable" offer of assignment if their agency has a "suitable job" which they can take by "bumping" or "retreat." Let's define those terms.

An offer of assignment is "reasonable" if the grade is not reduced, or if the grade reduction is the least that can be made under the regulations. The agency is required only to make a reasonable offer of assignment — not necessarily the job the employee would prefer to have.

A suitable job is a job of the same or lower grade in the same competitive area for which the employee is fully qualified and able to do the work without undue interruption to it. Bumping means taking the job that is occupied by an employee in a lower subgroup. An employee can retreat to — or take back — a job that he or she was promoted out of (or a job substantially the same) as long as it is occupied by an employee with a later service date in the same subgroup.

To illustrate how some of these actions may occur, take the case of a career GS-4 stenographer who is to be released. There are no jobs for which the stenographer qualifies that are held by lower-ranking employees at the GS-4 level. However, there are career-conditional employees holding GS-3 clerk-typist jobs for which the stenographer qualifies. The agency must offer one of these jobs unless it can offer the stenographer some other GS-3 job. . . .

Exhibit 14-2a. Letter from Congressman Rice

CONGRESS OF THE UNITED STATES
HOUSE OF REPRESENTATIVES
WASHINGTON, D.C. 20515

April 17, 1978

The Office of Administrative
Affairs, Claims Division
U.S. Department of Internal Affairs

Gentlemen:

It was very disturbing for me to note during my recent visit that the majority of CD employees who I talked with stated, ''their morale is low primarily because of poor management and the absence of an official agency statement regarding the proposed reduction in force and downgrading.''

I have grave concern about the proposed reduction in force as well as the possibility that a number of employees will be downgraded, and therefore, I am requesting that you send me immediately your plans for implementing the reduction in force and downgrading at CD.

There is tremendous apprehension among the employees Grade 4 and below, that they will be disproportionately affected by your plans for reduction in force and downgrading. It would be very tragic if CD implemented a plan that downgraded lower grade employees disproportionately to upper grade employees, and it would be a prima facie case of discrimination if lower grade employees are laid off, disproportionately to upper grade employees.

Thank you very much for your cooperation, and I trust you understand that your decision to downgrade an employee from Grade 3 to Grade 2 will have a greater impact upon that employee as opposed to your decision to downgrade an employee from Grade 13 to Grade 12. If the lower grades, which are heavily populated with Blacks, are forced to bear the brunt of your reorganization decisions, then it will appear that CD's management is racist, and I sincerely trust that this will not be the case.

I look forward to receiving your plans and please inform me if I can be of assistance to you in resolving these matters.

Sincerely,

Howard Rice
Member of Congress

Exhibit 14-2b. Profile on Congressman Rice

Congressman Howard Rice represents the 7th district, which includes that portion of Arlington wherein many Claims Division employees live. The district is 74% Black, with a median family income of $7,841.

Rice was first elected in 1970, a time when a number of more outspoken Congressmen came into office. He was recently chairman of the Congressional Black Caucus. He is a member of the House Banking and Currency Committee.

In his home district politics, he has frequently run unopposed, and in 1976 took 94% of the vote against an independent challenger.

Information adapted from *Almanac of American Politics 1978,* Michael Barone, Grant Ujifusa, Douglas Mathews

Exhibit 14-3. Department of Internal Affairs: organization chart

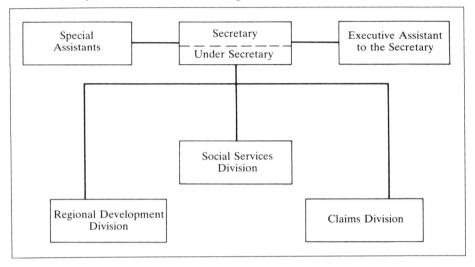

Exhibit 14-4. Claims Division: organization chart

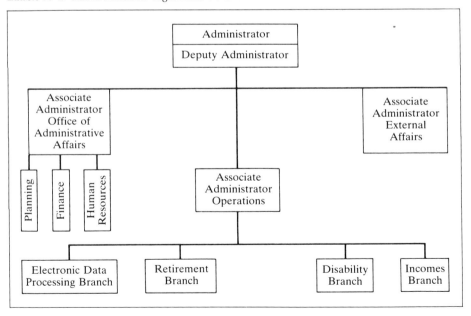

Exhibit 14-5. Composition of EDP workforce: January 1978

Total employees in EDP	8,000	100%
Total employees GS-5 and below	6,160	77%
Female employees	6,800	85%
Black employees	3,920	49%
Total minority	4,320	54%
Minority female	3,840	48%
Minority male	480	6%
Non-minority female	2,960	37%
Non-minority male	720	9%

Exhibit 14-6. Actual EDP employed vs. End of Year (EOY) employment ceilings

ORGANIZATION	ON DUTY 1/20/78	EOY CEILING FY 1978	DIFFERENCE VS. ON DUTY 1978	EOY CEILING FY 1979	DIFFERENCE VS. ON DUTY 1979
Office staff	23	23	0	23	0
Data operations centers (field)	1378	1238	140	881	497
EDP operations	5891	5080	811	3609	2282
TOTAL	7982	6341	951	4513	2779

Exhibit 14-7. Redeployment action plan prepared by Human Resources

```
                    Redeployment Action Plan

— Develop retraining efforts aimed at qualifying EDP employees for vacan-
  cies in other components for which they do not otherwise qualify. — OMA

— Prepare and submit a request to the Civil Service Commission to waive
  X—118 qualification requirements for employees who are excess to work-
  load needs.

— Freeze all non—career promotions and all outside recruitment (from CS
  registers, reinstatements, and transfers from other government agencies
  including other parts of DIA) for positions for which EDP employees
  qualify.

— Reassign EDP employees on a voluntary basis to vacancies in other com-
  ponents through either a formal or an informal announcement procedure.

— Canvass EDP employees to determine interest in switching to part—time
  employment in order to fully utilize current all—other ceiling.

— Prepare a submittal to the Civil Service Commission (through DIA) re-
  questing early out authority at GS—11 and below in CD headquarters. If
  approved, pursue a vigorous publicity campaign to assure that all eli-
  gible employees are aware of this option.

— Develop a plan to reassign EDP employees to vacancies in other compo-
  nents on the basis of directed reassignments when there are insuffi-
  cient volunteers.
```

Exhibit 14-8a. Excerpts from Federal Personnel Manual: RIFS

APPENDIX E. VOLUNTARY RETIREMENT OF
CERTAIN EMPLOYEES DURING A MAJOR
REDUCTION IN FORCE

E-1. Legislative Provisions

a. Authority. Section 8336(d)(2) of title 5, United States Code, permits the immediate voluntary (i.e., optional) retirement of certain employees of agencies found by the Commission to be undergoing a major reduction in force. *Major RIF retirement option,* as used in this appendix refers to the option provided in section 8336(d)(2) of title 5, United States Code, which reads as follows:

"(d) An employee who is separated from the service—

"(1) involuntarily, except by removal for cause on charges of misconduct or delinquency; or

"(2) voluntarily, during a period when the agency in which he is employed is undergoing a major reduction in force, as determined by the Commission, and who is serving in such geographic areas as may be designated by the Commission;

after completing 25 years of service or after becoming 50 years of age and completing 20 years of service is entitled to a reduced annuity." The annuity payable under section 8336(d) is reduced by 1/6 of 1 percent for each full month the employee is under age 55.

b. Major RIF voluntary retirements vs. discontinued service retirements. (1) Employees who meet the age and service requirements of section 8336(d) are eligible for a discontinued service annuity under paragraph (1) of the section if they are reached for separation in reduction in force. These employees have the option of retir-

ing voluntarily under paragraph (2) of the section even though they are not reached in the reduction in force, if they are serving in any position for which the major RIF retirement option has been authorized.

(2) When an employee exercises the major RIF retirement option his retirement will be treated as optional. If he is later reemployed, his pay on reemployment is reduced by the amount of the annuity. On the other hand, if the employee retires for discontinued service after involuntary separation and is later reemployed, he acquires a new retirement right if the reemployment is not excluded from retirement coverage. An employee, when advised about the major RIF retirement option, should be informed of this difference in his future retirement rights if he should later be reemployed. (For additional details, see FPM SUPPLEMENT 831–1, subchapter S15.)

c. Purpose of major RIF retirement option. By permitting employees to exercise the major RIF retirement option, an agency will be assisted in carrying out a major reduction in force with less than usual disruption to the workforce. This is accomplished by allowing eligible employees over a large part of the organization to volunteer for retirement before a reduction in force actually is effected, thereby permitting the employing agency to determine in advance the overall effect of retrenchment in a particular geographic or occupational area. These voluntary retirements will thus reduce the number of involuntary separations that must be made.

E-2. Responsibility for Determining When an Agency is Undergoing a Major Reduction in Force

a. The Commission has the responsibility and authority to determine the period

(Exhibit continues on following page.)

Exhibit 14-8a. Continued

and designate the geographic areas in which an agency is undergoing a major reduction in force. However, the initiative is with the agency undergoing the reduction in force to request the Commission to make a major reduction-in-force determination, submitting full justification for the reasons why the reduction in force is considered major, the geographic location where use of the major RIF retirement option would be authorized, and the time span within which the major RIF retirement option can be effectively utilized. The Commission will *not* determine that any agency is undergoing a major reduction in force without first receiving a written request from the agency head, or his designee, that the determination is wanted (see regulation 831.109).

E-3. Coercion

a. Voluntary decision. All retirements under the major RIF option are *truly voluntary* on the part of the employee. The employee must not be directly or indirectly coerced into deciding to give up his retention rights for retirement (see FPM SUPPLEMENT 752–1, section S1–2, on voluntary and involuntary separations and reductions). Retirement applicants under the major RIF retirement option will be fully informed of their retention rights before or while the reduction procedures are in process.

b. Agency monitoring. Authority for use of the major RIF retirement option will be issued by the Commission with the understanding that agency heads will take all possible steps to ensure that no coercion is exercised by any manager in the use of his authority. The letters of authority will request agencies to furnish the Commission with copies of noncoercion policy statements and issuances and notification

statements to employees advising them that retirements under the major RIF authority are voluntary.

E-4. Requesting a Determination that the Agency is Undergoing a Major Reduction in Force

a. Where to send a request. After an agency head determines that a reduction in force is necessary, and has issued a general or public notice of reduction in force, the agency head or his designee may, before resorting to the prescribed reduction-in-force procedures, or while such procedures are in progress, request by letter that the Civil Service Commission make a determination that the agency is undergoing a major reduction in force. The request should be addressed to the:

Director, Bureau of Recruiting and Examining
U.S. Civil Service Commission
Washington, D.C. 20415

b. Information to be submitted in the request. It is up to the agency to inform the Civil Service Commission about what the agency wants to do, what the problems are, and the extent of the authority desired. Therefore, the agency will provide the following information as appropriate to justify its request for the major RIF retirement option:

(1) Reasons for considering the reduction in force to be major.

(2) Time limit in which the reduction in force must be completed.

(3) Time limit desired within which the major RIF retirement option can be exercised.

(Exhibit continues on following page.)

Exhibit 14-8a. Continued

(4) Parts of organization, occupations, and geographic locations where the agency wants the major RIF retirement option. The agency may request geographic areas larger than the competitive area involved but must present a persuasive case for doing so. Justification for requesting a geographic area larger than the competitive area must show how the agency intends to use the extended geographic area to reduce the impact of the reduction in force (e.g., vacancy freezes, outplacement efforts, expanded placement and referral systems).

(5) Total number of actual employees (not positions) in the competitive area before the reduction in force and the target number to be achieved after completion of the reduction in force. Also, the number of losses anticipated to occur broken down by those through attrition and those through the reduction-in-force process.

(6) Other information which indicates the extent of disruption to the operations of the agency such as the estimated number of employees who would be transferred, reassigned or downgraded.

(7) Assessment of the probable effect of the reduction in force on the affected labor market, including information on the extent of the total Federal presence in the local labor market.

E-5. Commission Action on Requests

a. Method of approval. The Commission will either approve, disapprove, or modify the request based on the facts submitted and notify the agency of its decision. A letter of approval will carry an au-

thority number which must be shown on all Standard Forms 2806. Individual Retirement Records, submitted under the authority. (See also FPM SUPPLEMENT 831–1.) The authority number will also be shown on the SF 50's. (See FPM SUPPLEMENT 296–31 for instructions on processing SF 50's.)

b. Basis for determination. The Commission will make its determination on an individual case-by-case basis which will be directed at assessing:

(1) The extent of disruption to the operations of the agency or installation.

(2) The extent of the agency's capability to effectively carry out its mission in the future.

(3) The extent of the impact upon the local community and economy.

c. Other considerations. (1) The geographic area where use of the retirement option will be authorized may include agency activities not directly affected by the reduction in force, if approval would assist in out-placement efforts. Depending upon circumstances, approval might be given for a single occupational group, a given geographical area, a geographical region or State, an entire agency, an entire bureau, or an entire department.

(2) The right to retire optionally may be exercised →only by an employee who was on the agency's rolls 30 days before the date of the agency's request to the Commission for the major RIF determination and only during the limited period determined by the Commission.← The purpose of this time limitation is to permit an employee to volunteer to retire before the reduction in force is actually effected so as to enable the agency to carry out the actual reduction ef-

(Exhibit continues on following page.)

Exhibit 14-8a. Continued

ficiently. An employee normally will not be able to defer his decision to retire optionally until the reduction is nearly completed.

E-6. Evaluation of Use of Retirement Option

a. The Commission intends to evaluate the effectiveness of the major RIF retirement option in alleviating the disruptive effects of a major reduction in force. Agencies will be instructed in their letters of authority on what information must be sent to the Commission. Generally, agencies will be required to report on:

(1) The number of retirements under section 8336(d)(2) of title 5, United States Code, broken down by agency, geographical location, and occupational series and grade; and

(2) An analysis of the extent to which these retirements contributed to easing the impact of the scheduled reduction in force; and

→ (3) The number, if any, of the retirees under subsection 8336(d)(2) who were subsequently reemployed by the reducing agency within 30 days.←

Exhibit 14-8b. Excerpt from Federal Personnel Manual: severance pay

SUBCHAPTER 7. SEVERANCE PAY

7-5. Computation of Severance Pay

a. General. Severance pay shall consist of two elements, a basic allowance and an age adjustment allowance. (1) The basic severance allowance is computed on the basis of one week's basic pay at the rate received immediately before separation for each year of civilian service up to and including 10 years and two weeks' basic pay at that rate for each year of civilian service beyond 10 years for which severance pay has not been received under this or any other authority. In computing an employee's total years of creditable civilian service the agency shall credit the employee with each full year and 25 percent of a year for each three months of creditable service that exceeds one or more full years.

(2) The age adjustment allowance is computed on the basis of 10 percent of the total basic severance allowance for each year by which the age of the recipient exceeds 40 years at the time of separation. In computing years of age over 40 the department shall credit the employee with 25 percent of a year for each three months that his age exceeds 40.

b. Creditable service. In computing an employee's civilian service under this subchapter, the agency shall include all service that is creditable for annual leave accrual purposes under section 6303 of title 5, United States Code. →This includes (1) periods during which a person was receiving compensation under 5 U.S.C. chapter 81; and (2) periods of absence due to military duty, provided these periods interrupt otherwise creditable civilian service and the employee resumes Federal employment within the period of statutory or regulatory restoration rights.←

c. Limitation. The total severance pay received shall not exceed one year's pay at the rate received immediately before separation. One year's pay means pay for 26 biweekly pay periods.

CHAPTER 15

Handling Misconduct: Fondle, Fix, or Fire?

Handling misconduct is difficult for managers. In many jobs it is hard to measure whether or not someone is doing an adequate job. Even when a manager knows that someone's job performance is inadequate, the cause is not always clear so a means of fixing the difficulty may be elusive. Thus, helpful action may be difficult to take. Once a manager decides to discuss the matter, it is not always easy to look someone in the eye and discuss the problem. The employee may disagree or be offended, the employee may blame the manager, and things may become unpleasant as a result. The manager even may be risking the violation of some rule in the way he or she conveys the message.

For all of these reasons and more, undertaking to discipline or otherwise modify behavior of a problem employee can be difficult. The lack of practice and the various interpersonal, operational, ethical, and procedural considerations that can surround it make employee discipline something that many managers are ill-prepared for or are unwilling to do. Yet in the long term, the consequences of doing nothing may be significant to the organization and the employee.

In the following case a well-regarded manager (in a disguised agency location) is faced with a discipline problem. An employee in one of her units has been performing badly and behaving in ways that are disruptive to his co-workers and first-line supervisor. While there are a multitude of procedures that could be invoked including suspension, firing, disability retirement, and transfer, to name a few, these procedures offer little guidance in deciding *which* avenue would be best to pursue. The manager still has to make a decision and take action based on her judgment of what is best for the individual and the organization.

Even though each party may say the other is at fault, the manager must make the best and fairest decision possible. Against a lot of pressure, confusion, and many technical requirements, Ann Sacco must balance the interest of the employee with the rest of her responsibilities.

With little precedent or structure in the agency for handling decisions of this sort, the circumstances have gotten confusing and difficult for all parties. By analyzing the managerial situation, the ethics, and procedural implications, perhaps a useful recommendation can be made to the manager in this case.

STUDY QUESTIONS

1. What problems is Lento causing?
2. What are Sacco's responsibilities in the situation? To whom?
3. What should Ann Sacco do to handle the problem as it stands at the end of the case?
4. How will that decision affect Scott Lento?
5. How will that decision affect other people and considerations within Sacco's scope of responsibility?

RECOMMENDED READING

Leonard Reed "Firing a Federal Employee: The Impossible Dream," *The Washington Monthly*, July-August, 1977.

Employee Misconduct
at the U.S. Civil Service Commission (A)

Introduction

In early April, Ann Sacco, Director of the Staffing Division of the Denver Regional Office of the Civil Service Commission,* sat at her desk pondering an employee problem. Scott Lento, a new employee of the Division, was just not working out and it was becoming increasingly clear that serious action would have to be taken. If the situation continued to deteriorate, Sacco saw that she had three options:

1. Transfer Lento to another office, where he might fit in better;

2. Consider seeking a disability retirement for Lento due to his somewhat bizarre behavior; or

3. Terminate Lento for cause — a so-called adverse action. Sacco was aware that termination in this manner would preclude his receiving retirement benefits.

The last of the three is an action not often used in the Federal Government. While Sacco didn't know the figure, she, like most government supervisors, was aware that firing was reputed to be extremely difficult, if not impossible. Still, she had to consider it, something she had never

This case was prepared by Thomas Fagan while a masters degree candidate at the John F. Kennedy School of Government under the general supervision of Jon Brock, Lecturer at the Kennedy School of Government. While based on field research, some of the facts and names of persons and organizational units have been altered in the interest of confidentiality.

*In 1979 the Civil Service Commission was split into two agencies. The agency which currently performs the functions described in the case is now called the Office of Personnel Management.

done before. Previously, when she had had troublesome employees, she had been able to talk with them and work things out, or, in one case, the person had simply left on his own volition. This time, it wasn't going to be easy.

Background

The U.S. Civil Service Commission serves as the central personnel office for all Federal departments. While individual agencies have their own personnel functions, these are guided by policies promulgated by the Commission itself. The Commission also retains exclusive control over several personnel functions. For purposes of administration, the Commission maintains ten regional offices throughout the country, including one in Denver which has responsibility for several western states. (An organization chart appears in Exhibit 15-1).

Among the functions of most regional Civil Service offices, including Denver, is the administration of tests to job applicants. This function is carried out by the Staffing Division. Tests for all federal jobs, from clerical to professional, are given in several locations throughout the country. The primary function of the tests is to screen and rank applicants for federal jobs, and to establish for each applicant the maximum GS grade level for which they are eligible. The Denver office is responsible for test administration throughout its region.

Tests in Colorado are given directly by test examiners of the Denver Staffing Division, or by other Commission employees hired on an *ad hoc* basis when the load is too heavy for the examiners. In the remainder of the region, state level area offices are responsible for test giving, but distribution and retrieval of test materials is done by the Denver Staffing Division. Twenty-five different tests are administered. In all, tests are given approximately 150 to 200 times each month, to some 1,000 to 1,500 persons.

For each test administered, material must be assembled, packaged, and sent to the test administrator. Materials sent include the tests themselves, answer sheets, written instruments for the test administrator, and an inventory sheet listing the contents of the package. All items, used and unused, are returned to the Staffing Division after the test has been given. To insure fairness and protect the secrecy of the test materials, strict accountability of all materials must be maintained. The loss of a single copy of a single test could result in the end of its usefulness in the region and throughout the country. Materials must always be protected from duplication.

Therefore, packages sent to test administrators must remain sealed until just before the test is given, and be immediately repackaged and returned to the Denver office after test administration. After being accounted for, answer sheets are sent off for electronic scoring, used tests destroyed, and unused tests and answer sheets returned to inventory. Since far more people sign up to take tests than actually appear, there may be as many unused as used sets of materials.

Filling the Job

Mailing, retrieving, and accounting for test materials is done by a supply clerk in the Staffing Division. The job was classified at the GS-4 level — approximately the same as an average clerk-typist. Ann Sacco, director of the division, explained that filling the position was unusually difficult and time-consuming. First, the nature of the position demanded that the person holding it be extremely trustworthy, meticulous in recordkeeping, and smart enough to ensure that no errors were made in handling the materials. However, the nature of the task (see Exhibit 15-2 — Job Description) was essentially counting out items and packaging them for mailing — highly repetitive and boring. Sacco noted that the position required a "great deal of responsibility, but the job was routine," and that "anybody with real brains is going to get bored." Consequently, she had begun the process necessary to upgrade the supply clerk position to a GS-5.

In addition, the job was classified as "critical sensitive," the highest such security designation in Civil Service. This meant persons selected for the position had to undergo a "full field" investigation, similar to the procedure required to gain security clearance in the military. Background review would be done and neighbors interviewed. This procedure, initiated only after a person had been selected to fill the job, took seven or eight weeks. Original selection of the person from lists of qualified applicants could take two or three months prior to beginning the investigation. In the meantime, members of the Staffing Division were responsible for the clerk's task, and the increased number of persons handling the materials made it more difficult to maintain security. Consequently, staff members directed to do the job over an extended period might begin to feel put upon, and further be unable to do those things for which they held primary responsibility.

In early Fall of 1975, the job of supply clerk in the Staffing Division became vacant. Having recently experienced continual turnover in the position, after the retirement of a 20-year veteran, Sacco determined that this time she would "get someone maybe a little slow, but dependable who would stay." And, she intended to do this quickly in order to end the disruption. Normally, vacancies are filled through an established and time-consuming procedure. This procedure involves submitting a request to the personnel office that the job be "posted" inviting applications from all interested persons; screening by the personnel office of applicants to find those most qualified; and establishing a list of those persons and giving it to the selecting official. The official is then compelled to interview those on the list, and indicate his or her selection to the personnel office, who then notifies the applicant and determines if the person is still available and would be willing to await final job placement while the full field investigation was conducted.

In order to fill the vacancy as quickly as possible and avoid much of this time-consuming procedure, Sacco decided to seek applicants from two sources who would be exempt from all but the full field investigation requirement — those Vietnam veterans classified "noncompetitive" applicants, and former government employees holding "reinstatement rights." The first source did not yield any candidates, but the roster of persons eligible for immediate reinstatement included Scott Lento, formerly employed as a supply clerk with the Commerce Department. Lento had been laid off from his GS-6 position when a nearby office was closed and had been unemployed for the ensuing one and a half years. Both Sacco and Mary Sweeney, who supervised the supply clerk and test examiners, interviewed Lento. They agreed that though Lento was "not a great ball of fire," he was well spoken and eager to work. Consequently, Sacco notified personnel to initiate a full field investigation to obtain "critical sensitive" clearance for Lento. Sacco expected the full field investigation to be quite thorough in its check of Lento's past performance, obviating the usual need for her own reference check.

Clearance was obtained and Lento placed in the position. Since he had twelve years of service in the Commerce Department, he was "reinstated" to full "career" status without the usual probationary period in the job, as well as without the arduous hiring process described above.

Conditions at Work

Lento reported to Sacco on his first day of work and was then taken to the small room which housed test arrangement sections of the Staffing Division (Exhibit 15-3). Sacco and Sweeney formally introduced him to the members of the Division. Lento, as well as the other section members, was under the direct supervision of Sweeney. Sacco described Sweeney as:

> an extremely hard worker and a conscientious supervisor. Her ability to make sound decisions is unusually strong for a first-level supervisor. Sweeney's sense of humor stands her in good stead among those with whom she deals regularly. However, she wants things done her way and is not overly receptive to suggestions for change.

Lento took issue with most instructions given, questioning why it was done in that particular way. At first, Sweeney took his questioning as a desire to fully understand what his job entailed. Later, she and other staff members saw his queries as purely argumentative. Typically, when given an instruction, he would ask why, and when told, he would say: "I don't know why we have to do that. It seems dumb to me."

While Sweeney reported directly to Sacco, there was another person who periodically entered the picture. On her immediate staff, Sacco had three individuals who, as part of their duties, had the responsibility of working on special projects with the various units in the division. The person who worked with the testing unit was Elliot Sardis—a shy man who was a technical expert with no management experience. In carrying out this duty, Sardis made it his habit to stop by the testing office several times a week to keep up with things. Sweeney said that while Lento would argue with her over everything, giving her a "real hassle, when Mr. Sardis came in, he [Lento] was very nice and would do anything. If Ann [Sacco] told him to do something, he would ignore it." Sacco felt that "Lento really had this thing about working for two women."

At first, Sacco was not aware that there was any problem in the testing unit. This was due to Sweeney's desire to try and handle it before raising the problem to the next level. Sweeney knew Sacco was very busy with other matters, and did not want to add to her burden. Consequently, Sweeney attempted to rectify the situation by talking informally with Lento to try and find out what the underlying problem might be. These talks did not change anything, however, as the problem grew in size and complexity. Not only was Lento continually argumentative, he was also lax in his work and exhibiting other behavior traits which were annoying and disturbing to his co-workers, especially the test administrators.

While Lento's attendance on the job was satisfactory and he invariably arrived on time, he would disappear for "coffee breaks" of one to one and one-half hours, and take an inordinately long time to complete simple tasks. Some were not completed at all, and Sweeney began to receive calls from test administrators who said that items were missing from the test packages. Since packages weren't opened until just prior to test administration, missing items could not be delivered in time to be useful. In some cases, machine-scored answer sheets were missing, meaning tests would have to be hand scored. In other cases, the instructions to the test administrator were missing, necessitating that they be read to the administrator over the phone. On several occasions, tests had to be rescheduled due to improper materials in the packages.

Additionally, Lento had become lax in his record keeping, often letting things pile up before making entries. The tight inventory system for the test materials began to break down, and,

while test booklets were not lost, there was no effective control over their whereabouts, greatly increasing the danger that loss would soon occur. These incidents increased as other staff members, who had originally given Lento a hand getting started in his job, began to spend less and less time helping him, reasoning that his "break-in" period was now over.

Lento's odd behavior was also beginning to grate on Sweeney and the other test unit members, all of whom shared the same work space. He would sometimes sit at his desk and laugh aloud, but when asked what he was laughing at, would deny he had laughed at all. Also, Lento often stood in the doorway of the office staring at the women going down the corridors — a practice which frightened and annoyed most of the women. One said:

> Before I'd go by that office, I'd try to look down the hall. If I saw him standing there, I'd go all the way around the building rather than go down that corridor. It was eerie.

He consistently complained about the placement of a pencil sharpener on top of a file cabinet, claiming it was a safety hazard. One day, when Sweeney was advance dating some material to be sent out, Lento danced around her desk, chanting "Mary doesn't know what date it is, Mary doesn't know what date it is." Sweeney said that Lento also began to hide completed test results, rather than sending them out immediately to persons with job vacancies to fill. When Sweeney would find them buried on his desk, he'd deny ever having seen them, and state that "I think the people from upstairs are coming up here at night to mess up my work." The test administrators, who had up to this time often helped Lento when he got behind, now refused to do so, and worried about leaving Sweeney in the office alone with him when they were out giving tests.

According to Sacco, "Lento also arrived at work sometimes disheveled and unshaven. I suspected he might have some personal problem causing his strange behavior.'' Sweeney said she didn't know ''whether the biggest thing was his strange behavior or the work being badly butchered.'' She did know that the problem was taking its toll on her. Plagued recently with constant headaches, she consulted a physician, who found she had high blood pressure. She began to wonder if maybe Lento was sick, or perhaps it was she. She began to ''. . . know what it's like to get up in the morning really dreading coming to work—really dreading it.''

Other employees began expressing their anger at Lento for the way he was abusing Sweeney. One employee, who was quite upset with several of Lento's remarks to Sweeney, almost punched Lento and had to be restrained by other office staff. One of the employees then went to see Sacco to discuss the incident and complain about Lento's behavior.

Consequently, Sweeney set up a meeting with Sacco to explain her strong feelings concerning Lento. Sweeney said:

> I have my rights too! This man is driving me crazy. Not only that, but the other staff members are complaining — and we have never had any problems in this office before.

Performance Appraisal

Finally, as difficulties continued, Sweeney went to Sacco again. Sacco ''wished she'd been told sooner.'' It was now mid-March. Lento had started on his job at the beginning of January. Sacco, faced with completing annual performance appraisals on all employees, called Lento in to talk with him about his poor performance. These annual ratings, required by statute, allowed only three possible levels of performance—outstanding, satisfactory, or unsatisfactory. Unsatisfactory ratings are rarely given, partly since they may set in motion a formal grievance procedure. In addition, that procedure would have to run its course prior to taking any other action as Lento would be allowed 60 days for improvement. Ironically, therefore, it would be procedurally easier

to terminate Lento, if that course of action were decided upon, if he received a satisfactory rating than if he received an unsatisfactory one. With this in mind, Sacco explained to Lento that she was going to give him a satisfactory, but stressed that it was borderline, and that she would be watching him closely, expecting improvement. She then went on leave (vacation) and found, on her return, that the situation had deteriorated. Sweeney reported that:

> Lento has begun to destroy records which he thinks are superfluous. He has taken to standing in front of the mirror in the office, commenting on his own good looks. I've really had it.

Courses of Action

At the end of April, Sacco determined she was going to have to take action. Her first thought was to seek reassignment for Lento. There was one similar position elsewhere in the Regional Office, but it was in a unit which was having its own problems. Sacco didn't want to saddle those people with more difficulties in the event Lento didn't work out there either.

As a second alternative, Sacco seriously considered seeking disability retirement for Lento based on his bizarre behavior. With disability retirement, Lento would be eligible for immediate benefits based on his 15 years of prior experience with the Commerce Department. Sacco sought advice from the regional employee counselor who strongly suggested that Sacco not raise the issue of Lento's behavior. This option, according to U.S. Civil Service Commission regulations, would require the agency to obtain a detailed medical report certifying not only that Lento was disabled, but that the disability precluded his discharge of his duties. In addition to the uncertainty of getting such a determination, a counselor advised, the whole process was a long and protracted one which would tie Sacco up for months. Furthermore, Lento would remain on the job throughout the proceedings. The counselor suggested maintaining a focus solely on Lento's inadequate work performance and seeking some disciplinary action on that basis.

The third alternative, then, was to attempt to terminate Lento for cause by relying on his poor performance. Unlike disability retirement, termination would not provide immediate benefits, and if misconduct were involved, it would also cause a loss of retirement and other benefits. This course could also involve a protracted procedure since Lento was protected as a career employee.

Sacco found that if adverse action leading to termination were planned, Lento would have to be notified of that possibility in writing, and that he was entitled to have a union representative at any meeting held concerning his work performance. Anticipating the possibility of an adverse action, Sacco decided to have a formal meeting with him. Therefore, Sacco notified Lento of a proposed meeting, giving him also the name and phone number of his union steward (Exhibit 15-4). Lento arrived at the meeting alone. Lento did eventually meet with union representatives, but they never became involved. Marianne Murphy, the Regional administrative officer, said this may be due to the fact that union membership is primarily from one section of the office — not the test unit. Therefore, she said:

> I don't think they do what they are supposed to do. They seem to be pretty picky about what they will do. They are primarily from one unit and pretty much just represent that very small division.

Beginning the Disciplinary Process

Sacco went over his deficiencies with Lento and informed him of the existence of the Employee Assistance Program to help if he were having some problems. She told Lento that: ''I am just warning you. If you improve, fine. If not, I might have to take some serious disciplinary action.'' Throughout the meeting, Lento sat smiling, saying not a word. Sacco wrote up a summary of the meeting for insertion in Lento's personnel folder, sending Lento a copy, and sending a note to the Employee Assistance Program, asking to be informed if Lento should go to them for assistance (Exhibit 15-5). Sacco's summary of the meeting contained a list of specific charges against Lento and warned him that, if he failed to improve, Sacco was going to institute action, perhaps including termination.

Sacco also now sought the advice and assistance of the Division's administrative officer, Marianne Murphy. While not a personnel official, Murphy, like many administrative officers, often handles personnel questions. Never having faced the termination of an employee before, Murphy consulted the office files and could find no record of any past attempts at all. She did, however, find the regulations contained in the Federal Personnel Manual's sections on Removals and Adverse Actions, which sets out procedures to be followed in removing employees for the ''efficiency of the organization'' (Exhibit 15-6). Essentially, there are two categories of charges under which termination may be sought — those related to job performance and those related to conduct. Both came under the rubric of ''efficiency,'' and often are difficult to separate. Sacco's charges, listed in the May 6 memo, include both types.

Meanwhile, Murphy also pursued the question of Lento's odd behavior. She spoke to counselors in the Employee Assistance Office, and told them of his somewhat odd habits, and asked them if there was any reason to believe Lento might have a psychological problem. The counselor said it was a possibility, but that nothing could be done unless Lento sought assistance. In spite of Sacco's frequent suggestions, he did not do so.

Seeking further help in the case, Murphy called the headquarters office in Washington for advice. They offered little help, and no legal assistance at that time, but did give one piece of advice which Sacco and Murphy thought crucial. They suggested Murphy find out which agency in Denver had the best track record in winning termination cases, and seek help from them. The agency turned out to be the Environmental Protection Agency which was located in the same building as the Commission. The EPA sent their person who handled terminations to meet with Murphy and Sacco. He offered several specific pieces of advice:

1. Make sure all orders given to Lento were specific, totally clear, and contained no other option than the specific intent.
2. Put all orders in writing.
3. Make sure Lento understands all of the orders.

Sacco then met with Sweeney and told her, "Put your instructions to Lento in writing — even the most simple orders." Sweeney complied (samples are included in Exhibit 15-7). For their part, Sacco and Murphy devoted two weeks of full-time effort, making certain they knew the procedure, and that they were on firm ground with the action they were taking. Sweeney later complained that: "I was spending so much of my time giving instructions to Lento and checking to see if they were carried out, I had little time to do my own work." During the ensuing month, Lento's performance did not improve (Exhibit 15-8). Indeed, it appeared as if he were trying to call Sacco's bluff. After receiving Sweeney's written directions followed with an oral explanation, Lento would complete the instructions in reverse order.

On May 26, 1976, Lento was observed quietly tearing up and destroying test requisition forms which he had been specifically instructed to retain. After being again told not to destroy them, he was seen later that day destroying more forms.

Exhibit 15-1. Organization chart: Denver Regional Office, U.S. Civil Service Commission

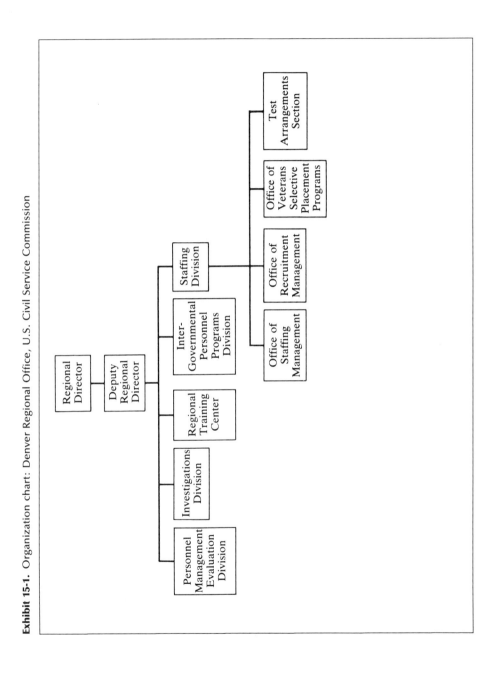

Exhibit 15-2. Job description: supply clerk

```
                     Supply Clerk, GS-2005-4

The incumbent works under the administrative supervision of the Chief, Staffing
Division and the technical supervision of the Staffing Clerk and is responsible
for the receipt, storage, binning, cataloging, inventorying, shipping and
distribution of a wide variety of tests and related materials for the Denver
Region.  He applies a good working knowledge of supply procedures for Commission
test materials and use of this material.

Working independently he controls the issuance, usage and return to stock of
expendable and nonexpendable test material requisitioned by the Commission Area
Offices and all appointing officers having personnel in the region.  Supervisor
is available for consultation in any unusual or difficult cases.

Specifically, incumbent performs the following duties:

Receives, places under control, and maintains security of test booklets and
related materials used or stocked for use in the Denver Region.  Verifies
quantities received and places material in appropriate bins after listing test
series number and quantity received on inventory cards.  Most test material
is of a confidential nature and for this reason incumbent must maintain tight
security and careful inventory on all material in the test storage area.

Receives requisitions for test material for tests scheduled; packs and ships
material; maintains control on material shipped or issued to the examiners.
Keeps a perpetual inventory of total quantity of all test material and control
records to show what material is in custody of each agency and examiner.  Closely
checks material returned from test point and notifies supervisor of any discrepancies.

Fills requests from agencies and examining offices for test booklets, directions
for conducting, answer sheets and related material, for a wide variety of
competitive, noncompetitive and direct recruiting purposes.

Makes periodic physical inventory to reconcile perpetual inventory records.  For
outstanding test material, entrusted to agencies or other Commission offices,
periodically requests those offices to submit any inventory of test material
on hand.  Reconciles those inventories with inventory cards.

Because errors in verification or shipping of material could result in exposure
or compromise of test booklets, as well as considerable embarrassment or expense
to the Commission, incumbent must exercise extreme care in his duties.

Assists the Staffing Clerk and performs the duties of that position
when Staffing Clerk is absent.

Incumbent must be able to lift 50 pounds.
```

Exhibit 15-3. Test Arrangements Section, Staffing Division

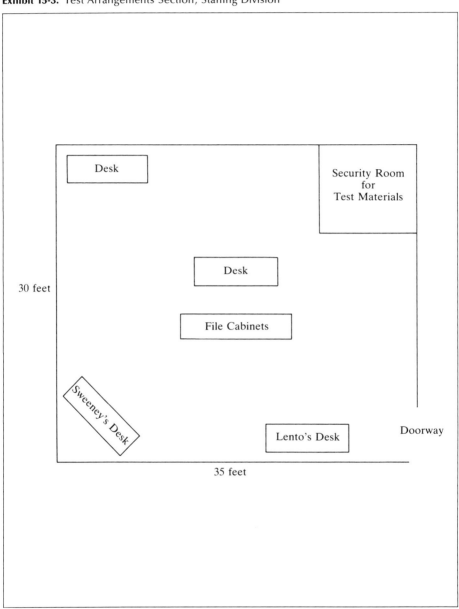

Exhibit 15-4. Memorandum to Scott Lento, April 27, 1976

United States Government
Memorandum

To: Scott Lento   4/27/76

Subject: Discussion of Work Performance

From: Ann Sacco
             Chief, Staffing Division

This is to confirm the conversation I had with you on Tuesday, April 27,
notifying you that I wished to discuss some unsatisfactory aspects of your
work performance which could lead to disciplinary action, and that I further
informed you that you have the right to have a union representative present
at the discussion. The name and phone number of the union steward in your
unit is Joy Clark and her phone number is 5-1166.

If it is agreeable with you, I would like to schedule the appointment for
2 P.M. Thursday afternoon, April 29. Please let me know if this is not an
acceptable time. Otherwise, I will expect to see you then in my office.

Exhibit 15-5. Memorandum to Scott Lento, May 6, 1976

UNITED STATES GOVERNMENT   U.S. CIVIL SERVICE COMMISSION

MEMORANDUM

Subject: Concerning Work Performance   Date: May 6, 1976

From: Ann Sacco
          Chief, Staffing Division
To: Scott Lento

The purpose of this memo is to make an official written record of the
discussion I had with you on April 29, 1976 when I admonished you concerning
several instances where you are not meeting my performance expectations for
your position and to confirm that I informed you that if your work does not
improve and if these types of errors do not stop that I will recommend you
be given a reprimand, suspended, or be separated.

Instances of performance not meeting expectations:

1) On April 22, my staff conducted a surprise review of the inventory record
    cards to see whether they were correct. Several cards (which you initialed)
    had inaccurate entries, reflecting mathematical errors on your part:

    a) Test 11 – Series 1A – card shows 101 on hand; balance should be 99;

    b) Test 135 – Series 4 (Action Sheets) – card shows 419 on hand;
        should be 427;

    c) Test 800 – Series 200 – card shows 2823 on hand; should be 2822;

    d) Test 800 – Series 181 – card shows 534 on hand; should be 574;

2) On April 12th, our test administrator in Area 6 appeared to conduct a
    blind PACE examination. The wrong material had been sent, causing great
    inconveniences to both the applicant and the administrator. The inventory
    sheet confirmed you had packed the material. The test was rescheduled.
    When the completed papers arrived, they were spot-checked because of the
    original mishap; all were in order. However, when papers were being
    cleared, the necessary papers for Washington were not there. Because they
    had been seen prior to this time, the test administrators conducted a
    search and found the papers in the waste basket.

3) On April 6th, insufficient answer sheets were packed for a high school
    examination conducted on April 13th. Photostatic copies had to be made
    to complete the examination. This resulted in the 16th Area Office having
    to hand score the papers instead of sending them to Macon causing a
    considerable waste of time and effort.

(Exhibit continues on following page.)

Exhibit 15-5. Continued

4) On April 19th, incorrect material (no DFC) was forwarded to the 12th Area Office for the summer make-up exam.

5) On April 19th, you packed some test material for 4th Area Office steno-typist to be held on April 21st and you failed to pack any notices of rating in the package.

6) On April 21st, specific written instructions which had been given to you as to which DFC should be used for a non-competitive examination were overlooked and the wrong material was used.

7) On April 22nd, I asked you specifically <u>twice</u> to go help the test administrators search for an apparently <u>lost</u> test booklet; in both instances, you directly ignored my request.

8) On April 23rd, a test administrator opened a test package to conduct a blind PACE exam: <u>Two</u> 2-D booklets were enclosed and no Record Sheet for Examiners. The record sheet shows that you packed the material.

9) On April 26th, two simple entries on record cards which should take no more than 8-10 minutes required 25 minutes to complete.

10) On April 23rd, several PACE packages were ready for mailing Friday; they were not mailed until Monday AM, thus losing two valuable mailing days.

11) On April 27th, it took two hours from 8-10 AM for you to set up two S & T exams and pack one; this should have taken no more than 30-40 minutes including packing <u>both</u> exams.

In all of the above instances, you had previously been shown the correct way to process the material and for the first 10-12 weeks you worked here, you were doing these and similar tasks without error. Furthermore, on April 27th, you were observed making five entries for Blind PACE in three minutes flat and then picking and packing these packages in seven minutes flat, a very good time frame. This situation demonstrates that you are quite capable of doing the work correctly.

As I told you, assistance is available to you for any personal or medical problem that is affecting your work or resulting in the errors listed above. You may contact the Employee Assistance Program for a confidential consultation by telephone or in person. You may also contact the Public Health doctor who is located in this building. I am advising the Employee Assistance counselors, by separate memorandum, that I suggested you contact them for possible assistance. A copy of that memorandum is attached.

(Exhibit continues on following page.)

Exhibit 15-5. Continued

A copy of this memo will be placed in your official personnel folder and will be withdrawn within one year after the date of signature. You may submit an explanation or reply at any time for inclusion in your official personnel folder.

You should note that this action is not a matter of permanent record. By good conduct in the future, and attention to duty, you have the opportunity to attain a clear record.

If, however, your performance does not improve immediately, I will have to recommend one of the disciplinary actions listed in the first paragraph of this memo.

Exhibit 15-6. Excerpts from Federal Personnel Manual

Chapter 75. Adverse Actions

Subchapter I. Competitive Service

Sec.
7501. Cause; procedure; exception.

SEC. 7501. CAUSE; PROCEDURE; EXCEPTION

(a) An individual in the competitive service may be removed or suspended without pay only for such cause as will promote the efficiency of the service.

(b) An individual in the competitive service whose removal or suspension without pay is sought is entitled to reasons in writing and to—

(1) notice of the action sought and of any charges preferred against him;

(2) a copy of the charges;

(3) a reasonable time for filing a written answer to the charges, with affidavits; and

(4) a written decision on the answer at the earliest practicable date.

Examination of witnesses, trial, or hearing is not required but may be provided in the discretion of the individual directing the removal or suspension without pay. Copies of the charges, the notice of hearing, the answer, the reasons for and the order of removal or suspension without pay, and also the reasons for reduction in grade or pay, shall be made a part of the records of the employing agency, and, on request, shall be furnished to the individual affected and to the Civil Service Commission.

(c) This section applies to a preference eligible employee as defined by section 7511 of this title only if he so elects. This section does not apply to the suspension or removal of an employee under section 7532 of this title.

S1-3. REMOVALS

a. Removals covered by part 752. Except as provided in S1-1, a removal within the meaning of law and the Commission's regulations in part 752 is a separation based on a decision of an

administrative officer (i.e., an involuntary separation). The following are examples of both disciplinary and nondisciplinary removals covered by part 752. Some other actions that may warrant removal are listed in S3-3.

(1) *Failure to accompany activity to another location.* The employee's failure to accompany his position in a transfer of function does not automatically terminate his services nor make any resulting separation voluntary. It is necessary to comply with appropriate adverse action procedures in removing him (see *Colbath* v. *U.S.*).

(2) *Failure to retain required qualifications or relationships.* When an appointing officer removes an employee from a noncareer executive assignment or a Schedule C appointment because the employee's qualifications or relationships required for the assignment or appointment change or cease to exist, or because the Commission revokes the exception of the position and thereby places it in the career service, the removal must comply with procedures in part 752 when the employee is covered.

(3) *Failure to qualify for conversion.* Employees who fail to qualify for conversion under section 315.703(a) of the Commission's regulations must be terminated within 90 calendar days after they complete three years of qualifying service. The termination, whether required by the Commission's finding that the employee does not qualify for conversion or by the agency's finding, is a removal within the meaning of part 752.

(4) *Failure to accept new assignment.* When an agency has found it necessary to assign an employee to a position in a different geographical or organizational location and the employee refuses to accept the new assignment, he may be removed for failure to accept the assignment. The new assignment must be from a competitive position to another competitive position or from an excepted position to another excepted position. Removal for failure to

(Exhibit continues on following page.)

Exhibit 15-6. Continued

accept a new assignment is appropriate when the employee refuses a position change that would carry out the terms of an established rotation policy or refuses any other position change which the agency has determined would serve the best interests of the service (see *Burton* v. *U.S.* and *Handler* v. *Secretary of Labor*).

(5) *Mental or physical disability.* Mental or physical disability may warrant removal under procedures in part 752. Before the agency initiates a removal for disability, however, it should be aware of the special provisions of this subparagraph.

(a) A definite duty devolves upon the agency to give retirement counseling to an employee who is unable to work satisfactorily because of ill health, if he has five years of civilian service and appears to meet the medical requirements for disability. If the disabling condition is mental, the agency must file disability retirement application on behalf of the employee if he will not or cannot file for himself (see FPM SUPPLEMENT 831–1 for the procedure). Under the rule laid down in *Anderson* v. *Morgan* and 39 Comp. Gen. 89, it is an error to remove for disability reasons the 5-year employee whose mental condition impairs his judgment and ability to make decisions without first applying for disability retirement on his behalf.

(b) If it is determined that removal (rather than reassignment or retirement) is in order, the agency should obtain a complete and detailed report of physical examination without cost to the employee. The employee should be referred for medical examination with a statement of the particular demands of the position and a statement of how the employee's performance or behavior fails to meet these demands. (See subchapter 1 of FPM chapter 339 for a discussion of arrangements for medical examinations by Federal medical officers or by other physicians.) This medical report is furnished to the Commission, upon its request, for appellate review of the removal or for other purposes.

(c) The agency has authority to direct an employee to take a fitness-for-duty examination. This authority is clearly implied by the language of section 01.3 of Executive Order 9830. Section 01.3 provides that "the head of each agency shall remove, demote, or reassign to another position any employee in the competitive service whose conduct or capacity is such that his removal, demotion, or reassignment will promote the efficiency of the service." The word *capacity* includes physical and mental capacity. The authority to require a fitness-for-duty examination is also implied in those sections of title 5, United States Code, which require that a person being removed from the competitive service be given reasons for the removal and in that section which authorizes agencies to apply for the retirement of employees on disability. To comply with the requirements of this Executive order and law, an agency that has a question about the physical or mental capacity of an employee should have a medical report from a physican who has examined the employee.

(d) If the employee refuses to submit to a medical examination, he may be removed for refusing (see *May* v. *USCSC* and *Yates* v. *Manale*). An agency, however, could not justify on appeal an adverse action against an employee who refuses to be examined by an agency-designated physician but who is willing to be examined by a physician of his choice selected under the provisions of subchapter 1 of FPM chapter 339 (paragraph 1–3c).

(e) If the employee refuses to submit to a medical examination or it is otherwise not practicable to obtain a medical opinion, action may be taken on the basis of deficiencies in performance or conduct.

(f) The agency must not rely solely upon a showing that the employee has a disabling condition, even when the agency has obtained a medical opinion of incapacity. Neither the placement of limitations on the duties which an employee is permitted

(Exhibit continues on following page.)

Exhibit 15-6. Continued

to perform nor medical conclusions about the employee's physical condition is sufficient cause for taking adverse action. The agency must establish a link between the medical conclusion and (i) observed deficiencies in work performance or employee behavior or (ii) high probability of hazard when the disabling condition may result in injury to the employee or others because of the kind of work the employee does. When an agency can clearly show high probability of serious hazard—for example, an agency has indisputable evidence that a truck driver with epilepsy is subject to grand mal seizures—the agency does not have to wait for the employee to have a serious accident on the job before taking adverse action. The medical evidence linked with the showing of potential hazard would be sufficient cause for taking adverse action. In all other cases, however, the agency must link the medical conclusion with observed deficiencies in work performance or employee behavior.

(g) The advance notice may include a summary of the medical opinion, when practicable, but not if the medical officer believes that the information might be harmful to the employee if it were released to him; in that case it should not mention the medical record but base the action solely upon those demonstrated deficiencies in performance or conduct which warrant removal.

(h) If the employee is not in a duty status, the advance notice may rely partially on the agency's need for the employee's services.

→(6) *Improper use of reduction-in-force.* When on appeal it is alleged that a reduction-in-force action was taken for personal reasons, such as inefficiency, that are improper, inappropriate, or contrary to the spirit, intent, or letter of Civil Service regulations on reduction in force, the Commission will consider these allegations in reaching a decision on the appeal. If it is found that the action was based on reasons personal to the appellant and the procedures outlined in part 752 were not followed, appropriate corrective action will be required.←

b. **Removals not covered by part 752.** As explained in S1–1b, some removals are not covered by part 752. The following are examples, with pertinent court cases:

(1) Removal excluded by 5 U.S.C. 7532, except the exclusion does not apply to a nonsensitive position (*Cole v. Young*);

(2) Disability retirement (*Ellmore v. Brucker* and *Murphy v. Wilson*);

(3) Voluntary resignation (*Popham v. U.S.* and *Rich v. Mitchell*).

Subchapter S3. Merit of Adverse Action

S3–1. GENERAL

a. **A cause.** Basically a "cause" for disciplinary adverse action is a recognizable offense against the employer-employee relationship. Causes for adverse action run the entire gamut of offenses against the employer-employee relationship, including inadequate performance of duties and improper conduct on or off the job. For certain extreme cases, causes have been specified by law, Executive order, or regulation. Examples of these appear in FPM chapter 731 (grounds for disqualification of an applicant) and FPM chapter 735 (conflicts of interest, etc.).

At the other extreme certain obviously improper causes for adverse actions have been prohibited by law, Executive order, or regulation (improper discrimination, for example). Between these two extremes what constitutes a proper or valid cause is essentially for the agency to decide. Section 01.3(d) of Executive Order 9830 makes agencies responsible for removing, demoting, or reassigning any employee whose conduct or capacity is such that one of these actions will "promote the efficiency of the service."

b. **A cause "as will promote efficiency."** Simply having an identifiable cause is not sufficient to warrant adverse action. In addition,

(Exhibit continues on following page.)

Exhibit 15-6. Continued

the action must be "for such cause as will promote the efficiency of the service." (As explained in *Kutcher* v. *Gray*, "service" as used here means the "public service.") A just and substantial cause is necessary for an adverse action and the action must be determined on the merits of each individual case. Differences in agency missions, in codes of penalties, or in other internal regulations may result in a cause and an action which combine to be perfectly proper in one agency being improper in another. For example, an offense involving a violation of law, which would warrant removal of a law-enforcement employee in an agency with a mission of law enforcement, might not warrant comparable action against a warehouse forklift operator in another agency. In every case the agency's action should be based on the conclusion that the adverse action is warranted and reasonable (i.e., the agency has a just cause for the action taken) and that the agency can establish, or "prove," the facts which support its reason for action.

c. **Prohibited considerations.** In no case may an agency discriminate against an employee on any of the following factors in deciding whether to take adverse action or in determining what action to take:

— Partisan political beliefs, affiliations, or activities (but this does not apply in taking actions required by law);

— Marital status (but this does not apply in taking necessary action against an illegally appointed spouse);

— Physical handicap (but this does not prohibit action against an employee whose handicap prevents him from performing his duties safely and efficiently);

— Race, color, religion, sex, national origin, or →age, provided that at the time of the action the employee was at least 40 years of age but less than 65 years of age.←

S3-2. INSUFFICIENT CAUSE

a. **Pitfalls to avoid.** Agencies should be alert to avoid such errors as the following:

(1) *Cause based on fact of arrest.* Generally, the mere fact that an employee was arrested for a crime does not provide a cause for taking

adverse action against the employee, even though the evidence of the arrest is fully recited and established. The employee may be innocent of the crime for which he was arrested. The agency action should be based, not on the fact of the arrest, but on the misconduct that led to the arrest, if there is sufficient evidence to prove misconduct or warrant suspension pending further investigation.

(2) *Cause based on criminal indictment.* Except when the agency suspends an employee indefinitely pending disposition of a criminal action, the agency should not base an adverse action on a criminal indictment or conviction. Instead, the agency should base the action on what the employee did that was wrong. If the cause relied on is a criminal indictment or conviction, then a subsequent acquittal of the employee or a dismissal of the criminal charge would, in effect, vacate the cause for action. However, if the cause relied on is the employee's acts of wrongdoing, generally the administrative action will not be affected by the subsequent court action on the criminal case (see S7–1c(2)).

(3) *Personal animosity.* In *Knotts* v. *U.S.* the court overturned the agency action because the administrative officer did not act in good faith. The court said: "In this case * * * we have reluctantly come to the conclusion that plaintiff's superiors in discharging her were motivated, not by the good of the service, but by personal animus."

b. **Cases the Commission found arbitrary, capricious, or unreasonable.** The following are examples of cases in which the Commission found that the agency's action was unwarranted under the efficiency of the service requirement.

(1) *No cause because no change in circumstances.* If an agency hires an applicant with full knowledge of certain facts concerning his fitness, it may not properly propose adverse action against the employee on the basis of those same facts at a later date if there is no change in circumstances. The agency would not have a cause for adverse action within the meaning of the regulations. In one case an agency hired an employee with full knowledge of his previous arrest record and later took action against him under subpart C of part 752 because of this record. Upon appeal, the Com-

(Exhibit continues on following page.)

Exhibit 15-6. Continued

mission found the action procedurally defective on the grounds that when an agency advances as the sole reason for adverse action facts known to it and accepted by it when the employee was hired, without any change in circumstances, the agency has not stated a reason for its action. Under the same reasoning, the Commission has found that agency adverse actions were unwarranted when the employee had been previously disciplined for the same offense. (This does not mean that if the employee commits a new offense the agency may not consider his past record in determining whether to propose adverse action or in assessing the appropriate penalty when the final decision is under consideration.)

(2) *Action unduly harsh for offense.* The Commission sometimes concludes that an adverse action was unduly harsh or severe for the reason for which the action was taken. In cases of this kind, the appellate office of the Commission does not recommend that a less severe penalty be substituted, even though the less severe penalty would have been found appropriate had it been imposed in the first instance. Instead, the appellate office decision outlines the basis for the determination that the action taken was not warranted and concludes by recommending that the action be canceled. After the cancellation the agency may use the same reason to impose a less severe penalty by initiating and completing a new action or may use that reason *in combination with one or more other reasons* to support the same penalty. →However, if the appellant alleges that the penalty imposed in a case is a clear deviation from agency policy or practice in similar situations, the Appeals Authority may reduce the penalty which was imposed by the agency. For example, if an agency separates an employee for an offense for which a three-day suspension is normally given, and the agency apparently has no good reason for this deviation from established policy or practice in similar situations, the Appeals Authority may reduce the penalty if the appellant raises this issue. The fact that the Appeals Authority may reduce a penalty when this question is raised by the appellant does not, however, relieve the agency from its responsibility to determine the appropriate penalty.←

(3) *Unlike penalties for like offenses.* In one case certain employees of an agency were found to have drunk intoxicants while on duty during a Christmas party. Although all the employees involved were substantially equal in guilt, some of them were removed while others were merely suspended or reprimanded. The Commission held that the removal actions were improper. Upon review, the Commission held that, in consideration of all the facts and circumstances—particularly the employee's record of satisfactory service in grade GS–3 clerical positions requiring only incidental typing and the presence of vacant clerical positions in grade GS–3 to which she could have been demoted and which she was willing to accept—the agency had acted arbitrarily in removing her from the service and, therefore, the removal action was improper.

(5) *Removal for a reason not substantiated by facts.* The reason given for a mailroom supervisor's removal was that, due primarily to his malfeasance and general negligence, a certain secret document was missing. Evidence developed through investigation and hearing showed that the employee had in some instances failed to adhere strictly to established procedures for safeguarding classified matter. However, the evidence failed to show that the employee ever had the particular missing document in his custody or ever had knowledge of its whereabouts. It was held that the evidence did not substantiate that the secret document was missing due primarily to the employee's malfeasance and general negligence, and that, accordingly, the employee's removal *on the basis of that reason was improper.*

(6) *Removal on inconclusive evidence.* An agency gave two reasons for proposing to remove a guard: (a) He had tampered with Government property by opening the time clock in his possession during a particular tour of duty and (b) he had unauthorized possession of a time clock key to open the time clock. Following consideration of the employee's reply, the agency dismissed the second reason but removed the employee on the basis of the sustained reason that he had tampered with his time clock. The Commission's investigation showed that the time clock had been tampered

(Exhibit continues on following page.)

Exhibit 15-6. Continued

with—there were perforations in the disc. However, it was brought out that, after insertion of the disc in the clock, the clock had been in the custody of other guards before being turned over to the employee. The record also showed that the agency had previously had no reason to question the employee's honesty or integrity. It was held that, while the perforations in the time disc gave the agency reason to suspect the employee of tampering with the clock and reason to check closely on his future behavior, such evidence was not sufficient grounds for the employee's removal from the service. The Commission found that the agency had acted arbitrarily in removing the employee on the basis of inconclusive evidence that he had tampered with his time clock during one tour of duty.

Subchapter S4. Notice of Proposed Adverse Action

S4-1. GENERAL

a. Giving fair opportunity to defend. (1) *Court rulings.* The courts have held in a number of cases that the advance notice must afford the employee a fair opportunity to defend himself against the proposed adverse action (*Baughman* v. *Green, Englehardt* v. *U.S., Norden* v. *Royall, Sells* v. *U.S.*). When an employee makes an exhaustive reply to the notice, this is evidence that he has understood the reasons for the proposed action and has had a fair opportunity to defend himself (*Schlegel* v. *U.S.*).

(2) *Regulatory requirement.* The regulations require the agency to assemble and make available to the employee the material relied on to support the reasons stated in the advance notice. This material may include, but is not limited to, statements of witnesses, documents, and investigative reports or extracts from the reports. If the employee's previous record forms part of the basis for proposing adverse action, the material relevant to that record must be made available to the employee. The agency is not required to wait until all the evidence in a case is obtained before proposing adverse action. The agency may issue a notice whenever it believes it has enough evidence to justify the action. Any additional supporting material obtained after the issuance of the advance notice may be introduced at a later stage in the proceeding. Also, when a case is one in which a crime may be involved, the requirement is not intended to extend the shortened notice period by requiring an agency to wait until all possible evidence is assembled.

It is sufficient in a "crime" case to make available the material on hand that supports the action proposed, e.g., a record or report of arrest and arraignment. The agency should not prematurely disclose evidence that could hamper proper law enforcement.

(3) *Use of restricted material.* Since all supporting material must be open to review by the employee, the agency must not support its reasons with any material which cannot be disclosed to the employee, or to his designated physician under section 294.401(b) of part 294. Material which cannot be shown to the employee because its disclosure would violate a pledge of confidence, or because it is in some way restricted or classified, cannot be used to support reasons stated in the advance notice. If the agency wishes to use information in a restricted or classified document, it must obtain this information in a form which can be made available to the employee for his review. If the agency wishes to use information in a Civil Service Commission investigative report which cannot be made available to the employee because it would violate a pledge of confidence, the agency may obtain the information independently in a form that can be disclosed. The agency may obtain the information by interviewing the employee, by contacting the sources named in the Commission's report and getting their permission to use the information and identify the source, or by contacting other sources.

b. Making clear why the action will promote efficiency. It is not always necessary for an agency to state specifically that the proposed

(Exhibit continues on following page.)

Exhibit 15-6. Continued

action will promote the efficiency of the service or to explain why it believes the action will promote the efficiency of the service. Factual statements of the actions of the employee which are the basis for the proposed action (i.e., reasons stated specifically and in detail) must make clear on their face why the agency is proposing to take action. In some instances, however, an agency should bolster its case by an express explanation of how the efficiency of the service will be promoted, especially when the adverse action is based on misconduct which does not directly affect performance of the employee's job tasks.

c. Avoiding errors. To prevent errors, an agency should require that a notice of proposed adverse action be prepared by, or reviewed before issuance by, an employee who has received training in the technical requirements of processing adverse actions. In addition, employees who prepare or review notices should be alert to such common errors as the following:

(1) *Reason for action not clearly shown.* Cases frequently occur in which the advance notice fails to state clearly just what the employee did that was wrong, and the employee is at a loss to know how to defend himself. An advance notice may state that a supervisor at a particular time and place during a tour of duty saw the employee talking on a specified telephone and an hour later saw the same employee sitting on the steps of a warehouse smoking a cigarette. While this is certainly specific and detailed, it does not clearly set forth a cause for action against the employee. The reason for proposing action may be that the employee was smoking in a place where smoking is prohibited. Or perhaps the employee was using a restricted phone without authority or justification. The fault here is that the agency stated what the employee was doing, not *why* what the employee was doing *was wrong.*

(2) *Using legal terms which connote crime.* It is very poor practice to state reasons exclusively in legal terms which connote crime. If, for example, an agency proposes adverse action for a reason such as "grand larceny," a legally defined crime, the agency may have to prove all the elements necessary to establish that the

crime has been committed. Similarly, an agency may create difficulties for itself if it uses as a reason "theft of Government property" when all it can prove is "unauthorized removal of property" or if it uses "assault and battery on a supervisor" when all it can prove is "striking a supervisor." Ordinarily it is preferable to specify in the notice what the employee did that was wrong without using legal terms. The agency then will merely have to show the employee's misconduct and why his acts justify taking adverse action against him.

d. Labeling offenses. (1) One way for the agency to avoid errors is to label the offense or offenses. In some cases, such as those involving specific acts of immoral conduct, the act may be stated without a label. In most cases, however, labeling the offense is good practice if (i) the label fits the facts, (ii) the label is not a legal term, and (iii) the agency keeps in mind that conclusions, or labels, will not satisfy the specificity-and-detail requirement. The following examples illustrate cases when labeling is good practice.

(2) When the administrative officer is being guided by an agency code of penalties, the nature of the offense and the number of times it has been repeated are important in determining the appropriate range of penalties. It is good practice to label the offense so that there is no question at present or any time in the future whether it is a first, second, or third offense of the same nature. The agency must be especially careful, however, to select a label that fits the facts and not to distort the facts to fit a specified offense in a code of penalties.

(3) Use of a label to describe the offense simplifies recording the adverse action on Standard Form 50, which becomes part of the official record of the case. The reason given on SF 50 must be consistent with the reasons stated in the advance notice and relied on in the decision.

(4) When the agency labels an offense, the employee knows how serious his offense is considered and the agency knows what offense it must prove. For example, an employee does not comply with a proper order on a specified occasion. The agency may conclude that the offense reflects deliberate, willful, and knowing

(Exhibit continues on following page.)

Exhibit 15-6. Continued

intent and label it "insubordination" if the agency can prove that the offense resulted from an affirmative act of will. Or the agency may conclude that the offense resulted only from negligence, or that there is not sufficient evidence to prove insubordination, and label the offense "failure to follow instructions." Either label would alert both the employee and the agency to the nature of the offense on which the proposed action is based and the kind of proof necessary to support the proposed action.

(5) When a repetition of irresponsible acts or failures on the part of the employee—rather than his most recent irresponsible act or failure standing alone—causes the agency to conclude that the proposed adverse action is the appropriate one to take, it is good practice to give a single basic reason and to cite all of the employee's offenses that are pertinent as facts supporting the basic reason. In some cases the offenses are all of the same general sort: Repeated absences without leave, repeated tardiness, repeated failure to carry out assignments. In other cases the offenses are various, such as insubordination added to previous instances of unauthorized absence and drinking on the job. These offenses could properly be labeled "repeated acts of misconduct."

(6) When an agency's reasons are based on an employee's past actions, the advance notice must label the actions the way they were treated when they originally occurred. For example, an employee on several occasions fails to call before taking leave. Upon hearing the employee's explanation, the agency charges the absences to annual leave or other forms of authorized leave. If there is a recurrence of the same offense and the agency initiates action against the employee, it would not be proper to label the offense "repeated instances of absence without leave," because leave was in fact granted in the previous instances. The offense should instead be labeled "repeated failure to get advance approval of leave."

S5–4. DUTY STATUS DURING NOTICE PERIOD

a. **General.** If at all practicable, an employee must be kept in an active duty status in his regular position during the notice period. However, in emergency situations (when circumstances are such that the retention of the employee in an active duty status in his position may result in damage to Government property or may be detrimental to the interests of the Government or injurious to the employee, his fellow workers, or the general public) the agency may believe that it should not allow the employee to continue in his regular assignment or even to remain on the premises. In this event, any nonduty status imposed by the agency must be in accordance with the provisions of paragraphs b and c of this section. (When an employee is absent for reasons that do not originate with the agency, the agency should first consider carrying him on appropriate leave—annual, sick, LWOP, or AWOL.)

b. **Emergency situations under subpart C.** An emergency suspension under subpart C of part 752 can often be completed in 48 hours, or even less. Subpart C of part 752 requires at least 24 hours' advance notice, an opportunity to answer, and a decision before the suspension can become effective. The agency may place the employee in a nonduty status with pay and without charge to leave for up to five calendar days while processing the suspension.

c. **Emergency situations under subpart B.**
(1) *Agency alternatives.* During the notice period required by subpart B of part 752 in an emergency the agency may:

(a) Assign the employee to other duties in which the problems that make his movement necessary will not exist;

(b) Place him on leave *with his consent* (the with-his-consent provision is based on court decisions indicating that, in general, an employee may not be placed on

(Exhibit continues on following page.)

Exhibit 15-6. Continued

enforced leave during the notice period (see S1–6c(4));

(c) Suspend him 30 days or less (see S1–6d);

(d) Suspend him more than 30 days (this would be an unusual alternative to follow because it would require subpart B procedures and could be used, therefore, only when the crime provision could be invoked to shorten the notice period for the suspension—in which event it would be quicker and simpler for the agency to follow alternative (e) below); or

(e) Curtail the notice period when the crime provision can be invoked and process only one action (see S5–4c(2) below).

The agency is not required to attempt to use these alternative methods of getting the employee out of his regular position, or off active duty entirely, in any particular order. When the facts warrant taking the employee out of his position, the agency may use whichever alternative it believes offers the quickest and safest relief. However, in view of the objective of keeping the employee in an active duty status in his regular position whenever practicable, it is good practice for an agency to use the alternative which most nearly approximates active status or otherwise causes the employee the least possible loss.

(2) *Use of "crime" provision.* When an agency believes an employee should not remain on the premises and can invoke the crime provision, it is better practice to shorten the notice period and process only one action—a removal or an indefinite suspension—than to suspend the employee during a minimum 30-day notice period and process two actions. Curtailing the notice period and processing

only one action avoids the procedural difficulties involved in simultaneously processing separate adverse actions, each having different requirements. It also avoids the difficulties in effecting a final adverse action before the employee has been in a suspended status for more than 30 days. Generally, to invoke the crime provision and process a removal or indefinite suspension with a curtailed notice period an agency would:

— Notify the employee he is being put immediately in a nonduty status with pay for no longer than five calendar days.

— Give the employee a notice either of (a) proposed indefinite suspension pending disposition of the criminal action or (b) proposed removal when the agency has sufficient evidence to warrant removal. The notice will tell the employee of the reasonable period for answer (no less than 24 hours).

— Issue a decision on the action after the employee has had an opportunity to answer and the answer, if any, has been considered.

— Complete the action before the employee has been in a nonduty status for more than five calendar days.

If the agency decides to suspend the employee and later, after the resolution of the criminal charges, decides to remove him, it must initiate a new adverse action to remove the employee. The agency may process the removal while the employee is still on indefinite suspension, if the advance notice and notice of decision for the suspension are worded to include this possibility.

Exhibit 15-7a. Memorandum to Scott Lento

To: Scott Lento

From: Mary Sweeney

Issued: 5/18/76   2:35 p.m.

This schedule should follow the duties on 5/17/76 work schedule which are at
this time still not completed -- Please show the time you begin and end
each chore. These are listed in priority order!!

1) Record, pack and ship Federal Protective Officers (2) to: Area 1 office
    (Time required -- 10 minutes)

2) Record and pack 4 requisitions necessary for Saturday, 5/22 exams in Area 10.
    2 - Steno-Typists @ 100 ea.
    1 - Dept. of State Steno
    1 - Recruiting Authority Steno
    (No more than 30 minutes required)

3) Record and pack Blind PACE material for 5/25 exam.
    (No more than 20 minutes necessary)

4) Record and pack Library Technician for 5/25 exam.
    (No more than 20 minutes required)

5) Record and pack special exam for 5/26/76 in Area 6
    (5 minutes required)

6) Record, pack and ship non-competitive computer operator to Area 3.
    (No more than 15 minutes required)

7) Record, pack and ship non-competitive Pace Booklets to Area 3.

8) Count returned booklets in the enclosed package from FAA. If you agree
    that the correct number of used booklets is enclosed, please enter the
    amounts on the stock cards and send booklets to the shredder.
    (material for 3 competitors -- no more than 15 minutes required)

Exhibit 15-7b. Memorandum to Scott Lento

Work schedule issued for 5/19/76

To: Scott Lento

From: Mary Sweeney

1)   I have had inquiries regarding papers of applicants who took the steno-
     typist exam in Area 15 on 5/12/76/ Please check to see if you have these
     in the shipping room. I am certain this is the package which you stated you
     did not have answer sheets for and you eventually located them. If they
     are still in the shipping room at this date, 5/19, please clear them and
     advise me. This involved 9 applicants and since it was counted in my
     presence, one week ago, it should not now involve more than 10 minutes
     if you still have it.

2)   The H.S. Steno-Typist conducted on 5/13/76 has not reached Area 2 yet.
     If you haven't cleared it, do that also!!
     No more than 10 minutes involved!!

3)   Stenographer-Typist conducted in Area 23 on 5/15 should and must be cleared.
     Another 10 minute task --

4)   Please check each requisition against each ATCS test package and
     determine which test point or test points are not yet in. I understand
     that this was done previously since I stayed with you to show you once
     again how it was done. I am certain that many more points are now in.
     If the class is complete -- clear it!! It it is not, report to me
     the point/s and requisition number/s not in. DO NOT go by previous
     checks or follow-ups. I repeat -- check each requisition against each
     test package. This check should not involve more than 20 minutes of
     your time!!

Exhibit 15-7c. Memorandum to Scott Lento

To: Scott Lento

From: Mary Sweeney

Tuesday, 5/26/76   11:05 a.m.

The Area Office called regarding a Pace Non-Competitive class of 39
competitors which you sent to them.

You did not include the 2090 with the answer sheets. Please send it to
Area 17. When you have done so, please sign off on this sheet and return
to me.

Exhibit 15-7d. Memorandum to Scott Lento

To: Scott Lento

From: Mary Sweeney

May 26th   Work Schedule

1) Yesterday I issued a sheet requesting that you forward a copy of the
    2090 which should have accompanied a class of 39 non-competitive
    PACE applicants which you shipped to Area 17. I asked you to return
    the slip when this was completed. I have not received the slip back --
    DID YOU COMPLETE THIS? IF NOT, PLEASE DO SO.

2) I also submitted a sheet asking you to send 3 booklets to Area 5 to
    make up the shortage in your shipment of Test 24. I have not received
    this sheet back as completed. DID YOU COMPLETE THIS? IF NOT, PLEASE
    DO SO.

3) Ship material to Area 13 for test at Marshall Senior High School.
    Include 2 copies of CSC 2090 in her package.

4) Please make a current check of Acct. Auditor exam. I am reasonably
    certain that some copies are in and you are showing them as out.
    What points are actually still out?

Exhibit 15-7e. Memorandum to Scott Lento

To: Scott Lento

From: Mary Sweeney

5/26/76

On 5/25/76 I requested that you send a CSC 2090 to cover non-competitive class of 39 Pace applicants. I also requested that you sign off on the sheet when it was completed. You did not sign off on the 5/25 work sheet. I was, therefore, forced to repeat this order on your 5/26 work sheet. You signed off "10:15 a.m." but did not include the date.

I have spoken to Area 17 today. They did not receive it. I do not need you to tell me that the 26th was not yesterday and not tomorrow -- what I do need is the 2090 to go to Area 17.

Copy to Ann Sacco

Exhibit 15-7f. Memorandum to Scott Lento

To: Scott Lento

From: Mary Sweeney

5/26/76

The 9th Area Office has phoned:
They did not receive and <u>must</u> <u>have</u>:

    CSC 2090 FOR PARK AIDE EXAMINATION HELD 5/25 AT FAITH HIGH SCHOOL

    CSC 2090 FOR LIBRARY TECHNICIAN EXAMINATION HELD 5/25 AT LOS ALTOS CENTER

<u>ALSO</u>:

    Technical Aids were sent there today without a cover sheet. The monitor
    there would like to know if this is a complete class. If not, what
    is remaining and why no cover sheets?

    Send to

    ADVISE ME WHEN COMPLETED!!!

Exhibit 15-8. Memorandum to Scott Lento about seeking medical advice

UNITED STATES GOVERNMENT   U.S. CIVIL SERVICE COMMISSION

MEMORANDUM   Date: May 24, 1976

Subject: Discussion with Scott Lento About Seeking Medical Help

From: Chief, Staffing Division

To: The File

On Friday morning, May 21, 1976, I spoke again with Scott Lento concerning the fact that his work performance had not improved at all since our discussion on April 29, 1976. I further told him that his behavior has changed so radically from the first 8-10 weeks of his employment that I wanted to be sure he had no medical or other health problems that were affecting his work performance.

I gave him the name and address of the Chief Medical Officer of the regional Public Health Service and told him that he would be excused from duty if he chose to go see him. I urged him to go today, if possible.

Lento gave no indication of whether he intended to go see the doctor or not. He thanked me for my time and left.

PART VII

Altering Practices for Managing People

CHAPTER 16 Civil Service Systems: Serving Managers or Protecting Employees?

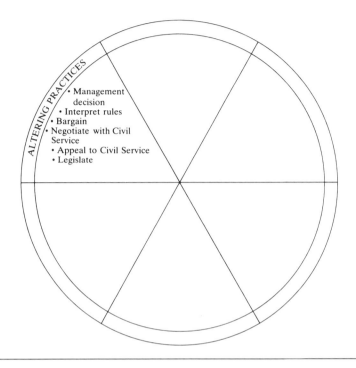

In public employment it is difficult to change the parameters of the formal personnel system. It may also be difficult to alter traditions and other informal organizational practices that affect people. Yet, as social values, institutions, and public policy change, it will be necessary to alter the management practices that affect people. Changed practices in human resource management may also be necessary to respond to changes in program or policy emphasis or changes in strategy. Change may be necessary also to loosen elements of a personnel system that may have become petrified, for no personnel system is timeless.

The case in Chapter 16 examines one aspect of the federal Civil Service Reform Act of 1978, focusing on the interpretation by a newly created agency of some of the reform provisions. The case suggests some of the implementation problems inherent in change of a formal personnel system. It also suggests that change in formal practices is not just a matter of passing a law but is a matter of dealing with the operational problems and outside actors that will influence the impact of such a change on day-to-day management. Thus, the case raises some practical problems.

Certain personnel practices in an agency or subunit can be altered without trying to alter basic civil service rules and regulations. Whether or not civil service systems respond easily, managers themselves will have to make adjustments if they are to attract and motivate employees in ways conducive to organizational success and individual satisfaction. As demographics and values change, forward-looking agencies, conscious of human resource management, will make such adjustments as they can within existing formal constraints. Standard hiring and recruiting practices usually can be altered to reflect certain labor market conditions; arrangement of hours worked and aspects of job content are also susceptible to change within most formal systems. Still, the formal practices are unlikely to keep pace. There are many practices that cannot be easily altered even if the need is obvious and great, and it is unlikely that a program manager as an individual can have much influence on the formal personnel system.

The following chapter provides some stimulus for thinking ahead and for anticipating the challenges and opportunities in altering management practices to reflect changes in the work force and in the needs of the public.

Civil Service Systems: Serving Managers or Protecting Employees?

Civil service reform is on the minds of many public managers and politicians these days. The 1978 attempt at federal civil service reform has generated interest in states and cities across the country. In general, civil service reform is intended to provide more flexibility to managers for deploying human resources in public agencies. The argument over civil service reform has usually pitted those in favor of increased management flexibility against those who are concerned with protecting employees from arbitrary actions, frequently couched in terms of ''political abuse,'' or from other violations of their employment rights.

For years, managers have complained that civil service rules protected workers even from management actions that would be in the employees' own professional interest and in the interests of the organization. Those in the personnel profession who administered the rules were considered by many managers to be insufficiently responsive to management's legitimate organizational needs. At the same time employee groups have claimed the opposite; in their view civil service rules have not offered adequate protection; worse, those administering the rules were considered insufficiently sensitive to employee rights. This apparent role conflict in the lives of those who administered civil service rules resulted in suggestions that the function of protecting employees be separated from those civil service functions that were intended to help managers, such as recruiting, testing, and examining.

In formalizing such a split, the Federal Civil Service Reform Act of 1978 created the Merit Systems Protection Board as a separate agency. The Board was to hear cases wherein management actions were appealed and to review the rules of the civil service system in an effort independently to protect the rights of employees. The separate Office of Personnel Management was to handle the management service functions of the old (pre-1978) Civil Service Commission.

The case, ''The Merit Systems Protection Board (A),'' focuses on the Board's first major decision, which concerned one agency's dismissal of employees for poor performance under the performance appraisal and expanded dismissal provisions of the Civil Service Reform Act. In addition to adjudication of an interesting appeal, some important policy and precedent questions are raised by the case with respect to the effects of reform. It is, therefore, a useful situation to examine in the context of assessing the implementation aspects of major changes in a formal civil service practice. The lessons from this case and the issues raised may have some utility as we consider the desirability, application, and difficulty of civil service reform at state and local levels.

STUDY QUESTIONS

1. As a member of the Merit Systems Protection Board, what are your responsibilities? to workers? to management? to the public? elsewhere?

2. As a member of the Board, what consequences do you see in connection with your decision on this case?

3. In view of your responsibilities and the consequences of this decision, what criteria would you use to decide the case?

4. What would you decide?

5. How would you articulate your decision to the interested groups? What message would you want them to receive? Why?

6. What effect do you think your decision would have on implementation or the intent of the Civil Service Reform Act? How will that affect employee protection? the use of performance evaluation? management flexibility?

7. Do you see any lessons in this case to be used in designing or carrying out civil service reform in other jurisdictions?

SELECTED REFERENCES

Staff Report of the President's Personnel Management Project, U.S. Civil Service Commission and Office of Management and Budget, 1978.

The Civil Service Reform Act of 1978, P.L. 95–454.

Report of the U.S. President's Committee on Administrative Management of the Government (U.S. Government Printing Office, 1937). Part II, "Personnel Management," pp. 7–13, especially pp. 9–10. Also known as the "Report of the Brownlow Committee."

The Hoover Commission Report (McGraw-Hill, 1949). Part VI, "Personnel Management," pp. 107–134. Report of the *U.S. Commission on Organization of the Executive Branch of the Government.*

The Merit Systems Protection Board (A)

It seems that during the first year of operation (various groups) set up a litmus test for you. . . . Everybody has a constituency. The Merit Systems Protection Board is without one. If one develops, we are probably not doing our job.

— Ruth Prokop, Chair, Merit Systems Protection Board

Within a couple of years it is likely that Uncle Sam will routinely fire more people for incompetence than all of the big guys — General Motors, U.S. Steel, etc. — put together.

— Mike Causey, "The Federal Diary," *The Washington Star,* January 28, 1980.

The Merit Systems Protection Board (MSPB) was established January 11, 1979, as part of the Civil Service Reform Act (CSRA). It, along with the newly created Office of Personnel Management (OPM), undertook responsibilities previously the function of the U.S. Civil Service Commission (CSC). Charged with the duty of shaping the new Board were its three members: Chairwoman Ruth T. Prokop, Vice Chair Ersa H. Poston, and Member Ronald P. Wertheim. Each of them had substantial public service experience.

Chairwoman Prokop had been General Counsel of the U.S. Department of Housing and Urban Development, and Senior Counsel to the General Telephone & Electronics Corporation. Prior to that she served in both the Kennedy and Johnson Administrations. Vice Chair Poston had been a United States Civil Service Commis-

This case was prepared by Thomas P. Sellers under the supervision of Jon Brock, Lecturer at the John F. Kennedy School of Government, Harvard University. It is based on a case originally prepared by Carol Ritter Thorn under the supervision of Mr. Brock. While based upon a factual situation, the names of some individuals are disguised.

sioner since 1977 and had previously served as President of the New York State Civil Service Commission, and as Chairperson of the President's Advisory Council on Intergovernmental Personnel Policy.

Mr. Wertheim had been in private practice for 10 years with a Washington, D.C., law firm. During that time he also served as advisor to the Secretary of Defense for Law of the Sea Negotiations and Alternate U.S. Representative to the United Nations Conference on the Law of the Sea. Mr. Wertheim served as Deputy General Counsel of the Peace Corps from 1964 to 1966 and as Peace Corps Director in Northeast Brazil from 1966 to 1968.

The case *Thomas W. Wells vs. Patricia R. Harris* presented an early challenge to the Board. It would be the first case to test MSPB's new powers, among them the authority to review — and invalidate if necessary — OPM regulations. The case was also the first challenge to the right of government supervisors to fire or demote employees for "unacceptable performance" under the new performance appraisal standards required by the Act. The Merit System Protection Board's ruling would carry weight throughout the entire federal service.

Background of Civil Service Reform

In 1883 the Pendleton Act created the federal civil service system as a reform of patronage. It established "merit" principles in the federal personnel system to prevent political abuse. Over the next century federal civil service became an outdated patchwork of statutes and rules that were not, at their root, designed to improve the management of a rapidly expanding bureaucracy. It was this entrenched system initially established for the right reasons, that President Carter took on in 1977.

413

Actually, the opening rounds in the battle had been fired by candidate Carter who pledged to "reform" the bureaucracy and ran as a Washington-outsider. Even though civil service reform was not a burning issue outside Washington, D.C., the bureaucracy was an issue producing a high level of public support for "reform" as measured by opinion polls and as perceived by major political leaders, not the least of which was Carter. "I am alarmed," noted Civil Service Commission Chairman Alan Campbell in 1978, "at the public attitude toward public employees and public service." Campbell was formerly dean of the LBJ School of Government.

Public support for generic "reform" and a combination of other factors resulted in an environment which supported the relatively swift passage of the Civil Service Reform Act. But, like many reforms, the CSRA involved a political process in which compromise shaped the final policy. The President's Personnel Management Project (PMP), bipartisan support in Congress, and initial support from the largest federal employee union, all played major roles in determining the structure, substance and potential for continued existence of the new rules.

Established in 1977, the PMP task force composed of academics and high-level careerists provided an independent and credible forum for developing reform proposals forwarded to the Congress. Members like Campbell, Chester Newland (professor of public administration at the Washington Public Affairs Center of the University of Southern California), agency representatives, business people and congressional staff members contributed both their operational expertise and their political relationships to the effort. In part, the PMP added to an overall climate which nurtured bi-partisan support for the Act among key members of the House Post Office and Civil Service Committee and the Senate Governmental Affairs Committee. The strength of anti-Washington public opinion stoked

by activist public interest groups was apparent to House and Senate members. Veteran's groups mounted a successful lobbying effort against certain provisions of the CSRA, thus ensuring the retention of veteran's preference in the new system.

After some *quid pro quos,* the Act also had the initial support of the American Federation of Government Employees (AFGE), even in the face of opposition from other federal employee unions. Limited to bargaining about work conditions and faced with steadily declining membership, AFGE felt it could achieve codification of employee rights in exchange for limited concessions to management flexibility that still included procedural protection for employees. However, AFGE's rank and file forced the leadership to withdaw support after President Carter limited FY1979 pay raises to 5.5 percent instead of an anticipated 8 percent or better. Because the withdrawal came a week after the House Committee acted favorably on the bill in a political climate favorable to CSRA, the AFGE action did not affect the adoption of the Act.

The Civil Service Reform Act was passed by Congress on October 3, 1978, and became effective January 11, 1979. The Administration promised federal managers that the Act would give them greater managerial flexibility. The general public was given the impression that the bureaucracy was "reformed," that firing incompetent employees would be easier and pay increases would be performance-based. The rights of employees to join unions and to engage in limited collective bargaining was established by statute. Also, several key institutions administering the federal personnel system had been reorganized.

Yet the CSRA was also a product of compromise, the result of a political process and an environment which required the coalition of constituencies with different interests. The reforms, in fact, were not as sweeping as President Carter wished. The law contained sufficient ambiguities and unanswered questions that its real impact would be determined by the way in which managers, unions, personnel officers and the new CSRA agencies interpreted and implemented their duties and responsibilities.

Merit System Protection Board

As part of the reform act, personnel functions previously handled by different subunits of the Civil Service Commission (CSC) were split up. The commission was renamed the Office of Personnel Management. Most labor relations matters became the charge of the new Federal Labor Relations Authority, fashioned after the National Labor Relations Board. Matters of ensuring that merit principles and other regulatory principles were followed were left to the Merit Systems Protection Board.

The Civil Service Reform Act of 1978 established the Merit Systems Protection Board (MSPB) as a quasi-judicial independent body charged with safeguarding merit principles and employee rights in the federal personnel system. The Board has the power under Chapter 12 of Title V in the U.S. Code to review regulations governing personnel policy, to adjudicate cases of alleged violation of the merit system, to enforce compliance with its orders, to order stays of personnel actions, and to conduct studies of civil service and other merit systems. In addition to direct appeals by employees, cases are brought before the Board by a Special Counsel, with significant independence, who is authorized to investigate allegations of prohibited personnel practices.

The MSPB consists of three members (no more than two from the same party) nominated by the president and confirmed by the Senate to serve seven-year non-renewable terms. The Special Counsel serves a five-year term and is also appointed by the President with Senate confirmation. The Board has subpoena power and is not subject to presidential directives in the performance of its adjudicatory functions. It may impose a range of sanctions where agencies and/or

individuals have violated merit principles including reprimand, removal, suspension, demotion, exclusion from federal employment for up to five years, and fines of up to $1,000. Agencies may also be ordered to pay an employee's legal fees under certain circumstances.

In addition to its new statutory responsibilities, the Board took over those functions of the Civil Service Commission intended to protect employees from personnel actions that did not conform with articulated principles of merit or otherwise were not in accordance with rights granted under Civil Service laws and regulations. The Office of Personnel Management retained that part of its mission to assist management in deploying and otherwise dealing productively with the work force. The separate creation of MSPB was intended to alleviate what many observers had for years identified as a role conflict within the CSC between helping managers and protecting employee rights, leaving the Board to discourage subversion of merit principles. Dwight Ink, Executive Director of the President's Personnel Management Project in 1977 called an independent and strong Merit Board "the cornerstone" of Civil Service reform.

Performance Appraisal

Congressional debate had acknowledged that any meaningful changes in the system required greater discretion for federal executives in personnel matters. Part of the debate focused on easing the requirements for removal, and on holding people accountable for their job performance. As a trade-off, however, the congressional drafters of the Act required that executives be held strictly accountable for exercising their discretion in accordance with merit principles. Seeking to make the process objective, the Act required agencies to establish fair and impartial performance appraisal systems which would identify the key tasks in an employee's job, called "critical elements," against which subsequent performance would be measured. "Performance standards" were to be established for each "critical element." Once these critical elements and the performance standards were determined, they were to be put in writing and communicated to each employee. If an employee failed to perform adequately according to these performance standards, removal could follow.

All performance appraisal systems are governed by Chapter 43 of Title 5 of the U.S. Code, as amended by the Reform Act. Title 5 USC 4303 allows agencies to reduce in grade or remove an employee for "unacceptable performance." It also provides that procedures for such actions will include 30 days' notice which identifies "specific instances of unacceptable performance . . . on which the proposed actions is based" and "the critical elements of the employee's position involved in each instance of unacceptable performance."

The Reform Act also changed the evidentiary requirements for taking adverse action against a federal employee for poor performance. The Act allowed removals or demotions to occur where there was "substantial evidence" of unacceptable performance, a less stringent standard than the previously required "preponderance of the evidence." In actual practice, the government often had great difficulty meeting the heavier evidentiary burden which, it was generally felt, resulted in the retention of incompetent employees. These new streamlined procedures became effective January 11, 1979, although agencies had until October 1, 1981, to fully implement performance appraisal systems.

Interim Regulations

For the period between January 1979 to October 1981, OPM gave agencies the authority to place in effect interim performance appraisal rules, including streamlined firing procedures, guided by OPM regulations. Because of the rush to get

regulations in place, the Director of OPM's Workforce Effectiveness Group was given one week to write them. Later she explained, "So I just sat down and dreamed it up. Nobody even thought anything of this. Nobody questioned any of it." The regulations were cleared by OPM's General Counsel H. Patrick Swygert, who would soon become the Merit System Protection Board's first Special Counsel.

On January 16, OPM issued its interim regulations on performance appraisal. (These were followed by final regulations issued on August 3, 1979.) They provided that before an agency takes a performance based action under 5 USC 4303 the Agency must:

— Identify the critical elements of the employee's position;

— Delineate the performance standards for those elements which the employee is not performing adequately;

— Communicate the critical elements and performance standards to the employee; and

— Provide the employee with a reasonable time and opportunity to improve his/her performance.

Action Against Thomas Wells

Acting under the OPM regulations, the Social Security Administration (SSA) initiated adverse actions against 41 employees, including Thomas W. Wells, of Shamokin, Pennsylvania. Mr. Wells was informed of the "critical elements and applicable performance standards" for his position by letter dated March 19, 1979. At the same time, he was informed that he was not performing any of these "critical elements" in an acceptable manner. On or about April 30, Wells received a notice of proposed removal on grounds of unacceptable performance. He was subject to discharge on or about May 31, the expiration of the notice period.

By May 15, 1980, SSA had formally proposed or effected the removal or demotion of 24 of the 41 employees. These included employees in several different states who had the same job title and position description. SSA took these actions based on "substantial evidence" of unsatisfactory performance, and used the streamlined firing procedures of the Civil Service Reform Act. The American Federation of Government Employees, AFL-CIO (AFGE) quickly protested the action against Mr. Wells and "other employees similarly situated." As the only major federal union to publicly support the 1978 Civil Service Reform Act, AFGE might have been interested in proving that it could also work to the benefit of employees.

The American Federation of Government Employees

AFGE is located in a modern, seven-story building on Massachusetts Avenue in Washington, where it presides over the union's 1500 locals, representing nearly 700,000 Federal employees. AFGE is the exclusive representative, in several bargaining units, for 72,000 SSA employees, and holds national consultation status with the SSA and Department of Health, Education and Welfare (HEW). Leaders of the SSA Council reported to AFGE headquarters that "wide-spread attempts" had been made by line supervisors to fire or demote employees in identical positions who had been subjected to diverse critical elements and performance standards. At least four of the 24 employees who had been affected were members of AFGE.

AFGE's Position

On May 15, 1979, AFGE filed a petition as an "interested person" with MSPB Special Counsel H. Patrick Swygert on behalf of AFGE's members and all SSA employees, nationwide. Under the Reform Act the Special Counsel had been given a broad charter to investigate and, where appropriate, prosecute cases arising out of the new personnel system. The petition requested that all SSA firings, demotions, or disciplinary

action based on "unacceptable performance" be blocked.

On the same date, AFGE petitioned the MSPB to review the interim OPM regulations "relating to agency actions based on allegations of unacceptable performance" and their implementation by the SSA. In their motion for an immediate stay and investigation, AFGE stressed, "Your immediate action is requested because of the imminent personnel action involving Mr. Wells and since other employees, similarly situated, may soon be discharged, if such action has not already been undertaken, within the next few days."

"The Union doesn't want to keep people on the payroll who aren't doing their jobs" explained AFGE staff counsel Jay Brusco. "Even in our constitution we state that an objective is to promote the efficiency of the service. But employees are entitled to protection provided by the law." AFGE maintained that the disciplinary actions against SSA workers on the grounds of alleged unacceptable performance had taken place without providing the workers their full range of rights under the Civil Service Reform Act.

AFGE Counsel Brusco noted "the regulations developed by OPM and their implementation by SSA have ignored totally the significant employee safeguards which Congress intended would be provided employees prior to any disciplinary actions on grounds of unacceptable performance." AFGE argued that Mr. Wells was granted only his procedural rights. AFGE requested the Board to determine whether OPM was obeying the law by allowing interim performance appraisal standards on an "as needed basis" before final standards were promulgated by the agencies.

Swygert's Actions

Special Counsel Swygert in turn petitioned the Merit System Protection Board to halt all firings and demotions based on interim standards until a hearing could be held to determine whether the performance appraisal standards were in accord with provisions of the Civil Service Reform Act. In seeking the stay, Swygert also asked the MSPB to require SSA to temporarily restore all affected employees to their previous positions and grades until the matter could be resolved. Swygert agreed with AFGE that the agency's actions violated the performance appraisal requirements of the U.S. Code and cited the following reasons:

— The SSA's guidelines violate OPM's interim regulations in that they allow individual supervisors to establish critical elements and performancé standards on an "as-needed basis";

— The SSA guidelines "may violate the rights of employees to equal protection of the laws as guaranteed by the Fifth Amendment";

— The agency, in its attempt to conform to the interim OPM regulations, "allows for disparate treatment of employees in identical positions performing identical functions in different regions of the SSA."

Initial Response by OPM and SSA

In a letter of May 25, 1979, to Special Counsel Swygert, OPM General Counsel Margery Waxman, argued that the stay should not be granted. OPM responded that its regulations reflected Congressional intent. Congress, Waxman argued, citing the legislative history, "recognized the difficulty in establishing performance appraisal systems but clearly stated that it expected that performance-based actions would be taken prior to the establishment of completed performance appraisal systems." OPM felt its regulations reflected the statutory requirements of 5 USC 4303 because they restate the procedural requirements in law.

Also responding to the initial complaint, HEW Secretary Califano and Commissioner of Social Security Stanford G. Ross explained:

[I]t is not reasonable to presume that Congress intended to penalize agencies to the detriment of the public welfare. It is unconscionable to suggest that Congress intended that agencies retain and/or pay employees at a grade level which is not warranted by the employee's performance. The public, as taxpayers, deserve to have a well-run civil service. SSA is not arbitrarily firing or demoting its employees. Management officials have consistently apprised their employees when poor performance has occurred. The employees have been told of deficiencies and informed of how they might improve. No personnel action has been taken without notice of a proposal, after the employee has had time to improve his/her performance.

MSPB Actions

On June 25, after reviewing the arguments from AFGE and the replies from OPM and SSA, Ruth Prokop, the Board's Chair, granted AFGE's petition and agreed to review the regulations. The MSPB then ordered HEW to stay all firings and demotions based on unacceptable performance and to offer immediate restoration of grade and position to all workers adversely affected.

Hearings before the MSPB on the *Wells vs. Harris* case were scheduled for September 27, 1979. The MSPB had solicited all "interested parties" for their comments concerning the case.

Thirteen agencies were represented, including SSA, the Department of Agriculture, Transportation, Army, Navy, and the Internal Revenue Service and Veterans Administration. An OPM spokesman indicated that their "political move" was to persuade as many agencies as possible to provide oral arguments to ensure that the Board had a full Executive Branch account. Rather than risk being overturned, many agencies had delayed disciplinary moves they had planned. Four unions presented oral argument, including AFGE, the National Federation of Federal Employees, National Treasury Employees Union, and FFA.

On September 26, 1979, Mike Causey wrote in his *Washington Star* column, "President Carter's civil service reform designed for government to fire 'incompetents' — undergoes a major, make-or-break test this week."

Arguments Presented by the Social Security Administration

The Social Security representative defended a March 15 memo addressed to all regional commissioners advising that during the interim period supervisors should develop critical elements on an as-needed basis, claiming this "did not constitute an open season on SSA employees by first-level supervisor." Out of 86,000 employees, SSA had taken action against 41 between March 15 and August 9. "Had SSA really intended to be arbitrary and to conduct a massive house-cleaning, it surely could have performed more acceptably than that," the lawyer maintained.

The March 15 memo advised managers that interim actions could be taken and laid down the following ground rules for such performance-based actions:

— Develop interim critical elements on an as-needed basis to implement the law;

— Have the interim critical element reviewed by a higher level of management;

— Provide the employee with the required 30-day notice to improve before taking action; and

— Coordinate any action with the servicing personnel office.

While the employees may not have been consulted in the initial development of critical elements in any individual case, SSA argued that if a supervisor communicated an element or standard to an employee which was not critical, realistic or job-related, the employee or his representative had an opportunity to dispute the standard:

— at the time they were communicated to him, thereby participating in the establishment of the standards,

— at the time the 30 days' advance notice of a proposal to take action was given to him, or

— in an appeal to the Board.

The Agency acknowledged that, in preparation for removal, it had identified the poor performers and constructed appraisal systems in such a way as to confirm a finding of poor performance, rather than implementing standards and judging performance by them. But their actions, they felt, were justified. The SSA contended that OPM's rules set an October 1, 1981, deadline for the new performance appraisal systems, and in the interim, permitted agencies to move against poor performers under the easier standard of "substantial evidence," even if new performance appraisal systems had not yet been fully established.

Arguments Presented by the Office of Personnel Management

While OPM's official line was to stand by its regulation and the Agencies, it hinted not so subtly during the hearings that it was not entirely pleased with SSA or its implementation of the regulation.

Their (SSA's) implementation did not violate the regulation; that doesn't mean, however, if the implementation was invalid, the regulations themselves were invalid. To invalidate OPM's regulations it must be shown that they require the commission of a prohibited personnel practice. To strike down an Agency's implementation of these regulations it must be shown that the implementation of those regulations has required any Agency employee to commit a prohibited personnel practice. It is not enough to determine that the method of implementation selected by the Agency is unwise or even that it may in the future make it easier for individual employees to challenge particular actions.

OPM argued that it was not necessary to have permanent performance appraisal systems in place until October 1981 under the deadline set by Congress, and that in the interim period agencies could set up temporary, streamlined performance appraisal systems to remove incompetent employees. After all, OPM reasoned, the intent of the Reform Act was to improve the efficiency and effectiveness of government by making it easier to identify "poor performers" and to demote or remove them if correction of the bad habits did not take place soon.

OPM cited passages of the legislative history which it said showed that Congress authorized adverse actions for "unacceptable performance" under the "substantial evidence" standard to take place prior to October 1, 1981. In addition, OPM argued, its interim regulations offer adequate substantive and procedural protections to employees. One lawyer spent considerable time discussing the merits of an issue crucial to OPM — developing critical elements and performance standards on a decentralized basis:

> Congress clearly intended to require Agencies to tailor their critical elements and standards to each employee's actual job duties. Elements and standards which did not reflect actual work performed would be meaningless and would continue the very approach Congress sought to end. . . .
>
> To burden the process of establishing critical elements and performance standards with a degree of centralization and uniformity will render them meaningless. Such an approach would make it impossible to achieve the meaningful performance appraisals based on actual work performed that was clearly intended by Congress. It is clear that nothing in the statute requires Agencies to adopt the same critical elements and performance standards for employees in the same series and grade, and even operating under the same position description. Rather, the relevant inquiry is to whether the standards and ele-

ments reflect the work actually performed by the employee, the employee's job duties; are they job-related?

Arguments Presented by AFGE

According to James Rosa, AFGE General Counsel, "The simple issue is, what is the effective date of the law?" "Congress went out of its way to indicate that they had a very true concern that nobody be removed under this new system until adequate safeguards . . . were developed," he argued. His interpretation of the law was that no one could be fired except for misconduct until the performance appraisal system was established and in place.

We (the union) have been characterized as delaying the Reform Act to the extent that no one could be removed until 1981. That's absurd; that's not our position. The law says that performance standards should be developed as soon as practical, not later than 1981. Only the Agencies have argued that the law says they have until 1981. Congress never said to drag your feet until 1981; it said act as soon as practical on all of this. I think our problem in this case is OPM has been dragging its feet by telling the Agencies they have until 1981, because OPM had these interim regulations which are going to hold everything up until 1981, and all you have to do is follow OPM's direction.

The only problem with Social Security Administration is that they have done it in sort of a hybrid fashion. They had done it without any recognition to employee participation. They probably could have done it even quicker if they had employee participation.

Furthermore, Rosa asserted that the Civil Service Reform Act makes it a prohibited personnel practice to remove or demote employees for inadequate performance before an agency develops objective performance appraisal systems. Their appeal charged that both OPM and SSA had taken improper action in adopting regulations "which were invalid on their face because they had not been communicated to employees." In addition, the union challenged OPM's right to give agencies such wide latitude in determining performance appraisal standards and noted that employees and their representatives had not participated in the establishment of those standards.

"The law requires the encouragement of employee participation in the establishment of performance standards. Those performance appraisals serve as a basis for training, rewarding, reassigning, and promoting employees," Rosa said. Finally, he acknowledged that the SSA may have taken the OPM regulation a step too far:

> What they (OPM) are saying is you can act without having a complete system. There's nothing that gives OPM the authority to pick and choose what provisions of law they will obey. Social Security went beyond even that, though. What they in effect were saying is there was no need . . . for either communication or the opportunity to improve. So I think what we have in the case of Social Security was going even further than OPM was encouraging or requiring the Agencies to go.

Before concluding the hearings, Chairwoman Prokop read the following passage from the House Report on the Civil Service Reform Act: "Between now and October 1, 1981, the Office of Personnel Management must insure that disciplinary actions against employees . . . are very carefully administered so that no employee can be disciplined when performance standards and critical elements have not been adequately defined by an agency."

Reaching a Decision

The three members of the merit Systems Protection Board left the hearings with general impressions formed. According to Chairwoman Prokop,

> It would have been much easier if Congress had devoted more time and clarity to

the issue. The legislation was not clear. Therefore, everyone was fighting battles here that they lost on the Hill. They began to focus their efforts on us, the implementing body. If an issue wasn't pursued on the Hill, they will try to get it through the administrative process. Each group will try to pressure you, so whichever way you rule you anger somebody.

Pressure came from various directions, primarily from the unions and public interest groups. Prokop commented, "Their (the union's) philosophy is that if they keep harassing you, you'll finally make decisions in their favor. You want to say 'quit pressuring.' You're not going to get it [your way] through the press." Although Capitol Hill was "remarkably quiet" throughout the Wells case, a few Congressmen contacted the Board on behalf of the union, primarily as an act of representation, rather than as a demonstration of any real depth or understanding of the issue.

The Office of Personnel Management, on the other hand, consciously chose to have no contact with the Board while it was considering the case. Rather, they felt it was better to try the case as lawyers in a professional manner. Few of their publications said an unfavorable decision would destroy Civil Service Reform, nor did the agency have a voice through the press. Explained an OPM spokesman:

> We didn't think they'd (MSPB) be impressed by rhetoric. We wanted to appear "legal" and demonstrate that we had integrity. We filed briefs that were moderate in tone and that were legally defensible. We adopted a moderate tone throughout the filing. Demagoguery doesn't pay.

In part, he continued, OPM was "writing to Ronald Wertheim," the MSPB member considered the expert on *Wells vs. Harris* because he did a vast amount of work on the case's legislative history and was the most involved in the case. Wertheim has also been described as the "scholarly, legal type."

From May to December 1979, the Board was actively involved in conducting a complete research of the legislative history of civil service reform. "We did the scrub work real clean and read the legislative activity as coldly as we could," Prokop said. Wertheim took the lead in drafting the decision. "I wanted to make sure I knew enough about it," Wertheim said of performance appraisal. "It was really a long, drawn-out process." This included making a list of the 10–15 questions at issue and discussing the pros and cons of each. "We began by discussing the structure of the Civil Service Reform Act. Most cases don't involve so many different provisions of the law," Wertheim stated.

Because of the complexity of the issues involved in this case, it took a long time for the Board to reach a decision. The union was becoming impatient, and would have liked to see a decision much sooner. However, according to Ms. Prokop, *Wells vs. Harris* would have a major government-wide impact, and "it's worth it to spend more time on these decisions because what's one agency's problem today is another agency's problem tomorrow."

This case also represented a testing ground for the Board's reputation as an independent agency. The members were aware their ruling would project an image of themselves. Offered Wertheim, "We are fighting a constant battle to maintain balance." "For an agency to have an independent status means it has no constituency," asserts Ms. Prokop. "You must ask: are you going to rule in your own best judgment, or try to build a constituency? In weighing the decision, we were aware of the question: 'are we going to be independent?' "